Shell Shocked

*For Adélaïde
and Louis*

Shell Shocked

The Social Response to Terrorist Attacks

Gérôme Truc

Translated by Andrew Brown

polity

First published in French as *Sidérations. Une sociologie des attentats* © Presses Universitaires de France, 2016

This English edition © Polity Press, 2018

The translation of this work was supported by funding from the REAT Research Project, granted by the 'Attentats-Recherche' committee of the Centre national de la recherche scientifique (CNRS).

Polity Press
65 Bridge Street
Cambridge CB2 1UR, UK

Polity Press
101 Station Landing
Suite 300,
Medford, MA 02155, USA

ISBN-13: 978-1-5095-2033-6
ISBN-13: 978-1-5095-2034-3 (pb)

Library of Congress Cataloging-in-Publication Data

Names: Truc, Gérôme, author.
Title: Shell shocked : the social response to terrorist attacks / Gérôme Truc.
Other titles: Sidérations. English
Description: Malden, MA : Polity Press, [2017] | Includes bibliographical references and index.
Identifiers: LCCN 2017019475 (print) | LCCN 2017025984 (ebook) | ISBN 9781509520367 (Mobi) | ISBN 9781509520374 (Epub) | ISBN 9781509520336 (hardback) | ISBN 9781509520343 (pbk.)
Subjects: LCSH: Terrorism–Psychological aspects. | Terrorism–Social aspects. | Toleration. | Cultural pluralism.
Classification: LCC HV6431 (ebook) | LCC HV6431 .T78513 2017 (print) | DDC 363.32501/9–dc23
LC record available at https://lccn.loc.gov/2017019475

A catalogue record for this book is available from the British Library.

Typeset in 10 on 11.5 pt Sabon
by Toppan Best-set Premedia Limited
Printed and bound in the UK by Clays Ltd, St Ives PLC

For further information on Polity, visit our website: politybooks.com

CONTENTS

CONTENTS

PREFACE TO THE ENGLISH EDITION

Perhaps, following a recent terrorist attack, you have taken to Facebook or Twitter to express your feelings and your support for the victims; perhaps you have even gone to the places where the terrorists struck in order to reflect, because you lived next door or were passing through the city, and then perhaps you left a short message, a candle or a bouquet of flowers; perhaps you also went out onto the streets to take part in a demonstration in homage to the victims, or to observe a minute's silence. Or perhaps you behaved in quite the opposite way: perhaps you felt that everyone was overdoing it; perhaps you waxed indignant at what you thought were inappropriate reactions; perhaps you found the litany of 'I am ...' statements on social networks ('I am Charlie' and so on) depressingly conformist, and remarked that we do not do as much for those who die every day in Syria or trying to reach Europe via the Mediterranean. It is probable, moreover, that you have successively adopted *both* of these positions in reaction to two different attacks; and that the people around you – friends, relatives, colleagues – reacted differently. Perhaps you tried to argue with some of them; you may perhaps have discovered that you did not share the same view of things, that the very definitions of these attacks and their causes were not as obvious to others as to you; and, as a result, perhaps you discovered how difficult it was to talk about it.

The reason is that terrorist attacks are not conducive to balanced discussions or to a sense of perspective. They are moments of social effervescence, of surging emotions, in which people get worked up and their positions harden. Each of us reacts to them immediately and viscerally, and we often cannot admit – let alone understand – that others, even more in our own circles, do not share our feelings. We lack the tools to grasp fully what is at stake, to understand what happens to us collectively and individually at such moments. The social sciences are generally dismissed as useless in such circumstances, since this is no longer a time for scholarly quibbles but one for taking moral and political positions. With or against terrorists: you just have to choose your side, and that's that. Comments are then reduced to generalities, in which we mix reflections on what we are and what we should be, about the 'trauma' suffered by the social body as a whole and the 'resilience' it is supposed to show; meanwhile, 'cultural conversations'[1] about the causes of terrorism replace empirically based explanations. The risk is therefore that we will be sucked into the maelstrom – to use the metaphor that the sociologist Norbert Elias took from Edgar Allan Poe[2] – created in the wake of terrorist attacks and that, for lack of perspective, we will gradually be drowned in it.

This risk is especially great since such attacks happen again and again. I am writing these lines a few hours after the Manchester Arena bombing, just over a month and a half after the attacks in Stockholm and two months after the attack in Westminster, while the Berlin attack is barely six months old and the first anniversaries of the attacks in Nice and Orlando have not yet arrived. More than ever, therefore, we need a 'sociology of terrorist attacks' to understand the effects of this type of attack on our societies better, and to help us to face them: this is what this book proposes.

At its heart is an inquiry conducted over several years into the reactions to the 9/11 attacks and those on Madrid in 2004 and London in 2005, from which I review a whole series of questions that arose in France following the attacks on *Charlie Hebdo* and the Hypercacher in January 2015. The manuscript was completed one month to the day before the attacks of 13 November 2015. Despite the scale of that later attack – which meant that some French journalists regretted having hastily described the attack on *Charlie Hebdo* as a 'French 9/11' – I did not consider it advisable to postpone the publication of this book. This was because, irrespective of the train of events, the sociological mechanisms that my investigation have laid bare remain fundamentally the same. It is precisely in this respect that sociological analysis offers a valuable perspective which makes it possible to look at the news differently – just as the news sometimes makes it possible to perceive the usefulness of this analysis better.

It will undoubtedly be better understood today, at a time when European societies are being subjected to an unprecedented series of suicide bombings, why it was necessary to begin this work with two chapters which scrutinize how the attacks of 9/11 were experienced on either side of the Atlantic and the role played by the analogy with this event in the perception of subsequent attacks in Europe, as elsewhere across the world. Although 9/11 took place over fifteen years ago, it marked a fundamental shift not only in the modalities of terrorism but also in the relationship of Western societies to terrorist acts, so that we cannot understand the way those societies now react to these acts without taking that initial event into account.

And if the reference to 9/11 seems to be less ubiquitous than it once was in commentaries on the attacks now facing Western societies, analogical thinking is still clearly in evidence. When Andy Burnham, mayor of Manchester, reacts to the bombing which has just plunged his city into mourning by recalling the precedent of the London bombings in 2005, he prescribes at the same time a particular form of behaviour to his fellow citizens: 'I was in the Home Office as a minister on that day and I remember how London felt on that day. I remember it very vividly. What I would say to people is, London pulled together. And in exactly the same way Manchester, in its own unique way, will pull together and we'll stand strong and stand together.'[3] Warding off any risk of division where it might arise, calling for unity: that is the function of political speech. But the fact remains that, behind such language, each citizen harbours his or her own feelings, opinions and reactions. Such is the role of sociological analysis, then: to see what is going on beyond political discourse, and to embrace the reactions of ordinary citizens in their plurality in order to shed light on what produces those reactions.

So I went again to the scene of the attacks of 13 November 2015 in Paris as well as those of 14 July 2016 in Nice to observe in situ the expressions of people's feelings. I found the same words as those left in New York, Madrid and London, words which constitute the raw material of this book. Short, impersonal messages, in the form of exhortations or incantations: 'Never again', 'No to terrorism', 'Peace for all', etc. Long letters in the first person, in dense handwriting. Invocations of the values of freedom, equality and fraternity, but also, and perhaps even more, calls for love, life and peace. Quotations from the Qur'an or the Bible, the Dalai Lama or John Lennon. 'We will not forget you', 'We are united' and 'We are not afraid.' Messages from foreigners who, in the name of their country or city, stand in solidarity with the victims and the city that has been struck. But also a solidarity that is expressed in the singular – 'I am Paris', 'I am Nice' – and on other scales: 'I am French' or 'I am human.' As I write these lines, I know that similar messages are now accumulating in Manchester. Assembled together, these utterances of 'we' and 'I' form the response of a society to the test, the ordeal, of terrorism. This book suggests an approach to understanding this response and a method for analysing it. In its own way, it is also a part of it.

Paris, 23 May 2017

ACKNOWLEDGEMENTS

This book is the result of a doctoral thesis in sociology at the École des Hautes Études en Sciences Sociales, supervised jointly by Daniel Cefaï and Louis Quéré. I would like to thank both of them for the intellectual generosity and attentiveness with which they followed my work. I have learned a huge amount from them. My thanks also go to my viva examiners: Yves Déloye, Jean-Louis Fabiani, Marie-Claire Lavabre and Étienne Tassin, whose remarks were invaluable when it came to producing this book.

My research would not have been possible without the support of a number of people and institutions. I am thinking first of the Casa de Velázquez, and I would like to thank its former director, Jean-Pierre Étienvre, as well as Xavier Huetz de Lemps and Stéphane Michonneau. I am immensely grateful to Cristina Sánchez-Carretero, who gave me access to the Archivo del Duelo, and Randall Collins, who invited me to come and work with him at the University of Pennsylvania. Thanks also to Stéphane Grimaldi and Marie-Claude Berthelot, of the Mémorial de Caen; to Meriam Lobel, of the 9/11 Tribute Center; and to my friend Guillaume Fournié, who greatly facilitated my periods of research in the London Metropolitan Archives.

This work benefited from exchanges of ideas with many researchers, and the help that some of them gave me. In this respect, thanks to Alexandra Bidet, Luc Boltanski, Mathieu Brugidou, Bruno Cautrès, Clément Chéroux, Vincenzo Cicchelli, Alain Cottereau, Béatrice Fraenkel, Sarah Gensburger, Liora Israël, Sandrine Lefranc, Denis Peschanski and Max Reinert. I was also lucky enough to have attentive and reliable reviewers, starting with my two intellectual travelling companions, Pierre-Marie Chauvin and Fabien Truong, to whom this book owes a great deal. Thanks also, for their observations and advice, to Sabine

Chalvon-Demersay, Arnaud Esquerre, Christine de Gemeaux, Claire Lemercier, Étienne Nouguez, Paul Pasquali and Thibaut de Saint Pol.

In conclusion, I would like to express my deep appreciation to those who made it possible for this book to see the light of day: Jean-Luc Fidel, for having helped me turn thesis into book; Serge Paugam, for having so kindly and enthusiastically agreed to publish it; Monique Labrune, for her confidence in me; Julie Gazier, for her patience and her meticulous revision of the manuscript; and my relatives, finally, for their support – especially to the grandparents of Louis, thanks to whom he will not have suffered too much from the final touches to the manuscript that took up so much of his father's attention, and to Adélaïde, whom I can never thank enough.

INTRODUCTION
TERRORIST ATTACKS AS A TEST

The silence was heavy, that night, contrasting with the never-ending bustle that is usually to be found in this area of Paris, both by day and by night. In the glow from candles and street lights, they had gathered there in the cold of January, brandishing pens and pencils, the front pages of newspapers and placards with 'I am Charlie' written on them. First there were just a few hundred of them, gathered in the late afternoon around the statue in the centre of the square, some looking meditative and all of them serious; eventually, by nightfall, there were tens of thousands filling the whole of the Place de la République and its adjacent streets. And thousands of others just like them, across France's major cities. All aghast and outraged. Shocked. Terror-stricken. Never before had a reaction of such magnitude been observed in France following a terrorist act. Soon, therefore, questions came tumbling out: how was it that the French had taken to the streets so rapidly and in such large numbers? What about the fact that the slogan immediately repeated by all of them, 'I am Charlie', was formulated in the first person singular, and not plural, as had happened after 9/11 with 'We are all Americans'? And was there even any sense in comparing this with the 9/11 attacks?

So the journalists turned to the sociologists, but they struggled to get any in-depth answers from them. In the fifteen years since 9/11, the sociologists, ultimately, had found very little to say – either in France or indeed in the US. Of course, in the US you find shelves full of works in bookshops and libraries devoted to the events of 9/11. But they are mainly journalistic narratives, collections of photos, the testimonies of survivors, discussions of the official report on the attacks, and technical arguments claiming to find support for the idea that it was all a conspiracy, together with investigations into Al-Qaeda and its networks. One searches in vain for a book that would study how American society and the rest of the world responded to the attacks, exploring the causes behind the solidarity shown towards the victims and analysing its intensity and scope. In short, a properly sociological book. Admittedly, studies do exist on specific aspects of 9/11 – the way it was treated in a certain newspaper or on a certain television channel, its impact on defence and security policies, on the aeronautics industry, etc. – but these studies were published in academic journals, meant for specialist audiences. The situation is the same when it comes to the two major attacks that have since been carried out on Western countries, preceding those that shook France in January 2015, namely the attacks of 11 March 2004 in Madrid and 7 July 2005 in London: there are as many books by experts on terrorist networks, essays by journalists, and narrative accounts as one could wish for; but when it comes to sociological analyses, there are virtually none. Indeed, the mother of a victim of the London attacks, in her preface to one of the very few academic books published to date on this event, laments this silence on the part of social scientists.[1]

Though I do not claim that it will fill this gap all by itself, my book looks back at the European reactions to the 9/11 attacks, and those in Madrid and London, so as to provide a certain perspective for what the French experienced in January 2015 and to come up with answers to the questions that arose then. Each of its chapters begins with a salient feature of the events of January 2015 and then sheds light on this by drawing on the results of an investigation into those three previous Islamist attacks in Western territory – an investigation that lasted several years. This book therefore proposes a *sociology of terrorist attacks*, rather than a sociology of terrorism as such.[2] It focuses on the attacks as events, on the way that ordinary individuals experience them and how they react to them, rather than on terrorism as a sociopolitical phenomenon, which is already the subject of many studies. The approach taken here is a quiet, 'cool'[3] appraisal of the effect an attack has on society: it aims to understand, compare and explain, but in no way to judge or deplore, as people are frequently all too quick to do, 'in the heat of the moment'. For the attacks are not very propitious moments for reflection, for a distanced view: people feel they are being called on to take a stand and choose sides. And as Emmanuel Todd's detailed analysis of the demonstrations that followed the attacks of 2 January 2015 will have demonstrated,[4] it is sometimes very difficult for a sociologist to remain objective in this area.

Testing social bonds

My book begins with a naive question, one which may seem morally aberrant: why is it that an attack does not leave us indifferent? Why do

2

we feel concerned by it when we are not victims ourselves, and do not personally know anyone who is? Why is it that we are shell shocked when we learn what has happened? Of course, it seems natural to us: we must be Charlie! How could we not be? How can we fail to be shocked when journalists and cartoonists are shot down by Kalashnikovs in our own country? So we have to be Charlie. And that, indeed, is what we all are: the front pages of the newspapers say as much. However, it rather quickly becomes apparent that some people are not Charlie, or not as much as other people would like them to be ... Then begins the hunt for who is or is not Charlie. Understanding what happens to a society when it lives through such moments requires us, first of all, to take a step back from our own reactions, as members of this society. We need to ask ourselves: *what exactly are we reacting to?* In other words: to what extent do media coverage of the attack and the way the authorities themselves react impact on our own reaction? And we must also ask: *what makes us react in this particular way?* What emotional springs are thus set in motion by the event?

This approach means considering the attack, from the sociological point of view, not only as an ordeal, but also as a test.[5] With it, a twofold uncertainty arises: an uncertainty that initially attaches, of course, to the attacked state, its ability to protect its citizens adequately and ensure peace on its territory,[6] but an uncertainty that also attaches, at the same time, to society itself. In striking some of its members, the attack calls into question the link uniting them to those who are not directly affected. Will the latter show concern for the fate of the victims? Will they feel solidarity? Or will they in fact demonstrate indifference? Or worse: will they actually take the side of the terrorists responsible for the attack? An attack, in this sense, reveals *what we are most attached to* – the things and the people that are dear to us, the values to which we collectively hold – which is at the same time *that by which we are most attached to one another*, i.e. what connects us to others, with whom we feel that we form a single community.[7] In short, it is a moment of truth for social cohesion.

But the reactions to the attacks that will be discussed in this book overflowed the borders of the countries where they occurred, sometimes to a significant degree. They are thus an occasion for us to investigate the role played by the sense of national belonging in reactions to an attack: not that we should necessarily minimize its importance, but rather so as to locate its rightful place among other emotional mechanisms that it may tend to obscure. For however significant the bond of nationhood may be, it is not – and has never been – the only link that connects us to others and is able make us sensitive to their plight. A foreigner may have felt that he or she was 'Charlie' for the same reason that a French person did, although this reason had nothing to do with the fact that one was French and the other not. And if a normative viewpoint will lead us to consider that no French person can fail to be 'Charlie', the fact remains that some French people felt more affected than others by the attack on 7 January 2015, and that it is unlikely (but not impossible) that this was because they felt more French. Conversely, behind some of the facile rhetorical responses that speak of a 'global emotion' involving 'the whole world' following an attack, there may be first and foremost the emotions of people who, throughout the world, are responding to a tragedy that has struck their home country.

To produce a sociology of terrorist attacks, then, involves asking what connects us to each other and makes us sensitive to the fate of others, in our own society as well as beyond its borders. In other words, it involves reconnecting with one of the founding questions of sociology, that of the relationship between individuals and groups, and of the mechanisms of solidarity in modern societies. This is a question which all classic writers in the discipline have had to face, starting with Émile Durkheim.

From one terrorism to another

The time when Durkheim was working on his first big book, *The Division of Labour in Society*,[8] was already marked by terrorism – not in those days Islamist, but anarchist. Before the 'bin Laden decade'[9] which marked the beginning of the twenty-first century, Europe experienced in the 1890s a 'decade of the bomb'[10] during which there was a series of attacks using dynamite (which had just been invented) targeting kings, presidents, ministers, judges, government buildings and public places. Durkheim defended his thesis and published *The Division of Labour in Society* right in the middle of the wave of attacks then hitting Paris, just a year after Ravachol's attacks in March 1892 and a year before the assassination of President Sadi Carnot by Caserio, on 24 June 1894.[11]

From 1891 to 1894, there were press articles on anarchist terrorism almost daily: not only information on attacks, arrests, potential threats and false alarms, but also editorials, and interviews with or portraits of anarchist figures. This terrorism was described in terms that vividly recall the language sometimes employed today about Islamists. One example is the attack on the Café du Terminus, at the Gare Saint-Lazare on 12 February 1894, carried out by Émile Henry: it featured in *Le Temps* – the forerunner of *Le Monde* – where it was called 'the continuation of the savage war declared by the sect on modern society'.[12] Like today's Islamist terrorism, anarchist terrorism in the France of that time represented the main threat to the social and republican order, and as such preoccupied Durkheim as he was writing *The Division of Labour in*

Society.[13] And, as today, this threat hung over a society riven by inequality, where the 'social question' seemed more urgent than ever.

There is, from the sociological point of view, an undeniable continuity in the problematic of terrorism: regardless of the cause defended by the terrorists, the way that their attacks put society to the test remains fundamentally similar. Writing against those who see *The Division of Labour in Society* as a now outmoded work, the American sociologist Edward A. Tiryakian has pointed out that the way American society reacted to 9/11 is a very clear illustration of the phenomenon that Durkheim portrays in that work under the name 'mechanical solidarity'.[14] Faced with the attack, Americans more than ever had the feeling of being united. This reaffirmation of national cohesion, an American 'we' that for a while took precedence over the singular 'I's that compose that community, was particularly reflected in the flourishing, in public space, of a symbol that was, as it were, erected as a totem: the Stars and Stripes. According to an often-quoted statistic, branches of Walmart sold 116,000 in the course of 11 September 2001 and 250,000 more the next day, almost twenty-five times more than in a normal period,[15] and a fifth of Internet searches in the hours following the attacks were looking for downloadable and printable versions of the flag.[16]

But Durkheim's analysis has found echoes in other places, too. Edward A. Tiryakian notes that, in the wake of the attacks, he received many emails of support from foreign researchers (French, German, Italian and so on), who had spontaneously written to him to express their condolences to the American people, and that his colleagues from other disciplines experienced the same phenomenon. History does not relate whether Durkheim himself received telegrams from US sociologists in August 1914, when Germany declared war on France, but he would probably have seen this, as Tiryakian suggests, as the demonstration of a solidarity that was not just mechanical, but organic – based on social differentiation rather than a sense of community, and spreading to an international scale, and perhaps thereby comprising the material for a new sociological study.[17] In one sense, it is a similar extension of Durkheim's analysis that I am putting forward in this book. Its raw material, in fact, is very similar to the messages I referred to just now.

The materials for a book

Essentially, this book relies on an atypical, unprecedented source: the countless messages that people addressed to the victims of the attacks of 9/11, Madrid and London, to express their solidarity. Just a few words or several pages long, collected on the actual sites of the terrorist attacks or on Internet sites, sometimes sent to newspapers or embassies that were asked to forward them, composed a few hours or days after the attacks, or sometimes several months or years later, these messages help us grasp at the individual scale the mechanisms of the collective response to the attacks, and thus to put into perspective what is nowadays observed, in such circumstances, on social media. What ordinary people say in order to show their support for victims, and the way they say it, if we pay proper attention, reveal how it is that they feel affected by the event, what sense of 'us' it involves, and how the meanings of 'I' and 'we' are related when attacks put us to the test.

However, one still needs to have the means to dominate the over-whelming plethora of relevant documents, tens of thousands in number, so as not only to identify a few cases that stand out from this mass, but to characterize the mass as a whole. So the heart of this book consists of an exhaustive analysis, using textual statistics software, of a corpus of nearly 60,000 messages written in reaction to the attack in Madrid, from the 'Archivo del Duelo', an archive created by researchers at the Consejo Superior de Investigaciones Científicas.[18] Its results have enabled me to develop an original grid of analysis and then explore other post-attack messages: those from the 'London terrorist attack 7 July 2005: memorials to victims' holdings in the London Metropolitan Archives, the messages from Operation 'Fraternally', an archive consulted at the Mémorial de Caen shortly before it went off to the United States to join the collections of the National September 11 Memorial & Museum, the 'visitor cards' of the 9/11 Tribute Center in New York, and finally a few scattered reactions collected here and there on the Internet.[19] In addition, I have worked my way through press archives (both in print and broadcast), and sum-marized the studies that have been published on the way the media treated the 9/11, Madrid and London attacks. The study could not have been complete without this, since the mass of individuals who were not directly victims or witnesses of the attacks actually reacted less to the attacks themselves than to what they perceived of them via the media.

This explains the architecture of my book. The first part, 'What is happening to us', explores the various facets of events comprised by the Islamist attacks in Western territory. Their treatment in the media is set in the context of all the operations of 'framing' to which they were sub-jected, on the part not only of journalists, columnists and intellectuals, but also of politicians and political institutions. Insofar as they impose definitions of the 'we' under attack, we will see that these operations convey the injunction to show solidarity and to feel concerned: these injunctions guide the reactions of ordinary people, but can also arouse their criticisms. While this first part of my book thus focuses on the question 'What are we reacting to?', the second turns to address the question 'What made us react that way?' Entitled '*What touches us*', this part analyses what it is that generates the widespread emotion that finds expression in the face of the attacks, the vectors through which we identify with their victims and the reasons why we are indeed sensitive to their fate. In so doing, this second part highlights the role played in our reactions to the attacks by a sense of being concerned that goes beyond the different senses of 'we' which media and political discourses emphasize rather unevenly, and exacerbates the sense of 'I'. Messages addressed to victims, as we shall see, are abundantly cited in support of the analysis. Giving them as large as possible a place in this book is also a way of paying tribute to those modest voices that, behind the din of bombs and Kalashnikovs, create great upwellings of solidarity.

Note on sources cited

Endnotes provide references to the following sources:

– *Mémorial de Caen, OF (Opération 'Fraternellement')*: messages from Operation 'Fraternally', consulted at the Mémorial de Caen and now held at the National September 11 Memorial & Museum, in New York.

– *Archivo del Duelo, DP (Documentos de Papel)*: documents on paper posted in the stations of Atocha, El Pozo and Santa Eugenia, in Madrid, from March to June 2004, consulted at the Consejo Superior de Investigaciones Científicas in Madrid and now held at the National Railway Museum in Madrid.

– *Archivo del Duelo, FD (Fotografías digitales)*: photographs taken in the stations of Atocha, El Pozo and Santa Eugenia, in Madrid, from March to June 2004, consulted at the Consejo Superior de Investigaciones Científicas in Madrid and now held at the National Railway Museum in Madrid.

– *Archivo del Duelo, EP (Espacio de Palabras)*: digital messages recorded from June 2004 to March 2005 via a computer set up in the stations of Atocha, El Pozo and Santa Eugenia, in Madrid, and the website masceranos.com, consulted at the Consejo Superior de Investigaciones Científicas in Madrid and now held at the National Railway Museum in Madrid.

– *London Metropolitan Archives, LMA/4469 / ...* : documents from the collection 'London terrorist attack 7 July 2005: memorials to victims' available from the London Metropolitan Archives.

– *9/11 Tribute Center, VC (Visitor Cards)*: messages written from September 2006 to June 2009 (date when the holdings were consulted) by visitors to the 9/11 Tribute Center in New York.

Part I

WHAT IS HAPPENING TO US

We do not know what is happening to us,
but this is precisely what is happening to us: the
fact that we do not know what is happening to us.

José Ortega y Gasset

— 1 —

UNDER ATTACK

There's been a massacre at the *Charlie Hebdo* offices. They say a dozen people have been killed … The circumstances are still vague. Nobody has any further details. You turn on the radio, the television; you look for news online. You ask the people around you, and phone round for information. Your day has been interrupted; you've already realized that things aren't going to follow their usual course today. This is the main characteristic of a terrorist attack: it 'brutally disrupts our tacit expectation that our environment will provide stability and continuity'.[1] Suddenly, without warning, violence, death and destruction break into the peaceful course of our lives, and radically undermine the 'routine grounds'[2] of our activities.

This phenomenon has probably never been as brutally clear as on 11 September 2001, since the terrorist attacks carried out on that day represented 'a radical transformation of the ordinary forms of terrorism':[3] rightly or wrongly, these attacks seemed to come from nowhere – there had been no warning signs, and they did not fall within the context of any familiar historical struggle. This was not true of the periodical *Charlie Hebdo*, which had been the focus of threats after it published caricatures of Muhammed. Likewise, the Spanish initially thought that the train bombings on 11 March 2004 were yet another ETA attack. And even before the 7 July 2005 attack in London, the British had had time to take on board the idea that, sooner or later, they would be targeted by Islamists. So it is impossible to understand the reactions produced by these attacks in Europe – the reason why, for example, the *Charlie Hebdo* shootings were seen as a 'French 9/11' – without having first taken the trouble to examine how the attacks on 11 September had been experienced on either side of the Atlantic. We need to focus on what was involved in this initial attack if we are to understand every new Islamist assault that occurs in a Western country.

9/11 live: Accident, terrorist attack, or act of war?

Even if some terrorist attacks come as less of a surprise than others, every attack, at the time it is carried out, creates a new and uncertain situation that needs to be defined. What is happening? What do I now need to expect? What should be done? Answering these questions requires what the American sociologist Erving Goffman calls a 'framework',[4] i.e. 'a cognitive and practical structure for organizing social experience, enabling us to understand what is happening to us and to take part in it'.[5] A framework is not just an interpretation, a representation or an after-the-event narrativization of what has happened. It becomes apparent in the very course of ongoing events, by way of describable activities – the framing operations – that help us to explain the events, specify which people are concerned by them, and decide on the best way to react to them. As one case of uncertainty as to the framework of a particular situation, Erving Goffman takes the example of the blackout that, on 30 November 1965, plunged the north-eastern United States into darkness: 'With the lights failing all over New York, the individual does not know whether there has been a technical failure, an enemy attack, or sabotage.'[6] It was exactly this same uncertainty that marked the first hours of 11 September 2001. When, a few seconds after 8.46 a.m., New Yorkers suddenly heard the noise of a loud explosion coming from the south of Manhattan,[7] and turned to look at the towers of the World Trade Center, they realized that the north tower was on fire. But the vast majority of them did not at that time know what had led to the blaze.

11 September 2001, 8.46 a.m.: The need to define a situation

The event instantly reached American newsrooms, which thereupon kept their cameras permanently trained on Manhattan. CNN was the first national channel to interrupt its programme, a few seconds before 8.50 a.m., to broadcast a static shot showing a thick cloud of smoke rising from the upper floors of the north tower of the World Trade Center into the clear blue sky of that Tuesday morning.[8] Superimposed on the image were the words 'World Trade Center Disaster'. At this stage, CNN journalists had no reliable information at their disposal. They spoke of 'something devastating' and mentioned the possibility of a plane crashing into the tower only as a hypothesis, stemming from 'unconfirmed reports'.

At the same time, CNN reporters were roaming the streets of Manhattan looking for eyewitnesses. The first hours of live media coverage of 9/11, on both television and radio, in the United States as in the rest of the world, would give a great deal of space to these eyewitness accounts gathered in the streets.[9] But these were partial and often contradictory: some people swore that the tower had imploded from within and confirmed that they had heard reports of a bomb, while others stated that they had seen a plane flying in over Manhattan at a very low altitude just before the explosion in the tower. But at that time, nobody had access to any image that would enable this to be confirmed with certainty.[10] So there was a plethora of hypotheses as to what kind of plane had been involved: a small tourist plane such as a Cesna, or an airliner, maybe a Boeing? In the former case, it might be an accident, but in the latter, it might have been a hijacked plane. Furthermore, the weather conditions, which on that morning were perfect, did not make an accidental crash seem likely.

Suddenly, at 9.03 a.m., just as one witness was on air stating that he had seen a big plane embedding itself in the north tower of the World Trade Center, a plane in flight surreptitiously appeared on the image for a fraction of a second, then vanished. The picture was interrupted for a moment, then the screen showed a ball of fire. The static shot broadcast by CNN did not distinguish between the Twin Towers, and so it was some time before the journalists gathered what had just happened: initially, they thought there had been a second explosion in the same tower. Then, when they realized that it was in fact the south tower that was now on fire, they again mentioned the possibility of a plane crash, but only as a hypothesis that needed to be verified. The framework of the developing situation was still very ill-defined.

However, this framework would become clear over the next half hour, as experts (especially those from air security and the FBI) were contacted by journalists, and press releases were issued by Associated Press and Reuters. The hypothesis of a hijacked plane gained ground, while an accident started to seem increasingly unlikely. Journalists were now talking in terms of a probable 'terrorist act'. At 9.29 a.m., President Bush, speaking from Emma Booker Elementary School in Sarasota, Florida, where he was visiting, made a brief statement in which he spoke of a 'national tragedy' and an 'apparent terrorist attack on our country'. Barely eight minutes later, at 9.37 a.m., journalists reported a new explosion, this time at the Pentagon, Washington. Less than one hour after the first plane had crashed, there was no further room for doubt: these were not accidents, and the United States was the target for several coordinated attacks.

The event now became international in its scope. In Europe, it was the middle of the afternoon, and TV channels interrupted their programmes to give way to special editions in which they broadcast, live, the images supplied by American channels, in particular CNN. France 2 was the

15

first channel to do so in France, at 3.33 p.m. (9.33 a.m. New York time, in other words just after President Bush's speech, and before the explosion at the Pentagon): this was just a few moments earlier than TF1. On all the television channels, journalists immediately spoke of terrorist attacks, and said the Twin Towers had been struck by airliners, probably hijacked by terrorists. For example, Élise Lucet, presenting the special edition on France 3, emphasized right from the start that President Bush himself was 'talking very clearly in terms of a terrorist action, and not an accident'.[11] The video of the second crash, involving United Airlines Flight 175 flying into the south tower of the World Trade Center, was immediately broadcast on a loop (at normal speed or in slow motion), continuously on TF1, and five times in ten minutes on France 2.

To make the developing event as intelligible as possible, journalists endeavoured to relate it to precedents or warning signs, so as to elucidate its causes, shed light on its meaning, and make conjectures as to its consequences.[12] This was also one way of assessing the extent to which this event marked a complete 'break' with the past, and of giving some idea of its more or less 'historic' character.[13] On all the French television channels, from the first moments of live transmission, one attack already carried out by Islamists on the World Trade Center in February 1993 was mentioned. Christian Malard, on France 3, justified this comparison, pointing out that the Democratic Front for the Liberation of Palestine (DFLP) had just claimed responsibility for the attacks. And, mentioning Al-Qaeda as another possible line of inquiry, he also referred to the attacks on the American embassies in Tanzania and Kenya in 1998, as well as the explicit threats to the United States uttered by the Al-Qaeda leader Osama bin Laden – whose name was starting to circulate in the media less than one hour after the first crash.

These first thoughts were, however, formulated while the towers of the World Trade Center were still standing. They no longer seemed adequate once these towers had been reduced to dust, and journalists had started to estimate the number of deaths at 40,000 or 50,000, while only an hour earlier, shortly after the crash of the second aeroplane, they had gone no further than a few 'hundred deaths' (the aircraft passengers).[14] One historical precedent then quickly emerged, overshadowing all others in the US media: the attack on Pearl Harbor.

'The Pearl Harbor of the twenty-first century'

It's a familiar story. On 11 September 2001, in the evening, before going to bed, President Bush noted in his private diary: 'The Pearl Harbor of the twenty-first century took place today.'[15] He was simply recording what had, in the course of the day, imposed itself on the United States

16

as the dominant interpretation of the situation: these attacks were not only an attack on the United States, but nothing less than a 'new Pearl Harbor'. It would be wrong to think that this analogy was a way of narrativizing 9/11 after the event. It played a major role in the course of events on the actual day: it made it possible both to determine the nature of what was happening (an unexpected act of aggression on the US), to point to those responsible (external enemies) and to allow people to surmise what the outcome would be (military retaliation).

This comparison of 9/11 with Pearl Harbor, the validity of which has sparked much debate,[16] may, with the benefit of hindsight, appear relevant in many ways: in both cases the United States were attacked by surprise, and by air (the use of hijacked planes rather than bombs was an element which clearly distinguished the 9/11 attacks from others); and the human toll of the two attacks turned out to be on a similar scale (nearly 3,000 deaths for 9/11, just over 2,400 for Pearl Harbor). The analogy nevertheless tends to overlook the fact that the 9/11 attacks mainly hit a civilian target, the towers of the World Trade Center, while the target of the Japanese attack of 7 December 1941 had been military. In so doing, the analogy undeniably helped to underpin the way the 9/11 attacks were viewed as true 'acts of war'.

The term 'war' emerged in public discourse only after the crash of American Airlines Flight 77 into the Pentagon and the collapse of the first of the two towers of the World Trade Center (the South Tower), at 9.59 a.m. If it had merely been a matter of President Bush's first speech, forty-five minutes after the first crash, and the comparisons being ventured at that stage by journalists with the attack on the World Trade Center in February 1993, or with the attacks on US embassies in 1998, the 9/11 attacks should have been seen as criminal acts – just like the most murderous attack in the United States before 11 September 2001, namely that perpetrated in Oklahoma City on 19 April 1995 (168 dead), whose author – Timothy McVeigh – was tried and executed by the Federal Government on 11 June 2001, three months to the day before 9/11. But the path followed was very different, and for that reason it was predictable that, even ten years later, bin Laden – named by the United States as the main figure responsible for 9/11 – would not be arrested and tried as Timothy McVeigh had been, but executed as part of a military operation. This too was the result of the way 9/11 was, from the very first hours of the event, viewed as an act of war rather than as a criminal act.

That same day, the political scientist Robert Kagan, a leading neoconservative intellectual, wrote a summons to war in which he stated that resorting to law and justice would be inappropriate in the face of the attack that had just been suffered by the United States:

One can only hope that America can respond to today's monstrous attack on American soil – an attack far more awful than Pearl Harbor – with the same moral clarity and courage as our grandfathers did. Not by asking what we have done to bring on the wrath of inhuman murderers. Not by figuring out ways to reason with, or try to appease those who have spilled our blood. Not by engaging in an extended legal effort to find the killers and bring them to justice. But by doing the only thing we now can do: go to war.[17]

The next day, when the *Washington Post* published this text, President George W. Bush stated that the attacks were more than acts of terrorism, they were authentic 'acts of war', and therefore demanded that an international coalition be set up to conduct military retaliation against the perpetrators of these attacks.[18] Almost simultaneously, the UN Security Council (based, let us remember, in New York) accredited this definition of the attacks of the day before as an act of war by unanimously adopting resolution 1368 authorizing the United States to exercise the 'right of self-defence'.[19] That evening, the NATO council activated for the first time the 'mutual defence' clause. Thus, on Thursday 13 September, Bush could say: '[N]ow that war has been declared on us, we will lead the world to victory.'[20]

There followed a whole week dedicated to forging national unity and preparing the United States for war; this contributed a little more to ratifying 9/11 as an act of war. A day of national mourning was observed across the United States on 14 September, during which a ceremony in homage to the victims was first celebrated in Washington Cathedral, before the president's visit to the ruins of the World Trade Center to praise the firefighters still searching the rubble in their hunt for survivors. That same day, the Senate unanimously authorized the president to use military force. Reservists were mobilized and American flags became increasingly visible across the country.[21] On 19 September, a national state of emergency was decreed. Finally, on 20 September, during a joint session of Congress, broadcast live on television, George W. Bush announced the end of the mourning and the beginning of the response: 'Our grief has turned to anger, and anger to resolution.'[22] Unlike the attacks themselves, which had arrived on screen unannounced, taking journalists completely by surprise, this solemn speech conformed to the canon of 'televised ceremony', carefully prepared, planned and announced in advance.[23] Regardless of its content, it was, by its very form, a response to the disruptive event: it helped to bolster the cohesion of the national community under attack while ratifying the resumption of control on the part of the US authorities. So the 'war on terror' could now begin.

Presenting 9/11 as an act of war on the United States would not have carried as much weight if it had been a matter of mere speeches; it also needed to be backed by these institutional operations. The report published in 2004 by the National Commission on Terrorist Attacks Upon the United States gave it ultimate confirmation,[24] placing 9/11 in the context of a fatwa pronounced by bin Laden in the name of the 'World Islamic Front' against the United States (and only against the United States). Previous events hitherto considered as negligible were here re-evaluated in terms of 9/11:

> At 10:02 that morning, an assistant to the mission crew commander at NORAD's Northeast Air Defense Sector in Rome, New York, was working with his colleagues on the floor of the command center. In a brief moment of reflection, he was recorded as remarking that 'This is a new type of war'. He was, and is, right. But the conflict did not begin on 9/11. It had been publicly declared years earlier, most notably in a declaration faxed early in 1998 to an Arabic-language newspaper in London. Few Americans had noticed it.[25]

The 1998 attacks on the American embassies in Nairobi and Dar es Salaam, in Kenya and Tanzania, and in 2000 on the USS *Cole*, were also redefined as the first battles in the war between the United States and the Islamists. In his address to the nation on 20 September, George Bush also mentioned the attack on the USS *Cole*, stating for the first time that Al-Qaeda was responsible.[26] It was also in the name of these previous attacks that military retaliation was deemed necessary.

The strength of an analogy

It must be emphasized that it was less the definition of 9/11 as an act of war which contributed to the success of the analogy with Pearl Harbor than the reverse. It would be wrong to think that because it was defined as an act of war, 9/11 could *subsequently* be integrated into a kind of 'heroic narrative' presenting it as a repetition of Pearl Harbor. In fact, viewing 9/11 as an act of war and drawing an analogy with Pearl Harbor were inseparable.

The term 'war' was pronounced for the first time on French television when live images of the huge cloud of smoke over Manhattan caused by the collapse of the south tower of the World Trade Center were broadcast. During the live coverage of the attacks on France 3, Patrick Hesters exclaimed, at the sight of these images:

19

Pardon me for interrupting you. Here is haunting image of Manhattan ... a Manhattan that looks, in fact, like a city coming under bombardment (*separating each syllable of the word*) during a war! And it's clear that what we have here really are acts of war (*emphasizing this last word*). These are not accidents. You don't get coincidences of this kind. They really are terrorist acts, but it's a terrorism of war (*emphasizing this word again*).[27]

Christian Malard, interrupted in his attempt to analyse the event from a geopolitical standpoint, unhesitatingly confirmed this: 'Patrick is right: it's an act of war.' After the crash of the fourth hijacked plane in Pennsylvania, United Airlines Flight 93 (at 10.03 a.m.), and the collapse of the second tower (at 10.28 a.m.), David Pujadas spoke on France 2 of 'war scenes' in New York and Washington, and supported his statement by referring to the soldiers mobilized in the streets, the fighter planes flying over Manhattan and the images of New Yorkers evacuating Manhattan on foot, which suggested, he said, an 'exodus'. Thierry Thuillier went even further, stating that 'since the end of World War II [...] the United States has never experienced such a panic or such a situation', adding 'perhaps even since the bombing of Pearl Harbor'.[28]

Soon after, on US television, the titles inlaid on the border of the live images (which is in a quite literal sense their 'framework') changed. They now read 'America under Attack' (which appeared on CNN at 10.57 a.m. precisely), or 'America at War'. This emphasis on war replaced the title 'disaster at the World Trade Center' that had been shown a few moments earlier. The tone now became much more melodramatic.[29] The word 'war' would be repeated a total of 234 times in twelve hours on CNN.[30] Around 2 p.m., New York time, the Republican senator from Arizona, John McCain, said that it was 'clearly an act of war', while the Democratic senator from Connecticut, Christopher Dodd, said: 'A day like this, that rivals – if it does not exceed – the Pearl Harbor attack, perpetrated 60 years ago [...] we are completely united behind our President and our Government.'[31] Witnesses interviewed in the street not far from the World Trade Center spontaneously made this connection, too: 'It's Pearl Harbor! It's war.'[32] Far from being invented by an inspired American president, the analogy with Pearl Harbor was, very early on, spontaneously and simultaneously, 'formulated by many different sources: the man in the street, teenagers, actresses, the TV presenter, and Henry Kissinger'.[33] If the analogy spread so quickly and clearly, this was because it corresponded to the experience that many Americans actually had of the attacks.

There is a fairly simple reason for this, which has been well documented since then:[34] the year 2001 marked the sixtieth anniversary of the attack that triggered the American entry into the Second World War. According to Emily S. Rosenberg, this sixtieth anniversary gave rise to a media coverage 30 per cent more extensive than that of the fiftieth anniversary.[35] American attention had been monopolized by the 'commemorative display' since January: the archival images, historical documentaries and testimonies of veterans had revived memories of that national tragedy, when the 9/11 attacks occurred. In particular, on 30 May 2001, the blockbuster of the year was released in cinemas: *Pearl Harbor*.[36] Produced by Disney, and made with colossal financial resources, its promotional campaign was more expensive than those for *Titanic* (1998) and *Jurassic Park* (1993), which had previously held the record. By the end of the summer, *Pearl Harbor* had accounted for 30 million cinema tickets in the USA. And this media hype did more than make everyone think of Pearl Harbor; it helped to revive and even update the images of that event, via the promotional campaign for the Hollywood blockbuster.

Thus the analogy between 9/11 and Pearl Harbor was suggested by the images themselves. Americans did not just *have the impression* that the 9/11 attacks were repeating the attack of December 1941: they *saw* as much. In the visual processing of these attacks, the historian of photography Clément Chéroux clearly established the predominance of the image of the fireball caused by the crash of United Airlines Flight 175 into the south tower of the World Trade Center and that of the cloud of smoke rising over Manhattan when the towers collapsed (figures 1 and 2): two images clearly echoing those of Pearl Harbor, the most significant of which showed the ships burning in the harbour and exploding when the flames reached their fuel tanks and ammunition reserves.[37] Together, these images of 9/11 occupied nearly 60 per cent of the front pages of American newspapers the day after the attack,[38] most often accompanied by an explicit reference to the 1941 attack, and in some cases with archival images reproduced facing them so as to strengthen the parallel.[39] Another snapshot later came to reinforce this visual reminder of Pearl Harbor. Taken by Thomas Franklin on the afternoon of 9/11, in it we see three firefighters hoisting an American flag on the ruins of the World Trade Center, in a posture reminiscent of the most frequently reproduced image in the history of the United States,[40] a symbol of revenge for Pearl Harbor: *Raising the Flag on Iwo Jima*, by Joe Rosenthal (figure 3).[41] The comparison was all the more obvious as, with the help of the context of commemoration, the bestseller of the time was a book whose subject was precisely this photo by Rosenthal: *Flags of Our Fathers* by James Bradley (later adapted for the cinema by Clint Eastwood).

Thomas Franklin's photo met with considerable success in the United States. A special stamp was published in 2002, with the words 'HEROES

Figures 1, 2 and 3. Front pages of the *San Francisco Examiner* (US) and the *Charleston Gazette* (US), 12 September 2001, and front page of *Newsweek* (US), special issue of 24 September 2001.

USA': almost 128 million copies were printed over the next two years. It is still reproduced these days on many commemorative objects sold in New York. But while, in the eyes of Americans, this photograph has become one of the main icons of 9/11, it is barely known in Europe. This is because 9/11 was, on the European side of the Atlantic, experienced and perceived as something other than a 'new Pearl Harbor'.

The view from Europe: From Western solidarity to a cosmopolitan perspective

'The "Third World War" has started': this was the title *Le Monde* gave to its international press review for the evening of 12 September. The use of the term 'war' to describe 9/11 was evidently not unique to the United States. As we have seen, the French journalists commenting on the events live on television also spontaneously used it. But in contrast to the US media, they immediately placed this war within a global perspective, focusing on the fear of further attacks in Europe. The framework they adopted, in other words, was not quite the same. For example, here is Daniel Bilalian on France 2:

> It's a national tragedy in the United States, the US president said so just now. But obviously, whether in Germany or in London, prime minis-

22

ters are now summoning their governments. It's also a state of alert. Perhaps they too fear attacks of the same style in their respective capitals? Well, we can't dismiss such a fear. At the moment, we can't rule it out.[42]

Thus, in Europe, the attacks of 9/11 immediately appeared as an attack not only on the US but more broadly on all Western countries.

Fear of a world war and Western solidarity

It is in the very nature of journalistic discourse to combine description with political analysis: while it frames the event (what is happening), it helps to constitute the collective subject of that event (the people to whom it is happening). Commenting on what was happening to 'us', the journalists and experts invited into TV studios play a leading role in the definition of this 'us'.[43] Thus, 9/11 resulted in the reactivation of a Western *imaginaire*[44] on the part of various European media that immediately, even before any politicians had expressed their opinion, presented the attacks on the United States as a declaration of war on *us*, i.e. not just the American nation, but the entire Western world. When the word 'war' was spoken for the first time on French TV, by Christian Malard, it was immediately used in this context:

It's an act of war. Today, these armed Islamist groups are at war with the West as a whole. The West [...], whose symbol is the United States. So they are at war with Western values, with the United States.[45]

This was echoed three days later in an editorial in Le Figaro:

This really is a war. And not only with the United States. It's the democratic West as a whole that is being threatened in the name of a conquering religion desperate to impose a system of values incompatible with ours.[46]

This way of framing the event was obviously not confined to France. It met with considerable success in Italy, through an article by Oriana Fallaci in Il Corriere della Sera that became famous, 'The Rage and the Pride'.[47] In Spain too: for example, the conservative newspaper ABC for 12 September put on its front page the words 'Islamic terrorism declares war on the West'. This was, almost word for word, the headline in the first edition of L'Express published after 9/11, in which we read:

The Third World War began on Tuesday 11 September on the East Coast of the United States. A world war of a new kind, unprecedented in history,

23

a war between terrorism, in all likelihood Islamist, and the West. [...] Tuesday 11 September 2001 is thus, in the scale of the assault and the victims it has created, the first day of the 'war of civilizations' between Islam and the West.[48]

The allusion to the thesis of the 'clash of civilizations' put forward by Samuel Huntington could not be clearer. The European success of this work by the American political scientist, published in the late 1990s,[49] certainly prepared the ground for this framing of 9/11. Before the attacks happened, there were already, in *Le Monde*, an increasing number of analyses that spoke in terms of the war of civilizations and religions, especially those written by Henri Tincq: on 6 July 2000, for example, a two-page article was dedicated to the '"hot spots" in the conflict between Islam and Christianity'.[50] And in the edition of *Le Monde* which appeared a couple of days after 9/11, another article emphasized that the events gave the impression that Huntington's 'prediction' was coming true.[51] But this framing was also strengthened by the first statements issued by various European heads of state, particularly British prime minister Tony Blair, who presented 9/11 as an attack on 'the free and democratic world',[52] and the German chancellor, Gerhard Schröder, who initially called it a 'declaration of war on the civilized world' and the next day, in the Bundestag, said it was a 'declaration of war on the free world'.[53] Such language is a clear allusion to the Second World War and the Cold War. The Allies of yesteryear were thus being called to unite against a new common enemy: after Nazism and Communism, this enemy was now, it seemed, Islamism.

This time, however, the reference to Pearl Harbor counted for nothing in the historical parallel: it was most frequently alluded to in quotation marks, and was mentioned only indirectly in the European media. In the aftermath of the attacks, for example, no French newspaper went for a headline that referred to the attacks explicitly, as opposed to their American counterparts who highlighted words like 'Infamy' and 'Day of Infamy', recalling the famous words used by Franklin D. Roosevelt the day after the Japanese attack. The idea of a historical debt to the Americans who had liberated Europe from the Nazi yoke, however, played an undeniable role. This is brought out by the messages collected through an operation launched the day after the attacks by the newspaper *Ouest-France* – usually France's bestselling paper, whose circulation stood at over one million copies at the time of 9/11 – in partnership with the radio station France Bleu and the Mémorial de Caen. Dubbed Opération 'Fraternellement' (Operation 'Fraternally'), it was intended primarily for the residents of the French regions most affected by the D-Day landings, as it was assumed these would inevitably feel particular solidarity with the Americans. But the appeal was relayed by TF1, France 2 and France Info, and ultimately reached a wider audience: almost 5,000 letters, a few words or several pages long, were received by the Mémorial de Caen between 12 September and 12 October,[54] from all over France (Corsica and overseas departments included) and several European countries (such as Belgium, the United Kingdom, Spain, Norway and Finland).

Almost half of these messages (46 per cent) did indeed mention the Second World War, and the generation to which their writers belonged played an obvious part: the figure rose to 96 per cent for messages from the elderly, who had experienced the Liberation, while fewer than 15 per cent came from teenagers.[55] So most of these messages showed a solidarity with Americans that was motivated by a sense of gratitude towards them. In the same way as the Americans had come to the aid of the French during the Second World War, the French now declared themselves ready to support the Americans in the new global conflict that was breaking out:

> In 1944, we needed you. [...] Today, we'll help you. As a symbol of THE FREE WORLD, rely on us. And let's fight together to bring terrorism to its knees.[56]

> It's the Western world as a whole that is in mourning, and our hearts are weeping in unison with our American brothers. We are one family and, together, we will face up to this attack that has killed our people. We weep, but we are erect and dignified, and we will stand up to the enemy. We extend our condolences to the American People and share, in its pain, its desire for revenge.[57]

> I am writing to you to express my thanks to the people and the Allies for the human sacrifices made during the Wars to restore freedom to the French. [...] Now, in September 2001, I offer my condolences to the Americans who are enduring these painful times, I want to extend to them my friendship and my full support; and I give my written pledge to be prepared to take up arms to fight at their side against their enemies.[58]

Such messages echoed the results of a poll conducted in the week following 9/11, according to which the French were, of all Europeans, those most in favour of an American military response (29 per cent, as against an average of 18.6 per cent in the European Union as a whole), and among the most inclined to see their army supporting the US (73 per cent in favour, just behind the British, 79 per cent of whom voiced the desire for such action).[59]

The Germans, while being notoriously pacifist (only 17 per cent of them were in favour of US military retaliation), nonetheless agreed (with a figure of 53 per cent) that their army should be committed alongside the American army, should the case arise.[60] This also shows the significance of the 'historical debt' to the US, something emphasized by German federal president Johannes Rau to a crowd of 200,000 Berliners gathered on 14 September, at the behest of the country's main political parties, to show solidarity with the victims of 9/11:

> No one better than you, here in Berlin, knows what America has done for freedom and democracy in Germany. We would not be here this evening, at the Brandenburg Gate, without the help that America gave us over many years, at a difficult time. That is why, here today, we send a message from Berlin to all Americans: America is not alone. [...] Here in Berlin, we remember the aid provided by the Americans after the war, their defence of the freedom of Berlin, and the great American contribution to German unity.[61]

And as soon as German Chancellor Gerhard Schröder learned the news of the attacks in the United States, he sent a telegram to the US president to assure him of his country's 'unlimited solidarity'.[62]

Although Germany and France were accordingly involved in Operation Enduring Freedom in Afghanistan, it is well known that they were among the fiercest opponents of the war in Iraq, a war that no longer appeared to be directly related to 9/11 and had not received the endorsement of the United Nations. This, as of September 2001, comprised the Achilles heel of Western solidarity. While the parallel with the Second World War (a parallel that meant 9/11 was experienced as a 'new Pearl Harbor') locked the United States into a unilateralist approach, it led the Europeans to turn instead to the UN, which after all had been founded in 1945 to prevent the world from ever being plunged again into a general war. The conclusions of the Extraordinary European Council Meeting held ten days after 9/11 clearly showed this: 'the European Union calls for the broadest possible global coalition against terrorism, under United Nations aegis'.[63] Thus, while an American riposte was 'legitimate', as these same conclusions pointed out, it was solely 'on the basis of Security Council Resolution 1368', and on condition that the actions be targeted. If the fight against terrorism were to be conducted outside the framework of the United Nations and international law, the risk was that the world would allow itself to be dragged into a destructive spiral of violence. Even those who read 9/11 in the light of *The Clash of Civilizations* agreed, with rare exceptions, that it was 'imperative to find ways and means of responding *without falling into widespread conflict*', as Denis Jeambar and Alain Louyot wrote in *L'Express*.[64]

'Apocalypse Now': How Europeans framed 9/11 differently

Thus, while 9/11 appeared to be part of a war situation both for Americans and for Europeans, a divergence between them in the way they framed this situation grew rapidly as the United States prepared to fight back. For the former, 9/11 designated a quite unique national tragedy, a surprise attack that was an act of 'infamy' that could be compared to nothing other than Pearl Harbor, and called for an adequate response. For the latter, however, it was a global event that did not concern the US alone and, if the Americans were not careful, risked plunging all mankind into a new, devastating war.

The two covers that *Paris Match* devoted successively to 9/11 clearly illustrate this trend (figures 4 and 5). The first shows the picture of the attacks most frequently published in the United States – that of the explosion caused by Flight 175 when it crashed into the south tower – with the title 'War'. This was in conformity with the aesthetics of the front pages of most US dailies published in the wake of 9/11. The cover of the following week, however, announced a report on 'These days that shake the world', on a background of smouldering ruins, with a fireman, his head lowered – the opposite of those firemen glorified in the photo by Thomas Franklin that was so wildly popular at that time in the United States. Inside pages, images of the collapse of the towers and the ruins of the World Trade Center bore captions such as 'It was suddenly night

Figures 4 and 5. Covers of *Paris Match*, 2730, 20 September 2001, and 2731, 27 September 2001.

27

time. It made you think of Hiroshima', or 'As at the end of world, the sun disappears in broad daylight.'[65] It is true that, in the American press also, these images were accompanied by phrases such as 'The day after' or 'Ground zero', both of which suggested a parallel with the devastation of a nuclear explosion. But what was different about the European treatment was the place that this apocalyptic *imaginaire* occupied in the media coverage of the event and the quite explicit parallels with Hiroshima to which it gave rise, giving the event a quite different meaning from that of being the 'new Pearl Harbor'.

This trend, too, was starting to become evident very early on, since the images of the ruins of the World Trade Center were presented twice over on the front pages of the French and US dailies in the wake of 9/11 (30 per cent of the front pages in France, as against 14 per cent in the United States).[66] And if we are to believe Aurélia Lamy, the word 'apocalypse' ultimately came up more often than the word 'war' in the language used by journalists commenting on the events live on French television: 'Daniel Bilalian calls the attacks a "veritable apocalypse", David Pujadas says that the drama gives "Manhattan the appearance of an apocalypse", he describes "a lunar, apocalyptic landscape".'[67] In the written press, the word was just as ubiquitous: 'Apocalypse in the USA', for example, was the 12 September headline in *L'Est Républicain*, with an image of the ruins: 'The terrorist apocalypse descends on New York and Washington', while *Le Figaro* and *Libération* called it 'Apocalypse in the heart of America'. Three days later, *Le Nouvel Observateur* was still telling the story of '120 minutes of apocalypse'.[68] The observation can be easily extended to the rest of the European press: in the UK, the *Daily Mail* and the *Independent* headlined with the word 'Apocalypse', while on its front page the *Daily Star* wondered: 'Is this the end of the world?';[69] in Italy, the *Corriere della Sera* titled one of its articles 'Apocalypse in Manhattan'; in Belgium, *De Morgen* opted for the headline 'Apocalypse Now'.[70] In short, there were innumerable examples of this, and so it is small wonder if the apocalypse theme was a commonplace in the essays written by 'French thinkers' about 9/11 straight after the events, given that their materials for thinking about this theme often did not extend beyond what they had seen on TV or read in the press.[71]

What is at stake here goes far beyond the mere demonstration of an apocalyptic tropism characteristic of Western societies.[72] A good example of this is the way *Apocalypse Now*, the title of Francis Ford Coppola's film on the Vietnam War, was used on the front pages of several European newspapers after the attacks (and it was also the title given by *Paris Match* to its first report on 9/11).[73] From an American point of view, the analogy with Pearl Harbor ruled out any comparison between 9/11 and any another moment in American history, particularly the Vietnam War;

from a European perspective, however, there were many other past events that could shed light on an attack that had brought the world to the brink of the Apocalypse.

So there was, first and foremost, the parallel with Hiroshima, which appeared as obvious to some people in Europe as did the parallel with Pearl Harbor to the Americans, as evidenced by the British writer John Berger:

> When on September 11 I watched the videos on television, I was instantly reminded of August 6 1945. We in Europe heard the news of the bombing of Hiroshima on the evening of the same day. The immediate correspondences between the two events include a fireball descending without warning from a clear sky, both attacks being timed to coincide with the civilians of the targeted city going to work in the morning, with the shops opening, with children in school preparing their lessons. A similar reduction to ashes, with bodies, flung through the air, becoming debris. A comparable incredulity and chaos provoked by a new weapon of destruction being used for the first time – the A-bomb 60 years ago, and a civil airliner last autumn. Everywhere at the epicentre, on everything and everybody, a thick pall of dust.[74]

The French historian Gérald Arboit said the same:

> The comparison with Hiroshima and Nagasaki was relevant. The same unity of time and place, the same way the media were united in the way they covered the events, even the absence of corpses and the same polarization of attention by another element in the drama: the atomic mushroom cloud.[75]

And, forty-eight hours after the attacks, Serge July was writing in *Libération*:

> A 'terrorist' Hiroshima carried out on a capital is now possible. This is the message of 11 September 2001.[76]

But there was also the first Gulf War, when the journalist Loïc Berrou saw the collapse of the two towers and stated, live on TF1: 'These scenes of chaos remind me of those witnessed in Jerusalem on the day the Gulf War was launched.'[77] Or the Kosovo War: 'It's Sarajevo on Wall Street', as *Paris Match* put it a few days later.[78]

While the US framing of 9/11 as a 'new Pearl Harbor' was clearly hawkish, the very different way it was framed in Europe seems more ambiguous. Without a doubt, the comparisons with Hiroshima and the wars in Vietnam and Kosovo could fuel anti-Americanism. In Greece, for example, the echo of the US bombing of Kosovo, which the Greeks had opposed, reactivated intense hostility to the United States (a hostility also roused by its role in the conflict in Cyprus). The Greeks were the least favourable of all Europeans to US military reprisals and to any possible involvement on the part of their own army,[79] and their newspapers tended to attribute responsibility for 9/11 to the Americans themselves, who, they argued, had created the global conditions for this terrorist attack.[80] At the very least, this alternative European framing suggested an equivalence between what the Americans were currently suffering and what, directly or indirectly, they had made others suffer in the past, or were still making them suffer in the present; the criterion for this was the suffering of innocent human beings. A few days after the attacks, *Le Monde* published a letter from a reader who, after denouncing the inhumanity shown by the terrorists in their massacre of the innocents, added:

> But I am not altogether sure, alas, that the atomization of the population of Hiroshima (about two hundred and fifty thousand victims) and Nagasaki (about eighty thousand) was a humane act of war. The time has come to remind the world that no cause, however just, can justify the massacre of innocent people.[81]

Even in a newspaper like *Le Figaro*, whose editorial line is pro-American and pro-Western, we read:

> Obviously, the atrocities in the United States are unforgivable. Nevertheless, when NATO bombed Baghdad, not only did this not affect us so powerfully, but some even found it entertaining, via CNN. If we add to this the passivity (apart from their words, of course) of the democracies when faced with the crushing of the Palestinian people, we can then understand how the conditions for hatred currently present on the planet can unleash terrorist fury. Yes, we should condemn the barbarity and stand alongside the Americans, but no, we should not relapse into a vulgar Manichean world view, with the angels on one side and the demons on the other.[82]

So this alternative way of framing things in Europe also stemmed from the fact that these comparisons flew directly in the face of the incommensurability that, from the American point of view, attached to 9/11. It reflected a conception of 9/11 not as an act of infamous aggression on the United States, coming out of the blue and comparable with Pearl Harbor alone, but as one massacre of innocent civilians *among others*, set in a geopolitical and historical context for which the United States, like other Western countries, undeniably bears part of the responsibility. Another reader of *Le Monde* stated that we needed to show as much solidarity with the Americans as we had with the Israelis in 1972 at the Munich Olympics and with the Palestinians at the Sabra and Shatila massacre in 1982. And we must ensure that we continue to show as much solidarity with 'Chechen, Iraqi, Afghan and Algerian civilians' if we do not want the ranks of terrorists willing to commit more attacks like those of 9/11 to swell.[83]

9/11 from a cosmopolitical perspective

What emerges through this alternative European framing of 9/11 is the point of view of the 'citizens of the world', one that aims to be as objective as possible. One might think that this is a response characteristic of intellectual circles. However, a study of data from the International Social Survey has shown that European countries are the only industrialized countries where, from 1995 to 2003, attachment to the nation weakened while the proportion of individuals claiming that they felt themselves to be 'citizens of the world' increased – where, in other words, 'cosmopolitanism is gaining ground against nation-oriented localism'.[84] Elsewhere (that is to say, in the United States, Canada, Australia, New Zealand, Japan and Russia) the complete opposite occurred, and this led the authors of this study to wonder whether the impact of 9/11 had been radically different across the world: had Europeans experienced it in their own specific way?

Obviously, in Europe there was a palpable tension between, on the one hand, a sense of compassion for the victims and solidarity with the United States, and, on the other, a way of envisioning 9/11 as a global event involving the whole future of humanity. Tzvetan Todorov put it extremely well:

> Solidarity must not be a vain word, and the United States is our ally. If France, my country, were attacked tomorrow, help would come from the United States, definitely not from Afghanistan. But solidarity does not mean justice. At the same time I say to myself that many cities throughout the world have suffered from American bombings in the twentieth century, and that the greatest novelty of these terrorist attacks is that they struck American territory and not that they killed 'innocent civilians'. [...] The inhabitants of Belgrade, Baghdad, Hanoi or Hiroshima felt as innocent vis-à-vis their government's policies as the inhabitants of New York; they all experienced the violence that struck them as a profound injustice.[85]

In other words, while it is obvious that the French had a sense of solidarity with the Americans in their tribulations, they also felt obliged to point out that a military response involving the killing of more innocent civilians would merely exacerbate the problem of terrorism rather than

31

solving it. In the week following 9/11, 76 per cent of Europeans expressed their preference for a judicial rather than military response to the attacks.[86] If they had the impression that 9/11 resembled the beginning of a third world war, most of them also hoped that this war could still be avoided. In Germany, rallies were held in the major cities – Berlin, Munich, Frankfurt – on the evening of 9/11 and over the following days, and placards were waved that stated, in English: 'No revenge please, no war', or 'No world war 3' (*sic*).[87]

This concern to preserve the conditions for peace in the world, linked to what I will be analysing later on as a 'banal pacifism' on the part of the Europeans,[88] was also reflected in the messages from French people collected as part of Operation 'Fraternally'. Nearly 20 per cent of those women and men who wrote to Americans did so to warn against the evils of taking an eye for an eye, urging them not to yield to the provocation of terrorists and asking them to carry out justice wisely. They did this in their own words and using less complex arguments than those developed in letters from readers of *Le Monde* or *Le Figaro* – a sign that this phenomenon was not limited to a few individuals giving themselves expert airs and addressing their geopolitical analysis to the editors of major dailies. Here are a few examples:

> We must ensure that we do not transform these barbaric acts into the trigger for a new war. We must, for we have no other choice, take them as an opportunity to rethink our vision of the world, to take more of an interest in what is happening beyond our borders. [...] It is with our hearts that we need to get together and ponder how to restore peace. For even if our desire for revenge is at present huge, the only value great enough that we can draw upon to oppose these barbaric acts, is peace.[89]

> What I wish to say to the US authorities, to you who will decide the fate of humanity, is that we must think and THINK again ... What about bin Laden? Is he not the reflection of our faces in the mirror? [...] I think the time of RECONCILIATION has come, it is a sad time, but the lessons we can learn from it are fundamental. [...] Let us gather all the countries in the world around the table of compassion.[90]

> We should not confuse the international outcry against these attacks with a corny pro-Americanism, but see them as an alarm call and a warning against a wave of blind, demonic violence spreading out in every direction. [...] Not all the victims were American 'bastards', but also Europeans, Africans, etc. Which shows how blind terrorism is. [...] As to retaliation, let justice be carried out wisely, without striking innocent civilians.[91]

All these messages were dated to the time around 14 September, the American National Day of Mourning; they expressed the concerns being voiced in Europe at the martial posture adopted by the United States.

The speech given on that same day by German president Johannes Rau in Berlin was another striking example of this.[92] When he said that the Germans would also meet terrorism with 'strength and determination', he immediately added:

> And with caution. Hatred must not lead us to respond with hatred. Nothing is more difficult to build, and nothing is easier to destroy, than peace.

Then he explained that it was primarily the state of the world at the beginning of the twenty-first century, the misery and despair in which some peoples were trapped, that fed into terrorism:

> Poverty and exploitation, wretchedness and lack of rights drive people to despair. Contempt for their religious beliefs and cultural traditions deprives them of any hope and any dignity. It leads some to violence and terror. It is already sowing hatred in children's hearts.

Hence his conclusion:

> The best protection against terrorism, violence and war is a just international order. The fruit of justice will be peace. [...] Our common goal is peace and security, justice and freedom for all peoples, wherever they live.

What the German federal president was appealing to, in order to eradicate terrorism, was not war, but rather the establishment of a true 'world politics', literally a *cosmopolitics*, backed by a principle of global justice.

European intellectuals subsequently sought to specify the shapes and modes of that cosmopolitan response to 9/11, including Jacques Derrida and Jürgen Habermas,[93] or Daniele Archibugi and David Held, who saw it as an opportunity to launch a worldwide 'Marshall Plan' whose main priority would be to reduce global inequality, effectively control the international circulation of arms and resolve the Israeli–Palestinian conflict.[94] Some of their US counterparts, such as Judith Butler, Edward Said and Immanuel Wallerstein, also spoke out in favour of this cosmopolitan response, but identified Europe as its spearhead.[95] Petitions also started to be circulated on 14 September, and met with some success: for example, in France, the petition launched by a young student at the elite Lycée Henri IV in Paris, Salim Abdelmadjid, or that of the 'cyber-actors', a pioneering organization for citizen activism 'online', created on this occasion by Alain Uguen, a local elected official from Quimper (also cofounder of the ecological party Les Verts).

The main result of these developments, which occurred over just a few days, was that they ultimately led, in Europe, to a shift away from the initial impression that 9/11 was part of a war situation. It is symptomatic in this regard that the word 'war' was completely absent from the conclusions of the Extraordinary European Council Meeting of 21 September 2001, where 9/11 was described in these terms: 'These attacks are an assault on our open, democratic, tolerant and multicultural societies. They are a challenge to the conscience of each human being.'[96] This text here endorses a divergence between the ways the United States and European countries framed the event. Rather than being an act of war, the 9/11 attacks were ultimately seen, in Europe, as a 'mass crime',[97] a sort of crime against humanity for which those responsible should be brought before the International Criminal Court.

From 'All Americans' to 'All New Yorkers'

'We are all Americans': the title of the editorial by Jean-Marie Colombani in Le Monde in the aftermath of 9/11 has become celebrated.[98] Exceptionally, Le Monde's circulation doubled (to over one million copies) and the editorial, widely circulated, set the tone for many of the reactions in Europe. Soon, however, in the face of the nationalist tenor assumed by US reaction to the attacks, this upsurge of European solidarity started to seem out of joint. It did not really have any place in the framework of a 'new Pearl Harbor'. American television channels focused on the grief and trauma felt in the US, with only a tiny amount of attention being paid to the repercussions of 9/11 in the rest of the world. One French TV viewer explicitly complained about this in a letter to Le Monde: if you believe the CNN images, he wrote, 'only the Americans have been hurt. Only the Americans are suffering.'[99] The different ways of framing the events emerging on both sides of the Atlantic also led to questioning of the words being used: thus, the political analyst Alain Joxe wrote, two weeks after the attacks:

> This does not affect the United States alone [...]. But to say that we are all Americans is absolutely false. We are Europeans, and yet we are shaken by these events, even though we do not have the same reasons for being shaken. The unity of the reaction stems from the fascist, genocidal nature of the act, not from shared political ideas.[100]

From the original 'We are all Americans', there was then an inadvertent slip to 'We are all New Yorkers.'

New York is seen as the 'world city' par excellence, and so claiming that 'We are all New Yorkers' better suited the European reframing of 9/11 as a global event affecting all of humanity. As the philosopher Jean-Paul Dollé wrote:

> *To attack New York is not to attack the US, it is to attack the world.* Not because, just as in Washington, all human affairs are to a greater or lesser degree affected by what is decided there [in New York], but because people from all around the world live there. From the beginning of its history, the city of New York has been a harbour and a haven where, after a long and perilous journey – from across the seas and across many lands – exiles, refugees, stateless people, and adventurers from five continents have been able to land. [...] *On 11 September 2001, at the time of the attack, all the ethnic groups of the earth were present in New York.* Workers of many nationalities occupied the storeys of the World Trade Center.[101]

Toni Negri, in an interview with the journal *Multitudes* a few weeks after the attacks, said the same:

> I don't think we can say that we are all Americans. I do think, however, that we're all New Yorkers. I feel this is really important. If we're all New Yorkers, it's not because we accept American culture, but because we accept the culture of New York, the culture of the melting pot, the Big Apple full of worms.[102]

Three years later, after the 11 March 2004 attack in Madrid, Daniel Cohn-Bendit also warned the journalists of *Le Parisien*:

> We need to be careful! There was some confusion after the 9/11 attacks. We shouldn't have said 'We are all Americans', but 'We are all New Yorkers.' Right now, I'm not saying that we are all Spaniards, but that we are all Madrilenians. It's not the same thing.[103]

But if there may have been some confusion in September 2001, it is also because a certain ambiguity slipped into the editorial by Jean-Marie Colombani, still reeling from the shock, in the night of 11 to 12 September 2001. Anyone who read on after the heading of the editorial came across these words:

> In this tragic moment when words seem too poor to express the shock that is being felt, the first thing that comes to mind is this: we are all Americans! We are all New Yorkers, just as certainly as John Kennedy declared, in 1962 in Berlin, that he was a Berliner.[104]

From the start, the editor of *Le Monde* used both formulations, with their reference to John F. Kennedy's celebrated speech in front of the West Berlin town hall on 26 June 1963 (and not, as Colombani mistakenly wrote, 1962): Kennedy was expressing his solidarity with a city, not a country: 'Ich bin ein Berliner.'

All the same, it is not altogether clear that saying 'We are all New Yorkers' was any more right and proper than saying 'We are all Americans' in the aftermath of 9/11. After all, the phrase ignores two of the four attacks that took place that day, marginalizing both the victims of American Airlines Flight 77, which crashed into the Pentagon (184 fatalities) and those of United Airlines Flight 93 (40 fatalities). While these two attacks killed only a tenth of those at the World Trade Center (2,753 deaths), they played, and still play, a crucial role in the American conception of 9/11. The crash of Flight 77 into the Pentagon, in particular, could not pass for anything other than an act of war:

> The assault is aimed at the war capabilities of the US empire. It is an act of war – not just terrorism – because it is evident that attacking the centre of the war machine does not merely terrorize the leaders of the US military, but is an indication that a full-frontal combat has been launched on them.[105]

And while New York is said to be the 'world city' par excellence, Washington is the US capital: attacking this city clearly means targeting the nation's nerve centre.

As for the crash of Flight 93 in Pennsylvania, it is, from the European point of view, a hijacked plane that missed its target (presumably Congress or the White House) and crashed into an empty field, far from the television cameras, just as the World Trade Center was collapsing and focusing all the attention on itself. From the American point of view, however, it is a perfect symbol of American heroism, as the passengers on the plane mutinied and thus foiled the terrorists' mission, and their plane crashed in Pennsylvania, the founding state of the nation, about 150 km from Gettysburg, the mythical battlefield of the Civil War which to the United States means roughly what Verdun means to France. With the benefit of hindsight, but very rapidly, the passengers of Flight 93 were treated as heroes of the American nation, and their story was brought to the big screen by director Paul Greengrass in his 2006 film, *United 93*. The widow of one of the mutinous passengers, Todd Beamer, was hailed by President Bush in Congress on 20 September, at the beginning of his speech announcing America's entry into war. And the site where Flight 93 crashed, in Shanksville, has become an important place of memory in the United States.[106]

Conversely, in the European media, these two crashes were soon side-lined. Forty-eight hours after the attacks, the crash of Flight 93 had dropped out of French TV coverage, while the particulars of the attack against the Pentagon were mere footnotes in comparison with the time devoted to events in New York.[107] In addition, the same day, survivors from the towers of the World Trade Center were interviewed, people whom European viewers could identify with – while, for lack of direct testimony, 'the Pentagon attack remained an event that happened to others; it was not an event that, even potentially, could have happened to us'.[108] The same was true in the printed press: between 12 and 14 September 2001, fifty-five articles on the attacks in New York were published in *Le Monde*, *Le Figaro*, *Libération* and *L'Humanité*, as against only fourteen on the attack on the Pentagon and four on the crash of Flight 93.[109] In some weekly papers, only the attacks on the World Trade Center were mentioned. In 2006, the sociologist Pascal Lardellier interviewed some hundred or so French people about their memories of 9/11, and found that not one of them mentioned the crashes into the Pentagon and Shanksville, as if the events at the World Trade Center had, for them, made everything else vanish 'into thin air'.[110]

So is it not uncommon these days for the attacks of 11 September 2001 to be referred to in France, in the media as well as in everyday conversation, as 'the New York attacks' or 'the dramatic events at the World Trade Center', rather than using the common expression '11 September' or '9/11'. This is absolutely not the case in the United States, where the date is always referred to this way. And there is another difference: '9/11' is, for Americans, a proper name that refers to a quite singular historic event, while in France and elsewhere in Europe, the date is frequently used as a common name for other events.[111] This, as we shall now see, was the case for the *Charlie Hebdo* attack.

— 2 —

EXPERIENCING YOUR 'OWN' 9/11

France too, it seems, experienced its 'own' 9/11. The front page of *Le Monde*, in the wake of the attack on *Charlie Hebdo*, attests this. But the newspaper, whose headline read, in capital letters, 'The French 9/11', was not the first to draw the analogy. Just a few hours after the shooting, it was already being used by people such as Michel Onfray, Philippe Geluck, Eric Zemmour and the president of the Racing Club de Toulon, Mourad Boudjellal. '9/11 for the press', '9/11 for cartoonists', '9/11 for freedom of expression': everyone went for their own version. 'This is a European 9/11' declared the president of the National Assembly, Claude Bartolone,[1] having obviously forgotten that the term had already been employed ten years earlier, for the attack on 11 March 2004 in Madrid, which remains the deadliest attack in Europe since 9/11.

And so, like the Spanish in 2004, we debated the merits of the analogy, made the list of similarities and differences between 9/11 and the tragedy that had hit us. But whether or not it appeared relevant, people generally failed to consider what this analogy involves, what it says of our relationship to 9/11 and the United States, and how it influences our response to Islamist attacks. While the attacks in Mumbai in November 2008 have also been described as an 'Indian 9/11', this is because one of the terrorists told the police that he and his associates had deliberately sought to replicate the impact of the attacks of 2001.[2] Nothing like this happened after the attacks in Madrid and Paris: it was the society affected that made its own comparison with 9/11. Could this have been avoided? If another attack occurs tomorrow in another European capital, is it doomed to be compared, yet again, to 9/11?

11 March attacks like a 'new 9/11'

On 11 March 2004, in the morning, four commuter trains leaving the station of Alcalá de Henares, in the southern suburbs of Madrid, were hit by ten bombs exploding in the space of two minutes. At 7.37 a.m., three bombs exploded successively in Train No. 21431, standing at the platform in Madrid's main Atocha station. At 7.38, three more bombs exploded in turn: two in Train No. 21435, in the station of El Pozo del Tío Raimundo, a few kilometres from Madrid, and one in Train No. 21713, a little closer to the capital on the same line, in Santa Eugenia station. A few seconds later, at 7.39, the last four bombs exploded in Train No. 17305, which was in Madrid, level with the Calle Téllez, approximately 500 metres from the Atocha station. These ten explosions caused the death of 191 people and injured 1,856 others – the worst toll of any attack in Spain since the Civil War.[3] The comparison with 9/11 thus seems to have been drawn by Spaniards straight away.

Spain's 9/11

It is probably not unfair to say that the reference to 9/11 was just as common in Europe as that to Pearl Harbor had been in 2001 in the United States; the involvement of European countries in the Iraq War in 2003 had only increased a little more the fear of a repeat in Europe of the 2001 attacks. Cathy Ceïbe, reporting from Madrid for L'Humanité, noted that 'comparisons between this 11 March 2004 and the tragic terrorist attacks of 11 September on New York are on practically everyone's lips',[4] from politicians to editorialists, via anonymous Madrilenians interviewed in the streets. Both in the special editions published by the main Spanish newspapers on the afternoon of 11 March and in those which appeared the next day, the reference to 9/11 was ubiquitous. There was not a newspaper that failed to mention it. ABC, for example, spoke of 'the shudder of 9/11 in the middle of Madrid', while El Mundo published an editorial entitled 'Our 9/11'.[5] Some newspapers put it straight onto their front pages – La Opinión de Zamora, for example, that headlined with 'El terrorismo resucita en Madrid el horror del 11-S' ('Terrorism revives in Madrid the horror of 11 September'), and Deia, a Basque newspaper: '11-M, el 11-S español' ('11 March, the Spanish 11 September').

It was the extent of the devastation caused by the explosions, first and foremost, that led to the comparison with 9/11, irrespective of any considerations about the identity of the terrorists. Here and there, as in September 2001, comparisons were drawn with bombings and scenes of war, and the analogy with 9/11 sometimes came with an evocation of the Spanish Civil War and, in particular, the bombing of Guernica. We also find traces of it in the French press, as shown by this excerpt from La Voix du Nord:

Nineteen Madrid hospitals have taken in 1,400 wounded and are experiencing the same scenes as if the city had undergone a real bombardment, an 11 September on 11 March, a new Guernica.[6]

So we need to avoid falling prey to a possible retrospective illusion: the Madrid bombings were not likened to a 'new 9/11' after the event, only once it had become clear that it had been perpetrated by Islamists, but the comparison was drawn immediately, even when it was still being attributed to ETA. This was the idea put forward throughout the day by the Spanish government, which fostered it among both journalists and foreign diplomats – witness the resolution unanimously adopted by the UN Security Council at midday, which condemned the attack, attributing it explicitly to ETA,[7] or the edition of *Le Monde* published in the late afternoon which, on the basis of information provided by the Spanish government, spoke of a 'bloody return of ETA' and did not speculate about any other possible perpetrators.[8]

The Spanish prime minister, José María Aznar, himself drew on the analogy with 9/11, beginning his speech on the evening of the attack with this sentence: '11 March 2004 now has its place in the history of infamy.'[9] Seeing the Madrid bombings as part of 'the history of infamy' clearly situated it as a direct extension of 9/11, provided we remember that 9/11 itself was viewed in the United States as a 'new day of infamy', i.e. a new Pearl Harbor. This comes down to presenting the Madrid bombings not only as a new 9/11, but even more as a new 'new Pearl Harbor', even though the reference to Pearl Harbor and the 'history of infamy' was perfectly foreign to the history of Spain. In this respect, José María Aznar was addressing, beyond his fellow citizens, more the Americans than the Europeans (in fact, his formula ended up on the front pages of several US newspapers the next day, while it was barely quoted in Europe). Without ever going so far as to mention 9/11 explicitly, he thus suggested that the attack just carried out in Madrid was an act of aggression on the Spanish nation equivalent to that suffered by the United States three years earlier; this therefore gave a little more justification for the support he gave the Americans in their 'war on terrorism', including the invasion of Iraq.

When reacting on CNN, the Spanish ambassador to the US, Javier Rupérez, made this way of framing the attack more explicit. He stated bluntly 'it is our 11 September' and concluded that the Spaniards would 'react exactly the same way as the Americans had reacted when they went through this terrible trauma'. Then, saying he was 'pretty sure that it is the terrorist group ETA' that was responsible for the attack, he added: 'I have the conviction that we are going to win the war.'[10] In the wake of these statements, the Spanish conservative newspapers adopted a hawkish rhetoric reminiscent of the American media in September 2001. *ABC*, for example, published an editorial by Juan Juaristi which saw the Madrid bombings as part of a world war between the friends of democracy and their enemies,[11] while *El Mundo*, inspired by the prime minister's speech, used as a headline, word for word, one that had been on the front pages in the United States following 9/11: 'The day of infamy'.

In the French press, the analogy with 9/11 was, to begin with, usually made in scare quotes, like the analogy with Pearl Harbor in September 2001. Two days after the attack, *Le Figaro* offered its 'Reflections on the Spanish "9/11"'.[12] In *Le Monde*, the front page 'Our 9/11', referred to the statements of the Spanish ambassador to the US,[13] while another presented this analogy as expressing a feeling specific to the Spaniards, based on a 'tragic coincidence in the calendar [which] has not escaped the notice of any city-dweller and has added a "historical" dimension to an unprecedented collective trauma'.[14] However, a few pages later, the analogy is also used without quotation marks, on a European scale this time: Daniel Vernet's editorial has the title 'Europe's 9/11'.[15] At the same time that this edition of *Le Monde* came out, on the evening of 12 March, an edition of *France Soir* read: 'The United States had their 11 September. *Now Europe will have its 11 March.*'[16] The same tone could be observed in Germany: on the morning of 12 March, the *Frankfurter Allgemeine Zeitung* initially referred to a 'Spanish 11 March [that] follows the American 11 September in the annals of terrorist monstrosities',[17] and the next day *Der Tagesspiegel* announced: 'In Madrid, Europe has experienced its 9/11.'[18]

This Europeanization of the analogy was especially justified by the way European institutions and elected officials responded to the attack. On the page facing Daniel Vernet's piece in *Le Monde*, an editorial entitled 'European tragedy' highlighted the 'immediate solidarity demonstrated at the European Parliament'.[19] The European and Spanish flags at the entrance to the European Parliament had of course been lowered to half-mast as soon as the news broke. Above all, at the opening of the plenary session scheduled for that morning, the MEPs began by solemnly observing a minute's silence. Just before, the president of the Parliament, Pat Cox, spoke in these terms:

> This morning in Madrid, at the height of rush-hour earlier today, there have been at least five bomb blasts at three railway stations. The worst of these was on a train entering the Atocha station in Madrid. Tens of people have been murdered; scores of people are injured. With each report, the reported casualty list is rising. This is, in terms of consequence, the worst act of terror in the history of Spain, the worst act of terror in memory in any European Union state.[20]

Then, noting that this attack came three days before a general election, he added: 'What happened today is a declaration of war on democracy.' The bombings in Madrid were framed as an attack not only on Spain, but on democracy itself and the founding values of the European Union, a feeling with which many other statements made by European leaders during the day concurred. Finally, after observing their minute of silence, the MEPs adopted a resolution to establish 11 March as a day of European commemoration for the victims of terrorism.[21] They themselves thus seemed to perceive the Madrid bombings as a 'European 9/11' even before the final toll had been established and before it had been settled whether Al-Qaeda was or was not behind the attack.

Europe versus Al-Qaeda

The term 'European 9/11' appeared for the first time in France on 15 September 2003, in an article published in *Le Figaro* by Michel Barnier, in his capacity as European commissioner (a few months later, he would be appointed French foreign minister).[22] Calling for a strengthening of the European policy on security and defence, he stated that he was responsible for introducing into the draft of the Constitution for Europe a solidarity clause between member states of the European Union in case of a terrorist attack on any one of them. A few months later, concluding his editorial in *Le Monde* entitled 'Europe's 9/11', Daniel Vernet recalled the existence of this clause and concluded that this was an opportunity for it to be adopted early.[23] In a context still marked by the deep divisions that had emerged within the European Union over the Iraq War, the Madrid bombings seemed, in the eyes of MEPs and European leaders, a de facto opportunity to show their unity. Javier Solana, then the European Union's high representative for common foreign and security policy, stated that 'unity against terrorism could be a way to cement' member countries of the European Union.[24] But if he used the conditional, this was because, if this 'cement' was to work over the long term, the terrorist threat had to be perceived as common to all European countries, and not as specific to only one of them.

This was the main idea expressed in an editorial by the British historian and essayist Timothy Garton Ash, published on the morning of 13 March in the *Guardian*: 'Is this Europe's 9/11?' According to him, the answer lay entirely in the identity of the terrorists responsible for the attack:

> If it was al-Qaeda, then few will doubt that this is Europe's 9/11. [...] If, however, those responsible were from the Basque terrorist movement Eta, or a radical splinter group, then there will be a strong temptation to say

that this is essentially a Spanish problem: just as most continental Europeans think the IRA is really a British problem, not a European one.[25]

If the Madrid bombings were originally seen as analogous to 9/11 because of their seriousness and the context in which they occurred, whether or not they really were akin to a repeat of 9/11 on European territory depended on this question, which appeared on the front page of *Le Monde* on the evening of 12 March: 'Madrid, 11 March 2004: Al-Qaeda, ETA?'

Now, at 6 p.m. on 12 March, i.e. just as this edition of *Le Monde* was coming out and Timothy Garton Ash was probably putting the final touches to his editorial, ETA, in a statement transmitted by telephone to the newspaper *Gara* and the Basque television channel ETB, formally denied any responsibility for the attack. Ninety minutes later, a man speaking Spanish with an Arab accent informed the channel Telemadrid that a video recording claiming responsibility for the attack was in a rubbish bin near the Islamic Cultural Centre in Madrid. On this video, a man, declaring himself to be the spokesman of Ansar Al-Qaeda, presented the Madrid bombings as a follow-up to 9/11 suffered by Spain for having allied itself with the United States. Twenty-four hours before, late on 11 March, the Arabic-language newspaper published in London *Al-Quds Al-Arabi* had received a statement by email signed by the 'Abu Hafs al-Masri/Al-Qaeda Brigades', claiming responsibility for the '"Trains of Death" Operation'. Even though the Spanish minister of the interior Ángel Acebes said on the evening of 12 March that he gave no credence to these statements, and even though he would continue to claim, until he left office (i.e. until the victory of the Socialist Party in the parliamentary elections of 14 March), that he thought the Basques were the most likely culprits, it seemed increasingly plausible from 13 March onwards that the Madrid bombings were indeed the repeat of 9/11 on the old continent that had been so dreaded by the Europeans.

In retrospect, it could even appear obvious. Two months after the attack, during a parliament debate, Jean-Louis Debré, then president of the National Assembly, said that 'the March 11 attacks in Madrid [clearly appear to be] an echo of 9/11'.[26] Three years later, the article in *Le Monde* on the start of the trial of the perpetrators of the attack also began with the words: 'it was like a repeat of 9/11: attacks against a big city just at the time people were setting off to work'.[27] In this respect, the analogy with 9/11 has played a particular role, in that it quickly became a crucial reference point. Right from the start, the scale of the attack and even more its modus operandi (simultaneous attacks on public transport in rush hour, clearly aimed to claim as many deaths as possible and to wreak spectacular havoc) did indeed arouse doubts whether ETA was responsible, unless it could be assumed that the organization had switched to 'hyper-terrorism' and, with this in mind, had perhaps collaborated with members of Al-Qaeda, as some people suggested the next day, purely speculatively.[28] But even more than that, the numerical coincidence seemed to indicate that the terrorists themselves had wanted to suggest a link between their activities and 9/11: an 11 March after an 11 September, four trains hit after four planes had been hijacked ... Commentators also pointed out that precisely 911 days had passed since 11 September, 2001: 911, just like '9/11'.

Reviving memories of its famous editorial published after 9/11 attacks, on the evening of 13 March *Le Monde* ran the headline: 'Europe facing the threat of Al-Qaeda. We are all Madrilenians.' 'All Madrilenians' was a formula that also appeared in the headlines of that day's *Libération*. The same phenomenon could be seen in the regional press. That same 13 March, *Nice-Matin* published an editorial by Alain Duhamel, 'Europe in the front line', where the Madrid bombings were presented as 'the first anti-European attack'.[29] Four days later, Duhamel developed this idea in the pages of *Libération*, in an article where he concluded by saying that 'Spain's misfortune has become a European tragedy.'[30] The term 'Europe's 9/11' or the 'European 9/11' then spread quickly, both in the press and on radio and television, in France as elsewhere, even appearing as the headline in the New York *Newsweek* on 22 March 2004.

For most of the journalists and politicians who resorted to it, this analogy was not simply meant to be a description giving the event its meaning and scope; it also had a normative value. It suggested that all Europeans *should* feel concerned by the attack, and respond with the same unity as the Americans had after 9/11. Basically, it expressed the hope that adversity could finally give birth to something like a European nation, or at least a community of peoples aware of what united them. The idea of 'we, the West' that was triggered by September 2001 was succeeded by a 'we, Europeans' in March 2004.[31] The discussions then under way on the drafting of the European Constitution obviously influenced this vision; witness an interview given by Noëlle Lenoir, minister for European affairs, to Radio Classique on 15 March. While the journalist did not herself use the term 'European 9/11' in the first question she asked, the minister said straight away:

It was right to describe the events of 11 March as a 'European 9/11'. It is a tragedy that affects us all [...]. The message is addressed to the democracies, because it is the democracies that have been targeted via the Spanish democracy. 'Wake up': this is the message sent to Europe. Europeans must agree. Europeans must be able to fight together effectively against terrorism.

44

Then, in her reply to the following question, she adds: 'Here I would like to make an appeal, as we no longer have the right, now, to retreat from the adoption of the European Constitution.'[32]

A (more or less) European 9/11

Apart from the reactions of European institutions and political leaders, it is a fact that the Madrid bombings did not receive the same attention in all European countries. Some more than others viewed it as a 'European 9/11', without this being necessarily related to their membership of the European Union. Romania, in particular, experienced it as a national tragedy, though it joined the European Union only in 2007. This is because Romania was, after Spain, the country that lost the most nationals in the attack: 16 of the 191 dead were of Romanian nationality. The embassy of Romania is thus the only one in Madrid where you can today see a plaque on its facade commemorating the event. It resulted in a lively debate in the Romanian press, on the causes of emigration that had led young Romanians to leave home only to die in Madrid, and also allowed Romanian politicians and media to emphasize the solidarity de facto uniting Romania and the existing members of the European Union, both in their mourning and in the fight against terrorism.[33]

On a smaller scale, this factor also played a part in Bulgaria and Poland, as both countries lost four nationals. It also had some influence in France as evidenced by the attention paid to the only person of French nationality who died in the attack: Marion Subervielle, a young woman from the Pyrénées-Atlantiques who worked at the National Library of Spain. Generally speaking, the fact that among the 191 people who lost their lives in the Madrid bombings, 27 (14 per cent) were nationals of European countries other than Spain[34] probably helped this attack to be likened to 'Europe's 9/11'. The 7 July 2005 attack in London, for its part, had plunged 'only' three other European countries into mourning outside the UK, as there were three female Polish victims, one Italian female and one French male in the 52 deaths (9.5 per cent; see table 1).

The nationality of those killed in the attack in Madrid does not, however, provide a sufficient explanation for the full effect. Although Italy did not lose of any of its nationals in the Madrid bombings, the latter were soon being seen in Italy as an echo of 9/11.[35] Other factors therefore played a part. The first among them was whether or not the country was involved in the Iraq War alongside the United States, as Spain was. The case of Norway illustrates this very well: while it is geographically remote from Spain and not a member of the European Union, its press gave a prominent place to the Madrid bombings. It was one of the first to accredit the claimed responsibility for the attack sent to

Table 1. Nationalities of those killed in each attack.

	9/11	Madrid bombings	London bombings
Nationals	85%	74%	79%
European countries	4.5%	14%	9.5%
Rest of the world	11%	12%	13.5%
Total of people killed	*2,977*	*191*	*52*

The nationality of those killed in the attacks in Madrid and London was determined from press obituaries (*El País* and *El Mundo* in one case, *The Times* and *BBC News* in the other). For 11 September, in contrast, obituaries published in the *New York Times* did not identify all of the dead and did not always refer to their nationalities, so the figures have been compiled by combining these obituaries with several other sources available on the Internet. Due to some cases of dual nationality, the figures do not always come to a total of 100 per cent.

Al-Quds Al-Arabi on the evening of 11 March and to criticize the attitude of the Aznar government in the way it managed information. Norway's leading newspaper, *Aftenposten*, supported the idea that Islamists lay behind the attack in its morning edition of 12 March, almost forty-eight hours before *Le Monde* or *The Times*.[36] Thus, the bombings in Madrid were soon being linked in Norway to the Iraq War; and the fact that Norway was, like Spain, involved in this war helped intensify the feeling that what was happening in Madrid could very well happen the next day in Oslo. Similarly, the Italian press placed even more importance on the attack as Italy had also taken part in the military coalition in Iraq, and the communiqué of the 'Brigades Abu Hafs Al-Masri' claiming responsibility for the Madrid bombings under the name Operation 'Trains of Death' simultaneously announced an Operation 'Black Smoke of Death' in Italy. In the UK, finally, the possibility that London would be the next city on the list of Islamist terrorists erased the usual editorial divisions between the conservative and the progressive press.[37] In all three countries, the Madrid bombings occupied more space in newspapers, and for a longer period, than was the case, for example, in Germany, which was not involved in the war in Iraq.[38]

How are we explain, on the other hand, that within the countries that had held back from the war in Iraq, French newspapers granted twice as much importance to the attack as their German counterparts?[39] The French press focused on debates over the identity of the terrorists, while the German press shifted its attention away from this after forty-eight hours, once Al-Qaeda's claim that it was responsible had been verified. Two other factors in all likelihood played a part here. The first was linked, of course, to the special relationship between France and Spain: a common border, centuries of shared history and a large immigrant population of Spanish origin settled in France. The second related to the place occupied by the question of terrorism in France, and more precisely, by the fact that France had itself experienced, some ten years previously, a series of bomb attacks perpetrated on public transport by Islamist terrorists.

The memory of Islamist attacks on the express metro line RER B in Paris, at the Saint-Michel and Port Royal stations, on 25 July 1995 and 3 December 1996 (together they claimed 12 dead and nearly 300 wounded) did seem to come to the minds of many people in March 2004. Witness this message posted on the forum of *Libération* the day after the attack:

> Last night I was watching the people in the metro in Paris, I imagine a lot of them were thinking about Madrid just then. Everyone who uses public transport on a daily basis can only feel a sense of solidarity for those enduring the current tragedy. [...] And I couldn't help having a thought for Saint-Michel and Port Royal, two RER stations that I often use and that my family used on the days when the attacks happened.[40]

A young woman who came to participate in a demonstration of solidarity with the victims in front of the Spanish embassy in Paris, on the evening of 12 March, also justified her presence there to *France Info* by evoking those precedents and referring to the threats of the mysterious 'AZF' group that hung over the French rail network:

> It could very well have happened to us here ... Just a few days ago, we heard about threats to the rail system in France, and practically all the train routes were under surveillance. So why not? There it is ... It might well have been that too. And then, we had 1995, 1996 ... We also know what it is, so ... There it is.[41]

The attack in Madrid, in fact, was similar to an intensified version of the bombings in the Paris RER in the mid-1990s, as was suggested by an expert who told *France-Soir* that what had happened in Madrid corresponded to 'attacks of the "Saint-Michel-Port Royal" type'.[42] In the same way in Italy, the Madrid bombings could seem an echo of the memory of the bomb attacks on trains or stations during the 'years of lead', especially the deadliest of them all, the one that occurred in Bologna on 2 August 1980 (85 dead and more than 200 wounded), which remains one of the worst attacks ever experienced in Europe.[43]

By recalling these precedents, journalists also contributed, in the countries where they took place, to sharpening public awareness of the event.

And, as we shall see in part 2, having yourself been, directly or indirectly, a victim or witness to a terrorist attack is one factor that inclines you to feel personally concerned by a new attack and thus express your emotions in the first person singular rather than plural.[44] Regarding the relationship of the French to the Madrid bombings, this homology of experiences intensified the sense of geographical closeness, as a message posted on the Internet forum of the association SOS Attentats suggests: 'May we, in France, remember that 1995 is not far away. And neither is Madrid.'[45] Even more generally, some people emphasized the fact that the victims were workers and students living in the suburbs who used public transport early in the morning to go to work – people everyone could identify with. MEP Anna Terrón i Cusí (a member of the Socialist Party of Catalonia) explained that if 11 March 2004 was indeed a 'European 9/11', this was because, in her view, it highlighted an 'undeniable emotional closeness' between Europeans, resting on the 'same way of life: we all take the metro, the train ... *We are all very close.*'[46]

If the analogy with 9/11 crossed the borders between France and Spain, then, this was not just because it enabled one to assess the Madrid bombings and relate them to an Islamist threat hanging over all the Western countries. It was also a way of suggesting that what happened in the Spanish capital might have happened to us, *to us, too*, all of us who take public transport in the morning to go to work and who have sometimes experienced such attacks in our own countries. The analogy operates as an instruction telling us to be concerned. All things being equal, the analogy fulfilled the same role for the attack on *Charlie Hebdo*. Saying it was a 'French 9/11' was certainly one way of describing the extent of the reaction to the event across the country, with thousands of French people gathering spontaneously in public places throughout the country after the attack. But it was as much a way of saying that *all the French*, and not just those who spontaneously took to the streets, not just the journalists, the Parisians and the readers of *Charlie Hebdo*, should be concerned about the event. In other words, it was the duty of the French people to be just as united at this time as the Americans had been in the aftermath of 9/11.

7 July 2005, a 'British 9/11'?

One year and three months after the Madrid bombings, on 7 July 2005, it was London's turn to see its public transport coming under attack. At 8.50 a.m., three bombs exploded within a period of about fifty seconds on three different Underground trains: one on train No. 204, on the

Circle Line between Liverpool Street and Aldgate stations; another on train No. 216, also on the Circle Line, which had just left Edgware Road station; and a third on train No. 311, travelling on the Piccadilly Line between King's Cross and Russell Square. A little less than one hour later, at 9.47 a.m., a fourth and final bomb exploded on the top floor of a bus on line No. 30 in Tavistock Square. Fifty-two people were killed by these four explosions and 784 wounded.[47] In terms of the overall number of victims, it was the worst terrorist attack ever perpetrated on the territory of the United Kingdom, and the deadliest since the 1988 Lockerbie attack,[48] thus also since 9/11. It exceeded the Omagh bombing of 15 August 1988, the worst in the history of the conflict in Northern Ireland (29 dead and 220 wounded). In this respect, its status within the United Kingdom was comparable to that of the attacks of 11 March 2004 in Spain, even if it was nearly four times less deadly. So it was easy to imagine that the 7 July attack, '7/7' as it is called in the UK, would go down in history as the 'British 9/11' or as the 'English 9/11' or even as 'a new European 9/11'. Why has this not been the case?

An analogy that did not catch on

The analogy, in the aftermath of the attack, did in fact appear in the British press. An editorial in the *Sun* – Britain's bestselling newspaper – spoke of 'Britain's 9/11', while another, in the *Daily Star*, referred to the attack as 'our 9/11'. But these phrases did not make it to the head-lines, they remained limited to the tabloids, and did not circulate in the rest of the media, either in the UK, or in Europe, or in the United States. The analogy, this time, did not catch on. There were several reasons for this. The first that comes to mind is that the element of surprise was far less when compared to the attacks of 9/11 and Madrid – or to what it might have been in January 2015 in France: even if they knew that *Charlie Hebdo* had been threatened, the French were certainly not as prepared for the suddenness of the attack as were Londoners in July 2005.

Once it was established that the Madrid bombings had been perpetrated by Islamists who probably wanted to punish Spain for its participation in the war in Iraq, it appeared clear that other European capitals could be hit in the near future, and that London was the most exposed of them. On 16 March 2004, the commissioner of the Metropolitan Police said that a terrorist attack in London was inevitable, even if the anti-terrorism agencies were doing everything in their power to prevent it. The mayor of London, Ken Livingstone, added that it would be 'miraculous' if London were spared by Al-Qaeda.[49] So the question was no longer 'What?', as for 9/11 , or 'Who?', as for the Madrid bombings,

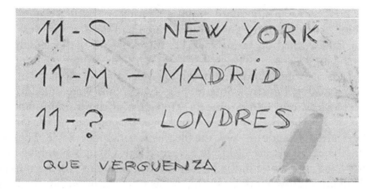

Figure 6. Message placed in the Atocha station after Madrid bombings. Archivo del Duelo, DP-2294. The final comment, 'QUE VERGUENZA', means 'the shame of it!'

but just 'When?', as suggested by a message left in the Atocha station in Madrid in March 2004 (Figure 6).

A second, less immediate explanatory factor, however, seems to have been more decisive: a greater number of British citizens died on 11 September 2001 (67) than on 7 July 2005 (41). Indeed, after the US, the UK was the country that paid the highest price in the 2001 attacks.[50] This was due to the closeness of links between the City of London and the New York business world: the Cantor Fitzgerald group, which occupied four floors at the top of the north tower of the World Trade Center and was therefore the most heavily hit by the attacks, has its headquarters in London. If the attack in London was not a 'British 9/11', this is probably because 9/11 itself had already been experienced as a national tragedy in the UK. On 14 September 2001 (while the figure of some five hundred British victims was going round), an impressive ceremony was held in St Paul's Cathedral attended by the queen;[51] in 2005, it took until 1 November, on All Saints' Day, for a ceremony to be organized in memory of the victims of the London attacks. In New York there is now a memorial garden specifically dedicated to the British dead of 9/11 (the British Memorial Garden, located in Hanover Square in the southeast of Manhattan),[52] and London is the only capital in Europe which houses a memorial to the victims of 9/11 (the September 11 Memorial Garden, in Grosvenor Square, next to the American embassy). It is thus likely, given the historical and cultural ties that unite the British to the Americans, that they share the feeling of an irreducible singularity attached to the tragedy of 9/11, with which no other event can really be compared.

In the eyes of the British, then, the London bombings remained to a fairly large extent overshadowed by 9/11. Just as the 9/11 attack was framed as a new Pearl Harbor, they, too, were immediately linked to memories of the Second World War, rather than to other terrorist attacks previously endured by London, particularly those perpetrated by the IRA.[53] The context, moreover, again favoured this historical parallel: the bombings came three days before the holding of official ceremonies marking the sixtieth anniversary of the end of the Second World War. The reference to the Blitz played exactly the same role in the British press in July 2005 that the reference to Pearl Harbor did in the US media in September 2001.[54] Tabloids like the *Sun* published photographs of the bombings opposite archival images from the Second World War, just as they had done in 2001 to substantiate the analogy between 9/11 and Pearl Harbor. And all mentioned the Blitz in the most explicit way imaginable. Here are just two examples:[55]

> We are under attack as surely as our parents and grandparents were during the Blitz. (*Daily Express* editorial)

> We survived the Blitz. We went through 30 years of IRA bombings … once again, the British will triumph over evil. (*Daily Mirror* editorial)

The analogy was also used by several public personalities, including Ian Blair, the then head of the Metropolitan Police in London:

> If London could survive the Blitz, it can survive four miserable events like this.[56]

But while the reference to Pearl Harbor in the case of 9/11 and to the 9/11 attacks in the case of the Madrid bombings had helped to broaden the scope of the events, the reference to the Blitz tended rather to minimize the effects of the London attacks. It allowed them to be framed as an act of war against the British nation, admittedly the deadliest in London since the Blitz, but far less significant than the latter; and, just as Londoners had not given in to Nazi bombs, they were not going to yield to these new attacks. The analogy with the Blitz reactivated the standard of behaviour that the British associate with the memory of the Second World War: the 'Churchillian' attitude of not letting yourself be intimidated and continuing your life as if nothing had happened; in short, feigning indifference. 'We are not afraid': such was the response to the attack.

Through this analogy to the Blitz, the attacks in London were resolutely made part of the war on terrorism being waged by the United States with its allies, the United Kingdom first and foremost: it was nothing other than a new battle. It is hardly surprising, therefore, that it was taken up and amplified in a sector of the American press: the *New York Post*, in particular, had the headline 'BLITZ' the day after the attack, while no British newspaper had gone that far. Conversely, the reference to the Blitz was mentioned only marginally in continental European newspapers, and always in quotation marks, or else in a purely allusive way, as in the headline that the editorial team of *Libération* chose for its 8 July 2005 edition: 'London under the bombs'.

This idea that the London bombings were just one battle in the war led by the United States and its allies against Islamist terrorists, triggered by 9/11 and ending with the death of bin Laden, is well illustrated by the film *Zero Dark Thirty* (2012), devoted to the tracking down of bin Laden by the US secret services: the London bombings are mentioned fleetingly, through some archive TV footage. In this, it appears to be part of the frame of events taking place 'in the background' while the United States sought to eliminate its public enemy No. 1. Conversely, the Madrid bombings, the so-called 'European 9/11', are not mentioned at any time in the film.[57] As if they were quite foreign to that story.

Cosmopolitanism versus Islamism?

However, it must be remembered that the day before 7 July 2005, London had just won the competition to hold the 2012 Olympic Games. So, while the analogy with Pearl Harbor had tended to be overwhelming in the United States in September 2001, and to frame 9/11 within a nationalist and hawkish context, the reference to the Blitz was counter-balanced, in July 2005, by the invocation of the 'great Olympic city', multicultural, open and tolerant. In the editorial of the *Guardian* which came out after the attack, the reference to the Blitz was followed by these words:

> Less than 24 hours before the bombs went off, London won a golden accolade from the rest of the world because it offered them an Olympic Games based on hope and inclusiveness towards all races, creeds and nations. [...] London has won the Olympics because it is an open and tolerant city. The way Londoners responded to the vicious attacks on them has vindicated the Olympians' confidence.[58]

Unlike the analogy with the Blitz, which focused on the 'Britishness' of London, the reference to the Olympics emphasized instead, as we see, the cosmopolitan character of the world city.[59] From this point of view, the London attacks could be seen less as an act of aggression on the British nation than as a new attack on a world city par excellence, and the people of all nationalities living there.

This was the framing of the event adopted by the mayor of London, Ken Livingstone, in the speech he delivered after the attacks:

I want to say one thing specifically to the world today. This was not a terrorist attack on the mighty and the powerful. It was not aimed at Presidents or Prime Ministers. It was aimed at ordinary, working-class Londoners, black and white, Muslim and Christian, Hindu and Jew, young and old. It was an indiscriminate attempt to slaughter, irrespective of any considerations for age, for class, for religion, or whatever. That isn't an ideology, it isn't even a perverted faith – it is just an indiscriminate attempt at mass murder and we know what the objective is. They seek to divide Londoners. They seek to turn Londoners against each other. I said yesterday to the International Olympic Committee, that the city of London is the greatest in the world, because everybody lives side by side in harmony. Londoners will not be divided by this cowardly attack. They will stand together in solidarity alongside those who have been injured and those who have been bereaved and that is why I'm proud to be the mayor of that city.[60]

It was more than a merely rhetorical issue. Unlike the attacks of 11 September and Madrid, those in London had been perpetrated not by foreigners, but by British citizens: three of them were born in the United Kingdom, of Pakistani parents, while the fourth was born in Jamaica, and came to the country as a child; all four spent all of their school years in the British system. So the attack appeared to undermine the multiculturalism of British society,[61] and while the Madrid attacks had not led to any significant increase of racism in Spain,[62] the London police noted in July 2005 a resurgence of racist assaults compared to July 2004.[63] To curb this phenomenon and ease community tensions, Ken Livingstone's call for unity was then reinforced in August 2005 by a public poster campaign with the slogan 'Seven Million Londoners, One London', followed a year later by the slogan 'We Are Londoners, We are One.'[64]

Thus, rather than an attack on the British nation or Europe, the London bombings could appear, ultimately, as an attack on cosmopolitanism itself, on the whole human race gathered together in this world city. There was objective evidence for this new way of framing the event. A study released six months before the attack had established that three hundred different languages were spoken in London and some fifty ethnic communities with over ten thousand members lived there,[65] leading the *Guardian* to conclude that 'London in 2005 can lay claim to being the most diverse city ever.'[66] It was estimated that a third of Londoners were born abroad, mainly outside Europe[67] – and this remains true today. The proportion of foreigners among the fifty-two people killed on 7 July 2005 corresponded quite well to the composition of the London population: 13.5 per cent of them were nationals of a non-European country, a greater percentage than for the attacks of 9/11 and in Madrid; and 9.5 per cent were foreigners from another European country, which was less than for the Madrid bombings (14 per cent).[68]

In other words, if we argue on the basis of those killed and *in relative values* (the number of people killed in each case was definitely not of the same order), 9/11 attacks claimed the largest number of national citizens, the Madrid bombings claimed the most nationals from European countries, and the London bombings claimed the nationals from the rest of the world. Thus, as *Paris Match* put it in July 2005, under a photograph showing posters of the dead in the streets of London:

> They have Polish, Pakistani, Japanese names ... The photos of these victims are a vibrant testimony to the cosmopolitanism of London, an open and tolerant city.[69]

Not only were there many foreigners among the victims of the attack, but as their names suggest, several of those with British nationality were of foreign origin. This observation was the starting point for the first article that *The Times* devoted to the victims, four days after the attack, entitled 'A grieving world in one city' (an allusion to the formula 'The world in one city' used to present London to the International Olympic Committee).[70] The nationality of the people killed in each attack does not explain everything, of course. But it nevertheless helps in understanding the force of the way 9/11 was framed as a 'new Pearl Harbor', the Madrid bombings as a 'European 11 September', and the London bombings as an attack on cosmopolitanism.

As well as these factors relating to the structure of the London population, there are others, more circumstantial, that explain why London could seem such an effective embodiment of cosmopolitanism in July 2005. In addition to the winning of the Olympic Games on the eve of the attack, there had been, in Hyde Park on the previous weekend, the big concert 'Live 8' which, according to the authors of the official report on the attack, 'had just sent a powerful and unprecedented message to the world's leaders about poverty in Africa'.[71] This concert was the culmination of a lobbying campaign launched by the movement 'Make Poverty History' aimed at putting pressure on the British government, president that year of the G8, and influencing the agenda of the summit held at Gleneagles, Scotland, from 6 to 8 July 2005. A few months earlier, in October 2004, London had also seen the Third European Social Forum, which had come into being shortly after 9/11 as an offshoot of the anti-globalization World Social Forum.

Some have seen these events as a way of implementing calls for a cosmopolitan response to the Islamist terrorism that struck on 9/11.[72] James Brassett also points out that activists, left-wing journalists and reformist politicians lamented that the terrorists of 7 July 2005 had disrupted the process aimed specifically at making the world a better place for 'them'.[73] They tended, in his view, to reproduce in their stance a schematic division between 'us' and 'them', and in so doing fallen back into a simplistic, Manichean vision of the world: the 'Either you are with us, or you are with the terrorists' uttered by George W. Bush after the 9/11 attacks had finally been followed, in July 2005, by the idea 'Either you are with "our" cosmopolitan values, or you are against them.' This was also what was intimated in Tony Blair's first public reaction to the attack, issued in Gleneagles before leaving the G8 summit to deal with the emergency:

> It is particularly barbaric that this [attack] has happened on a day when people are meeting to try to help the problems of poverty in Africa and the long term problems of climate change and the environment.[74]

While the United Kingdom was the main ally of the United States in the war against terrorism and the war in Iraq, presenting the G8 summit as the place where a 'cosmopolitics' was being invented allowed the British prime minister to thwart in advance any attempt to link the attack to his foreign policy. But by suggesting that the terrorists wanted to strike the host nation of the G8 rather than the ally of the United States, he simultaneously drew an opposition between 'civilized cosmopolitans' on one side and 'barbaric terrorists' on the other.[75] There then resurfaced a principle whereby the world was split and humankind divided into two camps – the very same principle which the idea of a cosmopolitan response to terrorism had attempted to combat in Europe after 9/11.

If the attacks in London were not experienced, as those in Madrid had been, through the prism of an analogy with 9/11, this was mainly because 9/11 itself was a greater tragedy for the British people than the London bombings, and because the reminder of the attitude of Londoners during the Second World War enjoined them not to give it too much significance. The fact that this attack, occurring as it did a day after the Olympic Games had been awarded to London, was also perceived as an attack on the cosmopolitanism of a world city par excellence (rather than on the nation of which it is the capital) did not favour an analogy with 9/11 either – even though the event was still interpreted in the light of a 'clash of civilizations'.

Why, then, can a terrorist attack sometimes be viewed as a 'new 9/11'? The first criterion is one of sheer impact: this attack should appear as the worst tragedy ever for a city, a country, or any community, at least since 2001. If the 18 July 2012 attack in Bourgas, on a bus of Israeli tourists, was also presented as a 'Bulgarian 9/11',[76] even though it claimed only six victims, this was because it was still 'the greatest tragedy of the last twenty years in Bulgaria'.[77] But this criterion is not enough: it must also be the case that this attack is perpetrated in a Western country, not only against its interests or nationals elsewhere. Neither the Bali bombings in 2002 nor those in Casablanca in 2003 gave rise to the analogy, while the events in Bombay in 2008 would probably not have been called an 'Indian 9/11' if the term had not been used by one of the terrorists. Islamist attacks perpetrated in the Middle East never appear to us as new 9/11s, however deadly they may be: the one that occurred in Ankara in October 2015, which only a few Turkish intellectuals or experts in Turkish affairs ventured to describe as a 'Turkish 9/11', was evidence of this: it simultaneously made it clear on which side of the world the Western media actually situate Turkey. The analogy thus draws on an opposition between 'us' and 'them' and carries with it, whether we like it or not, the idea of a war of civilizations. In this respect, it expresses a Western-centred view, which contradicts the desire to promote a cosmopolitan point of view. And this contradiction has become constitutive of our relation to the Islamist attacks.

— 3 —

TO SHOW, OR NOT TO SHOW, VIOLENCE

The image will endure: the death of a man lying on the ground in central Paris, Police Lieutenant Ahmed Merabet, shot dead by terrorists in a burst of Kalashnikov gunfire while trying to stop their flight. It was on the front pages of the most important European dailies in the aftermath of the attack on *Charlie Hebdo* – *The Times*, the *Wall Street Journal* and all the British tabloids, *Bild* in Germany, *Corriere della Sera* in Italy, *El País*, *El Mundo* and *La Vanguardia* in Spain, etc. – while their French counterparts all opted for front pages in black, as a sign of mourning, or for cartoons, as a tribute to the murdered cartoonists. The weekly *Le Point* was severely criticized for putting it on its cover. It was taken from a video posted on Facebook barely a few moments after being recorded, and its author quickly apologized for making it public. Was he right to regret his action? Should this scene even have been filmed? Should the most graphic images of an attack be shown, or not?

As old as photojournalism, these debates about the exhibition or concealing of violent images are most often related to a change in sensibility with respect to suffering and death that is said to characterize Western societies as a whole.[1] However, we lose something if we address the issue in such general terms. Variations in the iconographic choices made to represent a single attack by one country or another also reflect differences of views on the event, its causes and its consequences. These choices, whether or not they are consciously raised, are definite stances, part of the framing of the event that help to guide the way a society reacts to it. If, in September 2001, images of the explosion of the south tower of the World Trade Center were the most reproduced in the United States, while those from the ruins of Ground Zero were reprinted most often in Europe, this is because the former were sticking to the idea of a 'new Pearl Harbor' while the latter were summoning up a post-apocalyptic fantasy.[2] Whether or not we choose to show the victims of an Islamist attack, in this sense, also says something about our relation to this terrorism.

The place of the dead

It has become a commonplace to say that terrorist acts are viewed more than ever as media events since 9/11. How people react to them when they are not victims or eyewitnesses depends very much on what they see via TV, the Internet and the newspapers. In this respect, the Madrid bombings were indeed the equivalent of 9/11, providing striking and spectacular images: gutted trains in the middle of a European capital. Admittedly, neither this nor any attack since has been a television event broadcast live in the way that 9/11 itself was: that day, viewers around the world could view in real time United Airlines Flight 175 as it flew into the south tower of the World Trade Center and the towers collapsed. But this does not mean that the images of the Madrid or London bombings were any less violent than those of 11 September – the opposite is true. It pays to distinguish between intrinsically violent images, that show the death and suffering inflicted on others, and images *of violence*, which let you imagine it but do not display it frontally.[3] The former may appear *intolerable*, leading us to look away, to turn off our TV or change channels, while the latter are, in the real sense of the word, *shocking* images, that leave us 'shell shocked' and mute as they go round in an endless loop. The images of the killing of Ahmed Merabet, or those of the executions carried out by Daesh, are violent images, but those of the planes hitting the towers of the World Trade Center are images *of violence*. They are certainly scary, terrifying even, but death and suffering are not directly perceptible in them. Should they have been supplemented by other images, showing the horror of the terrorist massacre more directly? This has sometimes been claimed in Europe. But was it even possible?

What we did not see on 11 September 2001

Clearly, the attacks of 9/11 had been planned so as to be not only destructive but also spectacular and, if we may put it this way, 'photogenic'. This resulted, in the wake of the attacks, in a much greater place being devoted in the newspapers to photographs, both more numerous and more visible than usual. US dailies reorganized their front pages to devote 60 per cent of the space to images.[4] Some newspapers, like *The Times* and *Libération*, even decided to print one double-spread panoramic photo, covering the front page and the last page of the newspaper. The same was true of the inside pages: in its edition of 12 September 2001, the *New York Times* published a good fifty photographs, as against the normal twenty or so.[5] Most newspapers followed suit. But if we are to believe Barbie Zelizer, there was only one precedent for this before 2001, and this, yet again, had to do with the Second World War: the liberation of the concentration camps in 1945. However, as Zelizer notes, in images of 9/11, 'bodies, human limbs, bloodied remains are absent. It is quite unlike the bits of corpses and gaping pits full of bodies that were endlessly shown in 1945; here the bodies are simply banished from the image.'[6]

Indeed, as we have seen previously,[7] the photographic treatment of 9/11 in the US press was dominated by two images: that of the explosion in the south tower of the World Trade Center when United Airlines Flight 175 flew into it, and that of the cloud of smoke caused by the collapsing towers. Clément Chéroux's study of the American dailies published in the aftermath of 9/11 showed that the photos that appeared on the front pages the day after can ultimately be reduced to six 'image-types' (in the form of photos taken from different angles): apart from the two afore-mentioned, corresponding to 41 per cent and 17 per cent of front pages respectively, they showed the ruins of the World Trade Center (14 per cent of front pages), Flight 175 approaching the south tower (13.5 per cent), scenes of panic in Manhattan (6 per cent) and finally the American flag floating over Ground Zero (3.5 per cent).[8] No dead or injured, with very few exceptions. Barbie Zelizer summarizes the finding in a striking formula: 'the towers overshadowed the bodies'.[9]

Yet those who followed the attacks live on television from the first moments were shown, also live, the desperate people trapped in the burning towers and jumping into the void. It is estimated that about 200 people died in this way.[10] In the moments just before the collapse of the World Trade Center, relatively long sequences, taken with zooms, were devoted to them. There are also photos of those who jumped from the windows, including one in particular that has passed into history under the title 'The Falling Man'.[11] Taken by Richard Drew at 9.41 a.m., in it we see a man diving head down, one leg bent and his body straight, perfectly aligned with the tower from the top of which he is falling. Published on 12 September in the morning in several American newspapers, including the *New York Times*, and on the front page of the *Herald* (published in Pennsylvania), the photo aroused strong reactions from their readers. These images of people jumping from windows, like the images of the wounded, were usually confined to the inside pages of the very first newspapers published after the attacks and have rarely been reproduced thereafter. A photograph by Todd Maisel that appeared in the *New York Daily News* on the evening of 11 September sparked an even livelier controversy: it shows a torn-off hand, its finger pointing, lying on the Liberty Street pavement before the towers collapsed.[12] There are a few other photographs of human body parts taken that day, even if these images could have been taken only over a very short period of time (from 8.46 a.m., when the first plane crashed, to 9.59 a.m., when the first tower collapsed) and in a very dangerous area.[13]

The way the material destruction seemed to take precedence over human suffering in media representations of 9/11 is not due to an absence of images of the wounded and the dead. These photos exist, but they were quickly set aside. It is unlikely that we can attribute this marginalization to a political censorship exercised by US federal authorities: in the panic and confusion of the first few hours, the administration was far from being in any position to filter images of the attacks itself, or to impose its will on the media.[14] The explanation lies rather in the self-censorship of American journalists themselves who felt that some images were not to be put into circulation,[15] coupled with an 'eco-censorship', as Clément Chéroux calls it,[16] resulting from the impact of economic and financial globalization on the media industry. One figure sums up the importance of this 'eco-censorship': 72 per cent of the images published on the front pages of American dailies on the morning of 12 September come from one and the same source, Associated Press, which supplied the whole world with images.[17] 'In European dailies, when the images do not come from Associated Press, they were generally provided by Reuters, or by AFP [Agence France-Presse].'[18] So it is ultimately through the eyes of these interconnected agencies, which occupy a quasi-hegemonic position in the world market of press images, that we will have seen 9/11. And so, of the 9/11 attacks, we will have seen only what they were willing to show us.

In the hours following the collapse of the towers of the World Trade Center, very tight control of the activity of cameramen and photographers in New York was quickly imposed. Access to hospitals and morgues was denied, and they were not allowed within a seven-hectare area around Ground Zero. They could enter the site only if they agreed to be part of the 'pools' supervised by the police and the firefighters who limited the kind of shots they could take – a practice imported from war zones. Don Emmert, then in charge of photography for AFP in New York, said:

> During the organized pools, we were allowed to film only what the authorities wanted to see filmed. Those who moved around freely were the military photographers of the US Navy and FEMA (Federal Emergency Agency). They provided the agencies with some very fine photos, but don't expect to see any dead bodies in them. Even if the American press continued to publish pictures of the ruins of the World Trade Center, all the

media, including the tabloids, have to settle for these pools so as to take photos from the distance and just showing wide shots of the site.[19]

The practice quickly stirred controversy in Europe, where there was criticism of the 'lack of access to reality' and 'American censorship'.[20]

To show the human dimension of the attacks, European journalists were therefore forced to do it with the few images of victims at their disposal. A photograph showing firefighters evacuating the remains of the body of a priest – Mychal Judge, who would be the first 'official' victim of 9/11 to be identified – was particularly highlighted in the French press: it was published in colour on the last page of *Le Parisien* the day after the attacks, then on a double-page spread in *Paris Match*.[21] It was also reproduced as a full page in major German newspapers to support an appeal for the benefit of those left orphaned by 9/11, launched by the Bertelsmann Foundation (this is linked to the major German media group and in particular works to strengthen transatlantic ties). Images of the 'jumpers' were also more commonly shown in the European than in the American press. *VSD* and *Paris Match* devoted several double-page spreads to them, and there was even one in *Le Monde*, a newspaper that is, nevertheless, reluctant to indulge in sensationalism, the day after the attacks.[22] Similarly in Italy, on 13 September, *Il Corriere della Sera* published a continuous header running across the pages showing photos of victims and survivors, as well as several images of 'jumpers' within forty-eight hours of the attacks.

However, 'just one picture of American dead was shown in the media, an image representing bodies in shrouds on the site of the Pentagon'.[23] This was the effect of the control over images exercised from above in the United States – a link back to an old iconographic tradition. As Susan Sontag notes:

> With our dead, there has always been a powerful interdiction against showing the naked face. [...] By the time of the landing in France – June 6, 1944 – photographs of anonymous American casualties had appeared in a number of newsmagazines, always prone or shrouded or with their faces turned away.[24]

The dead of 9/11, in short, will therefore have been entitled to the same photographic treatment as US soldiers who died in combat.

What we saw on 11 March 2004

The day after 11 March 2004 in Madrid, some Spanish papers, inspired by a phrase used by José María Aznar,[25] repeated verbatim titles adopted by some of their US counterparts after 9/11, such as 'Infamy' or 'A day of infamy'. But if we compare the front page of *El Mundo* on 12 March 2004 with that of an American newspaper published on 12 September 2001, it is obvious that, while the titles are the same, the images are radically different (figures 7 and 8). The image with which *El Mundo* leads bears no reference to Pearl Harbor or the American memories of that 'day of infamy': no explosion or cloud of smoke, this time, but dead bodies lying in the wreckage of a train, their faces exposed. While the dead of 11 September had been almost invisible, those of 11 March appeared immediately on the front page of one of the major Spanish dailies. But perhaps this was an isolated case?

A calculation based on a sample of front pages published on the day after the Madrid bombings, similar to that made by Clément Chéroux for those published on 9/11, clarifies the situation:[26] 11 March also led to the recycling of several typical images, reproduced on the front page of all newspapers. As for 9/11, there were six of these typical images (see table 2, p. 66). The main one of them (on 38 per cent of front pages in Spain) shows the gaping hole caused by one of the explosions in a

Figures 7 and 8. Front pages of *Tulsa Word* (US), 12 September 2001, and *El Mundo* (Spain), 12 March 2004.

train when it was level with Calle de Téllez, shortly before it entered Atocha station. The following two image-types show corpses in the rubble of one of the train's carriages – as on the front page of *El Mundo* – and the bodies in black shrouds, lined up next to the trains, ready to be transferred to the morgue. Between them, these three image-types comprised almost 80 per cent of the front pages published in Spain after the Madrid attacks. Then came close-ups of the wounded, wide shots of the gutted trains and, finally, those of the injured being rescued on the tracks, down the length of the train. Together with these six image-types, a seventh was found in other European countries and the United States: Spaniards taking to the streets to demonstrate their opposition to terrorism (4.5 per cent of European front pages and 7.5 per cent of American front pages). The images of the dead were undeniably more visible in March 2004 than they were in September 2001. But one image-type was even more visible, and was in fact the most widely reproduced picture of the Madrid bombings: it showed the gaping hole caused in one carriage (figures 9 and 10).

Elevated into a symbol of 11 March, the image of this 'eye of hell'[27] has often been reprinted since to illustrate articles commemorating the

Figures 9 and 10. Front pages of the *New York Daily News* and *New York Post*, 12 March 2004; the photographs were taken by Christophe Simon (AFP) and Paul White (AP) respectively.

attack. Of all the images of the Madrid bombings that have been put into circulation, this is probably the one best suited to reminding the French of the wave of attacks in the RER, or the Italians of the Bologna attack. But its success was mainly due to its ability to give visual support to the idea of a repeat of 9/11, inasmuch as it gives precedence to material destruction (the train gutted by the explosion) over human suffering. Thus, while images of 9/11 had directly recalled those of Pearl Harbor (the same fireballs, the same cloud of smoke, etc.), the memory operated rather indirectly this time – or, more precisely: it was in a *negative* fashion that this image of 11 March 2004 could remind people of the images of 11 September 2001. Several press cartoons tried to make this explicit: the trains gutted by bombs seem to echo the towers pierced by the aircraft, with, in addition, the horizontality of the former evoking the verticality of the latter (figure 11).

So this picture would become even more important in the United States: in fact, the proportion of the photographs corresponding to this image that were published on front pages on 12 March 2004 rises to 56 per cent, as against 38 per cent in Spain and 24 per cent in other European countries. (In comparison, we should remember, the most reproduced image-type of 9/11, that of the explosion in the south tower

Figure 11. Cartoon by Chapatte published in *Le Temps* (Switzerland), 12 March 2004.

of the World Trade Center, reached 'only' a figure of 41 per cent.) The photographic treatment of the Madrid bombings was thus more balanced in Europe than in the US: the picture-type of the 'gaping hole' was about as widely reproduced as two other pictures that directly showed human suffering: that of a bloodstained casualty and that of the railway tracks where, amid the wounded passengers who had been rescued, we can clearly distinguish fragments of human bodies and corpses. Each of these images accounted for 18 per cent of the front pages of non-Spanish European newspapers, but only 2 per cent and 3 per cent of the photographs published on the front pages of American newspapers. If the image-types of Madrid attacks were much the same on both sides of the Atlantic, the hierarchy between these images differs greatly (table 2).

Aside from a gaping hole in a train carriage, Europeans and Americans ultimately did not at all see the same images of the Madrid bombings. While in March 2004 the European media directly showed the dead bodies and the blood they had not been able to show in September 2001, the American media again decided not to use these images. In this sense, we can conclude that the Madrid bombings were an opportunity for the European media to reveal the *reverse* of 9/11, i.e. the human suffering eclipsed in 2001 by material destruction and its symbolic value. A song by the French rapper Abd al Malik puts it well: 9/11 is referred to in each refrain through the image of the 'Twin Towers [which] have collapsed'. And when, in a couplet, he suddenly mentions the Madrid bombings, it is with these words: 'And bodies collapsed in Spain'.[28]

Table 2. Main image-types published on the front pages of newspapers in Spain, in the rest of Europe and the United States on 12 March 2004.

	Gaping hole	Wreckage	Shrouds	Wounded	Trains	Tracks
Spain	38%	23.5%	16.5%	9.5%	5%	2.5%
Europe	24%	11%	9%	18%	11%	18%
USA	56%	1%	20.5%	2%	8%	3%

'Thank you for showing us the dead'

This difference between the photographic treatment of Madrid bombings and of 9/11 did not fail to revive the controversy over 'American
censorship', something criticized by European journalists in 2001. In
one of the letters to the editor of *Libération*, two days after the attack,
we read:

> There is nothing voyeuristic or gory about my message. I am simply writing
> to thank the European media for showing in a dignified way what the
> United States refused to show us: the dead. It is obviously not nice to see
> blood, a limb, a body lying lifeless or mangled; but that is the reality of
> terrorism and I think it is important to see these images. I experienced
> September 11 very, very close up, and if I hadn't used my wits just before
> the first tower collapsed, I might not be here today. In any case, to have
> been a direct witness of the killing of thousands of people and yet to have
> never seen, either on TV or in the papers, any bodies – at most just a few
> bloodstains–, well, I can say that this greatly disturbed me.[29]

If journalists this time showed the violence of the attack directly, this
was mainly because they were given access to the site of the tragedy.
While Catherine Nayl, main editor of the 1 p.m. news on TF1, regretted
that in September 2001 journalists did 'not even have access to hospitals
and morgues',[30] in March 2004 they were able to get into the makeshift
hospital in a sports centre just opposite the train that had exploded level
with the Calle Téllez. It was also possible for them, in the first moments
after the attacks, to go right up to the gutted trains, directly on the rails,
amid the dead and injured. This freedom of access led to the creation of
some particularly harsh images: the day after the attacks, on the inside
pages of the newspaper *ABC*, there were pictures of bloodstained casualties waiting to be attended to, and in *El País*, images of still smouldering
carriages strewn with dismembered and disfigured corpses.[31]

It is statistically undeniable that the dead and injured were much more
visible in Europe after the Madrid bombings than they had been in the
United States after 9/11. If we aggregate the proportions of all image-
types that showed the dead and injured, it turns out that they were visible
on 52 per cent of front pages in Spain on 12 March 2004, and 58 per
cent of them in the rest of Europe, whereas, with very few exceptions,
they had been totally absent from the front pages published the day after
9/11. The situation was the same on television: the reports broadcast on
the TV news on channels TF1, France 2 and France 3 on 11 March 2004
mainly showed (as was indeed the case throughout the day on Spanish
TV channels) lifeless bodies in and around trains, and the wounded near
stations and in hospitals. The second main image-type in Spain was that

66

of dead bodies lying in the train wreckage, with their faces exposed, as on the front page of *El Mundo*. And while the image of the 'gaping hole' was reproduced in several photographs, shot from different angles, the image of corpses was shown in just one photograph, which thus happened to be the one that was most reproduced on the front pages of Spanish dailies on 12 March 2004 (just this one photo accounted for 14 per cent of front pages in Spain, and 9 per cent in Europe): this was the photograph taken by Emilio Naranjo and showing the corpse of a woman embedded in the wreckage of a carriage, with two firefighters in the foreground covering bodies. Although it was used by the European Pressphoto Agency, Associated Press and Reuters, it made the front page of just one American newspaper in the sample studied, which happened to be a Spanish newspaper aimed at the US Latino market: *El Nuevo Herald* (figure 12).

This very same concentration on a single photograph could also be observed at the same time for the other two most reproduced image-types in the rest of Europe. The first of these was a photo taken by José Huesca and published by Associated Press, having appeared in Spain on the front page of *La Razón*. It shows a young man bleeding from the head, his eye swollen, holding a mobile, sitting alongside a young woman who was gazing anxiously at him (figure 13). In the US, this photograph made it onto the front pages of very few dailies, but as it was probably the least shocking of all the images showing the human devastation caused by the attacks, it was also published in a small version, at the side of a larger picture, on the first page of 18 per cent of US dailies. (This had already happened after 9/11 for several of the less shocking images of the wounded.)[32] As for the second image-type, it corresponded to a photo taken by Pablo Torres Guerrero barely minutes after the explosion of the train level with the Calle Téllez. Amid the rescued casualties on the ballast, human body parts can clearly be seen and, in the background, corpses lying on the train (figure 14). In Spain, *El País* alone, which had exclusive use, had published it on its front page, before it was put into commercial circulation by Reuters. It appeared on 18 per cent of front pages in Europe, but only 3 per cent of them in the United States (see table 2, p. 66).

This photograph (figure 14) deserves special attention as it was digitally cropped and retouched in a variety of ways that stirred controversy.[33] Among the newspapers that published it on their front pages, a certain number did cut out the whole of the foreground, such as the *Virginian Pilot* and the *Baltimore Sun*, so as to remove the fragment of the human body contained therein – most likely a femur. The *Irish Independent* preferred to remove the top of the image and the bodies that could be seen in the background, leaving the femur visible in the

EL PAIS

Infierno terrorista en Madrid:
192 muertos y 1.400 heridos

Interior investiga la pista de Al Qaeda sin descartar a ETA

Figures 12, 13 and 14. Detail of the front page of *El Nuevo Herald* (US, Miami), 12 March 2004, showing a photo take by Emilio Naranjo; the front page of *Libération* (France), 12 March 2004, showing a photo taken by José Huesca; and the front page of *El País* (Spain), 12 March 2004, showing a photo taken by Pablo Torres Guerrero.

foreground. Others decided to change the colour balance to make the blood less visible (*Toronto Star*), to use the graphics palette to colour the femur grey (the *Guardian*) or to publish the image in black and white (*International Herald Tribune*), while several newspapers opted for the outright digital erasure of the distressing detail, as did the Belgian newspaper the *Gazet Van Antwerpen*, and several British dailies, including the *Daily Telegraph* and *The Times*. A final strategy consisted in placing the heading over the femur, as did various weeklies such as *Time Magazine*, *Paris Match* and *Der Spiegel*. One Israeli newspaper, *Yedioth Ahronoth*, even went so far as to combine all these practices, cropping the photo, retouching it digitally to remove the femur, and placing the heading at the top to conceal a dead body (figure 15).

Finally, there were few European newspapers which followed *El País* in publishing Pablo Torres Guerrero's photo without any retouching or with a simple cropping that did not delete any of the macabre details: in the sample studied, only *La Libre Belgique*, the *Morgunbladid* (published in Reykjavik, Iceland) and the *Potsdamer Neueste Nachrichten* did so. In the United States, the photo was very rarely published on the front page, but when it was, the most common editorial choice – made by the *Washington Post*, the Los Angeles *Daily News* and the *San Antonio Express News* – was to reproduce it just as it was, without retouching or cropping. The situation could thus be summed up as follows: for

Figure 15. Eight front pages of daily papers published on 12 March 2004 showing the photograph by Pablo Torres Guerrero that was disseminated by Reuters.

European journalists, the main point was to show human suffering, even if the harsher images were retouched, while for American journalists, it was essential to conceal this suffering and not to use these images. Sometimes, descriptions have allowed them to evoke the horror without having to show it, as had been the case in September 2001. The *New York Post*, for example, reported the words of eyewitnesses who saw 'a baby torn to bits' and 'bodies [...] littered across the floor'.[34]

So images of the dead and wounded thus represented, in total, only 26 per cent of the photos of the Madrid bombings published on the front pages in the United States – this was half the proportion in Europe. Above all, almost all of the images were those of corpses in black shrouds. While the dead and wounded appeared with their faces exposed in 35.5 per cent of front pages in Spain and 47 per cent of them in the rest of Europe, this was true of only 6 per cent of cases in the United States (see table 2, p. 66). This finding recalls vividly the treatment of 9/11 by the US media, since the only image of dead bodies from these attacks that were circulated was a picture of bodies in shrouds on the site of the Pentagon. It is obvious that in their treatment of the Madrid bombings, the vast majority of American dailies again conformed to the rule that in a war, you do not show the dead on your own side, much less with their faces exposed. In this respect, they evidently considered the attack to be a 'battle' in the 'war on terror'. Conversely, the European media, by hiding nothing of the horror of the Madrid bombings, were in all likelihood seeking to try and counter the way 9/11 had been framed, as they had in 2001, without being able to back this up in visual terms. Through various iconographic choices, we can thus also detect different views as to the nature of terrorism and the way we should respond to it.

The ethics of iconographic decisions

'Photographs lay down routes of reference', writes Susan Sontag.[35] The importance assumed after the 9/11 attacks by the images of explosions and smoke (in the United States), and by images of the ruins of the World Trade Center (in Europe), were due in effect, as we have seen, to the capacity of the former to evoke the memory of Pearl Harbor, and of the latter to summon up a post-apocalyptic fantasy.[36] To characterize more precisely the power some photographs have to generate a sensation of 'déjà vu', such as Thomas Franklin's picture of firefighters hoisting an American flag at Ground Zero, irresistibly reminding the spectator of Joe Rosenthal's *Raising the Flag on Iwo Jima*, Clément Chéroux proposes that we use the concept of 'inter-iconicity', which can be defined as a relationship of co-presence between two or many images, most often through the effective presence of one image in another.[37] To what extent can this concept help us also to understand the importance assumed by certain photos of the Madrid bombings in Europe? Indeed, their success was probably due to their ability to remind us of other images and thereby to guide our perception of the event.

Showing so as to denounce

How can we explain that, following the Madrid bombings, Emilio Naranjo's photo of the body of a woman lying in the wreckage of a train was the one most often reproduced on the front pages of Spanish newspapers? First, we can think about the turning point represented in the history of war photography by the Spanish Civil War, to which both Spanish and French newspapers made specific reference in their accounts of the attacks. It was during that war that photographers began to capture images of the fighting from really close up, so that this war marked the beginning of the era of 'photo-evidence', attesting to the reality of violence – and not just photo-documentation or illustration. This era reached its culmination in the Vietnam War.[38] Robert Capa's famous photo, *Loyalist Militiaman at the Moment of Death*, where we see a soldier being cut down by a bullet as he charges forward, 'emerged as the symbol of the Spanish Civil War, and indeed of all wars'.[39] This war also represented a pinnacle in the use of images of dead civilians for propaganda purposes:[40] following heavy bombing of Getafe and Madrid by the German Luftwaffe on 30 October 1936, photos of children's bodies were reproduced in tens of thousands of copies by the Commission for Propaganda of the Generalitat de Catalunya to denounce the fascist crimes; they thus circulated round Europe on posters and leaflets, in newspapers and books, edited by Communist organizations.[41]

This first explanatory element is linked to a second: the way Spanish journalists became accustomed to use images of the victims of ETA attacks so as to delegitimize its violence in the eyes of Spanish public opinion. This other factor is more directly relevant, since at the time journalists chose to publish Emilio Naranjo's photo on their front pages, many people thought that ETA was responsible, in line with the view of the Spanish government. Also, some of the images on the front pages of 12 March 2004 that are the most difficult to look at echoed others that were published after the worst attacks of the Basque separatist group, from the mid-1980s, when ETA started to carry out mass killings that struck increasing numbers of civilians, and journalists decided to stop concealing its atrocities.[42] So the photographs of corpses lying in the wreckage of the trains on 11 March 2004 reminded Spaniards of others that had in their time been quite traumatic: civil guards killed in their buses in one of ETA's deadliest bombings on the Plaza República Dominicana in Madrid on 14 July 1986 (figure 16), or those showing a little girl aged twelve, Irene Villa, lying in a pool of blood after being hit on 17 October 1991 by an attack targeting her mother (figure 17). This change in the photographic representation of terrorist violence could also be observed in France, as Gérald Arboit notes:

> Until the mid-1980s, then, the press merely showed fire engines, the choreography of nurses and ambulance men. A change then occurred, as evidenced by the 1995 Paris attacks. The spectacle focused on the new 'Holy Innocents' of democracy in the face of terrorist barbarity. The camera could get right up to the blood, even hampering, if necessary, the rescue work.[43]

These images both aimed to denounce the horror of terrorist violence and also, as a result, helped to turn the victims into martyrs.

Figures 16 and 17. Front pages of *La Vanguardia* (Spain), 15 July 1986, and *ABC* (Spain), 18 October 1991.

But while this second factor is sufficient to explain the decision made by many Spanish newspapers to publish images of dead bodies on their front pages, it does not account for the way Emilio Naranjo's photo could appear to the editorial board of *Newsweek* magazine, according to Lynn Staley (then deputy editor-in-chief), as 'one of the most beautiful, haunting, and amazing images that we had seen'.[44] There is some reason for finding this a strange judgement, referring as it does to the image of the corpse of a woman in the wreckage of a train. What it expresses, in fact, is an aestheticization of suffering, that is to say an apprehension of someone else's suffering in the mode not of moral indignation or pity, but of the sublime.[45] And, based on the genealogy that Luc Boltanski sets out, the Spanish school of painting turns out to have contributed powerfully to this aestheticization of suffering, particularly the work of Francisco de Goya, who represents a real turning point here.[46] And indeed, among the thousands of people who, after the Madrid bombings, came to leave messages, candles and various objects in memory of the victims in the Atocha station, one person did not fail to make the connection between the images of atrocities in the press and one of the Spanish master's most famous paintings, *Saturn Devouring his Son*, which hangs in the Prado, just a few hundred metres from the railway station. This analogy inspired a drawing where Saturn devours, not his child, but a train (figure 18).

Seeing the bloody images that made the headlines of European newspapers after the Madrid attacks as reminiscent of Goya's imaginary world is thus not part of what Jean-Claude Passeron ironically calls a 'hermeneutics of mood or sensitivity'[47] which directly deduces what the public perceives in an image from what scholarly criticism detects in it. This drawing, found in the Atocha station, attests to a perfectly real way of perceiving the images of the attacks – one that was probably not limited to just one person. For twenty years, Goya has been unusually popular in Spain, something of a craze.[48] It is therefore more than likely that, when Naranjo took this photo, he had in mind the iconographic tradition of which Goya is the most prominent representative, and in any case this tradition was obviously part of the context in which the photograph was perceived in Spain.

Figure 18. Drawing left in the Atocha station after the Madrid bombings. Archivo del Duelo, DP-0291.

If, however, we seek to specify in more detail what phenomenon of inter-iconicity made the success of this photo possible, it seems to draw less on a work by Goya himself than on one of the most famous paintings in the Prado Museum, by the founder of the school of Spanish painting, El Greco. In the overall composition of the image, in the posture of the corpse in the middle (the right shoulder coming forward), in the draped white sheets in the foreground and in the distribution of colours (red at bottom right, white and blue in the top left, yellow at the top and grey below), we can glimpse as it were an echo of *The Trinity* (figures 19 and 20).

Dolorism and pacifism

Even though the inter-iconicity in Naranjo's photo is less clear than the equivalent process in the now symbolic photo by Thomas Franklin of the 'new Pearl Harbor' for the Americans, it is still suggestive – even more so in that El Greco had himself drawn inspiration for his painting from Michelangelo's *Pietà*. And the *Pietà* is not only one of the most famous works in the history of art, but also one of the recurring iconographic themes in consciousness-raising campaigns for humanitarian appeals[49] – something that may have helped give Naranjo's photo its

Figures 19 and 20. Photo by Emilio Naranjo circulated by Associated Press and Reuters; and El Greco's *La Trinidad* (1579).

success beyond just a Spanish public. The religious dimension of these two icons (Goya's *La Trinidad*, Michelangelo's *Pietà*) also echoes the lively popular piety in Spanish society, which was manifested through its reaction to the Madrid bombings: in solidarity with the victims, there were many people who came to Atocha station and the other places hit by the bombs to leave religious icons.[50]

The special case of a photograph published on the front page of two Andalusian newspapers, *Granada Hoy* and *Diario de Sevilla* (which belong to the same press group), is also a good example of this religious dimension. It is the portrait of a woman in tears, hand on mouth (figure 21), whose quality as information is very poor (it provides no contextualization), but which clearly evokes a *Mater Dolorosa*, and refers, in the Spanish context, to the icons of Mariolatry and Christian dolorism that are widespread in Andalusia (figure 22). As Deborah Puccio-Den notes, 'in Spain, the main antonomastic image is that of the Virgin: so much so that, to designate the latter, the word *Imagen* is simply used by itself'.[51] Another example of the importance of this iconographic context in the visual framing of the Madrid bombings is provided by one of the images used to illustrate the home page of the website of the photographic project 'Madrid in Memoriam'[52] (figure 23): it shows a girl with a delicate, soft face standing in the rain during a demonstration of solidarity with the victims, which also evokes a Marian image (figure 24).

The aestheticization of suffering and Christian iconography are deeply linked. That is why the phenomenon of inter-iconicity at work in the images of the dead and wounded from the Madrid bombings is not specific to them, but brings them into a much broader tradition, which Susan Sontag describes in these terms:

> To feel the pulse of Christian iconography in certain wartime or disaster-time photographs is not a sentimental projection. It would be hard not to discern the lineaments of the Pietà in W. Eugene Smith's picture of a woman in Minamata cradling her deformed, blind, and deaf daughter, or the template of the Descent from the Cross in several of Don McCullin's pictures of dying American soldiers in Vietnam.[53]

In other words, the images of the Madrid bombings that were omnipresent in Europe but eclipsed in the United States are part of the same iconographic tradition as some of the most famous pictures of the Vietnam War, which marked a sharp break in the American iconographic tradition of not directly showing the deaths on your own side.[54] The American framing of 9/11 as a 'new Pearl Harbor' had allowed a veil to be drawn over sixty years of US foreign policy, the Vietnam War in particular; now, the images of the Madrid bombings, three years later,

Figures 21, 22, 23 and 24. Front page of the *Diario de Sevilla*, 12 March 2004; Ntra Señora de la Hiniesta Dolorosa (Seville); photo of the Madrid in Memoriam project; and synthetic image available on various Catholic Internet sites.

provided a European counter-framing suggesting that wars conducted by the United States since 9/11 constituted a sort of 'new American quagmire' which, far from producing the desired results and making the world a safer place, were fuelling a worldwide spiral of violence.

While the inter-iconicity of the images of the material destruction of 9/11 was historic and photographic, or even filmic (archive footage of the attacks on Pearl Harbor updated by the Hollywood industry, the Joe Rosenthal photo of Iwo Jima), the inter-iconicity of the images of human suffering on 11 March 2004 was pictorial and religious (Goya, El Greco, Christian iconography). And while the former fed into the nationalist and bellicose tone of responses to the attacks in the United States, the latter was, in Europe, a response imbued with cosmopolitanism and pacifism,[55] reactivating in particular, as we shall see below, the movement of opposition to the Iraq War. The firefighters in Thomas Franklin's photo are the heroes of an America preparing for war; the lifeless woman in Naranjo's photo is the martyr of a Europe that wants peace. The London bombings only confirmed this divergence of views.

The two faces of 7 July 2005

The attack on 7 July 2005 is known to have been the first event after which photos taken by amateurs with their mobile phones were printed on the front pages. Most of the explosions took place underground, in the dark tunnels of the London Underground, and not in the open as in Madrid, so it was impossible for professional photographers to produce images equivalent to those of the 'gaping hole' that had made the headlines after the Madrid bombings. To fill this gap, the media turned to the images created by survivors. *Paris Match*, for example, exclusively published seven photos of a French survivor, and used them to compose an iconographic record strikingly similar to the one which the same magazine had devoted just ten years earlier to the bombing of the Saint Michel station (figures 25 and 26).

In July 1995, *Paris Match* had already managed to publish exclusive images taken within the station just after the explosions by an eyewitness – something that was unusual at a time when not everyone went around with an apparatus capable of taking photos or filming.[56] At the time, these amateur images had not made it onto the front pages, while the day after the London bombings, one such picture was published on the front page of the *New York Times*. But it found its way there more probably because of its documentary value than because of its aesthetic qualities: all you can make out on it are human shadows in single file in the light of a smoky tunnel ... And that is why, even if these photos by survivors have been widely discussed, they actu-

Figures 25 and 26.   Covers of *Paris Match*, 2930, 13 July 2005, and 2410, 3 August 1995.

ally appeared on only 2 per cent of front pages worldwide on the day after the London attacks.[57] Faced with this difficulty, the European and American media opted, from the same set of photos available, for radically different solutions.

The image that made the front page of the *New York Post* the day after the attack, under the title 'BLITZ',[58] was the bus that had exploded in Tavistock Square just under an hour after the Underground trains were hit. Of the four explosions that occurred that morning in London, this was the only one occurring in the open and of which professional photographers produced great quantities of images. These images were thus the only ones to be immediately available to show the material destruction caused by the London bombings[59] – and it is therefore hardly surprising that they correspond to the image-type most frequently reproduced on the front pages of American dailies the following day (31 per cent) (table 3). They do, however, have one major defect that explains why they did not have the same success as the picture of the gutted trains in March 2004 or that of the explosion of the south tower of the World Trade Center in September 2001: they did not capture the heart of the event, since three of the four explosions occurred in the Underground, and not in buses, and furthermore the explosion in Tavistock Square was

Table 3. Main image-types published on front pages in Europe and the
United States on 8 July 2005.

	Woman with mask	Man in suit	Three faces	Evacuated casualties	Gutted bus
Europe	39%	9%	1.5%	6%	27%
USA	28%	6%	3.5%	3.5%	31%

Statistics based on a sample of 322 newspaper front pages (256 American and 66 European).

not the deadliest of the four. So it probably did not seem right to use it as the visual synecdoche of the London bombings.

Thus, European journalists went for another iconographic decision, representing the attack through its victims, even more than they had done for the Madrid bombings. As they had been unable to access the Underground tunnel, it was mainly victims being evacuated and given first aid near the stations that reporters sent there endeavoured to photograph. As the front page of *Le Parisien-Aujourd'hui en France* (figure 27) or of the *Gazeta Poznańska* (figure 28) clearly show, it was, on the day after the 7 July attacks, primarily images of the wounded that Europeans saw on their front pages. Just four different image-types of casualties account for over 55 per cent of the front pages published in Europe on that day (see table 3). This was more than after the Madrid bombings.

That said, these four images did also make it to 41 per cent of American front pages. This can be understood only in the light of the constraints we have just mentioned, and if it is borne in mind that these images are all images of the less seriously wounded, where there is no blood visible. In this respect, they are substantially different from the images of the wounded from the Madrid bombings and closer to those of survivors of the World Trade Center that appeared on a few American front pages as vignettes after 9/11. In particular, one of these images of the injured was reproduced much more than others the day after the London bombings, accounting by itself for 39 per cent of European front pages and 28 per cent of US front pages: in it, we see a woman holding a protective mask over her burnt face while a man holds her in his arms as he guides her along. Her face, therefore, is hidden, unlike those of the dead and wounded on the front pages in March 2004. These pictures of

Figures 27 and 28. Front pages of *Le Parisien-Aujourd'hui en France* and the *Gazeta Poznańska* (Poland), 8 July 2005.

the victims of the London attacks, finally, are not images of the dead. As in September 2001, the few photos of dead bodies that actually exist[60] did not make the front pages.

The London bombings, from the photographic point of view, thus embodied a kind of halfway house between 9/11 and the Madrid bombings, and consequently endorsed a divergence of points of view between Americans and Europeans when it came to Islamist terrorism and the suffering it engenders. Somewhat schematically, we might say that, in the case of 9/11, then of the attacks on Madrid and London, the US media mainly showed burning towers, a gutted train, and a bus with its roof blown off, while the European media showed burning towers, then the dead and wounded. For some, the heart of these events was the material destruction and its symbolic significance; for others, it was ultimately human suffering and the compassion it engendered. The front page of the *Gazeta Poznańska* the day after the London bombings is particularly eloquent in this respect (figure 28): to illustrate this trilogy of attacks, it uses a photo of 9/11 very different from the standard image-types on the front pages in September 2001. It does not show the Twin Towers on fire, but a young woman in tears, clutching an American flag. It is isolated and without a caption, so it is not clear that everyone would see it as an image of 9/11. But juxtaposed with the photo of another young woman survivor of the London Underground attacks, and that of a wounded man from the Madrid bombings, bleeding from the head, it allows us to see on the same level three events which, from the point of view of their destructive force and the number of victims involved alone, were not comparable. While 9/11 remains an irreducibly singular event for the Americans, the trigger for the start of a war in which the attacks on Madrid and London were mere battles, the human suffering that was entailed, from a European point of view, meant the three attacks could be equated.

This principle of equivalence, however, is not without its ambiguity. On the one hand, it tends to depoliticize the attacks, and may refer, in a cosmopolitan perspective, to the idea that humanity itself, at the beginning of the twenty-first century, is a vast 'community of tears and suffering'.[61] Potentially, it does not know any borders. But on the other hand, it also tends to suggest that the West and Europe, in the face of these attacks, are asserting themselves as 'communities of mourning', whose cohesion is strengthened by the experience of a 'shared suffering'. This is an ambiguity from which we have still not emerged.

— 4 —

DEMONSTRATING SOLIDARITY

The demonstration of 11 January 2015 will go down in history. Nearly four million people took to the streets after the attacks: never had France seen such a demonstration. But Europe had: on 12 March 2004, in the aftermath of the Madrid bombings, a full eight million Spaniards demonstrated, two million of them in Madrid, as many as in Paris in January 2015 – a record for both cities. In proportion to the population of the two countries, the demonstration on 12 March 2004 was even bigger than on 11 January 2015, since Spain has twenty million inhabitants fewer than France.[1]

In either case, the magnitude of this civic display contributed to underpinning the analogy between these events and 9/11: when *Le Monde* headlined with 'The French 9/11', this was against the backdrop of an image of demonstrators gathered in Paris on the evening of the attack on *Charlie Hebdo*, closely resembling the demonstration on 12 March 2004 on the front pages of French newspapers that presented the Madrid bombings as a 'European 9/11'.[2] The underlying idea was the same each time: these demonstrations testified to a sense of community drawing strength together in adversity and grief. 'Suffering in common unites more than joy. In the case of national memories, grief is better than triumph.'[3] In March 2004, as in January 2015, the demonstrations seemed to echo those famous words of Ernest Renan uttered in the Sorbonne on another 11 March, 122 years, day by day, before the Madrid bombings. While there is certainly some truth in this interpretation, is it sufficient? Ten years after the 'time to demonstrate'[4] observed in the aftermath of the Madrid attacks enable us to decide.

The attacks as a 'time to demonstrate'

After 9/11, too, millions of people testified to their solidarity with the victims by taking to the streets. People gathered throughout the

United States, and in the rest of the world, notably in front of American embassies, where they came in silence to lay flowers and light candles in memory of the dead. This was particularly true in Canada, Japan, Russia, Israel, India, Australia and Europe, where the phenomenon was particularly evident in Germany and the United Kingdom.[5] In addition to the specific links between these two countries and the United States, they were also the ones which, out of all the European countries, feared having the greatest number of their own nationals among the victims of the attacks.[6] In the forty-eight hours following the attacks, several thousand Germans took part in silent gatherings in Munich and Frankfurt, as well as in Berlin, in front of the American embassy and the town hall of the Schöneberg district from the balcony of which John F. Kennedy made his famous speech in 1963. The same was true in London, where on 13 September some three thousand people gathered in front of the gates of Buckingham Palace to watch and listen as the military band played the American national anthem during the traditional Changing of the Guard. Is it possible, however, to place such gatherings on the same level as the demonstrations of 12 March 2004 and 11 January 2015? In France too, straight after the attack on *Charlie Hebdo*, on 7 January, gatherings were held in Paris and several other French cities: were they simply prefiguring the great demonstration of 11 January, or were they of a different nature? In short: what are we talking about? What exactly does it mean to show solidarity after an attack?

Spontaneous gatherings and post-attack demonstrations

Strictly speaking, a demonstration is defined as 'a collective displacement organized on the public highway for the purpose of creating a political effect through the peaceful expression of an opinion or a demand'.[7] No doubt this canonical definition is a little too restrictive, given that it is often difficult, in practice, to draw a distinction between a static gathering and a procession in motion.[8] The major demonstration that took place in Madrid on the evening of 12 March 2004 brought so many people out onto the streets of the Spanish capital that it was soon impossible for the demonstrators to advance, and instead of being a procession to the Atocha station, it evolved into an immense static gathering that occupied the entire city centre of Madrid. However, that leaves two essential criteria, namely the degree of organization of the gathering and its intention: these make it possible to differentiate between two main types of post-attack mobilizations.

On the one hand are gatherings resulting from the convergence between individuals who feel the need to go out and pay a public tribute to the dead, and who come on their own initiative to the place that seems to them the most appropriate for this purpose. Some of them place flowers in their memory, or a message, a candle or some other object, thereby creating what are known as popular memorials or spontaneous sanctuaries,[9] similar to those that took shape at the foot of the central statue in Paris's Place de la République on the night of the attack on *Charlie Hebdo*. The phenomenon was thus as visible after the attacks of 9/11 as after those on Madrid, London and Paris, and in cities struck by the terrorists as elsewhere in the world. But it is not specific to those attacks: it is found each time a society is confronted by collective deaths, whether accidental or criminal,[10] or the death of a famous person, such as Princess Diana[11] or Pope Jean-Paul II.[12] These gatherings are therefore less 'demonstrations', in the political sense of the word, than rituals of collective mourning.

On the other hand, there are the demonstrations called out by organizers at a specific date and time, with an explicit slogan and a political purpose. These are not simply about coming together to pay tribute to the dead, but about sending a message to the terrorists and the rest of the world. The call for a demonstration may come directly from the government of the country hit by attacks, as was the case after the Madrid bombings: that same evening, José María Aznar asked Spanish citizens to demonstrate the next day 'with the victims, for the constitution and for the defeat of terrorism'. In response to the *Charlie Hebdo* massacre, it was the main political parties and trade unions of France, as well as several associations, which called for participation in what was presented as a great 'republican march'. In this respect, these calls to demonstrate were part of the way the event was framed by the authorities – the slogan 'for the constitution' implied a tacit condemnation of the separatist group ETA, the call for a 'republican' demonstration turned the attack on *Charlie Hebdo* into an attack on the French Republic as a whole – something that exposed it to criticism: in the procession on 12 March 2004, placards asked 'What does the constitution have to do with it?', while in January 2015 some people denounced the 'political recuperation' of an outburst of spontaneous solidarity.[13] The absence of any call to protest in the aftermath of an attack also makes sense from this point of view: after the London bombings, this was a way of displaying the impassiveness of British citizens in the face of the attacks – though this did not prevent them from also gathering in silence to honour the memory of the dead.

After 9/11, too, there were calls for demonstrations. The 200,000 Berliners who gathered at the Brandenburg Gate on 14 September 2001 did so after an appeal from the main German political parties, under the slogan 'No Power to Terror – Solidarity with the United States of

America'. But the success of this demonstration was also due to the fact that it allowed a pacifist message to be sent to the United States: witness the speech (already quoted earlier) given by German federal president Johannes Rau, as well as the demonstrators' placards, on which you could read 'Peace' or messages in English such as 'No revenge please. No World War 3.'[14] In the United States, while rallies in memory of the dead were observed throughout the country from the evening of the attacks onwards, demonstrations in the strict sense did not begin until the weekend of 15 September, which was also a way of rejecting violence and vengeance and calling on George W. Bush to be cautious in his desire to punish those responsible for the attacks. Organized at the behest of American pacifist associations, Protestant churches, and left-wing organizations such as the online mobilization platform *MoveOn*,[15] the placards read: 'Break the cycle of violence', 'War is not the answer', 'It's time for reflection, not revenge' and 'An eye for an eye leaves the whole world blind.'[16] These demonstrations, the biggest of which took place in New York and Berkeley, California, to media silence, were more *reactions to the reaction* of the US government than to the attacks in themselves, contrary to those which were to be seen in the aftermath of the Madrid bombings in March 2004 or Paris in January 2015.

So it is necessary to pay some attention to a 'myth of spontaneity', which ordinarily attaches to street demonstrations, of whatever kind,[17] and which was more prevalent than ever in the case of the demonstrations that were held in response to an attack. The dominant impression seems to have been that the emotion felt after the attack would in some way *naturally* impel citizens to leave their homes and demonstrate their solidarity with the victims. However, there is no clear correlation between the number of people who take to the streets to demonstrate after a killing, whether or not of terrorist origin, and the number of individuals killed.[18] If, in modern societies marked by moral individualism, an attack on the life of even one man can seem like a sacrilege,[19] and if it is a fact that the most significant demonstrations observed in France since the beginning of the twentieth century were all, until the one held on 11 January 2015, aimed at protesting against a killing, the fact remains that, as the historian Danielle Tartakowsky notes, the demonstrations organized for example after the execution in the USA, in 1953, of the Rosenberg couple, accused of spying for the USSR, were not as big as those which had followed the death of the anarchists Sacco and Vanzetti in 1927.[20] Other factors, part of the sociopolitical and historical context in which the demonstration took place, must therefore be taken into account. The 'time to demonstrate' observed in reaction to the Madrid bombings is a good example of this.

12 March 2004: Replaying an(other) 'historic' mobilization

Before 'the spirit of January 11', there was 'the spirit of Ermua' and 'the spirit of Atocha'. The scale of the demonstrations held the day after the Madrid bombings was due firstly to a classic phenomenon: the institutionalization of demonstrating against terrorists. In the 1990s, the Spanish got into the habit of going into the streets to protest at each new ETA attack: this was commonly called 'the spirit of Ermua', from the name of the home town of Miguel Ángel Blanco, whose murder, on 13 July 1997, led some six million Spaniards to take to the streets.[21] This was why, on 11 March 2004, José María Aznar, as head of the Spanish government, himself called on the Spanish to protest. But even without his appeal, they would probably have done so, as taking to the streets has become a reflex for many Spaniards after an attack. A teacher of Spanish at a business school in Poitiers, who organized the demonstration of solidarity with the victims that took place in this city, told a journalist:

> The best way to react is to take to the streets in silence, as is the practice in Spain after ETA attacks. Ultimately, whether it's Al-Qaeda or ETA, the consequences are the same and we undeniably have 200 dead.[22]

The gesture of the 'manos blancas' (clean hands – which means that the citizens, unlike the terrorists, do not have blood on their hands) was very evident in the demonstrations of 12 March 2004, and it very clearly connects those demonstrations with the 'repertoire of collective action'[23] forged by Spaniards in the face of the ETA attacks: it appeared for the first time in the student demonstrations triggered by the assassination of the professor of law at the Autonomous University of Madrid, Francisco Tomás y Valiente, on 14 February 1996, and it was also ubiquitous in the protests of July 1997 in reaction to the assassination of Miguel Ángel Blanco. With reference to this 'spirit of Ermua', Spanish journalists in March 2004 evoked a 'spirit of Atocha'[24] – the name of the station considered to be the epicentre of the attack – an expression already used in 1977, in the midst of the transition to democracy, in connection with the (at that time unprecedented) demonstration of 150,000 people indignant at the assassination of five left-wing lawyers in their office in the Calle de Atocha in Madrid by far-right terrorists.[25]

To this structural factor, connected to the history of Spanish society and of terrorism, we need to add a second, more contextual element: the still fresh memory, at the time of the Madrid bombings, of the opposition movement to the war in Iraq. The biggest demonstrations in this worldwide movement were in Spain: it is estimated that 18.5 per cent of the

Spanish population took part in them.[26] At the demonstration on 15 February 2003, which marked the summit of the protest movement worldwide, one million people marched through the streets of Madrid.[27] There were still 500,000 marching a month later, on 15 March 2003, almost a year to the day before 11 March 2004 (as against 65,000 in Paris and 2,000 in London).[28] Because the date of the Madrid bombings recalled that of 9/11, and even more because it coincided, give or take a day or two, with the first anniversary of the beginning of the war in Iraq, many people had the feeling right from the outset that this attack had not been carried out by ETA, whatever the Spanish government might say, but by Islamist terrorists seeking to punish the way Spain had joined the United States in the war in Iraq.[29]

Thus, in May 2004, 64 per cent of Spaniards thought that the Madrid bombings would not have taken place if Spain had not supported the United States in the Iraq War (only 23 per cent did not agree with this position).[30] And when asked what in their view the main reason was for Islamist terrorists to strike Spain, the war in Iraq was cited most often (26.4 per cent), ahead of religious fanaticism (20.4 per cent) and US foreign policy (18.7 per cent).[31] So taking to the streets was, for some of them, not only a way of demonstrating their solidarity with the victims and their rejection of terrorism, but also at the same time of emphasizing their opposition to the war in Iraq, which they regarded as an indirect cause of the attacks. Hence, elected representatives of the Popular Party were harassed in several cities and sometimes forced to leave the demonstration. José María Aznar himself, at the head of the procession in Madrid, was booed by demonstrators who held him responsible for the attack, as he had stubbornly insisted on committing troops to Iraq in spite of massive public opposition.

The fact that, in the rest of Europe, the Madrid bombings also brought several thousand people out into the streets may be related to the local presence of Spanish immigrants and expatriates. If we look at the regional details of the demonstrations observed in France,[32] it can be seen that there were more of them, and they were better attended, where there was the biggest population of Spanish origin, i.e. in the south of France, and particularly in the south-west. According to the 2009 census figures, 0.4 per cent of people residing in France were immigrants born in Spain, whether they were of Spanish nationality or had acquired French nationality. Only six regions came in above this average; with the exception of the Île-de-France, they were all in the south (see table 4). In addition to the demonstration outside the Spanish embassy in Paris (2,000 demonstrators), the biggest demonstrations in France, after the Madrid bombings, took place in Toulouse (also 2,000 demonstrators) and Bordeaux (1,000 demonstrators). There were

Table 4. Proportion of immigrants born in Spain, by metropolitan area of France, in 2009.

Region of France	Immigrants born in Spain	Total population	Proportion of population born in Spain (per cent)
Languedoc-Roussillon	46,928	2,610,890	1.8
Midi-Pyrénées	27,327	2,862,707	0.95
Aquitaine	28,825	3,206,137	0.90
Provence-Alpes-Côte-d'Azur	25,619	4,889,053	0.52
Rhône-Alpes	27,282	6,174,040	0.44
Île-de-France	47,773	11,728,240	0.41
Auvergne	4,398	1,343,964	0.33
Bourgogne	4,693	1,642,440	0.29
Centre	6,401	2,538,590	0.25
Alsace	4,516	1,843,053	0.25
Champagne-Ardenne	3,108	1,337,953	0.23
Lorraine	4,772	2,350,112	0.20
Franche-Comté	2, 254	1,168,208	0.19
Limousin	1,384	741,785	0.19
Corse	521	305,674	0.17
Picardie	3,077	1,911,157	0.16
Poitou-Charentes	2,366	1,760,575	0.13
Haute-Normandie	1,906	1,832,942	0.10
Nord-Pas-de-Calais	3, 349	4,033,197	0.08
Basse-Normandie	1,024	1,470,880	0.07
Pays-de-la-Loire	2,443	3,539,048	0.07
Bretagne	1,905	3,175,064	0.06
Metropolitan France	251,870	62,465,709	0.40

Source: INSEE, 2009 census.

400 demonstrators in Montpellier, Castres and Saint-Jean de Luz, 300 in Albi, Nîmes and Marseilles, and several hundred in cities such as Perpignan, Béziers, Cahors, Agen, Tarbes and Bayonne. Finally, there were countless micro-demonstrations, even in small towns with barely 6,000 inhabitants, each bringing together between several dozen and a hundred or so people, in various areas of the Midi-Pyrénées and Languedoc-Roussillon, the two French regions with the biggest Spanish population (more than twice the national average in the Midi-Pyrénées and more than four times in Languedoc-Roussillon).

Where these demonstrations were not called out by associations of Spanish immigrants (as was the case in Paris and Toulouse), it was the consul (for example in Montpellier) or the mayor who issued the request for them, in these cases going out of his way to emphasize the 'strong' or 'historical' links between his city and Spain – as when Philippe Bonnecarrère, mayor of Albi, mentioned in his appeal that the 'Hispanicity of the city' should be highlighted. Elsewhere in France, and particularly where the Spanish presence was significantly lower than the territorial average (Brittany, the Loire, Upper and Lower Normandy, Nord-Pas-de-Calais), demonstrations of solidarity were usually based on a small isolated settlement of Spaniards, as in Vannes (Morbihan) where 200 people gathered at the invitation of the association 'Amitiés Vannes-Spain' and the 'Association Culturelle pour l'Échange et l'Amitié entre les Peuples' ('Cultural Association for Exchange and Friendship between Peoples').[33] Finally, in places where the Spanish community was not organized into associations and where the local authorities did not take the lead, these demonstrations were the result of isolated initiatives taken by Spanish immigrants, who thus assumed a role, one might say, as entrepreneurs of solidarity. In Poitiers (300 demonstrators), this was a teacher of Spanish; in Rennes (200 demonstrators), students involved in the Erasmus exchange;[34] in Villefranche-sur-Saône (some fifteen demonstrators), it was a 'young woman from Madrid resident in Calade'.[35] This observation can be extended to the rest of Europe: in Copenhagen, the 200 people who gathered on the square in front of the city hall did so on the initiative of a Spanish national;[36] in Turin and Liverpool, the demonstrations that brought together some hundred people were apparently organized by Erasmus students, etc.[37]

The same phenomenon was at work in the reactions to the Paris attacks in January 2015. While these attacks triggered demonstrations in Europe and the rest of the world that were even bigger than those after the Madrid bombings (with the number of demonstrators amounting to 20,000 in Brussels and 18,000 in Berlin),[38] this was obviously, first and foremost, because of the symbolic impact of an attack on journalists, which led the authorities, political parties and media of several Western countries to issue their own calls for a protest. But where they did not do so, as in Spain, it was French nationals who ensured action was taken: the demonstration of solidarity held in Puerta del Sol, in the centre of Madrid, on 11 January 2015, was organized on the initiative of French Erasmus students. Of course, this does not mean that only French people took part in this event, any more than there were only Spaniards in the demonstrations observed in Europe after the Madrid bombings. In front of the Spanish embassy in Paris, on the evening of 12 March 2004, there were several people who had no direct link with Spain, as witnessed by a young woman interviewed by France Info:

> My name is Diane, I have no connection with Spain, I don't even speak Spanish, but it's really a matter of showing solidarity with a people that, like ourselves, is today affected by the same networks as happened in other countries, through terrorism. We may all have a loved one, or a friend, or just someone who didn't ask to die at that time and in those conditions. So it's really solidarity ... simple solidarity.[39]

Similarly in Nancy: whereas, according to the 2009 census, there were exactly 162 residents in this city who had been born in Spain,[40] almost 800 people gathered on the Place Stanislas at noon on 13 March 2004,[41] at the initiative of the mayor as relayed by a local Franco-Spanish association. So we should not confuse organizing demonstrations in response to attacks with taking part in them: if nationals of the countries hit by attacks may take the initiative and call for demonstrations where they live, this in no ways prejudges what prompts others to respond to their call.

Why demonstrate after an attack?

In view of the above, the question of participation in post-attack demonstrations may not actually seem to arise. Or rather: we may forget to ask it. The outrage triggered by an attack and the impact of injunctions to feel concerned by it in political and media discourses might seem sufficient explanation for the protests. In addition, as the case of the Madrid bombings illustrates, recourse to demonstration in this sort of situation can be a kind of institution for a certain society. Most members of that society would argue: 'There has been an attack, we have to demonstrate', and everything else must take second place.[42] However, there is no reason not to apply the paradox of participation in collective actions, also known as the 'Olson Paradox',[43] to this situation as well: everyone can imagine that they are only a drop in the ocean of solidarity, and whether or not they join the demonstration will not really change its impact – especially when the demonstration has the status of an institution and everything impels us to take part in it.[44] In an attempt to resolve this paradox, emphasis is generally laid on the psychological comfort brought about by taking part in a demonstration after an attack and the collective trauma caused by such an event.

What 'collective trauma' does not explain

Indeed, studies have shown that taking part in demonstrations after the Madrid bombings had a positive impact on Spaniards' perceptions of the social cohesion and overall 'emotional climate' of their country. More specifically, a longitudinal survey of Spanish students and their families came to the conclusion that, two months after the event, those who had participated in the demonstrations tended, all other things being equal, to have a positive perception of their environment (i.e. to declare that they trusted other people, felt hope for the future and had a sense of solidarity with others rather than feeling isolated).[45] The authors of this inquiry concluded that, in general, taking part in a post-attack demonstration reinforces, in the medium term, the feeling of social integration and, in the longer term, the ability to move beyond the trauma of this attack. The 'paradox of participation' in these demonstrations is, in their view, resolved by the mere fact that these have a 'positive effect' on the participants: they lead them to feel more socially supported, united in adversity; they reinforce their beliefs and prevent them from yielding to feelings of impotence and confusion.[46] Individuals therefore participate in these demonstrations because these *help* them 'feel better' when they are confronted with a 'traumatic event' such as a terrorist attack.[47] But this trauma, which should give rise to this need, is a presupposition of the authors of the survey: nothing in their work helps us to understand exactly what it is, what impact it may have, or why, among those who are not directly victims of the attack, some are more 'traumatized' than others, so much so that they go out and demonstrate.[48]

It seems certain that those who took part in demonstrations of solidarity after the Madrid bombings did, according to these studies, present higher scores, in terms of 'positive emotional feeling', than those who had not taken to the streets: they declared that they felt closer to other people, and more inclined to trust them. But the problem is that we have no information on the emotional state of those people *before* the attacks took place. Nothing says they had not already, *before the attacks*, been more inclined than others to have a 'positive emotional feeling'. What appears as an effect of participation in the demonstrations could therefore, to a certain extent, to be the cause of it: we have every reason to believe that persons who, as a general rule, are more trusting towards themselves and others, who are less likely to be subject to isolation or even depression, and who have a more extensive and richer social life, are more inclined than others to participate in demonstrations, of whatever kind. Here as elsewhere, the event and its 'traumatic' quality would reflect pre-existing socio-biographical determinants.[49]

The so-called 'cultural trauma' theory that is fashionable in the United States,[50] and which was promptly applied to 9/11, does not avoid this damaging criticism.[51] Of course, it has the undeniable merit of drawing attention to the fact that, however traumatizing certain events may be for those who suffer them, there are no 'traumatic events' as such for a society or a community taken in their entirety. For an event to come to be perceived as traumatic – including, for the proponents of this theory, an event like 9/11 – people need to mobilize in order to impose the idea that this event has irrevocably and profoundly marked the identity and collective memory of the group – in the case of 9/11, the American nation.[52] But this theory also leaves us at a loss as to how one individual can be more sensitive than another to this socially constructed 'cultural trauma'. In the end, emotions, both individual and collective, occupy a marginal place in the analysis, even though they are at the heart of the phenomenon under study.[53]

It has long been established by sociologists that the socialized character of our affects, even the most intimate ones, means that intimately felt emotions and public emotions are inseparable.[54] Randall Collins has shown that the propensity of Americans to demonstrate their solidarity with the victims of 9/11 could not be grasped independently of local contexts of sociability within which this demonstration made sense. While there is a tendency to view American farmers as more nationalistic than city people, it was ultimately at the doors of houses located in towns, rather than those of farms in rural areas, that he counted most American flags flying after 9/11.[55] This is evidence of the way that displaying a flag as a symbol of solidarity is meaningful only within a dense social environment: what counts is that the neighbours can see the flag from their homes, and that the person flying the flag knows that the neighbours can see it: the social control that operates in the neighbourhood also works as a reciprocal incentive to feel concerned and to show this by demonstrating your solidarity. Conversely, because farms in rural areas are isolated from one another, there is no point in showing a flag that no one will see. Randall Collins draws the following conclusion:

> Although the symbol displays solidarity with the national group, not ostensibly with one's local ties, the local group is what sustains the display.

> People make their displays of solidarity with distant groups by acting together in local groups rather than as individuals.[56]

This may seem obvious, but it is all too often forgotten: in the aftermath of a terrorist attack, one does not show solidarity in a vacuum, but *to others*. Without a public seeing us demonstrate our solidarity, it loses its meaning.

The same applies to street demonstrations, whether after a terrorist attack or in other circumstances: we know they are 'the result of multiple mobilizations and social incentives related to the interactions of daily life'[57] – something which finds expression in the fact that people often take part in them in small groups rather than alone.[58] This is why the correlation between the scale of the demonstrations of solidarity observed in France after the Madrid bombings and the local presence of Spanish immigrants or expatriates does not mean, as I have already noted, that these demonstrations mobilized only Spaniards, but rather that the presence of persons from Spain in their environment will have encouraged French people to take part in these demonstrations of solidarity. It may also, quite simply, have made them more sensitive than other French people to the tragedy that had struck Spain. The solidarity demonstrated on a transnational scale is in this sense very clearly based on local solidarities.[59] And as the observations made by Randall Collins in the United States after 9/11 show, the same is true of the solidarity demonstrated on a national scale, even though this tends to be thought of as a feeling of shared belonging to the nation under attack, a feeling that supposedly exercises its influence uniformly among the population, at least among all 'decent citizens'.

Arguing in terms of a sense of national belonging (and collective trauma, which usually goes with it) tends to conceal the fact that people's reactions to the terrorist attacks stem rather from a *feeling of closeness* to the event and those who are victims, both inside a country and beyond its borders. A feeling of national belonging can of course influence this feeling of closeness, but it is not the only decisive factor, and so they cannot be seen as identical. Even if the authorities and the media present it as an event that concerns *all* of us, a terrorist attack taking place on the public transport system of the capital of my country may remain foreign to me because of geographical distance (I live at the other end of the country, I never set foot in this city) or social distance (I never use public transport, the victims and I do not have the same lifestyle, so I do not have the impression that it might just as easily have happened to me). A journalist from *The Times* investigated, shortly after the London bombings, the way they had been perceived in rural areas, and summarizes the general feeling that he found in Derbyshire:

London is another place, where other folk live. Cities are cities. New York was, too, and so was Madrid. People think that it is awful, shocking, what has happened in London, but there is not quite – nearly, but not quite – the impression that it happened to *us*.[60]

This phenomenon was less perceptible in the case of the Paris attacks in January 2015, since the symbolic dimension of the first attack on *Charlie Hebdo*, carried out on journalists and thus infringing the freedom of expression, immediately awakened the 'national imaginary',[61] as had happened in the United States after 9/11.[62] However, a French person with family in Paris may well have felt more concerned by the events, and therefore more inclined to demonstrate, than someone with no family connections in the capital, just as a French person may whose circle includes journalists, Jews or policemen, compared to someone who does not.

A question of closeness

Ten years on, this much is clear: it was this phenomenon on a European scale that the demonstrations of solidarity in response to the Madrid bombings brought out, rather than a barely articulate sense of common belonging to Europe, as some people said at the time – and today we can see how little of that remains ... All sociological studies on the subject agree that, if national selfishness has been on the wane for several years in Europe, this is not because any new supranational identity is emerging: Europeans do not feel they 'belong' to Europe.[63] For example, Sophie Duchesne and Virginie Van Ingelgom have shown that French-speaking French and Belgian people do not 'really (any longer) perceive [nationals of other West European countries] as competitors, likely to arouse negative emotions – though this does not mean that, on the European level, a community imagined as sovereign encompassing them all has emerged'.[64]

While it plays a part, on the microsocial level, in local configurations of social relationships and the interactions of everyday life in which each of us takes part, the feeling of a greater or lesser closeness between Europeans also lies, on the macrosocial level, in the links that may have been established between some countries more than others. A mass terrorist attack taking place tomorrow in Berlin or Brussels would without the slightest doubt bring more French people out onto the streets than an attack in Vilnius, even if the last killed more people. That France was the country where there were the most demonstrations of solidarity outside Spain after the Madrid bombings – to such an extent, indeed, that the authorities in Madrid later had an insert published in the French national press saying: 'THANK YOU FRANCE. Madrid will never forget the demonstrations of solidarity and the support of the French after the attacks of last 11 March'[65] – cannot, in this respect, fail to be connected to the fact that Spain was, at the end of 2003, the European country which French people most liked (48 per cent of them, compared with 23 per cent of all Europeans).[66] However, seeking to determine the origins of this type of positive feeling between certain European countries, Bruno Cautrès comes to the conclusion that it cannot be related merely to the length of time those countries have been part of the European Union, something that would have given rise to a shared sense of belonging between their inhabitants; rather, it stems from links that have been forged between countries over time, often fostered by a shared border:

> Trading with another country, exchanging resources, capital, or goods with it is at least as important, if not more so, in the way we imagine it than knowing that it is now part of the same integrated political group.[67]

There is a historic precedent for this: the upsurge of solidarity aroused in France at the end of the nineteenth century by the floods in the region of Murcia that caused the deaths of more than 1,000 people in October 1879. In response to a subscription campaign launched by Spanish newspapers to help those affected, some 43 million old pesetas had been collected in France. And in order to explain what was considered even then to be an unusual display of solidarity, some observers, such as the Marquis de Molins, former ambassador of Spain to France, had noted the 'personal and material links' between the French and the Spanish, links which had intensified over previous decades thanks to the improvement in means of telecommunication and transport. 'Spain is wounded, France bleeds; the blow striking Murcia has reached Paris', as Victor Hugo summarized the situation in a text published for the benefit of the victims.[68] An erudite reader of *La Nouvelle République du Centre Ouest* who exhumed this text the day after the Madrid bombings did not fail to emphasize that Hugo would probably not have written anything different in March 2004.[69]

In this regard, the press clearly plays a significant role as a mediator, now as much as before. Thus, French regional newspapers systematically reported on the Madrid bombings in terms of these concrete, personal and material links, helping to bring the victims closer to their readers (this was also the case for the French national media, but in a less overt way). Many articles focused, for example, on how 'local' Spaniards experienced the event. This was obviously the case in regions of France where there was a significant community of Spanish immigrants, well established and structured: 'The Spanish community between pain and revolt' (*Midi Libre*, 13 March), 'The Spaniards of France return home to support their families' (*La Provence*, 13 March), 'The Spaniards of France in mourning' (*Le Progrès de Lyon*, 12 March). But it could also be witnessed where the Spanish presence was less in evidence. In Burgundy, for example, where the proportion of immigrants born in Spain is less than the national average (0.29 per cent), *L'Yonne Républicaine* devoted its front page on 18 March to 'The grief of the Spaniards of Auxerre'. Similarly, in the Limousin region (where the proportion of immigrants born in Spain is 0.19 per cent), *La Montagne* published on 13 March an article devoted to the 'little Spanish colony' of Limoges, which was 'devastated'.

This way of making the terrorist attack more familiar to the reader also worked the other way round, by highlighting the 'people from here' who were 'present there', in Madrid, at the time of the bombings. First among them was Marion Subervielle, the only Frenchwoman to have been killed in the Madrid attacks: a native of Mourenx, in the Hautes-Pyrénées, her funeral was on the front pages of *Midi Libre* and *La Dépêche du Midi*. Then there were those people who could have been in the trains hit by the explosions: 'The lie-in that saved the life of Manu, the student from Narbonne' (*Midi Libre*, 12 March); and 'Ghislaine, the miraculous survivor of the 7.30 a.m. train' (*La Provence*, 12 March), a young woman from Martigues and working in Madrid who missed her train on the morning of the attacks. Finally, there are those who were given the status of main witnesses such as Danielle Segalen, a teacher of French from Carantec, in Brittany, who had been based in Madrid for thirteen years, who was interviewed by a journalist from *Le Télégramme de Brest* a month after the attacks, while she was on holiday in her native region. A passage from this interview is worth pausing over. To the question 'How did your acquaintances in Carantec react [to the news of the attack]?', Danielle Segalen replied:

> My mother received a lot of sympathy calls. 1,500 kilometres away from Madrid, there was another surge of solidarity! I was very surprised, and very touched.[70]

And so, in this region of France, where the proportion of Spanish immigrants is the lowest in all of France (0.06 per cent of its inhabitants were born in Spain), people immediately thought of Danielle Segalen at the moment when they learned that an attack had been carried out in Madrid. Knowing someone who worked in Madrid will have made them feel closer to the event and its victims: hence, perhaps, a more important emotion, giving rise to that 'other surge of solidarity' which, fundamentally, was no different from the one that had led other French people to take to the streets at this time.

The concrete ties established between France and others can, in this sense, be transformed into *vectors of solidarity*, offering the French a way of showing their solidarity with those who, in one of these countries, have been victims of a terrorist attack. This is very clear in the particular case of twinning arrangements between the municipalities or institutions of different countries. Of course, they are often essentially institutional links, which do not, in such circumstances, involve anything more than one mayor (or head of an institution) sending a letter of support to another. Thus, two days after the Madrid bombings, *La Dépêche du Midi* reported that the mayor of Tarbes had written to his opposite number in Huesca. One could quote dozens of similar examples. And the London Metropolitan Archives of London overflow with letters sent in July 2005 to the various boroughs in Greater London from the mayors of their twin towns and districts.

But in some cases, when it goes somewhat deeper, a twinning link may also play a more important role. For example, in Sommières, in the Gard, it was at the initiative of the twinning association Sommières–Callosa de Segura that a silent march was organized in March 2004: the twinning between these two towns was based on strong ties established through seasonal migrations (with Spaniards from Callosa de Segura coming every year to harvest in Sommières and eventually settling there), and because in September 2002, when Sommières had been the victim of devastating floods, the inhabitants of Callosa de Segura had themselves demonstrated their solidarity.[71] Likewise in Auxerre, students in the fourth year of the Saint-Joseph secondary school were especially affected by the Madrid bombings as they had been to the Atocha station the October before and, through a twinning arrangement with the San José del Parque de Madrid school, established links with Madrilenians of their age and their families who had hosted them during their stay. Upon learning of the attack, they observed a minute's silence in class, and drafted words of support in Spanish addressed to their friends in Madrid.[72]

What leads people to take part in gatherings or demonstrations after a terrorist attack, both within and beyond the borders of the stricken country, thus proceeds above all from these concrete, personal and material links between countries, institutions, towns and individuals – links that bring us closer to the victims. This does not mean that these gatherings and demonstrations do not mobilize feelings of belonging; even less does it imply that taking part in them does not help to strengthen such feelings at the time. But regardless of the territorial scale on which this mobilization is observed, it is initially on the local level, step by step, that it operates. To see it as the mere expression of a national unity, or the sudden epiphany of a European or even global collective awareness – as was sometimes said after 9/11 – is nothing more than an additional way of framing the event comprised by the terrorist attack: a way for authorities and journalists to decide on its meaning and to guide people's reaction to it. Because we support it, because we believe in it, this framing has real effects. People could undeniably feel they were, as never before, part of a national community – 'we, the French'- by participating in the demonstration of 11 January 2015. It may even have given them goose-bumps or brought tears to their eyes. But at the same time, as everyone knows, those of us who were there all had our different reasons: we were not there simply *because we are French*, and some people, although they were just as French as we were, were not there. The minutes of silence declared by the authorities after a terrorist attack stir the same tensions; but because, in many contexts, it is obligatory to observe them, these can take a more problematic turn.

— 5 —

OBSERVING SILENCE

A minute's silence was observed throughout France at noon on Thursday 8 January 2015 to pay tribute to the victims of the attack on *Charlie Hebdo* and mark a day of national mourning declared by the president of the Republic. Just one minute's silence, then hours and days of debate. Why did they observe a silence for the dead of *Charlie Hebdo* but not for so many others in the world? Why did they not observe another minute's silence after the attack on the Hypercacher (the kosher shop)? And then there were the schools where this moment of reflection caused 'incidents', the young people who refused to 'be Charlie', those professors who tried to justify a mourning which ought to have been self-explanatory, etc. Questions, in short, that had already been asked in September 2001, the last time that the president of the French Republic had issued such a decree, and then again in March 2004 and July 2005 after the attacks in Madrid and London. Questions that, in all likelihood, will need to be asked again …

The minutes of silence that the authorities ask us to observe after terrorist attacks make it possible to display the community of mourning and, in doing so, to establish by a symbolic action the 'official' framing of the attack: if all Europeans observed a silence after the Madrid bombings, this was because the attack concerned all of them; if France observed a silence the day after the attack on *Charlie Hebdo*, this was because it was an attack on all French people, and not only on the editorial board of a magazine. But for this very reason, these minutes of silence gave rise to criticism.[1] By displaying a community of mourning, they were an opportunity to question the validity of the boundaries assigned to it. By treating the honoured dead differently from those who were not honoured, they posed a problem of moral equivalence which affects the very foundations of individualistic societies: the idea that all human beings are equal by nature, and that no human life, of whatever kind, can in principle be worth more than another. In other words, they force us to face our contradictions. When you profess universalist ideals, and when you have defended the adopting of a cosmopolitical point of view on 9/11 and the reasons behind Islamist terrorism, how can you justify being more inclined to observe a silence for some of the dead rather than others?

A ritual of collective mourning

Asking citizens to observe a minute's silence seems to have become a reflex on the part of the authorities after a terrorist attack. Appearing in Europe at the end of the First World War, this ritual of collective mourning has been spreading ever since, until it has nowadays become almost commonplace.[2] It differs from mere spontaneous gatherings of citizens in one essential point: its solemn character. Organized and convened by the authorities, the minutes of silence resemble 'ceremonial gatherings', just like funerals or openings of buildings, rather than mere 'demonstrative gatherings', such as those discussed in the previous chapter.[3] They have, in this respect, the power of establishing a community of mourning: if all French people observe silence on the same day and at the same time after a terrorist attack, this is because all French people are affected by it, and France itself is in mourning. But contrary to what we might believe, it has not always been so. While young French people born at the end of the 1990s have regularly had to observe a silence for this reason – at primary school after the Madrid bombings, in secondary school after the attacks of Mohammed Merah in 2012, in sixth form college after the attack on *Charlie Hebdo* – this was not the case for previous generations. In the past, only the National Assembly held a minute's silence after a terrorist attack, as it did after the attack on the Saint-Michel RER station in July 1995, the most deadly in France until that against *Charlie Hebdo*. From this point of view, 9/11 marked an undeniable turning point.

Establishing a community of mourning

Your grief is also ours: this was the message that the European authorities wanted to send to the Americans the day after the 9/11 attacks. As we have noted earlier,[4] Friday, 14 September 2001 was a day of national mourning in the United States, with a major national ceremony in honour of the victims in Washington Cathedral and a candlelit vigil in the streets of New York.[5] But within the European Union, too, it was officially a

100

'day of mourning and solidarity with the American people'. Multiple ceremonies in homage to the victims were organized and all European citizens were called on to observe three minutes' silence at noon. At that same time, the main European radio and television channels interrupted their programmes, several stock exchanges stopped trading, and public transport in many cities came to a halt.[6] In Spain and Portugal, this mourning was officially extended to forty-eight hours, while in France, it was the subject of a decree signed by the president of the Republic and the prime minister, published in the *Journal Officiel* immediately after the attacks.[7] Thus, 14 September 2001 was turned into a 'day of national mourning', as if France had itself been affected by the attacks, whereas such decrees had until now been reserved for the deaths of heads of state. Since then, only the attack on *Charlie Hebdo* has once more led to the publication of such a decree.

The flags on public buildings were thus flown at half-mast for four days, and a ceremony was held in the courtyard of the Élysée Palace at noon on 14 September; here, the three minutes' silence was observed by the president of the Republic, alongside the US ambassador, and the American national anthem was played by the Republican Guard – never, in the history of the French Republic, had a foreign national anthem hitherto resounded in the court of the presidential palace.[8] In London, the American national anthem was played during the Changing of the Guard at Buckingham Palace (another first), while on 14 September, a ceremony to commemorate the victims was celebrated in St Paul's Cathedral, in the presence of the queen and the prime minister. Some 3,000 people attended, and nearly 30,000 gathered outside the cathedral. Major religious ceremonies in the presence of heads of state also took place in other European capitals, including the American Church in Paris.

Similar events were held in March 2004, after the Madrid bombings, which was the subject of three days of national mourning in Spain. The president of the European Union, Bertie Ahern, called on all member states to observe again, just as in September 2001, three minutes' silence at noon on 15 March 2004 – which was also a way of symbolically marking that 11 March 2004 was indeed the equivalent of 9/11 for Europe. As three years earlier, the media again reported silent assemblies in city squares throughout Europe, with stock exchanges suspending their activities, public transport coming to a halt, and television and radio channels interrupting their programmes. Flags were flown at half-mast in the member states of the European Union, as well as at the headquarters of NATO and various European institutions. In France, the new day of mourning did not on this occasion lead to the publication of an official decree: it was simply announced by a press release from the presidency of the Republic. But the victims of the Madrid bombings did have the right to one honour that had not been granted to those of 9/11: a 'national homage' celebrated in Notre-Dame-de-Paris on the evening of 13 March.

The main difference between these solemn acts and those already observed in Europe in September 2001 is that the latter had not been presented as establishing a European community of mourning, but rather as part of a worldwide accord. In completely symptomatic fashion, in the edition of *Le Monde* for 14 September 2001, the fact that the European Union announced a 'day of mourning and solidarity with the American people' was not treated as a subject in itself, but was included in an article entitled 'The whole world expresses its solidarity with the American victims.'[9] Similarly, when Italian television channels interrupted their programmes at noon on 14 September, they spent three minutes re-broadcasting the images of the attacks, while scrolling a banner with the words:

> These acts of barbarism constitute an attack not only on the United States of America, but on humanity as a whole, and the values of freedom which are common to all.[10]

Europe is therefore merged into a community of mourning identical with the whole of humanity or, at the very least, with a community of values. This was because, in addition, the Council of Europe had immediately joined the initiative taken by the European Union, and the call to observe three minutes' silence in memory of the dead of 9/11 concerned a total of forty-three countries, not just the fifteen member states of the European Union in September 2001. The European media could thus lead with headlines on 14 September reading '800 million Europeans showing solidarity',[11] with Europe now meaning less a clearly defined political community, the European Union, than a geographical and civilizational area including even Turkey and Russia. So Europe was in mourning, but it did not yet form a *community* of mourning.

This is what changed in March 2004. This time, the minutes of silence observed within the European Union were highlighted to support the idea that Europe had just experienced its 'own' 9/11, and that a collective European consciousness was emerging in the sharing of suffering and mourning. An article published in an online newspaper a week after the attack show this particularly well:

> A collective European consciousness [...] has come to life in the shared mourning over the victims of Madrid and in the demonstrations of solidarity which followed the tragedy. We have seen, of course, the official reac-

102

tions [...]. We have also seen individual and collective solidarity: asking for news of friends, holding demonstrations in front of embassies, sharing incredulity, feeling others' pain. And three minutes' silence, observed by schoolchildren in Northern Ireland and by the aircraft engines at Heathrow on Monday 15 March.[12]

The significance of the minutes of silence observed after the Madrid bombings must be related to the efforts made by European institutions, especially on the basis of the Maastricht Treaty, to strengthen 'European feeling' through symbolic policies borrowed from the national model (flag, hymn, Festival of Europe, motto, etc.).[13] But the problem with promoting identification with Europe, modelled on the nation-state, is that it runs the risk of coming into conflict with national institutions, which is exactly what happened at the time of the London bombings.

The British government decided that a day of mourning would be observed one week to the day after the terrorist attacks, i.e. on 14 July 2005, and the governing bodies of the European Union once again called for member states to join in. But 14 July is, of course, the date of the French national holiday. The French authorities were thus faced with an unprecedented dilemma: how to ask the French to observe a moment of silence in memory of London's victims in the middle of a day supposedly meant to be wholly devoted to the self-celebration of the national community? The problem, of course, would not have arisen if it had been a question of commemorating the victims of an attack carried out in France or against French people. But in the present case, the European community of mourning came into conflict with the national community. If we are to believe the testimony of Bruno Le Maire, Jacques Chirac, then president of the Republic, reacted in these terms:

This idea of a minute's silence on 14 July is utterly incredible! Personally, I'm shocked. Really. A minute's silence for terrorist attacks, on the day of the national holiday! [...] It's totally absurd! 14 July is a holiday for all the French. We are not going to commemorate terror attacks. What did we do for the dead in Beslan? Nothing. And for the dozens of victims killed every day in Iraq? Nothing. It's ridiculous. But since everyone is against me, let's go along with it![14]

As in March 2004, it was ultimately through a simple communiqué – this time released on the day before it was due to take effect – that the presidency of the Republic called on the French to observe a moment's commemoration at midday:

The president of the Republic has expressed the desire that all of our fellow citizens will be able to join the tribute, in association with the other countries of the European Union, in memory of the victims of the attacks committed on 7 July 2005 in London: two minutes' silence will be observed on Thursday, 14 July 2005 at 1 p.m.

But given the circumstances, those minutes of silence passed almost unnoticed in France. And by way of national ceremony, the traditional 14 July reception in the gardens of the Elysée Palace was simply interrupted for a short time, at 1 p.m., to enable the president of the Republic to stand in silence alongside the ambassador of the United Kingdom.

In general, while other official ceremonies of this kind were organized on that day in the member states of the European Union, these minutes of silence had, outside the United Kingdom, none of the magnitude of those observed in 2001 and March 2004. To take just one example: while in Brussels between 3,000 and 4,000 people gathered in front of the European Commission building on 14 September 2001 and 15 March 2004, on 14 July 2005 there were at most 300 of them. It was mainly in London that the day was marked: after having gathered in silence at midday, thousands of Londoners gathered in the late afternoon in Trafalgar Square to pay tribute again to the victims for over two hours, some of them staying there all night long in the candlelight – just as New Yorkers had done on the evening of 14 September 2001 in Union Square. The community of grief that actually forms as a consequence of an attack, therefore, is not always the community which the authorities, both European and national, intend to create. Calling on citizens to observe a minute's silence is one thing: whether they actually respond to this call, and how, is another.

Observing (or not) a silence on 15 March 2004

The reports on the observing of silence comprise a separate genre in journalistic literature. They include descriptions of behaviour that are better written than those usually in the newspapers (they show an attention to the reciprocal adjustments between individuals, to their efforts at coordinating their physical activities, to the glances and non-verbal signs that they exchange). But they also sometimes involve ascribing mental states in a way that can be confusing. The description in Le Monde of the three minutes' silence observed on 14 September 2001 at the Gare d'Austerlitz in Paris is representative in this respect:

Everyone understands that this is a serious time. [...] There is a brief moment of awkwardness, and after a few furtive glances at their neighbours, everyone assumes a dignified pose of detachment: the minute's silence is observed in a quite unassuming way. [...] [Then] everyone resumes the movement they had been making before the pause, without a smile, with a studied naturalness, wondering whether or not he really observed three minutes' silence, and whether he will dare to say so.[15]

Yet, just as one cannot, from the observation of a cheerful crowd, deduce individual enthusiasms – as journalists still sometimes tend to do when they report, not on minutes of silence, but on the way French presidents go on walkabouts[16] – it seems problematic to draw, from the mere observation of a crowd standing in silence, conclusions as to what 'everyone' is thinking or feeling in their heart of hearts. On what basis can it be asserted that some are genuinely commemorating the dead while others are calculating the effect their behaviour will have?

One of the great merits of Erving Goffman's sociology is to have taught us that the boundary we think we can trace between a 'sincere' and a 'cynical' attitude is, basically, irrelevant.[17] With regard to life in society, what counts is that individuals understand what is expected of them in a given situation, and observing whether they comply with this or not. And from that point of view, observing a minute's silence is clearly part of what Simmel called 'the negativity of collective action':[18] when an instruction is given requesting that people stand silently for a few moments as a tribute to the victims of a terrorist attack, failure to respect it may be interpreted as a mark of indifference towards these victims; but if individuals comply with this instruction, it does not necessarily mean that they are personally mourning for them. It simply means that they are following instructions. In so doing, there is a good chance that they really will feel the emotion that the posture they are adopting is intended to express publicly: standing with their arms by their sides, head bowed, as a sign of remembrance, in the midst of a crowd that is doing the same, can awaken in people a sense of affliction that they had not felt seconds before; just as, when you force yourself to weep, it often happens that you end up being unable to hold back your tears.[19] But who can say if this affliction and these tears are 'sincere' or not? The real challenge is to understand what leads people to follow the instructions to observe a minute's silence, when they might very well not do so. Focusing on the case of the minutes of silence observed in France after the Madrid bombings, I started with a very simple question: where were these minutes of silence observed, and where was this not done? Where did they actually give rise to solemn gatherings?

Regional press archives turn out, yet again, to be valuable resources, as for the study of demonstrations of solidarity. In this particular context, when national and European authorities call for minutes of silence following a terrorist attack, even the absence of a gathering is an event on the local scale: 'No gathering at Belley', said Le Progrès on 16 March

105

2004, after the Madrid bombings.[20] The article relates that in this small town of 8,000 inhabitants located in the *département* of the Ain, 'at noon, in spite of the siren announcing the beginning of the commemoration, only Jean-Claude Travers, mayor of the city, and some members of his town council observed the three minutes' silence in front of the Town Hall of Belley', without any of the locals joining them. And the journalist wondered: 'Indifference or lack of information?' The question deserves to be asked, since in Sélestat, in the Bas-Rhin, the local media argued that the information had arrived too late to be relayed properly to the population, so that the few inhabitants to join the local elected representatives in the Place d'Armes of the town on 15 March did so 'by chance', according to the *Dernières Nouvelles d'Alsace*.[21] Newspapers also mentioned technical problems in some towns, notably Colmar, Vénissieux and others in the Rhône area, where the siren that should have announced the beginning of the period of silence never sounded.[22] Therefore, a journalist from *France-Soir* went so far as to write of an 'initiative [that had been] unequally relayed' across France.[23]

Conversely, the editions of *Midi Libre* and *La Dépêche du Midi* were filled with articles, often accompanied by a photo, which reported numerous gatherings in the squares of the towns and villages of the south-west of France at noon on 15 March 2004. For example, in Bizanet (Aude), a town of 1,250 inhabitants, some 50 people observed three minutes' silence on the square in front of the town hall, but there were similar demonstrations in Sauvian (Hérault, 4,000 inhabitants), Coursan (Aude, 6,000 inhabitants), Bédarieux (Hérault, 6,000 inhabitants), Lavelanet (Ariège, 6,000 inhabitants), Lézignan-Corbières (Aude, 9,000 inhabitants) and so on. As a general rule, these articles noted the strong links between these towns and Spain and mentioned the presence, at the sides of the municipal authorities, of a representative from associations of Spanish immigrants, or from Spanish cultural centres. For larger cities such as Toulouse, Perpignan, Narbonne, Agen, Tarbes, Sète or Carcassonne, longer articles described in conventional terms the conversations that came to a halt on the terraces of the cafés, the passers-by standing motionless in the streets, and the cessation of activities in schools, stations and shops.

In Vandœuvre-lès-Nancy, which is, in terms of population, the second largest town in the urban community of Greater Nancy and Meurthe-et-Moselle (30,000 inhabitants), there were, however, at the most a dozen people gathered in silence in the town centre at noon on 15 March.[24] And in Mulhouse, with its 111,000 inhabitants, a hundred or so gathered on the Place de la Réunion, i.e. as many as in certain towns of the south-west with one tenth as many inhabitants.[25] As for post-terrorist demonstrations, then, a correlation can be observed between the greater or lesser local implantation of a population of Spanish origin and the extent to which the minutes of silence were observed. Again, the realization of the ritual of collective mourning is not uniformly observed within society, but depends on the local social configurations, where there is a varying sense of closeness to the victims of the attack. It is also observable in businesses. If in Vénissieux and Saint-Priest the production lines of Renault Trucks stopped for three minutes after the Madrid bombings, this was because Spain is the second biggest market for that company, and the only foreign country in which it has a factory.[26] On the other hand, the employees of the Doux group in Brittany complained publicly that they had not been able to observe even one minute's silence in memory of the Madrid victims: the management refused it on the pretext that the request had been made too late by the trade union.[27]

All indications therefore are that the three minutes' silence at noon on 15 March 2004 was observed more if family members, friends, colleagues or peers had spread the news and reminded people. In some contexts, particularly town halls and local government buildings, the question of whether or not to associate oneself with the minutes of silence simply did not arise: people did so because they felt obliged to do so. On the other hand, things were quite different in the impersonal streets of large cities, where social control is not so tight, even in cities where there is a strong Spanish presence:

> In Montpellier, as the sirens sounded, life did not stop (it had not done so after 9/11, either), even if there were some passers-by who stopped on the pavements or people standing on the terraces of cafés. [...] It was mainly in local government buildings and universities that the commemoration was most respected.[28]

What happened in Montpellier (where 0.83 per cent of the inhabitants were born in Spain[29]) was substantially equivalent to what could be observed in a town markedly less affected by Spanish, such as Puy-en-Velay where, apart from the fifty people gathered in front of the town hall and in the courtyard of the departmental council, 'it does not seem that our citizens felt very concerned by this call to commemoration', given that 'you could count on the fingers of one hand the passers-by who, on the Place du Breuil, stopped and observed the three minutes' silence'.[30]

Between these two extremes, public institutions on the one side, the anonymous streets on the other, there was a whole range of places where the incentive to observe the minutes of silence was more or less powerful. In shopping centres and railway stations, announcements broadcast via loudspeakers generally reminded people of the request, but could pass unnoticed. At the train station in Valenciennes, for example:

107

On the platforms of the station, the travellers came and went, and nobody
there seemed to hear the sound of the sirens crying out with the pain of
the Spanish people at 12 noon, drowned out by the noise of trains passing
through.[31]

In the concourse, the journalist noted that the women in the ticket office
rose to observe the minutes of silence but only one traveller did so.
Similarly, at Nancy station, a photo published by *L'Est Républicain*
showed a man in a posture of commemoration on a platform while
behind him people continued to walk and talk.[32] Or take the Montparnasse
station, in Paris: some people rose and adopted postures of contempla-
tion, while the brasserie continued to serve customers and a mother
loudly scolded her child, reported a journalist from *France-Soir*; meanwhile, the salesman in a clothing store had endeavoured to respect the
moments of commemoration, but told the journalist that he had not had
time to switch off the music in his shop and had been disturbed by a
security guard who came up to chat.[33]

In a shopping arcade in Villeneuve d'Ascq, in the north of France,
information about the minutes of silence was also broadcast in the
morning, then, at noon, the background music was switched off in all
the shops, 'generating a certain calm straight away'. But, notes the journalist of *La Voix du Nord*, 'the vast majority of customers continued on
their journey and carried on with their conversations'.[34] Finally, on the
campus of the Arts Faculty in Nancy, where a reporter from *L'Est
Républicain* noted that at noon on 15 March 2004 there was 'the usual
hubbub', one woman went off by herself into the park to observe the
moment of commemoration when the sirens began to sound.[35] As this
last example suggests, respecting the minutes of silence is, in some contexts, a personal matter. Thus individuals can sometimes play a role as
entrepreneurs of solidarity by ensuring that the request for silence is
collectively respected. On a Madrid–Marseilles flight, for example, the
three minutes' silence was observed at the express request of one woman
passenger, supported by the pilot-in-command.[36] And it is in such cir-
constances that it may become necessary to justify silence to those who
do not see why they should respect it, just as teachers experienced with
their pupils the day after the attack on *Charlie Hebdo*. This need for
justification may appear intolerable, in so far as it calls into question the
moral foundations of Western societies.

A problem of moral equivalence

The situations where the instruction to observe minutes of silence is
explicitly issued are particularly interesting from a sociological point of

view insofar as they give rise to criticism. Some people may ostenta-
tiously refuse to follow it, and then find they have to explain their decision. Thus, on the platform of Nancy railway station on 15 March 2004,
a reporter from *L'Est Républicain* who asked a couple why they had
refused to observe the three minutes' silence in memory of the victims
of the Madrid bombings drew this retort:

> Because nobody's doing so for a certain lady, now in hospital, in the last
> stages of cancer, and because nobody did a thing after the massacre of the
> Rwandans. In fact, it would take a lifetime of silence![37]

The objection deserves our attention, since it is far from being marginal
or trivial. This is exactly the same type of argument which teachers
sometimes heard from their pupils the day after the attack on *Charlie
Hebdo*, just as fifteen years before, after 9/11: why do we keep silence
for these dead when we do nothing for the dead in Palestine, Iraq or
Syria? And, as I noted earlier, we will find that this was also the argument put forward by President Jacques Chirac himself to challenge the
principle of minutes of silence meant to be observed in the aftermath of
the London bombings on a 14 July ... This is, in short, a problem of
moral equivalence between the dead who are honoured and those who
are not honoured, a problem which touches on one of the essential
foundations of Western societies: the idea that all human beings are
equal, and that no human life can be worth more than another.[38] The
contradiction, in the context of the post-9/11 period, is all the more
striking as this idea presides over the cosmopolitan point of view which
Europeans endeavoured to defend against the nationalist and hawkish
reaction of the Americans, and against a reading of the terrorist attacks
in terms of a 'clash of civilizations'.

'Why is nothing being done for the dead in Iraq?'

The problem, it should be emphasized, is specific to minutes of silence.
One can very well, after a terrorist attack, participate in a demonstration
without seeing any problem in this, but still hesitate to associate with
the minutes of silence decreed by the authorities. Thus, after the Madrid
bombings, someone who took part in the demonstration in front of the
Spanish embassy in Paris on the evening of 12 March wondered about
the situation:

> Madrid: 200 deaths: 3 minutes' silence. Uganda: 192 deaths massacred in
> a refugee camp: and what? Bali: 180 deaths: and what? New York: 2,800
> deaths: 3 minutes' silence.

Though I've been able to join the silent demonstration from the Trocadéro to the Spanish embassy, to show all those who advocate violence as a solution that the proponents of non-violence are more numerous than they are, I am asking myself questions about these three minutes' silence decided on by our head of state ... Why not decide on a minute's silence each time there's a terror attack, a massacre in a country, of whatever kind? Are these minutes' silence a reflection of our own fears, as the attacks in New York and Madrid are too close to us? And what about people living in other countries? They have less value in our eyes?[39]

This question clearly stems from a cosmopolitan point of view, similar to the question that was raised in the European media after 9/11. If the minutes of silence which the authorities call for appear more questionable than a demonstration of solidarity, conversely, this is because, unlike the latter, they implicitly assume that the dead of Madrid are worth more, in the eyes of the French, than all the other dead in the world, for whom they do not observe any silence.

In the register of condolences made available to the public in those places where the silent gatherings took place in tribute to the victims of the London bombings on 14 July 2005, you can also read:

WHAT ABOUT ALL THOSE KILLED IN IRAQ SOLDIERS + CIVILIANS? London Metropolitan Archives, LMA/4469/A/01/003.

Around 100 people died and they got a garden, what do the thousands of innocent civilians in Iraq get?[40]

Rest in peace. And may the 24,865 civilians killed in Iraq since March, 20, 2003, also rest in Peace.[41]

The way different human lives are weighed against each other is here more precise: it focuses on the difference in treatment between those killed by the attack and those who, at the same time and in much greater numbers, were dying in Iraq. But if the protest against the war in Iraq without any doubt sharpened just a little more this concern for moral equivalence among Europeans, it was obviously already present at the time of 9/11. In Brussels, for example, as 4,000 people gathered on the Schuman roundabout, in the European Quarter, to hold a silent commemoration at noon on 14 September 2001, 'in front of the seat of the Council, a small group held up a poster asking for tribute to be paid to all victims: the Americans but also the Serbs and the Iraqis', as a reporter from *Le Soir* noted.[42]

Similarly, in France, on 21 September the newspaper *Ouest-France* published in its Ille-et-Vilaine edition a reader's letter, in this case from the Breton intellectual Gérard Prémel,[43] who confesses that he felt 'uneasy' about the three minutes' silence. Not that he thought it was wrong, in itself, to pay tribute to the dead of 9/11, but, as he explains, it was just as he was closing his eyes to remember them in silence that it 'seemed that an endless cohort of atrocious shadows was suddenly descending on the scene': the hundreds of thousands of Africans who had died of AIDS and famine caused by global warming, the civilians who had died under US bombs during the Gulf War, the assassinated Tutsis in Rwanda, the Palestinians massacred in Sabra and Shatila and in Beirut, Bosnians, Chechens, etc. The conclusion that he drew from this, couched as a mock-naïve question, deserves to be quoted at length:

> I realized then, thinking of these countless 'human brothers and sisters' who had died tragically, that at no time had the highest authorities of my country asked me to pay tribute to them by observing three minutes' silence. Should I conclude that all these dead people were not 'human brothers' in the eyes of my country's authorities? Such an idea seemed too frightful for me to contemplate. Then I thought: it must be an oversight. And I decided, in the solitude of my office, to repair this oversight.[44]

Others did not react the same way, but used this argument to justify their refusal to observe the minutes' silence in memory of the victims of 9/11.

Already at that time, as after the attack on *Charlie Hebdo*, articles in the French press were reporting incidents in some schools. Echoing these articles, the editorial offices of *Libération* and *Le Figaro* both decided in March 2004 to publish exactly the same letter – a fact undoubtedly unusual enough to be emphasized – from a history and geography teacher from the suburbs of Paris:

> On Monday 15 March, at my middle school in Val-Fourré, Mantes-la-Jolie, I told my year seven pupils what the minute's silence that we were going to observe meant: the injustice of terrorism that cuts lives short at random. I suggested that they write short texts that I would send to the Spanish embassy. Some of them moaned a bit, then almost all of them wrote their little messages. Overwhelming messages: 'Why so much violence? Don't lose heart!' 'I am asking the group that committed this crime: what's the point of killing innocent people for nothing?' 'It's terrible, we are all born equal, but it seems that this is not true for terrorists. Why so much hate?' [...]. The names of these pupils are Hassiba, Marouan, Houlemata, Chidi, Pinar, Nordine, Jebril, Sullivan, Samy, Karim, Darina, Thomas. Working in a 'sensitive' school also means being in contact with sensitive pupils. Quite simply human.[45]

From the left-wing point of view of *Libération*, this testimony was probably important because it reminded everyone of the elementary humanity of suburban schoolchildren, too often depicted as 'savages', and yet being *just* as capable of showing compassion in the face of human suffering and indignation at the 'injustice of terrorism', which knows no boundaries. From the right-wing point of view of *Le Figaro*, it was no doubt seen as an exemplary illustration of the fact that minutes of silence are part of a form of civic education, insofar as they contribute to turning these schoolchildren, mostly from immigrant families (as their first names indicate), into future 'good citizens', whose sensitivity already testifies to their attachment to some of the cardinal values of French society. The fact is that school, along with the family, is an essential institution of socialization and training in citizenship, and as such, journalists now pay particular attention to schools whenever minutes of silence are to be observed after a terrorist attack. This was made clear yet again from the excessive media coverage of incidents in schools in the aftermath of the *Charlie Hebdo* attack – incidents which were, in themselves, far from exceptional.

Justifying silent commemoration to school pupils

The question of the merits of the minutes of silence held in tribute to the Western victims of Islamist attacks perhaps never arises as acutely as to teachers responsible for getting their pupils to observe them. A debate between teachers, transcribed and published in *Les Cahiers Pédagogiques* after the minutes of silence of 15 March 2004, is clear evidence of this.[46] Their initial question is how to respond to pupils who refuse to join in with the moment of silence, and how to explain in class the European dimension of the mourning that they are then asked to observe. There are two clearly opposite points of view. There is, on the one hand, Jean-Michel, for whom the minutes of silence are a good opportunity to make the pupils aware of the fact that they belong to a community of values:

> We need to show that condemning or defending terrorism is not a matter of opinion but rather a way of locating oneself in relation to values that are those of democracy and humanism.

Thus, the fact that all Europeans observed these three minutes' silence at the same time attested to the fact that, in his view, 'Europe offered a community of civilization.' And if this community, he went on, 'represents an opening' towards a wider horizon of common humanity, he also added a little later that we must not forget what brought Europeans together: the need 'to oppose the enemies of democracy'. For this reason, this community could not refuse to take part in the fight on terrorism, which is 'a fundamental struggle of civilization'.

Several of the debaters, on the other hand, produced a cosmopolitical argument. Philippe, who experienced 9/11 at the Lycée Français in New York, where forty nationalities are represented, explained:

> The victims of Madrid as well as those of New York came from all corners of the planet. The pupils must be encouraged to reflect that one in every four inhabitants will be confronted with this phenomenon of migration that raises problems whose solution lies in a combination of diversity and universality rather than in antagonism over identities, an antagonism that lies behind all crusades.

He continued his argument by saying that he was always shocked by the fact that 'in distant wars, the victims are named only by their supposed group membership. They are "Rwandans" or "Chechens".' He then pointed out that there might be a 'pedagogical virtue' in getting pupils to understand that in these wars, as in terrorist attacks, it is always individual human beings who die, men and women with first names and family names. Philippe thereby linked the cosmopolitical point of view to a singularization of victims: as we shall see, this is an important factor in our reactions to terrorist attacks.[47] Jacqueline fully agreed, adding:

> If you refuse to reduce everything to a question of identity, this doesn't mean you negate identity. Quite the opposite: it's a way of accepting complexity. It then becomes essential to recognize others as fully fledged individuals with their differences and the realities that make them exist.

Those who defended a cosmopolitical point of view agreed on the need for recognition of the 'other'. Élisabeth stressed that it was essential, in her view, not to let pupils think 'that Europe will be constituted by the opposition to "the other" considered as a threat', and to ensure that it 'is not perceived as a place of defence "against" other cultures'. Unlike Jean-Michel, for whom the minutes of silence observed in homage to the dead of Madrid provided an opportunity for pupils to understand that they belonged to a community of values and a shared civilization needing to be defended against its enemies, Élisabeth took the view that this silence raised questions about the place of teaching world cultures and civilizations at school, which alone could prevent equating Arabs with terrorists. She believes that, as teachers, their role is to help pupils put themselves 'on the side of knowledge and respect for what is foreign to us or, simply, for what we do not know'.

113

On one hand, therefore, the minutes of silence are clearly accepted as a symbolic gesture to help strengthen a sense of belonging; on the other hand, they are in a way relativized by being set in a global and universal perspective. But how then, in the latter case, can we still justify observing a silence *specifically* for the dead of Madrid, and not for all those who are dying elsewhere in the world? Marie-Christine formulated the question this way:

> We are indeed drawing attention to an event that is valued more than others. That's what I want to question. It is true that I feel really awkward if a pupil says: 'Why not a silence for Chechnya?'

Considering that it is not possible, contrary to what Jean-Michel states, to answer this legitimate question by 'an argument dictated by a moral point of view', she comes to the conclusion that 'the only argument that can be made is that of cultural closeness'.

An argument based on *closeness*, yet again: such would be, ultimately, the only answer that can be given to the problem of moral equivalence without renouncing a cosmopolitical point of view. We feel closer to certain victims than others – this is just a fact – and that is why we can wish to pay them a particular tribute, while still remaining aware that these are just some tragic deaths among many others in the world that are more distant from us. To speak of '*cultural* closeness' as Marie-Christine does in connection with the Madrid bombings may, admittedly, seem to converge with the 'civilization-based' argument put forward by Jean-Michel, and as such seem unsatisfactory. Indeed, it is not at all certain that this argument will suffice to convince pupils or any other persons who refuse to observe minutes of silence. But let us also remember the MEP Anna Terrón i Cusí, who referred to an 'emotional closeness' based on the same way of life, on the fact of using public transport every morning, as did the people killed in Madrid and London.[48] It is undeniable that such a sense of closeness may have helped make it easier for some French people to observe silence after the Madrid bombings than after 9/11.

In 2001, many French companies had attempted to avoid any internal tension by making it clear that their employees were free to associate themselves or not with the minutes of silence: this was what the national rail company, the SNCF, and the Paris public transport system, the RATP, had done. However, when interviewed by a journalist from *France-Soir* on the eve of 15 March 2004, an RATP employee explained that on this occasion he would join in with the three minutes' silence in memory of the victims of the Madrid bombings, even if his management had not explicitly asked him to do so. To justify himself, he added:

114

We feel closer to the victims than in 2001, perhaps because, ultimately, Europe does mean something.[49]

Here, as in the declarations of Anna Terrón i Cusí, this sense of *emotional closeness* to the victims of the terrorist attack seems to come down to a sense of *common belonging* to Europe. There is an ambiguity to be clarified here because, as Laurent Thévenot points out, closeness and common belonging are after all two distinct modes of relationship to the 'other'.[50] Two individuals can come together within the same group without this in any way altering their relationship to this collective. And although the two things are often confused – even by sociologists – the feeling of being close to someone does not necessarily involve a sense of 'us', nor does it automatically produce anything collective. If this does happen, then it is a collective that is formed 'step by step, without any guarantee it will be carried over',[51] with fuzzy, shifting borders: in other words, something different from a community of belonging.

The recurrence of this issue of closeness to the victims, which, as we saw in the previous chapter, is also the issue underlying post-attack demonstrations and gatherings, means we need to take it seriously. What needs to be understood, in short, is how, for Europeans subjected to the ordeal of Islamist attacks, a feeling of belonging to the same community, whether national, European, civilizational or other, drawing a boundary within mankind between 'us' and 'them', relates to a mere feeling of closeness built up step by step, and not necessarily in opposition to the 'other' – as if it were always in principle open to one's neighbour. Might this not also be the meaning of 'I am Charlie'? 'I feel close to Charlie, I am personally affected by what is happening to him, that is true, but I don't feel I am blending into a clearly defined "we"'? If solidarity with the victims of a terrorist attack has ultimately found public expression in the first person singular rather than plural, this is also because, behind the injunctions to feel concerned through the intermediary of some 'we' that is fostered by the way the attacks are framed by politicians and the media, everyone can feel that they have reasons of their own to feel close (or not) to these victims.

115

Part II

WHAT TOUCHES US

It would seem that the sentiment of humanity evaporates and weakens as it is extended over the whole world, and that we cannot be touched by calamities in Tartary or Japan as we are by those of a European people.

Jean-Jacques Rousseau

— 6 —

TERRORIST ATTACKS AND THEIR PUBLICS

> Basically I can't really understand why, since I didn't have any family members working at *Charlie Hebdo* or even friends. But at the gathering in Madrid, the French all sang the Marseillaise together. And, well, without knowing why, a tear ran down my cheek. And then I realized that other people were crying too. I doubt they had any family members involved, either. But everyone is to some extent affected by an event like that.

These are the words, published on Facebook, of a French student on the evening of the attack on *Charlie Hebdo*. It expresses a form of paradox: I don't know any of the victims, *and yet* I cry, I'm moved, I feel concerned. It is this same paradox that, consciously or unconsciously, all those who write messages to the victims of an attack to express their emotion and show their support are trying to resolve. How can we convey our feelings to them? We don't know them and yet we feel close to them, we feel concerned by what happens to them. 'Finding the right words', as they say, involves managing to say how and why we feel concerned.

These messages are, in this sense, the traces of a personal experience of the event, and thus a prime source of material that will help us understand the different ways in which the public at large feels concerned by a terrorist attack – to grasp, in other words, what makes this attack a public event, and not just a private tragedy for its victims. Terrorist attacks happening throughout the world are reported regularly by the European media, but do not, in our view, constitute public events, since no one in our country is directly affected or feels concerned by them. These attacks are immediately forgotten and disappear in the continuous flow of 'international news'. And we don't write anything to their victims. On the other hand, the messages which were addressed to the victims of the 9/11 attacks, and those on Madrid and London, enable us to identify several types of public, concerned in different ways, that take shape when an Islamist attack occurs in the West.[1]

From written reactions to the concerned publics

Like the observation of minutes of silence, the opening of books of condolence is akin to a reflex on the part of the authorities to situations of collective mourning. After the Madrid bombings, some of these books were made available to the public in France, in Spanish consulates and cultural centres, and in town halls. This was obviously true of places where there was a significant Spanish population (in Toulouse, no fewer than five books of condolences were filled from 12 to 18 March),[2] but also elsewhere: in Saint-Mandé and Nogent-sur-Marne, both near Paris, for example.[3] As a general rule, the local press relays the initiative, pointing out that these books will be transmitted to the families of the victims, via the competent authorities. After the attack of 7 July 2005, the London City Hall collected hundreds of books of condolences from the United Kingdom and the rest of the world. Added to those opened in various public places in the British capital (town halls, churches, parks, sometimes even supermarkets), they occupy eleven metres of shelving in the capital's archives. It also happens frequently that the media themselves call on the public to send them messages of support for the victims: as we saw earlier, this is what the newspaper *Ouest-France* and the radio station France Bleu did in France, in partnership with the Mémorial de Caen, in the aftermath of 9/11.

Reacting to the attacks in writing

Some messages received by the Mémorial de Caen following this appeal show that these initiatives were responding to a real need. A young man from Rouen who presented himself as a student of philosophy began his letter by exclaiming:

> Finally, an address, heard on the radio, to which everyone can send their messages of solidarity towards the American people, subjected to such a terrible ordeal![4]

Similarly, a 21-year-old woman from Brittany wrote:

> The sight of what has just happened has made me very upset and the only way I have found to express it is to put it in writing.[5]

Some describe this need to write as something literally physical, such as this Frenchman, also writing after 9/11:

> It's six o'clock in the morning, I cannot sleep because this weight I've had on my chest for three days is stopping me living normally, I'd like to cry, scream, I can't. It's as if my family were affected by this dreadful attack.[6]

Or this woman from Madrid, after the 11 March attacks:

> I'm a 25-year-old student, like many of those who came to journey's end here. I'm writing this message because I am heartsick, because I am crying every day and because I want, one way or another, to be with the families that have been broken for no reason.[7]

Resorting to writing thus corresponds to a spontaneous form of public response to the attacks, a response that seems to be less triggered than channelled through the provision of books of condolences or the publication of calls to forward people's messages.[8]

Confronted with an imperious need to write, people sometimes act on their own initiative and send their messages directly through the post to an approximate address – such as 'Atocha Station, Madrid', for example – and rely on the postal services to get their messages to the right recipients. Others turn to the Internet, and post their message on the public forums of major newspapers or embassy websites. So, in the aftermath of the London bombings, one American woman sent this email to the secretariat of the British embassy in Dublin:

> I tried to find a condolence books on your web site but may have missed it. I just wanted to let you know that you are all in my thoughts and prayers. America will always be by your side.[9]

Many of those, finally, who lives in cities hit by the attacks place or post their message directly in the vicinity of the scene of the tragedies, or in the public squares where rallies are held as a tribute to the victims. This was observed by Parisians after the attacks of January 2015, both in the Place de la République and in the Rue Nicolas Appert, the site of the premises of *Charlie Hebdo*, on the Boulevard Richard Lenoir, where the policeman Ahmed Merabet was killed, and outside the Hypercacher at the Porte de Vincennes. After 9/11, the streets of Manhattan were filled with written messages in quite unprecedented quantities.[10] And although it did not have the same magnitude, the phenomenon was just the same after the attacks of 11 March 2004 and 7 July 2005. In London, King's Cross Station and the other sites of the attacks also saw hundreds of messages pile up,[11] while books of condolences were made available to the public in various parts of the city. As for Madrid, the stations where the trains exploded, those of Atocha, Santa Eugenia and El Pozo, were transformed into real mausoleums, filled with candles, flowers and objects gathered in memory of the victims, with walls and windows covered with thousands of messages pasted, glued or directly inscribed on them, like graffiti.[12] One week after the bombings, the French newspaper *Libération* devoted a long double-page spread to these writings, illustrated with five photographs, with the evocative title: 'Meeting evil with words'.[13]

In New York, these writings were withdrawn and destroyed by order of the mayor after a month – provoking many protests. Similarly in London: everything that had been deposited in the vicinity of the sites of the attacks was removed after two weeks and the last books of condolences closed in mid-August. In Madrid, however, the messages remained in place for three months, until the beginning of June 2004. But the impact of the attacks of 9/11 and 11 March 2004 was such that even several months and years afterwards, many people continued to feel the need to address the victims in passing through New York or Madrid. For several years, messages thus continued to be glued or directly inscribed on the walls and fences around the site of Ground Zero, in spite of signs prohibiting this,[14] while St Paul's chapel, located just next door and rapidly becoming a centre for mourning rituals after 9/11,[15] made available to the public a large picture equipped with a roll of paper. Above all, the 9/11 Tribute Center, a small museum that had opened its doors on Liberty Street in September 2006 on the initiative of the September 11th Families' Association,[16] dedicated its last room to messages that visitors to Ground Zero sometimes still wish to write: cards and pens are placed at their disposal on a large table, while a selection of the previous messages is displayed on the walls and searchable in binders. On average, one out of ten visitors to the museum writes something.[17] By the end of 2011, over 200,000 cards had been collected, in 48 languages and from 120 different countries. The museum's leaders published a book-length selection on the occasion of the tenth anniversary of 9/11.[18] In Madrid, computer terminals were installed in June 2004 in each station hit by the attacks of 11 March 2004, in order to collect directly in digital format the messages that some people still wished to address to the victims. This unprecedented arrangement, called 'Espacio de Palabras', remained in place for over three years and consisted of four computer terminals – two in Atocha, one in Santa Eugenia and one in El Pozo – operating from 7 a.m. to 11 p.m. and connected to a website (www.mascercanos.com)[19] on which it was also possible to record a message from any computer. This arrangement was an immediate success. Three days after its inauguration, 10,000 messages had already been recorded. And when the website went offline, at the end of 2007, its counter had registered a total of more than 113,000 messages.

Messages written in response to terrorist attacks thus stem from an 'act of writing'[20] which can be carried out in very varied ways. Therefore, even if their content appears repetitive at first glance, we can see, on closer inspection, that they range from the most formal to the most personalized, and from the most succinct to the most loquacious. Some people write a long letter or a poem on a piece of paper, in the tranquillity of their own homes, while others merely add a few conventional words and their signatures to a book of condolences opened in a public place. Messages of condolence, support or solidarity: by the way, it is not always easy to know how to describe them as a whole. And researchers do not always know what to do with them, either, especially when there is such an overwhelming quantity of them. Pierre-Yves Baudot, who worked on the reactions written in response to the deaths of French presidents, noted:

> Faced with this impressive collection of testimonies of grief, the researcher finds himself paradoxically at a loss. Whether they are of a distressing banality – a long litany of 'heartfelt condolences' – or more personalized, as when the sincerity of emotion is expressed by the originality of the words used, these messages are a tricky source to use.[21]

Thus, it is often enough to discard the messages that appear the most stereotypical, and to relate the contents of the rest to a thematic grid based on prior hypotheses.[22] But nothing says that this grid is ultimately the best adapted to the corpus, and it is quite possible, by proceeding in this way, to miss the point. Another solution is to leave out the content of the messages, and to focus instead on their modalities of utterance and signature, taken as singular indices of commitment in a collective act of writing.[23] The approach followed here is closer to this second option, though it does not neglect an analysis of contents. It consisted in using the textual analysis software Alceste in order to produce inductively, from a comprehensive analysis of a total of nearly 59,000 messages written in reaction to the Madrid bombings via the 'Espacio de Palabras', an analytic grid linking the contents of the messages and the positions of utterance, and then applying this grid to the other messages collected.[24]

The Alceste software has this particularity: it does not aim simply to identify the vocabulary used in the corpus submitted to it to restore lexical fields, but to derive from them classes of meaning that are characterized by the proximity of repetitive elements, whether lexical or discursive.[25] In very concrete terms, it creates a table that contains, in rows of calibrated segments of text (i.e. sentences or phrases) called 'units of elementary context' ('uec's), and in columns the nouns, verbs, adjectives and adverbs, rendered in their canonical form (that is, in technical terms, lemmatized, so that, e.g., 'world' – both noun and adjective – and 'worldwide' – both adjective and adverb – are counted together). This table is then reorganized (according to the principles of a top-down hierarchical classification) so as to obtain stable and coherent classes. If it is interesting to use this software to analyse messages written in response to terrorist attacks, this is because it makes it possible to locate exactly what recurs again and again in them, apart from conventional formulas such as 'Sincere condolences', 'We will never forget you' or 'Rest in peace', without on principle excluding from the analysis those formulas which 'give form to the difficulty of saying, and allow everyone to express themselves even if they do not know how to express themselves or cannot do so'.[26]

In return, we need to agree to meld all the messages for analysis into one and the same corpus: it is in fact from sentences or phrases (the 'uec'), not from messages as such, that software builds classes. For example, a message will most often include sentences that link it to different classes, sometimes more to one class than to others and, in some cases only, to one and the same class. The messages corresponding to just one class may be (but are not necessarily) the shortest. To the extent that messages written in response to terrorist attacks are of very unequal length, this method also has the advantage of placing all messages on an equal footing, regardless of their size (without assuming, for example, that the longest ones are also the most interesting). The classes produced by the software define a discursive space in which it is then possible to place each message and, behind the message, a person who has responded to the attack.

What gets written after an attack, and how it is written

The corpus submitted to the Alceste software contained exactly 58,732 messages recorded on the site 'mascercanos.com', via the computer system set up in the railway stations after the attack and placed directly online, from the start-up of the system, on 9 June 2004, until the first anniversary of the Madrid bombings, on 11 March 2005.[27] This represents nearly 99,000 words and 6 million characters. Given its imposing size, this corpus had to be analysed several times. An initial analysis made it possible, on the basis of the classification carried out by the software, to divide it into three sub-corpuses:[28] two sub-corpuses with rather indistinct content and of equal size (42 per cent and 47 per cent of the 'uec's retained by the software in its analysis), and a third, residual sub-corpus (11 per cent of the 'uec's), bringing together messages written in different foreign languages which the software immediately distinguished from the mass of those written in Spanish. (The following analyses on this residual sub-corpus led to a more refined classification by language.) Then each of the two first sub-corpuses was subjected to a new analysis, with convincing results: in both cases, the software revealed, in the same order and in extremely close terms – something that attests to the robustness of the results[29] – three classes of messages. And a final analysis of the corpus bringing together all the 'uec's classified previously confirmed this result by coming up with the same three classes.[30]

The first of these classes (representing 31 per cent of the corpus analysed and classified by the software at the end) corresponds to formulas of the following type:

There are times when lives separate. But we must look to the future, for a world without innocent deaths in wars waged by terrorist governments. So that it never happens again, and that we can all be happy. The lives of righteous people deserve more worthy deaths.

We will continue to struggle for non-violence. Peace and love for all. No more wars, which end up spreading terror in all the countries of the world and make people suffer from horrors like those of 11-M and 11-S, and many others.

No to terrorism. No terrorism can be justified. YES TO LIFE. I believe in a world of freedom, tolerance and equality. One day, may all these deaths not have been in vain.

CLEAN HANDS FOR PEACE. We want a free world, without terrorism. Only monsters blinded by their beliefs and feelings are capable of committing such attacks. Let's struggle for a free world, for world peace, against the barbarity of death which strikes blindly and against all existing ways of killing.

What is expressed here is wishes for a better world, without violence and without war, where terrorism would no longer exist, the sources of division and injustice between human beings would have disappeared, and all would live in peace and freedom, with respect and mutual love. The terms most often found in this class are: world, human, violence, hatred, religion, war. And, to a lesser extent: peace, better, freedom, tolerance, respect, innocent, race, love. Moreover, personal pronouns, adjectives and adverbs are less present in this class than in the rest of the corpus, while there are more nouns written in capital letters. The sentences are often in the future, use impersonal turns of phrase ('may all

127

these deaths ...') and short sentences, sometimes simple slogans ('No to terrorism. Yes to life').

Conversely, the second class (26 per cent of the corpus analysed and classified) is characterized by more personal turns of phrase, and sentences generally in the present or in the past. These are direct references to the attack, as well as the mourning and trauma it caused:

> Now we have 11-M, which should never have happened. I believe that it was a real massacre, many people left on that day to go to work and never went back home, and the worst thing was seeing children lose their parents. In my opinion, we were all in those trains.

> As always, passing trains, packed full of people. As in a film, a jolt on the cable, three explosions, and, all of a sudden, stupor, confusion, and fear.

> Every second of this atrocious day is like an hour of my life, everything stopped as in those trains which should never have exploded.

Here, the speaker frequently addresses the dead themselves or their relatives:

> Dear friends who are still here with us, we will not forget you. I felt the attack closely because I live in Azuqueca and normally I take the train in which there was the bomb, but on that day I could not be with you.

> I send you a cordial *abrazo* of friendship and support, accompanied by tears that did not fail to spring from my eyes on this fateful 11 March. A part of each of us died in these trains. We will not forget you.

Some messages in this class are sometimes even directly addressed to one dead victim in particular:

> I've been crying for three months. Everyday. I can't sleep in the train anymore. I will continue to cry every day, with your parents, your brother and your fiancée, until I have no more tears left.

The most characteristic terms in this class are: train, day, tear, cry, sky, star and Atocha; followed by: journey, station, soul, life, why, thank you. The sentences here contain more adjectives, adverbs and markers of intensity, markers of person too. They are at the same time less contextualized (fewer prepositions than in the rest of the corpus) and better structured (more conjunctions of coordination) than in the other classes. Very often, speakers seem to share with the victims of the attack the condition of being users of trains in the suburbs of Madrid. In short, two formulas that are repeated from message to message summarize these expressions of mourning fairly well: 'We were all on this train' ('Ibamos todos en ese tren') and 'We will not forget you' ('No os olvidamos' – more literally, 'we do not forget you').

The third and last class, the largest in volume (43 per cent of the corpus analysed and classified), appears to be made up of messages of condolence in the strict sense, that is to say messages that assure those who have suffered the loss of a loved one that they have the writer's support:

> To all the families of the victims, with whom we stand forever, an *abrazo*. We will not forget. From Cordoba, with all our hearts. We will not forget.

> We send you all our support and all our strength to continue to move forward. A very big hug. From Euskadi. Solidarity with the victims.

> From Tenerife, we would like to offer our most sincere condolences to all the families of the victims such a brutal attack. We will keep you all in our memories.

> I'm a 15-year-old teenager and I am writing this message to give my support to all those who have been affected by the brutal attacks of 11 March.

The words that fall into this class are: family, support, condolence, victim, affected, friend, courage, dear, sincere, attack and *abrazo* (a very common term in Spanish that means roughly 'hugs'). And they are more strongly associated with this class than the characteristic words we quoted above were with theirs – which amounts to saying that of the three classes, this one is lexically the most stereotyped. Two other characteristic features of this class are that they include more sentences in the first person (singular or plural), with formulas such as 'I want' or 'we would like to', and the sentences are shorter and less elaborate than in the previous class (which, again, can be taken as an indication of the stereotypical nature of the formulas used).

Last but not least, this last class is marked by the presence of several names of localities (countries, regions, cities). The examples quoted above clearly attest to this: 'from Cordoba', 'from Euskadi', 'from Tenerife'. This concern for localization is found in a large number of messages, including handwritten ones, where some go so far as to indicate their full address. The frequent choice of a postcard as the medium, when the message is sent by post, is further evidence. Like the fact of specifying one's age, this can be interpreted as an additional mark of personalization. But it also expresses a greater distance between the speaker and the victims of the attack than in the previous class. These are no longer fellow travellers of the victims who might have been in the trains hit by the explosions. This is why we particularly find here the statement of the paradox mentioned at the beginning of this chapter: *although* neither they nor any of their relatives were directly affected by the attack, the authors of these messages also feel really touched by them.

> I come from the Canary Islands and, among the victims, there is no one close to me, but I felt and I continue to feel that all of them are like my family or friends. My sorrow is very great.

> Although we have not suffered the loss of any loved ones in this terrible attack of 11-M, we stand in solidarity with all these families who have lost a loved one.

> Although they were not close to me, I felt something special for all these people, the victims as well as those who helped them during the attack. All my support to the families and courage to all. We will always keep you in our memories.

The messages that tend towards the latter class thus come from non-Madrilenians testifying their support for the families of the people who died in the 11 March attacks, while those in the previous class are messages from Madrilenians writing directly to the deceased. As for the messages tending towards the first class, it seems that anyone could have written them and that, while addressing the victims, they are potentially intended for everyone. Thus, from the mass of tens of thousands of messages written in response to the Madrid bombings, we are starting to see different figures of the public emerge.

The space of the public reactions to an attack

In order to characterize these publics more clearly, a diagram enabling us to visualize the oppositions and proximities between the three classes was produced by means of factor analysis of correspondences (figure 29).[31] The first axis of this factor analysis (reproducing 59 per cent of the total inertia of the scatter plot) contrasts the class of condolences addressed to the families of the victims with the class of wishes for a better world. This contrast seems to reflect a greater or lesser degree of personalization of the messages: on the one hand, there are messages written in the first person and localized, and on the other, more impersonal messages, mobilizing collective entities and general categories, such as 'humanity' or 'the law'. In the middle of this axis, as it were, we find the many variants on 'We were all in those trains', falling into the class of expressions of collective mourning. The second axis of analysis (41 per cent of inertia) expresses a greater or lesser distance from the attack: a concrete lexicon (train, station, Atocha, morning, going to work, tear

Figure 29. Graphical representation of the factor analysis of correspondences applied to messages written in response to the Madrid bombings from June 2004 to March 2005.

[as in shedding tears], etc.) is contrasted with a more abstract lexicon (world, war, race, love, human, but also attack, victim, deceased ...). Simplifying somewhat, we could say that on the one side of this axis the messages refer to the bombs that exploded in the Madrid trains, while on the other they talk about terrorism in general.

Through this twofold polarization that accounts for the essential characteristics of the messages written in response to the Madrid bombings (the two axes of the factor analysis cover 100 per cent of the inertia of the scatter plot), this graphic has the essential merit of helping us to schematize the space of public reactions to a terrorist attack. The system of relations and oppositions that it displays enables us to distinguish, unilaterally accentuating each pole, between:

131

(1)   those who are distant from the attack and who react to it in an impersonal mode;

(2)   those who are distant from the attack and who react to it in a personal mode;

(3)   those who are close to the attack and who react to it in an impersonal mode;

(4)   those who are close to the attack and who react to it personally; in other words: those who are generally referred to as its victims.

This typology calls for two remarks. First, it might seem to be strange to consider the victims of an attack as part of its 'public'. This helps to denaturalize the socially constructed category of 'victims',[32] making it continuous with the rest of society. The victims of the Madrid bombings, organized within the 11-M Afectados del Terrorismo association, themselves reject any 'victimization' and insist on being seen as 'citizens affected', neither better nor worse than the others, in other words as a 'public' in the political sense of the word, as conceived by John Dewey.[33] In addition, there is in general a blurred border between those who are personally affected by an attack and those who are affected on a more impersonal or indirect level: the friends or cousins of deceased persons, for example, may well be placed, and place themselves, on one side or the other. Some will consider that the only 'victims' are the dead and injured, while others will argue for a more extensive use of the category, to include the parents of the deceased or those survivors suffering only from psychological after-effects.[34] Finally, it is evident that the status of an attack as a public event is inseparable from the way in which its victims react, whether or not they mobilize to obtain compensation from the state, to ask for an independent investigation to be carried out into the causes of the event, or request that a memorial be built.

The second point is that it is important not to confuse the classes identified by the Alceste software within the messages reacting to the Madrid bombings with the different modes of participation in the public of this event. If efforts are made to induce the latter from the former, this does not mean that we have the right to see them as the same. Nothing illustrates this better, no doubt, than the absence of a lexical class in the part of the diagram that corresponds to the 'victims' (bottom right). This does not mean that the victims of the Madrid bombings did not react publicly, but simply that, with rare exceptions (cases where those who lost a loved one react by writing to the deceased), they did not do so by writing to themselves! Let us not forget, indeed, that the messages on which the analysis is based have all been recorded through a computer system that invited people to show their solidarity with the victims of the Madrid bombings. These classes, moreover, should not be reified. They are absolutely not hermetically sealed from one another:

as I have already pointed out, most of the messages, from one sentence to another, combine several classes; and while it is possible (thanks to Alceste) to say which class each message most inclines to, only a few fall exclusively into one of them. On the other hand, each author of a message occupies one, and only one, position within the public of the attack when he or she reacts to it through an 'act of writing', and the best indicator of this position is usually his or her signature. Therefore, the analysis carried out using the Alceste software must be extended by a study of the modalities of signature of the post-attack messages.

In what capacity an attack concerns us

The contrast between messages with more or less personal content and wording, as identified by Alceste, proves invaluable when we try to organize the great variety of signatures that we meet in the messages written in response to terrorist attacks. We can distinguish between two particular cases: on the one hand, the anonymous messages, without signature; on the other hand, messages that include not only a named signature, i.e. one allowing the author of the message to be identified, but also a means of contacting him or her (full postal address, email address or, more rarely, telephone number). Between these two extremes lie the vast mass of messages signed with one name, with initials or an illegible scrawl, and more or less information about the identity of the signatory, usually city of residence and country of origin, and sometimes also age.

Anonymous solidarity and personal messages

Messages signed with a name and containing indications of the signatory's home address, and even more the messages which indicate a means of contacting the signatory, are generally close to the class of condolences addressed to the victims' families:[35]

> The Reyes *** family from Palma de Mallorca shares the pain of all the relatives and friends of the victims of the terrible catastrophe of 11 March. (*email address*).[36]

> That day I turned 21, I will never forget that day. In Jaén too, we are crying like everyone else in Andalusia. We are with you and we will never forget you. (Javier *** – *postal address*).[37]

> We are Ricardo and Begoña, from Pamplona. We have just got married and wanted to complete our honeymoon in Madrid, near all those people

133

who have lost a part of their lives. We want to offer them our hope and support. Your suffering was ours. Forever in our memories ... (*email address*).[38]

These are messages written in a more personal style than others: they frequently include, like these last two examples, an explanation of the *personal reasons* for the authors of the messages (who may be collective authors: a couple or a family, in particular) to feel concerned by the attack although they were not directly affected by it. Here we find a criterion of distance, since those who, in reaction to the Madrid bombings, signed their messages in this way were none of them Madrilenians and experienced the attack from a distance. Whether they were Spanish or foreign, on the other hand, was of little importance:

> I am French, daughter of a Spanish republican father, I still have cousins and aunts who live in Spain. I am still very upset when I think about the victims of the Atocha bombs. [...] (Maria-José *** – *email address*).[39]

> I can't express the pain and anger I feel for what has happened here. As a US American who has lived and loved in Spain, March 11th was just as painfull and shocking as that day in September, 911 days before. I stand with Spain and I will do all I can to make sure the 'war on terror' changes, because it surely isn't working the way it's going now. (Valeria *** – *postal address*).[40]

The solidarity with the victims that these messages express must therefore be conceived, in Durkheimian terms, as an *organic solidarity*: that is to say, a solidarity based less on the resemblances than on the differences between individuals – on the recognition of the fact that they are all singular individuals, who occupy their own place within society.[41] This solidarity does not involve the invocation of a common belonging, but rather a *common singularity* shared by the victims of the attack and the authors of the messages: all are unique human persons, with a first name, a family name and an origin. The giving of a precise address, from this perspective, can be interpreted as a means of eradicating any possible homonymy and thus ensuring the singularity of the message. The authors of these messages are thus reacting to the terrorist attack first and foremost in their own name, *in a personal capacity*, and thus form what can be called a public of 'singular persons'.

At the other extreme, anonymous messages have a more impersonal content, and are found more often in the other two classes previously identified, namely expressions of collective mourning and wishes for a better world. What they express is closer to what Durkheim called *mechanical solidarity*, resting on the sharing of the same state of mind within a given group and on the effacement of individualities behind the collective.[42] Authors of the message are then conceived as just so many links in a chain of solidarity that transcends them. Therefore, rather than making a show of their singularity, they melt into the mass. Rather unusually, the 'postscript' of a message received by the Mémorial de Caen in the framework of Operation 'Fraternally' after 9/11 formulates this explicitly:

> PS: This letter does not contain a signature, I find such a thing superfluous given so much anonymous solidarity, courage, and mutual aid.[43]

The expression of solidarity thus involves spotlighting not 'who' is personally the author of the message, but 'what he or she is', socially. Anonymous messages written in reaction to the Madrid bombings were thus very frequently signed in a formulaic way, by 'a worker', 'a citizen', 'a user of public transport' or 'a Madrilenian'. Sometimes associated with a mere first name or initials, these formulas ultimately indicate *in what capacity* the author of the message feels concerned by the attack and commiserates with the fate of its victims. When this capacity is not mentioned in the signature, it may also appear at the start of the message (built on the model 'As a(n) ..., I would like to ...'). The named identity of the signatory is less important here than this facet of a social identity which links the signatory directly to the victims and makes him or her feel solidarity with their fate. Thus a reaction to the Madrid attacks may end: 'With affection, from a Madrilenian like you';[44] likewise, in a book of condolences opened in the wake of the London bombings, we read: 'From one Londoner to other's. Deepest Sympathy.'[45]

Some people go further and accentuate the negation of their singularity a little more by adding 'any' or 'among others' to the capacity in which they are writing. For example:

> We will never forget what happened. For me the only culprit is the intolerance of religions. (Any Madrilenian).[46]

> Terrorism will disappear when hunger disappears. Power implies responsibility. We are the relatives of poor countries. Let's accept this and help others so that everyone will love us. Terrorism is the war waged by the poor. (A citizen among others).[47]

> Once you have seen the horror, it is impossible to forget. We will always keep you in our memories. (Any citizen).[48]

There is, of course, a form of modesty in such signatures. But it can also be seen as a way of suggesting that the message assumes its full meaning only by being joined to others. It also contains a normative dimension: to sign in this way is to suggest implicitly that any other person sharing the same social identity should be able to write the same thing. What we find here is the idea of a state of mind common to all members of the same group, and a certain form of injunction to conformism, characteristic of so-called 'mechanical' solidarity. Conversely, other signatories modulate the generic title by personalizing it. In a book of condolences opened in London in July 2005, we find for example the following signatures: 'A Londoner born in Madrid', 'A Scot by birth but a Londoner at heart', 'A Dutch Londoner', etc.[49] 'Who' the signatory of the message might be can be glimpsed behind 'what he or she is'; and the mechanical solidarity is then tinged by an organic component.

The contours of an imprecise community

As Béatrice Fraenkel noted in New York in September 2001, 'everyone affirms him- or herself as the member of an imprecise community' when adding a message to the thousands of others.[50] But if this community seems imprecise, it is indeed because not everyone acts in the same way: not only are organic and mechanical solidarities interwoven in each message, but several types of mechanical solidarity are also mentioned. There is the solidarity which unites the companions of the same train, the solidarity which unites the inhabitants of the same city, and the solidarity which unites the fellow citizens of the same country, to name but three. So not just one but several communities are involved here, with porous boundaries that are partly revealed or reconfigured by the terrorist attack itself; this power to reveal and reconfigure communities stems precisely from the public nature of the attack.

The community formed by the fellow travellers of the victims, i.e. all those who daily use the public transport networks hit by terrorists in Madrid and London, did not pre-exist the attack. In normal circumstances, these users do not consider that they form a distinct collective, they have no 'group consciousness'. But the indifference to others which usually marks the 'blasé attitude' of the urban dweller[51] can, under the impact of the event, become a feeling of closeness, a vector of concern:

> I probably passed you on the street, we probably took a tube ride together and we may have sat next to each other on the bus. You were my neighbours. May you rest peacefully now. (Melanie, London).[52]

Some people then start to feel a sense of common belonging to the group of transport users:[53]

We don't normally think of ourselves being 'together': we avoid brushing against each other; we avoid eye contact and we definitely don't speak to each other – but we are together – because this was meant for ALL of us ANY of us. We don't forget you. (Blake, another passenger).[54]

In the attempt at an 'autoethnography' she wrote after 9/11, sociologist Carolyn Ellis also noted:

Flying on a plane during the attacks made me feel as though I *were* a participant in the terrorist attacks. Part of this feeling came simply from the obvious commonality of being in the air I shared with some of the direct victims of the attacks. [...] When I did find out, it was easy to think, 'That could have been me' and to identify with those who died in the crashing planes.[55]

For the same reason, those who use the public transport systems of major European capitals every morning may well have felt more concerned by the bombings in Madrid and London.

But such a feeling, obviously, does not persist beyond a few weeks. It is therefore advisable to consider the collective of the fellow travellers of the victims of the attacks less as a stable and lasting 'community', in the ordinary sense of the word, than as a fleeting and ephemeral 'public', formed as a result of the ordeal and graspable only through its manifestations, such as the messages I just quoted. It is precisely *under the impact* of the emotion aroused by the attack that some people come to realize that taking the train, the Underground or metro, or the bus every morning to get to their work makes them, in fact, feel in solidarity with the people hit by the bombs. Like Blake, who signs as 'another passenger', these people can finish their message with a formula such as 'a fellow Piccadilly line commuter',[56] 'a fellow traveller on the train in the Santa Eugenia district'[57] or 'a daily train user'.[58] If not, they leave an anonymous message similar to these:

My most sincere tribute to you all, fellow travellers.[59]

In memory of all the fellow travellers who, on that day, did not reach their destination.[60]

Similarly, a London woman who signs her name did not deem it necessary to indicate her exact address, but did specify which Underground line she regularly uses (one of those hit by the terrorists):

It could have been any one of us on those trains or the bus. We're all in this life together, and peace, love and understanding should begin with each of us. (Maryam ***, London, ***, Piccadilly Line).[61]

If the community of co-users of the same Underground line pre-existed the attack, messages signed in this way would be more numerous. But other people who share with the victims the condition of being public-transport users also choose to emphasize their capacities as fellow citizens of the same city or country:

> I am one citizen among others who, some time ago, occasionally took one of these trains, and my wife was a daily user. On the fateful day, the first thing I thought of was that she or I could have been there at the time of the explosion.[62]

> TO ALL LONDONERS INCLUDING MYSELF. We stand shoulder to shoulder going to work every morning in our beloved city. Then came this tragic bombing on the 7th day, 7th month 2005.[63]

There is thus no strict determinism that lays down the capacity in which each person responds to a terrorist attack. It is not *because* a person takes each morning one of the London Underground lines struck by terrorists on 7 July 2005 that he or she *necessarily* signed their message as a co-user of that line, or even that he or she felt obliged to send a message in response to this attack.

It seems rather that all those leaving messages opt to write in the capacity that appears to them personally as the most *relevant* at the time, while they have several choices. Otherwise, it becomes impossible to understand why many Spaniards chose to sign their messages in reaction to the Madrid bombings as a 'citizen of the world' or a 'human person':

> For a better world and more solidarity, and let us stop killing each other. Mankind is already a few thousand years old and it seems that we have learned nothing. (Fores, citizen of the world and human person).[64]

> Solidarity at a distance from Barcelona, with the closeness of a citizen of the world. (José Luis, Barcelona).[65]

> For the missing, they have left a void in a home, a bed, at a table, in an armchair, in the street and in many hearts. But they have left a living message for the world. Peace and non-violence, here and throughout the world. (Ruben, a citizen of the world).[66]

> Although this attack has no justification and is vile, to make it the last, collaborate with the rest of the world. Poverty + Hunger + Lack of Education + Religions = Barbarism. (A citizen of Planet Earth).[67]

Among these messages signed by a 'citizen of the world', we note a predominance of formulas wishing for a better world. Those who responded in this capacity all obviously considered the Madrid bombings as a global event, which reinforced them in their conviction that national and community affiliations (especially religious ones) are merely factors of division artificially setting human beings against each other, and that it was therefore necessary to move away from them so that all human beings will realize that they belong to one single great family and finally manage to live in peace.

Thus there are also messages which express a cosmopolitical conviction in the most traditional of veins, such as these anonymous messages left at Atocha:

11-M / MY COUNTRY IS THE WORLD / MY FAMILY HUMANITY[68]

WITHOUT DISTINCTION OF NATIONALITY OR RELIGIOUS BELIEFS WE WILL NOT FORGET YOU[69]

We are all human beings. No matter where from.[70]

Similarly, in London, in July 2005:

There is ONE race, the human race. Let us value life, the future, the young, the old for we are ONE & our shared humanity is deeper than anything that divides. (Many humans of London).[71]

From London, Paris, the World, we are all part of the family of the victims.[72]

From Bilbao, we will remember them, and we must know that *borders and races do not exist, there is only one world*. (Asier).[73]

Those who respond in this way to the attacks are obviously driven by the conviction that all human beings form one and the same family, and by what Hannah Arendt called 'love of the world'.[74] They point out that it is mainly insofar as they share the same world and the same human condition with the victims of the attacks that they feel solidarity with them. Whether they live, like the victims, in London or Madrid (and use public transport on a daily basis) is then merely a contingent factor likely to accentuate their personal concern, but not the main source. They therefore take care to sign 'José Madrigal, citizen of the world who lives in Madrid',[75] 'Ariana, citizen of the world, living and working in London for better or for worse',[76] without claiming to be a 'Madrilenian' or 'Londoner' as others do. Or they insist particularly on their status as a human being, something that takes precedence over the rest – one example is Glen, who writes:

I am a Londoner, a Christian and foremost a member of the Human race.[77]

On the basis of this study of the different ways in which messages are signed, it becomes possible to characterize more precisely the three main

Table 5. Typology of modes of participation in the public of a terrorist attack (in parentheses, the impulse of the reaction).

	Personal	*Impersonal*
Close	Victims (directly affected)	Fellow travellers and fellow citizens (sense of common belonging)
Distant	Singular persons (sense of common singularity, personal reasons)	Citizens of the world (sense of common humanity, love of the world)

modes of participation in the public of a terrorist attack previously mentioned (see table 5): those who experience the attack from a distance but respond to it in a personal way are part of the public as 'singular persons'; those who experience it from a distance but react in an impersonal way are part of it as 'citizens of the world'; and finally, those who experience it from close up and respond to it in an impersonal way do so as 'fellow travellers' or 'fellow citizens' of the same city or country. The last two ways of participating in the public are based on the same factor of concern, namely a sense of *common belonging*, the scale of which varies. The public of the 'citizens of the world', on the other hand, relies instead on a 'love of the world' that all other human beings share, and a sense of *common humanity*. As for the public of 'singular persons', finally, it is moved by a sense of *common singularity*, which leads those who participate in it to make explicit the specific reasons why they feel personally concerned by the attacks even though they are not directly victims: these reasons stem from their socio-biographical trajectories.

This typology can be applied to any terrorist attack that has the status of a public event in the West, and probably also elsewhere in the world. Thus it helps us to see more clearly into the maelstrom of reactions to the January 2015 attacks in Paris. The slogan 'I am Charlie' made more obvious than ever the formation of a public of 'singular persons', feeling concerned by the attack mainly in a personal capacity. Others may have been concerned in a more impersonal fashion, through the mediation of a common belonging, bringing them closer to the victims: as journalists, cartoonists, Jews or policemen. Still others may have experienced it in the same way, but as Parisians, French people, and even – why not? – as Europeans, or Westerners. Even if the effects of the way the event was framed, as we saw in part I, guide our reactions and seek to give priority to certain modes of concern over others, it is important not to reduce to a single schema, that of a sense of common belonging to the nation under attack, the vast range of modes of reaction actually triggered by a terrorist attack within a certain society. Likewise, we should not forget, at the same time, that some people responded to the January 2015 attacks, in France as elsewhere, simply as human beings, distressed by the events and worried about the downward plunge the world seems to be taking at the beginning of the twenty-first century.

THE MEANINGS OF 'WE'

The same basic slogan varied with the event: 'I am Charlie, a Jew, a policeman, a Muslim.' And why not, after all, 'I am French'? Or simply 'I am human'? What would we have said if the terrorists had struck in the Paris metro at rush hour? 'I am a Parisian'? Or maybe something like the slogan adopted by the Spaniards after the Madrid bombings: 'We were all in those trains'? Joachim Roncin, the inventor of the formula 'I am Charlie', has since explained his slogan on several occasions: he was not trying to do any more than express his deep feelings, his feeling of being shell shocked half an hour after the attack. And if other people took it up, it was because they saw themselves in it, and it reflected what they felt too.

Our first reactions when we learn the news of a terrorist attack – what makes us, before hearing any official reactions, immediately feel shocked, affected, concerned or not – are irreducible to the discourse of the media and the politicians who strive very quickly to frame the event. The fact that the *Charlie Hebdo* attack was presented as a 'French 9/11' did not mean that it was immediately experienced by the French as an attack on their nation as such. Thus the article devoted to the slogan 'I am Charlie' on Wikipedia has been the subject of several hundred changes soon after it was first created, all on just this issue, and it aroused a fierce discussion between the various editors of the online encyclopaedia.[1] Likewise, if the Madrid and London bombings were presented by political leaders and journalists as attacks on Spain and the United Kingdom as such, or even against Europe itself in the case of the Madrid bombings, they were in fact experienced on different scales by the general public: as we saw in the previous chapter, some people initially reacted as users of public transport, others as citizens of the world or members of the human race. The fact that we live in societies characterized by a process of social differentiation, where we are all part of a multitude of groups, implies that the meaning of 'we' is never simple or unambiguous. This is also what terrorist attacks reveal, especially when they strike great international metropolises such as New York, Madrid, London or Paris.

Above and below the level of the nation

Let us start with a statistical observation. If we do a simple survey of the 59,000 or so messages reacting to the Madrid bombings that were directly recorded in digital format between June 2004 and March 2005, by both Spaniards and foreigners, we find that the word 'world' is used more than 5,800 times. In other words, it appears in almost 10 per cent of the messages. The word 'Madrid' is mentioned 2,600 times: this is clearly less frequently, of course, but it is still twice as much as the word 'Spain', with just 1,290 occurrences. That leaves the word 'Europe', found a mere 45 times among the 59,000 messages: this is surprisingly little for an attack that was viewed as Europe's '9/11'! The collective entities which appear relevant to ordinary individuals, whether Spanish or foreign, to express what they feel after this attack are, above all, the world, and the city of Madrid. And the wave of solidarity that swept through the European Union, as after the January 2015 attacks in Paris, did not involve any focus on a sense of common belonging to a 'Europe' which the terrorists had struck by attacking Madrid.

The ambiguity of the European 'we'

Clearly, it is ultimately in their reactions to 9/11 that Europeans most often expressed their solidarity *as Europeans*. In everyday life, it is already more natural for the French to present themselves as Europeans when talking to Americans rather than to Spanish or British people. It is also well known that Erasmus student exchanges between European universities, far from reinforcing a feeling of shared belonging to Europe, tend rather to sharpen, among their beneficiaries, the awareness of all that differentiates Europeans from one country to another, or from one cultural area to another (northern Europeans differing from those of the south, as the Germanic peoples differ from the Latin), and that it is only when they have the opportunity to discover another continent that these students come to think of 'the Europeans' as a group to which they belong.[2] So there is nothing more logical, on a daily basis and for most people, than the way the proposition 'I am French' appears to have more meaning than 'I am European'; and this made the sociologist Norbert Elias say at the end of the 1980s:

Think of the difference in emotional charge between the statements: 'I am an Englishman', 'I am a Frenchman', 'I am a German', and the statement: 'I am an English, French or German European'. All references to the individual European nation states have a strong emotive value to the people involved, whether positive, negative or ambivalent. Statements like 'I am a European, a Latin American, an Asian' are emotively weak by comparison.[3]

But he added at once that it did not seem to him unrealistic to imagine that, in the future, these statements could take on a greater emotional significance, insofar as social life increasingly tends to take place against a global horizon, where humanity appears as the ultimate relevant social unit.

It is therefore unusual to see a message of reaction to the Madrid or London bombings signed 'as a European', but when this does happen, the term 'European' never appears alone: usually, it is included in a continuum of scales of identity of the signatory, which resemble concentric circles nested within one another, ranging from the most local to the most global (or vice versa), that is, to a common humanity. This is the case, for example, in this message from a Spanish man after the London bombings, which deserves to be quoted in full:

I was in New York, I was in Madrid, and I'm in London. Many of my friends and companions have died. It could have been any of us. No more violence. No more war. Enough of fanaticism, of old rancours and wounds that never close. Let us turn our world into a place of peace, where justice, equality and reason govern human beings. No more behaving like animals. We are all human beings. Let speech be our best weapon! For justice. May these acts of violence be the last in the world!

A human being,

　　A citizen,

　　　　A European,

　　　　　　A Spaniard,

　　　　　　　　Someone from Guadalajara. (Luis ***).[4]

Three messages reacting to the Madrid bombings end with a similar formula:

Enough of intolerance. Let us wager on dialogue, peace, respect. Is this possible? We need to believe in it. To stand ready. (Maria – ***, Murcia, Spain, Europe, Earth).[5]

For peace, freedom, equality and love. ALL UNITED. (A Madrilenian, Andalusian, Spaniard, European and CITIZEN OF THE WORLD).[6]

We are with all the families of the deceased, it could have been us. No to terrorism. WE WERE ALL IN THOSE TRAINS. (Wicky – Fuenlabrada, Madrid, Spain, Europe, THE WORLD).[7]

It is important to note that all three messages were written by Spaniards; unlike the French, for example, they do not need to draw on their European identity in order to feel in solidarity with the victims of the Madrid bombings. If they mention it anyway, this is because it allows them to signify that they are reacting not only as Spaniards – this is just one reason *among others*. In each of these signatures, as in that of the first quoted message, the term 'European' is mentioned as an intermediate level between a local and national identity, on the one hand, and being a human being, a citizen of the world or an inhabitant of planet Earth on the other. Moreover, the way some people mention this last identity in capital letters suggests that it is in their view the most important, the only one that is not relative, in short, so that their identity as Europeans assumes its full meaning only in relation to it, from a cosmopolitical perspective.

In the body of the messages, too, Europe is mentioned as a collective entity in mourning *among others*, in a continuum that extends from the city to the entire world, via the nation and Europe:

Courage Madrid, courage Spain, courage Europe, courage dear Planet. The tears shed will be the sap that will nourish the hearts of those we love. ENOUGH OF ALL THIS BARBARISM.[8]

Spain will not forget, nor Europe, nor the whole world. Let us show more solidarity and let the world be at peace.[9]

Madrid, Spain, Europe and the World wept and suffered with you all on 11 March 2004. Rage in the face of barbarism, pain and helplessness were mixed with feelings of solidarity and love. I want to continue to believe that tomorrow will bring us a better, less unjust and more peaceful World.[10]

But in this way, Europe is also personified, as the real subject of the event: she will not forget, she weeps, she suffers. Thus she can gain autonomy and free herself from this cosmopolitical horizon of which she is always otherwise a part, as is the case with the few who acclaim her in the way one normally acclaims one's country:

Long live Spain and long live Europe. Together let us fight against war. Solidarity, love and life.[11]

145

Hello, I am French; sorry, I do not speak Spanish. But I am wholeheartedly with you. Long live Europe![12]

The French people who signed these two messages of reaction to the Madrid bombings are not all that close to Spain: the first notes in his signature that he left this message during his 'first visit to Spain', while the second recorded it via the Internet from Paris, and neither of them wrote it in Spanish. They seem to have felt impelled to highlight a common sense of belonging to Europe as the best means of expressing their solidarity with the victims in Madrid in the absence of any closer bond – a default position, one could almost say.

The case of another message recorded in the Atocha station in the spring of 2004, including the words 'Long live Europe', but written in Spanish, is somewhat different. This is indeed one of the very rare messages collected at this station which take up the idea of a clash of civilizations and suggest that immigrants and terrorists are more or less the same.

Long live Europe! [...] [This attack] was the product of fanaticism and barbarity. Because they hate us. They hate our freedom, our democratic system, our values and our culture. Uneducated fanatics who hate us so much that they come to Europe in search of a better life and want to impose their culture, create insecurity, and undermine the rule of law. No, no, no, you will not overcome the West and still less Spain, which is united in its people's hearts. Long live Spain![13]

The reference to Europe then functions as an extended nationalism, a kind of 'nationalism squared', which implies a principle of exclusion and opposition of what is foreign to it, a contrast between 'us' and 'them', the terrorists, 'uneducated fanatics'.

The very rare messages of reaction to the Madrid bombings which mention the European 'we' are thus evidence that this 'we' is a problem insofar as it is torn between, on the one hand, a *cosmopolitanism in miniature* – Europe conceived within a global horizon, whose project is based on the ideal of peace and universal brotherhood between all people – and, on the other, an *extended nationalism*, with Europe defined by the sharing of '*our* values', '*our* culture', '*our* democratic system', to which others will always be foreign. Messages that bypass this difficulty do so by invoking Europe *only* as a community of mourning and tears, as in the messages left in London in July 2005 by, respectively, a Spaniard and a German:

All Europe shares your grief.[14]

ONE LONDON, ONE EUROPE. WE STAND ON YOUR SIDE.[15]

Or in these two other messages left by French people in Madrid during the summer of 2004:

> In memory of that terrible morning in March 2004 which echoed throughout Europe as a deep sorrow. In memory of the victims.[16]
>
> Your dead are our dead. All Europe suffered with its Spanish compatriots.[17]

The formulation of this latter message is particularly clear: what is expressed here is a form of European patriotism (the Spaniards are described as 'compatriots'), but one that is striving not to be confused with a European *nationalism* that would reproduce a form of xenophobia. We should rather understand it, it seems, as an 'open' or 'humanistic' patriotism, a 'small part of cosmopolitanism', in the words of Durkheim.[18] But this is just an exception – one message from among tens of thousands.

Solidarity at the level of cities

Unlike 9/11, the Madrid and London bombings were not coordinated attacks on several points of a national territory and did not target symbolic and strategic objectives in Spain and the United Kingdom. While speaking of the 'New York attacks' to designate 9/11 induces a bias of perspective, speaking of 'the Madrid attacks' and 'the London attacks' is the same as speaking, as the Spaniards do, of '11-M', and the British of '7/7'. Thus these two attacks were perceived more as attacks on these cities in themselves than on the nations of which they are the capitals, while 9/11 was experienced, throughout the world, as an attack on the United States.

After the Madrid bombings, the slogans that recur the most often, from message to message, are 'Todos somos Madrid/Madrileños' ('We are all Madrid/Madrilenians') and 'Íbamos todos en ese tren' ('We were all on that train'). People who are not of Spanish nationality thus show their solidarity, on behalf of their country of origin, with Madrid and its inhabitants rather than with Spain: 'Ireland weeps for Madrid', 'France is with the Madrilenians', 'Madrid is in the thoughts and hearts of the people of the UK', 'Ecuador is with you, Madrid', etc.[19] And when they do not express solidarity with the city, this is because they feel closer specifically to the victims or to an indistinct 'you', but never explicitly with the Spaniards: 'Portugal with the victims of 11 March', 'Scotland Has Her Arms Around You All', 'Bulgaria is with you', 'Portugal weeps with you', 'Hungary: we weep with you'.[20] The Spaniards themselves very often express their solidarity as stemming from that of their city or their province with Madrid, rather than reacting as if they had been directly attacked as Spaniards:[21]

> From Alicante, we stand in solidarity with the city of Madrid. On 11 March, we were all Madrilenians. May this never happen again, anywhere.[22]

> We, Valencians, will always keep you in our hearts. We are with Madrid and we love you.[23]

Among the thousands of messages recorded at Atocha station after the attacks, there are countless examples of this type: 'Cartagena is with Madrid', 'Murcia with Madrid', 'Segovia with Madrid', 'Oviedo weeps for Madrid', 'Galicia with Madrid', 'The Canaries in solidarity with Madrid', 'Catalonia with Madrid',[24] etc. The city, personified, is sometimes directly addressed:

> Madrid, the Asturias are with you!!! Peace!!![25]

> Malaga and all its inhabitants are with Madrid, today more than ever. We won't forget you. Every day, every moment, we keep you in mind. A big hug from us. Courage Madrid, you will get through![26]

Some messages even border on a declaration of love:

> From afar, I miss you, Madrid. You will always be in my heart. I love you.[27]

> From Lanzarote, we are wholeheartedly with the victims and their families. We love you MADRID.[28]

> Why did the oil of Iraq turn into blood in Spain ... Much sorrow, much sadness, and many tears have poured from the depths of my heart. TODAY MORE THAN EVER, MADRID I LOVE YOU, MADRID I ADORE YOU!![29]

Here again, there is hardly any difference between Spaniards and foreigners, since the following two messages collected at the Atocha Station were originally in French: 'MADRID RESISTS'[30] and 'MADRID MY LOVE'.[31]

There was much the same phenomenon in London in July 2005. The television reports in which the messages left near the scene of the bombings appear give an immediate overview, as do the descriptions of them in the press, which highlight formulas such as 'Palestinians in solidarity with London' or 'Afghans are with London'.[32] Messages left in the books of condolences by strangers passing through the city at the time of the bombings are also a vivid demonstration of this. For example, two Spaniards wrote:

> We come from Spain, we want to express our rejection of terrorism, because we understand your pain better than anyone else. Spain is with you.
>
> SPAIN IS WITH LONDON. (Irène and Pilar).[33]

While it might have seemed logical for these two women to express their solidarity from one country to another country, from Spain to the United Kingdom, or maybe England, it is London and Londoners that they actually address. The fourth page of a book of condolences from Westminster City Council offers another good example: four messages dated 14 July 2005, the authors of which indicate that they come from Limerick (Ireland), Espoo (Finland), Seville (Spain) and Bredon (Netherlands); and all explicitly address their message to the victims and/ or to Londoners, none to the English or the British.

If we look at the books of condolences collected in the London Metropolitan Archives, we can see that, even for the British themselves, the 7 July 2005 attacks were perceived more as an attack exclusively on London rather than on the British nation as a whole. This is shown by the differences in tone and formulation between the books of condolences opened in the boroughs of Greater London and those from the different counties of the United Kingdom. Only the London books are characterized by a massive use of the lexicon of unity and social cohesion, and by the repetition of formulas such as 'We are not afraid' and 'United we stand', which are almost absent from the other books, those of Nottinghamshire and Scotland, for example. These books are ultimately much closer to those made available to the public in the Republic of Ireland, the United States, the Netherlands or even Nigeria. The formulas that repeat themselves are rather 'Our thoughts are with you', 'God Bless You', 'Rest In Peace', 'You won't be forgotten', etc. On the one hand, the victims of the attacks are embraced within an incantatory 'we', while on the other, as soon as we leave London, they are designated in the second person, 'you', as if they were outside the group of the person addressing them.[34] This was also, as we have already noted,[35] remarked on by a *Times* reporter walking through the English countryside after the attack: in rural areas, there was not the same impression that the London bombings were something that had happened to *us*.

If the terrorist attack of 7 July 2005 thus sharpened the sense of 'we', this was confined to London rather than extending to the British nation as a whole. Among Londoners, it found particular expression in a sense

149

of pride in belonging to this city – a common reaction when the group to which one belongs publicly displays its cohesion in the face of an ordeal,[36] something which many Parisians experienced in January 2015, and which we can also see at work in Madrilenians in 2004:

> I just want to say that I feel proud of my city, Madrid, and all the Madrilenians. They will not take away our freedom! Madrid is also a 'Ground Zero', its asphalt has been bloodied a thousand times, but it is an example of righteousness and solidarity.[37]

> I have always loved my city but I have never felt so proud in my life to be a Londoner. London is united against these terrorists in the memory of those who lost their lives.[38]

> I am hurt. I am angry. I am fearful. But I am also proud. Proud that the peoples, races and faiths of London, the UK and the world came together to say no to this act of barbarity. Proud that our sometimes petty differences and rivalries have been forgotten in the face of evil. Proud to be born and working in one of the greatest and most tolerant cities in the world.[39]

> Once again I am so proud to call myself a Londoner, and to come from a family of Londoners who have survived with this city from the Blitz, through the IRA years, and now this.[40]

A French resident in London also signed her message with this formula:

> A French, a European, but above all *an extremely proud LONDONER!*[41]

This woman's European identity, though mentioned here, seems less important than her being a Londoner, a fact which she emphasizes by writing this in capital letters and underlining it three times, to indicate how much, in these circumstances, it takes precedence over the rest.

In the case of immigrants, the attack was thus an opportunity for them to express for the first time their sense of belonging to the city:[42]

> After 10 years in this city 7/7 marked the day I became a Londoner for the first time. Like millions of others I felt my city had been attacked, like my way of living had been threatened, like my desire to live in the most successful, diverse, exciting city was being put at risk. But like millions of others I only feel strengthened; ready to stand up for this city – its way of life, and, for the first time, call it my own.[43]

> It could have been me. I was born in Italy. London welcomed me six years ago. I am a Londoner today. I am a Londoner because I feel for all of you hurt. For all of you who are not in this beautiful city anymore. There are no words right enough to express my feelings. But I am with you. Love.[44]

In the face of terrorism, London seems to assert itself as a community of life and mourning both for Londoners 'born and bred' and for immigrants from throughout the world.

The large silent gathering in Trafalgar Square to pay tribute to the victims on the evening of 14 July, in particular, embodied this community. The assembled crowd provided the participants with the sense of a unity in diversity that would give London the strength to resist terrorists, and fuelled their sense of pride:

> Today London is as tolerant, diverse and life-affirming as ever – a city that no form of bigotry or fascism can ever hope to thrive in.[45]

> Today we stand united as one, regardless of our religions, faiths, or beliefs.[46]

> Today London is beautiful and people are out on the streets for you. London lives and your memory lives.[47]

On the eve of the great demonstration of 11 January 2015, Parisians would undoubtedly have been able to write similar things. That is why, even if similar demonstrations took place throughout France, many of the participants refused to see them as a demonstration of 'national unity': in their eyes, it was first and foremost the people of Paris who were gathered there, a people that was comprised of all origins, all denominations and all nationalities.

World cities and the test of terrorism

The predominance of a 'we' at the level of stricken cities in the reactions to terrorist attacks has one essential characteristic: it makes it easier for people of foreign nationality to identify with the victims. The existence of a national community, indeed, always implies that of an outgroup: the word 'national' means that there must also be 'foreigners'. Apart from people of dual nationality, identification with a nation is exclusive. Conversely, identification with a city is inclusive: modern cities, especially metropolises like Madrid and London, are, by nature, places of social mixing, open to all, cosmopolitan.[48] Being a member of a nation is not the same as identifying with a city, and so the two things do not come into conflict. So it is possible to say 'the Belgians are also Madrilenians'[49] or 'I am German, but I am also Madrilenian',[50] whereas declaring that 'the Belgians are also Spaniards' or 'I am German, but I am also Spanish' would strike many people as a logical contradiction.[51]

As a result, while in 2001 the Europeans had hesitated between saying 'All Americans' or 'All New Yorkers', in 2004 and 2005, things were straightforward. As one Frenchman wrote in a London book of condolences on 10 August 2005:

We are all Londoners, as before we were Madrilenians.[52]

As we have already seen, the slogan 'We are all Madrilenians' flourished in the European media in the aftermath of the Madrid bombings. It was also found in many messages, whether written by Spaniards or by foreigners, just as, after the attack of 7 July 2005 in London, many people wrote, out of solidarity, 'I am a Londoner' or 'We are all Londoners.' On the other hand, in both cases, formulas such as 'We are all Spaniards 'or' We are all British' are more or less non-existent. In this sense, the attacks in Madrid and London ratified the decision to give 'We are all New Yorkers' priority over 'We are all Americans', mirroring a certain conception of 9/11.

New York – Madrid – London ... and Paris?

Two days after the Madrid bombings, the president of the SOS Attentats association, Françoise Rudetzki, appeared on the programme *Tout le monde en parle* ('Everybody's talking about it') on TV channel France 2. Reacting to her intervention, a viewer wrote on the association's website forum:

We have all been New Yorkers, we are all Madrilenians, we are definitely all human. That's one thing, at least, that's good about globalization. We are part of the same species, the same human community. And it is the whole world that trembles when the World Trade Center collapses.[53]

It is particularly clear here: identification with the victims of these terrorist attacks at the level of cities is linked to a cosmopolitical point of view, in which these attacks are seen as world events concerning the whole of humanity, events that affect all of us as members of the same 'human community'. But at the same time, through this reading of events, 9/11 is more than ever reduced to the tragedy of the World Trade Center. This is also very clear from the message that a woman from Barcelona addressed to the victims of the Madrid bombings:

On 11 September we were all in the Twin Towers in NY and on 11 March in those trains in Madrid. NO TO TERRORISM, YES TO PEACE.[54]

It is also evident in the message that Madrilenians left at Ground Zero in March 2008:

> We Spaniards, we feel that, sadly, we are the brothers of the city of New York, because on 11 March 2004 the terrorists blew up 3 trains in the city of Madrid. [...] MADRID ♥ N.Y.[55]

It is the cities of Madrid and New York which, from their point of view, feel solidarity with one another, united by the terrorist ordeal, rather than the Spanish and American nations.

Divergences between American and European points of view on the Islamist attacks perpetrated in the West appear to have become more pronounced since 2004, with some people arguing in terms of nations and others more in terms of world and cities; the contrast could sometimes prove to be particularly striking. On the one hand, when Europeans express their solidarity at different levels, they sometimes purely and simply forget the national level: 'To the Victims, the Citizens of London, the rest of the World', as one Londoner wrote in July 2005.[56] On the other hand, when Americans react to terrorist attacks in European cities, they evidently tend more than others to do so in national terms that stand out against the rest of the messages. Thus, in Atocha after the Madrid bombings, some American tourists left this unusual message in the spring of 2004:

> People of Spain: American hearts are suffering for you.[57]

Similarly, on a notice with multiple messages retrieved in August 2005 from Tavistock Square, where bus no. 30 exploded, we read: 'America loves England so Much',[58] while thousands of messages in the London books of condolences attest to the fact that, aside from those Americans, almost nobody perceived the London bombings as an attack on England. On the contrary, in one of these books, a New Yorker who had survived 9/11 wrote:

> As a survivor of the attacks on the USA, 11 Sept 2001, my hearts and prayers go out to the families of the victims of these vicious attacks in London and to all the people of London.[59]

While he presented 9/11 as an attack on the United States, it is striking that, unlike other Americans, he was addressing his message of solidarity to Londoners, and not to the English or the British, as if the fact that he himself had been affected by 9/11 as a New Yorker made him more inclined to adopt a non-nationalist perspective on the London bombings.

Thus a triptych 'New York – Madrid – London' took shape in Europe after the attack on 7 July 2005. 'I was in New York, I was in Madrid, and I'm in London', wrote one Spaniard at the beginning of the first message quoted in this chapter. Another also expressed his solidarity with the victims of the London bombings in these terms:

> I wept for New York, I wept for Madrid and my friends, now I am weeping for all of you. As of now and forever, we are brothers.
>
> NEW YORK – MADRID – LONDON: We are all brothers!
>
> We will always miss you and I will remember you until the day I die. We love you![60]

And a Londoner began his message thus:

> NEW YORK, MADRID, LONDON – DIVIDED BY OCEANS, UNITED BY GRIEF. WE WILL REMEMBER THEM ALL.[61]

Given the connection that some people had drawn between the attacks that occurred in Europe and the war in Iraq,[62] Baghdad was sometimes added to the triptych:

> New York, Madrid, London, Baghdad, we are all one city and one people, united in sorrow for the victims and in determination to live free in spite of terrorists.[63]

The link between the victim cities could also be suggested otherwise than in writing: on the outskirts of Tavistock Square, for example, after the London bombings someone placed a keyring with a photograph of the Twin Towers and the inscription 'I LOVE NEW YORK – W.T.C.'[64] Placed there, it was enough on its own to give concrete form to the idea of a grieving community uniting New York and London, the American 'world city' and the European 'world city'.

This triptych corresponded to a period, that of the 'bin Laden decade', of 9/11, the war in Iraq, and their repercussions in Europe. While the attacks in Paris in January 2015 may have given rise to an analogy with 9/11, they were not seen in the context of those previous Islamist attacks on European capitals. Quite the opposite: they tended to reveal how much the attacks in Madrid and London, ten years later, had already been forgotten in France. Nobody wrote 'New York, Madrid, London, Paris'. This, of course, is also due to the fact that identification with the victims first had been expressed on the level of the magazine that was attacked – 'I am Charlie' – before it moved to the level of Paris and assumed the variant, later on, of 'We are all Parisians' (although this was used here or there, notably by foreign politicians, including the mayor of London, which is obviously a detail of some significance). However, it would have been relevant to recall these precedents, since it is true that the reactions to the attacks in January 2015 also involved an attachment to a European metropolis and what it embodies in the eyes of the world.

European metropolises, the beacons of humanity

While it was possible throughout the world to identify with the victims of the attacks in New York, Madrid and London, and more recently in Paris, this is because these cities are not simply geographical and social entities among others, but also spiritual entities which embody certain values.[65] The messages quoted in this chapter are reminiscent of the anecdote told by Georg Simmel in his 1908 work *Sociology* as he reflected on the self-preservation mechanisms of social groups:

> During the Spanish-American War in the summer of 1898 as the Spanish fleet seemed to threaten the American east coast, a Bostonian away from home was asked what he would think about his city possibly being bombarded. 'Bombard Boston!' was the response. 'You talk as though Boston were a locality. Boston is not a place; Boston is a state of mind. You can no more shoot it with a gun than you could shoot wisdom, or justice, or magnanimity.'[66]

There are thus many who, in reaction to terrrorist attacks, emphasize their attachment to the values symbolized by the cities attacked. For instance, after the London bombings a Tunisian wrote:

> London is the most safe, peaceful and tolerant city in the world. [...] O Londoners, your capital is a great city, a city of peace, fairness and tolerance, to many people of the globe London is the capital of the world.[67]

'Capital of the world': this is exactly what some said of Paris on 11 January 2015, while demonstrators renamed the Place de la République 'la place de la liberté d'expression' (the 'place' of freedom of expression). The reference to this value, of course, stemmed from that fact that the terrorists had just murdered journalists, but the news, unfortunately, continues to show that their actions would not have produced a reaction of such magnitude had it taken place elsewhere in the world. It is also because this attack took place in the 'city of Voltaire', in the capital of the 'nation of the Enlightenment and human rights', that it triggered an unprecedented and outraged reaction well beyond French borders.

Our reactions to the Islamist attacks on European cities also arise from the fact that in our view these cities embody, more than any others in the world, values such as freedom, tolerance, justice and peace. The emergence of humanist values is in fact historically linked, according to Claude Lefort, with the rise of an 'urban civilization' in late medieval Europe.[68] He is here drawing on the work of three authors: Max Weber, first of all, for whom the European city was the place of freedom, and above all of commerce, which allowed capitalism to develop (unlike Chinese and Russian cities);[69] Marc Bloch, who viewed these cities as the birthplace of a particular 'type of man', the bourgeois, attached to the principle of equality at a time when the feudal hierarchy was gradually dissolving;[70] and, finally, Aldo Schiavone, who thinks that 'the European cities of today represent the direct continuation of their medieval contexts',[71] that is, built on the principle of equality among all men, as opposed to Roman slave-based society.[72] Thus, Lefort concludes, the European city 'embarks on a singular experiment in the sense that it establishes connections between all those in it, so that anyone can encounter anyone else' and promotes by doing so an 'openness to the world'[73] or, in other words, a cosmopolitan ethos.

It was thus in 'properly European' cities[74] that the values associated with this ethos seem to have developed. Lefort mentions, among others, Florence in the fifteenth to sixteenth centuries, the birthplace of Machiavelli and the cradle of civic humanism, and Amsterdam a century later, a major home for migrants and a city symbolizing freedom, one which sheltered Spinoza, Descartes and Locke. We could also add Berlin at the turn of the nineteenth–twentieth centuries, the city that Georg Simmel had in mind when he described metropolises as 'the seat of cosmopolitanism',[75] or the Vienna of Freud and Wittgenstein, at the same time, about which Stefan Zweig wrote:

> It was sweet to live here, in this atmosphere of spiritual conciliation, and subconsciously every citizen became supernational, cosmopolitan, a citizen of the world.[76]

And there is of course London in the twentieth century – for, as a message in reaction to the attack of 7 July 2005 notes:

> This is the city of Karl Marx; this is the city of GANDHI. Now, this is my city too. Even when I return to India (or anywhere else).[77]

The triptych New York – Madrid – London then appears in a new light: the common thread between the three cities – to which Paris could now be joined – and the real target for Islamist terrorists, is ultimately the humanist values associated with the cosmopolitan ethos of urban civilization.

156

This was already the interpretation that emerged from certain readings of the 9/11 attacks in the winter of 2001–2, when, in response to the 'nationalization' of 9/11 that was observed in the United States, the European tendency to distinguish the attack on the World Trade Center from the rest of the events became clearer. As Xavier Crettiez and Isabelle Sommier put it:

> It is also the humanism of a city, the living incarnation of the modern city, which is attacked. It is the double symbol of this 'living together' that was best embodied by the twin towers of Manhattan, both practically, as the fusion of individualities in a city with a cosmopolitan reputation, and unconsciously, as a universal representation of the southern tip of Manhattan, as the road to the American Dream, which is targeted.[78]

Similarly, when Jean-Paul Dollé states that 'we are all New Yorkers', but not 'all Americans',[79] he goes on to explain that what, in his view, drives the terrorists, more than a hatred of America, is a 'hatred of world cities'. Then he adds:

> Gradually, the hatred of world cities becomes a hatred of what they permit, that is to say sexual and thus social mixing, urbanity, civilization. That is why attacking New York means attacking not just a global metropolis located in the USA, but attacking each of those who feel or aspire to feel part of the same human civilization.[80]

Since some people think that this 'human civilization' was born in Europe, it seems that such interpretations were an attempt in some way to claim New York as the most European of non-European metropolises, the final crowning of the historical process analysed by Claude Lefort. But in doing so, as can be seen from the words of Dollé, we fall back into the idea that the world is divided between 'us', *cosmopolitan civilized people*, and 'them', the terrorists who hate cosmopolitanism and are not part of this 'humanist civilization' – a contradiction which, as we have seen, largely characterizes our relationship to Islamist attacks.[81]

It might therefore be asked whether, in the ordeal of Islamist terrorist attacks perpetrated on their territory, the cosmopolitanism of the Europeans might not turn out to be nothing but the umpteenth avatar of their propensity to arrogate the universal to themselves and to set themselves up as speaking on behalf of all humankind.[82] The idea that humanist values are linked to a properly European urban civilization is actually still highly controversial. Some, such as the anthropologist Jack Goody, consider that this is a pure and simple fable that has allowed Europe to claim a prerogative over values which have nevertheless developed concomitantly in other parts of the world.[83] Patrick Le Galès also,

157

drawing on the work of the historian Bernard Lepetit, sees this less as a historical truth than as a founding myth, one that was developed recently so as to provide a frame of reference in which to think about contemporary social transformations, in particular the erosion of national borders in European societies.[84] But basically, from a sociological point of view, this is not what counts. The important thing is that many people around the world, and not only in Europe, believe in this myth, and that this belief produces real effects, such as their reactions to terrorist attacks.

— 8 —

THE VALUES AT STAKE

Pens and pencils brandished as a sign of solidarity, demonstrators with their mouths taped up and gagged: it's freedom of expression that's being murdered! Whatever you think of *Charlie Hebdo*, whether or not you have ever read it, whether or not you like it, no one can tolerate the members of the editorial staff of a newspaper being murdered in cold blood. One of the main reasons behind the reactions to the January 2015 attacks in Paris was the attachment of the French to one of the cardinal values of their Republic, constitutive of their culture and their history. And yet, if they had been asked only a few days before the terrorist attacks, in the context of a survey, what in their view the most important values were, there is nothing to say that freedom of expression would have been the value most often cited. It was in the heat of the moment, in the face of an attack of such a nature, that the French, and others with them in the world, came to realize how dear to them was this thing called 'freedom of expression'.

Terrorist attacks are major ideological moments in the life of a society: values, ideals and moral principles find themselves, for a few days or weeks, at the centre of attention. The president and prime minister constantly appeal at these times to the fundamental values of the society under attack, values which the terrorists could not shake. But beyond that, the feelings of ordinary citizens also show a commitment to certain values – not necessarily the same as those invoked by political leaders – since '[I]t is by experiencing emotions that we reveal our values to ourselves.'[1] Those of them who express their feelings in writing often do so by explaining which values in particular they think should be defended in the face of the terrorist ordeal and, in some cases, how these values must be defended. In this respect, their messages appear as valuable indices of what Émile Durkheim called the 'moral sensitivity' of a society.[2]

Reactions to terrorist attacks as value judgements

On the evening of the attack on *Charlie Hebdo*, François Hollande spoke of an attack on freedom of expression and democracy, but also of 'an ideal of justice and peace' and a 'message of tolerance' that France brings to the world.[3] Two days later, he called on all citizens to take part in the republican march of 11 January in the name of 'the values of democracy, freedom, and pluralism, to which we are all attached'.[4] Similarly, if the attack of 11 March 2004 in Madrid could be seen as a 'European 9/11',[5] as we saw earlier, it is because European leaders presented it as an attack on the values embodied by the European Union. Romano Prodi, then president of the European Commission, declared in reference to the minutes of silence observed on 15 March 2004:

> Whoever the perpetrators of these attacks, and whatever their motivation, it is clear that they have struck against the fundamental principles of all European states ... against the values on which the European Union is built. [...] This has been an attack against the respect of human dignity, liberty, democracy, equality, the rule of law and respect for human rights.[6]

The attacks of 9/11, on the other hand, were immediately described by George W. Bush as an attack on freedom itself, and the 'war on terror' triggered in return was justified by the need to fight all the 'enemies of freedom' wherever they may be throughout the world – so not just those responsible for the attacks – and to defend the 'universal values' associated with it.[7] The first military operation launched by the United States after 9/11 was, let us remember, known as 'Enduring Freedom'.

The call to values, from this point of view, is also a way of framing the event, helping to determine its meaning and our response to it. By simultaneously giving the attack a more intense and symbolic resonance, it also makes it possible to raise the cause of the attacked country to a more general level, so as to gain as much support as possible in the actions it would undertake in response to this attack.[8] But the place of values in reactions to the attacks is far from being limited to this incantatory and rhetorical dimension: they also play a central role in the way each of us, on our own level, experience the event. It is because we have the direct feeling that the terrorist attack is imperilling important values, because we then come to realize how much we ourselves are attached to those values, that we feel shell shocked, horrified and indignant – even before our political leaders have made the least statement.

Realizing what we are attached to

As the philosopher John Dewey pointed out, the idea of freedom seems to be very abstract apart from the possibility that everyone in a democracy can indulge in 'free gatherings of neighbors on the street corner to discuss back and forth what is read in uncensored news of the day'.[9] And so it is only when we find ourselves deprived of such a possibility that we come to realize how much we are attached to this value. This applies to what has been interpreted as a 'republican surge' after the attack on *Charlie Hebdo*: thousands of people became aware of the importance to them of the way that, living in France, they could stop at a kiosk at the corner of their street and buy (or not buy) *Charlie Hebdo*, like any other newspaper. If people are not always aware of what in this sense constitutes 'values' for them, it is precisely the emotions they feel in moments of ordeals such as terrorist attacks which reveal to them what they hold especially dear, things that they can then summarize in one word: 'freedom', 'peace', 'democracy', 'respect' and so on.

Realizing at the same time that they are not alone in being attached to these values, they become aware of just how much what we are attached to is also what we are attached to one another *by*[10] – what allows us to form a society. After the attack on 7 July 2005, some Londoners wrote:

> It is in times of severe adversity that we come to realise the true values of our society.[11]

> The attack on our city will not stop us holding true to what is important to us. Multi-cultural, Freedom, Hope, the ability to fulfil your dreams. God Bless the people of London.[12]

Similarly, a Spaniard wrote after the Madrid bombings:

> We think of you every day of our lives, in every station, in every train, in countless situations. Our values have been strengthened; Madrid and the whole of Spain were united that day. If only it could have been for a different reason![13]

Already in September 2001, anthropologist Béatrice Fraenkel noted of the messages that had invaded the streets of New York that they plunged their readers into a 'great bath of values'.[14] We could say the same of the messages written in reaction to the Madrid and London bombings, which refer to the values of a 'we' facing the attack as well as to 'human values' in general:

I hope it will make us reflect on human values.[15]

Let your death make our values stronger, which are better, and not weaker.[16]

For a better world in which peace and human values would be preserved, we all say NO to TERRORISM. We all felt we were Madrileneans this 11 March.[17]

Evil people can destroy bodies but they will not destroy our values.[18]

God bless London and all those who share its values.[19]

A few even mentioned 'European values', as did one German after the London bombings:

No terrorists can destroy European values and thoughts of freedom and liberty.[20]

But alongside these generic values, others are more exactly evoked, as we can see, such as freedom or peace. Indeed, this is the general case. Most often, the values under attack are specifically quoted in groups of two, three or four, or even more in some cases. Placed on the same level, these values take on meaning in their interrelationships. Sometimes, one of them is detached from the others, and sometimes highlighted. It then appears as a superior goal to which the other values are subordinate, the goal to which the author of the message is attached *above all*. Some values are quoted from message to message, as ends in themselves or means to another end, contributing to the achievement of some ultimate goal.[21] It is peace which appears most often as this ultimate goal, as in these messages of reaction to the Madrid bombings:

Peace is the fruit of love, tolerance and freedom.[22]

We must reach peace through the path of tolerance, freedom, respect, love and solidarity.[23]

For a better world where freedom, tolerance and dialogue ... and all that is necessary for peace are our main values. Let us not forget that we form one big family and that those who perished in these trains were our brothers.[24]

This may also be the case for democracy, as in this message left in London in July 2005 by a Greek person:

Democracy as an ideal has survived and existed for over two thousand years. We will not allow fifty years of terrorism to prevail, as long as we never forget our humanity and great values of life.[25]

The places occupied by each of these two values in popular reactions to Islamist attacks in Europe are, however, incommensurable. The word 'peace' occurs more than 14,500 times in the nearly 59,000 messages recorded in digital format after the Madrid bombings up until March 2005 (admittedly, it occurs approximately 1,800 times as part of a 'Rest in Peace' formula), while the word 'democracy' is used only 77 times.[26] This is rather surprising, especially given the fact that the Madrid bombings were explicitly described by European political leaders as an attack on democracy, like all other Islamist attacks in the West. This needs to be seen as further evidence of the discrepancy between the reactions of ordinary people and the institutional reactions to terrorist attacks – a discrepancy that proves that it is not possible to deduce the former from the latter.

The same applies to freedom, albeit at a lower quantitative level. Systematically invoked by heads of state after every Islamist attack, freedom appears only 1,555 times in the messages of reaction to the Madrid bombings, not as much as other values, which do not appear in the national mottoes of Western countries, or the treaties of the European Union: these are values such as love (cited more than 2,200 times) and life (cited more than 2,500 times).[27] Thus, value judgements formulated by ordinary individuals in response to the attacks are not merely variants, or repetitions, of those conveyed by the public framing of terrorist attacks: they have their own autonomy, and thus often mark a critical distance from official discourse. Messages that refer to freedom are an especially clear demonstration of this.

Defending freedom first and foremost?

If there is a constant element in the official reactions in the West to the Islamist attacks that have occurred since 9/11, it is indeed the reference to freedom. On the evening of the attack on *Charlie Hebdo*, François Hollande concluded his speech by stating:

> Freedom will always be stronger than barbarism. France has always vanquished her enemies when she has managed to stand up as one for her values.[28]

These words are reminiscent of those used by George W. Bush after 9/11:

> Tonight we are a country awakened to danger and called to defend freedom. [...] On September the 11th, enemies of freedom committed an act of war against our country. [...] [But] as long as the United States of America is determined and strong, this will not be an age of terror; this will be an age of liberty, here and across the world.[29]

163

Ordinary individuals, of course, drew on the same rhetoric for their own purposes, such as this Frenchman who, after having visited Ground Zero, wrote to the victims of 9/11:

> Rest in peace, you who gave your lives for freedom. America will continue to rebuild magnificently what others sought systematically to destroy: FREEDOM.[30]

Bolstered by the parallel with the resistance of the people of London to Nazi bombs during the Second World War,[31] these references to the defence of freedom against its enemies are particularly common in the reactions of Londoners to the bombings of 7 July 2005:

> As Londoners we stand together in the free world.[32]

> Sandwiched between July 4th (Independence Day) and July 14th (Bastille Day), surely this is [7/7] 2005.[33]

> Liberty, democracy and freedom from terror. These are London's deepest values – yesterday, today and tomorrow.[34]

> We will not be swayed in our rights and choices to live in freedom, and unafraid.[35]

The mayor of London himself presented the bombings as an attack on a city of freedom, to which people from all over the world flock simply 'because they come to be free', 'to live the life they choose', 'to be able to be themselves'[36] – a debatable view of things, to say the least.[37]

We know the famous saying of Paul Valéry according to which freedom is 'one of those detestable words that have more value than meaning'.[38] It has to be said that what we have observed in Western societies since 9/11 suggests that he was right. Continuously intoned by the United States and its allies to justify the war on terror and then the war in Iraq, freedom as a humanist value, in the sense in which Kant understood it, that is, as the foundation of cosmopolitanism and the hope of universal peace between men, has finally lost its meaning in the eyes of many. As Yves Citton notes, 'it is in the name of Kantian values of freedom, law and democracy that war was waged in Iraq, but also that war was opposed'.[39] That is why, in the reactions to the Madrid bombings in particular, freedom was sometimes mentioned less as an ideal to defend than as a debased value:

> Freedom! Freedom! How many crimes are committed in your name![40]

> The cause of freedom turns into a farce if the price to pay for it is the destruction of those who should enjoy freedom.[41]

When it is invoked positively, this is most often together with peace, as if to counteract the belligerent use that has been made of it since 9/11. One slogan in particular, forged by the Spaniards during the conflict with ETA, comes in many variations: 'For peace and freedom, no to terrorism!' The defence of freedom is also generally related to a more long-term struggle:

We must continue to fight for freedom.[42]

We will never forget, and we will always continue to struggle for freedom.[43]

Nothing at all can stop us loving those who are dear to us, you will always be in our hearts. We will continue to struggle for freedom.[44]

And this struggle for freedom, in view of which the Madrid bombings is part of the Spanish people's endeavour to assert its sovereignty, against Franco and then against terrorism, must also be understood as a joint struggle for peace, as was stressed by some writers:

You will always remain in our hearts and, in memory of you, we will continue to fight for PEACE and FREEDOM. Until we meet again!!![45]

Your memory gives us strength to continue to struggle for peace and freedom.[46]

Similarly, a Madrilenian who had moved to London wrote in July 2005:

NO to violence, long live freedom! They will NOT move us, never again, we will continue to struggle, onwards, peace will overcome. With all my heart, from a Madrilenian and Londoner. MADRID IS WITH LONDON AND NEW YORK.[47]

When peace and freedom are mentioned together, it is notable, moreover, that peace is almost always put first, as if there were between these two values a natural precedence.

Given that the struggle for freedom is at the same time a struggle for peace, it cannot therefore be confused with war. As if to further deconstruct the discourse of 'the war on terror in the name of freedom', some writers emphasize in their messages that war and terrorism, like any form of violence, are the opposite of peace and freedom, for which it is thus impossible to fight unless one resorts to non-violent means:

NO TO WAR, NO TO VIOLENCE, NO TO TERRORISM.

YES TO PEACE, YES TO CONCORD AND YES TO FREEDOM.[48]

165

NO TO TERRORISM, NO TO VIOLENCE, NO TO WARS.

YES TO PEACE, YES TO TOLERANCE, YES TO FREEDOM. FOR A BETTER WORLD.[49]

NO to WAR, NO to TERRORISM, NO to HUMAN BARBARITY.

NO to MURDERS carried out because of a Faith, Belief or Religion.

YES to PEACE, YES to FREEDOM of EXPRESSION and RESPECT for ALL.

LIVE and LET LIVE.[50]

In short, what is here being expressed is what one might call, to draw on the words of Michael Billig,[51] the 'banal pacifism' of the Europeans, that is, a pacifism which is not simply a matter of *pacifist* conviction, but is also rooted in the their daily lives, in their experience of a *peaceful* shared life, and their attachment to what makes this possible. And because the defence of freedom is intrinsically linked to the preservation of this state of peace that terrorist attacks challenge, it seems to some people that this struggle must take the form, not of the use of force and violence, but of the promotion of humanist values.

The banal pacifism of the Europeans

'Peace, freedom and tolerance', 'Peace, freedom and cohabitation', 'peace, freedom and solidarity', 'peace, freedom, love', 'peace, freedom and LIFE', 'Peace, hope and freedom', 'Love, Freedom and Justice', 'freedom, love and union among peoples', 'freedom, tolerance, humanity', 'Freedom, Peace and Equality', 'Love, Life and Freedom', 'for peace, freedom, solidarity and love', 'freedom, respect, trust in the human being, love', 'for the right to life, freedom, and respect for others', 'peace, humanity, freedom, love and life':[52] these are some of the groups of values put forward in messages addressed to the victims of the Madrid bombings. While in the speeches of George W. Bush after 9/11, freedom is always invoked as an end in itself, it here appears as one value *among others*, and these other values define its meaning. Thus it can be again linked to a cosmopolitical ideal:

May peace, justice, freedom, brotherhood, solidarity and love reign over the entire planet.[53]

For freedom, respect, understanding, love and peace. Is there anything greater in this world?[54]

Solidarity and respect are the principle of our freedom. For a peaceful multicultural world.[55]

166

These reactions to the Madrid bombings are in line with the 'love of the world' that was expressed in Europe after 9/11:[56] 20 per cent of letters sent by French people to Americans through Operation 'Fraternally' had also referred to peace and/or humanistic values. Colette, for example, concluded her message with this list of values that in her view should serve as a guide in the dark times following 9/11:

LOVE – FRIENDSHIP – FRATERNITY – RESPECT – COMPASSION – FREEDOM in RESPECT for the OTHER. These are true values.[57]

Colette's letter was dated 26 September, six days after George W. Bush's speech to Congress announcing America's entry into war. Her need to specify 'freedom *in respect for the other*' can be interpreted as a reaction against the way American leaders used 'freedom' in a loose way to legitimize the war that was about to start. In the same way, on 13 September 2001, a young man from Rouen, who presented himself as a philosophy student, wrote to explain that, contrary to what the American president had declared that day, the coming struggle was not that of 'Good against Evil', but 'that of freedom, of democracy and peace, that of the values in which we believe and that we believe to be the most just and generous' – a struggle which, he insisted, needed to be subordinated to 'the preservation of the very idea of humanity', as the terrorists, however 'bestial' their acts might be, were nonetheless 'an integral part of our humanity'.[58]

Tolerance, respect, love

This refusal to divide humanity into two camps, 'us' and 'them', is consistent with a cosmopolitical point of view, and leads some people to present the promotion of humanist values (particularly education) as the only answer, in the long run, to Islamist terrorism. One German thus wrote after the London bombings:

9/11 or the 7th of July in London – there is no difference. We are all deeply touched. We all belong to one World and we should become one people. But the only way to make this come true is education. Let's spend lots of money in all the world if we want to live free. 'I have a dream', Martin Luther King said, and I share his dream. But I want to add: Let this global village be one.[59]

Similarly, a resident of Valencia wrote after the Madrid bombings:

Education is what underlies tolerance. Let us all, as much as we can, use it to make sure that the events that took place here are never repeated. For a society of respect. No to violence.[60]

167

And a teacher, as one might expect, also writes:

> On March 11, your voices fell silent, but the teachers will preserve your memory by educating our pupils in peace and tolerance, to build a world where hatred and terror no longer have any raison d'être.[61]

The defence of freedom, for some people, thus disappears behind these humanist values, the transmission and dissemination of which appear to be more than ever paramount since 9/11 to achieve an ideal of universal peace, i.e. to ensure that the peace that Europeans enjoy between themselves can become the peace of the whole world.

In fact, many writers in reaction to the Madrid bombings mentioned these values alone, without any reference to freedom:

> I simply want to say that two values such as tolerance and solidarity can change the world … that's all … and express my thanks to all.[62]

> Enough violence! More respect and solidarity! Another world is possible![63]

> We want RESPECT and TOLERANCE to be the predominant values in this society … We are with you.[64]

> With tolerance and respect, we will overcome hatred and injustice. EVERYONE AGAINST TERRORISM.[65]

> I feel great sorrow for the deceased. I do not understand terrorism. We must spread the values of TOLERANCE, RESPECT AND LOVE.[66]

Even if in a somewhat more marginal way, the same phenomenon is observed in the reactions to the 7 July 2005 attacks, in which London is not exclusively presented as a city of freedom, but also, in accordance with its world-city status, associated with the values of tolerance and respect:

> London today is as strong as it ever was. A colourful, multinational city of freedom, tolerance, and respect. This will never change. [67]

> We live in a diverse, cosmopolitan city where tolerance and respect must prevail.[68]

Tolerance and respect, moreover, are – when they are mentioned – almost always cited together, as these messages attest. If these are not the values most often mentioned in the reactions to the attacks (both appear barely 400 times in the corpus of 59,000 messages collected in response to the Madrid bombings), their association deserves to be pondered.

168

The philosopher Michael Walzer, in his *On Toleration*, distinguishes four types of tolerance, each corresponding to a degree of acceptance of the difference of the other: a simple 'resigned acceptance of difference' (which arises from the exhaustion of those who have hated and confronted one other for too long), a stance of being 'benignly indifferent to difference' (which corresponds to what Simmel referred to the 'blasé attitude' of the city-dweller),[69] a 'stoicism' that puts up with difference, and finally, a real openness and curiosity towards the other, 'perhaps even respect', writes Michael Walzer. In other words, respect seems to be a limit case of tolerance, to some extent its most successful form: beyond this, we switch to an enthusiastic support of difference, a form of love for the other, which is something other than tolerance.[70]

If tolerance is so often associated with respect in the reactions to the Madrid and London bombings, this is so as to ensure that it is understood in a maximalist sense, closer to a friendly reception than a veiled hostility. Indeed, in the minimal sense, which is also its original meaning, tolerance as 'resigned acceptance' refers first and foremost to the wars of religion that scarred Europe in the fifteenth and sixteenth centuries. It is 'a *Christian* virtue, or for that matter a *Catholic* virtue. The Christian must tolerate the non-Christian, but, even more so, the Catholic must let the Protestant be', as Jacques Derrida points out.[71] Of course, this original meaning generally affects the place occupied by tolerance in the Western reactions to the Islamist attacks, at the level of ordinary citizens as well as at the level of politicians and the media. As Derrida rightly points out:

> Since we today feel that religious claims are at the heart of the violence [...], we resort to this good old word 'tolerance': that Muslims agree to live with Jews and Christians, that Jews agree to live with Muslims, that believers agree to live with 'infidels' or 'nonbelievers' (for this is the word 'bin Laden' used to denounce his enemies, and first of all the Americans). Peace would thus be tolerant cohabitation.[72]

The problem, however, is that tolerance retains from its original meaning the trace of an asymmetric relationship between the one who tolerates and the one who is tolerated: tolerance is always on the side of the 'reason of the strongest',[73] as the French dictionary *Littré* demonstrates by defining tolerance as a form of condescension or indulgence. That is why Jacques Derrida ultimately continues to be somewhat wary about the word and the discourse that it structures in the post-9/11 context.

169

It seems as if Europeans were attempting to overcome this reservation in their written reactions to the attacks in Madrid and London by adding respect to tolerance, or indeed, as even more of them did, that they in turn eclipsed tolerance, retaining only respect and associating it with love, always in a cosmopolitical perspective:

> Peace in the world, brotherhood between peoples, and respect between persons.[74]

> Solidarity, love, peace and above all respect for others.[75]

> Let all the lives fallen along the way lead us, not only to reflect, but also to restore the values of respect and love between different races and conditions, [for] we forget that in the end we form but a single human race.[76]

These examples taken from reactions to the Madrid bombings are echoed by other messages from the books of condolences opened in London in 2005, such as this one:

> We *must* learn to Love & respect one another
> – A global community – Hate will eat away our souls.[77]

Or this message signed by an Italian woman:

> We must fight terrorism, but the most important thing is to love and respect one another.[78]

In this same spirit, a message left at the Atocha station in Madrid concludes by inviting us to 'take care of each other',[79] while in response to the London bombings a Londoner argued that 'the only answer is to open our hearts to one another'.[80] Another Londoner, finally, wrote:

> The things that we throw we get back. If we want respect, throw respect and love, then we will get back the same. For those that [have] gone, 11-S, 11-M, 7-J, Iraq, etc. [81]

Europeans are thus called upon to live up to their ideals. If they truly want human beings to live at peace in a world cleared of all violence, they should themselves start by sowing love and respect around them. It is therefore by way of example, and not only in words, that the values that Europeans hold dear must be promoted. Gandhi's famous dictum, 'There is no way to peace, peace is the way', is quoted in many messages, as are the words of Saint Augustine: 'It is not enough to be peaceful, you must be a builder of peace.'

The expression of a Christian tradition

It would of course be difficult not to see in these injunctions to love one another, which sometimes sound like sermons, the traces of religious convictions, in particular Christian convictions. They raise, in fact, the question of the role that such convictions may play in the reactions of some of us to terrorist attacks, but they also refer, on a more cultural level, to the Christian sources of the cosmopolitical ideal of universal peace.[82] This love invoked by Europeans in the face of the terrorist ordeal is clearly *agape*, that is to say, universal love as a generalized state of peace, as it is understood in a theological perspective.[83] Loving one another is strictly synonymous, in this sense, with living in peace with each other – witness the fact that the values of 'love' and 'peace' are placed on the same level in certain messages, like this one, which a Frenchwoman wrote in response to 9/11:

Love, Peace should be the only existing values![84]

These messages of Europeans invoking love and peace – there were more of them, we should remember, after the Madrid bombings than those calling for the defence of freedom – would thus be an expression of this 'vocation of Europe' which, according to Emmanuel Levinas, consists in realizing 'peace as love of the neighbour',[85] i.e. peace as agape. The 'neighbour', in this perspective, is conceived as being detached from 'any close relationship of family, friendship or nation':[86] the neighbour is an 'other' than me, another than ourselves, and must be loved in all his or her otherness and strangeness.

In the face of an Islamist attack, this propensity for agape is expressed by the refusal to see the Muslim 'other' as an enemy. Thus, the sociologist Nilüfer Göle noted of the demonstrations of 11 January 2015:

Without a slogan against Islam or immigrants, without even any mention of the murderers [...], these were not gatherings to protest against an adversary, but the expression of a society affirming itself.[87]

Similarly after 9/11, only a tiny minority of messages sent by the French to the Americans via Operation 'Fraternally' included content of a racist or Islamophobic kind (0.4 per cent). Indeed, none of the publics that are formed in response to an Islamist attack, of the kind that has been identified through written reactions to the Madrid bombings, is characterized by a posture of denunciation or incrimination.[88] Some people, admittedly, wrote to the victims that they would be avenged or furiously condemned the terrorists, but this kind of message is very marginal with

171

regard to the whole. When popular vindictiveness was expressed after the Madrid and London attacks it was aimed more at Western political leaders than at the terrorists: José María Aznar, George W. Bush and Tony Blair were vilified because of the war in Iraq, without which, some believed, these attacks would never have occurred – as if these were, in short, dramatic misunderstandings, since nobody in principle could have any reason to wish to attack Europeans, who want peace for everyone in the world.

From the point of view of agape, however, the question of who is responsible, whether directly or indirectly, for the attacks is of little importance. Those who preach this universal love stand in the present and do not care about past offences. It is not so much that they forgive, but that they quite simply consider that what is done is done, and that looking for culprits would serve no purpose. Some messages express this very well, for example:

> There are no culprits,
> There are victims.
> There is no hatred,
> There is pain.
> There is no war,
> There is selfishness.
> We do not want violence,
> We want PEACE.
> We need PEACE.
> We deserve PEACE.
> For us,
> For them,
> For you,
> For *everyone*.[89]

In a different style, this is also what two young Spanish women said:

> We are Ines and Lourdes. Learn how to give importance to the things that are really important, and LIFE is one of them. We must give thanks when we get up every morning and make the most of every minute as if it were the last. We must not look for culprits, the damage has been done. Not all Muslims think the same way.[90]

These messages which claim that no one is guilty here should of course not be taken literally. They are not judgements of fact but *judgements of value*. They do not mean that no one is to blame for what has happened, as if the attack had been a mere accident, but rather that, from the perspective of agape, knowing who is guilty is not what matters. This is because the rejection of a binary partition of the world and of humanity between 'us' and 'them' can also lead us to think that we all may be, deep down, a little guilty for what has happened, as some people pointed out after the Madrid bombings:

> There was a train full of victims, we were all victims, all a bit guilty. My respect for those who have died, my solidarity with those who are still alive.[91]

> Life is so wonderful that absolutely no one deserves to have it taken from them. We might come to think that we are all a little bit guilty for what has happened.[92]

In this respect, as noted by Luc Boltanski, agape contrasts particularly clearly with justice.[93] It is interesting to note here that the first military operation of the war on terror, Operation 'Enduring Freedom', was initially baptized by the United States 'Infinite Justice' and that on the day President Barack Obama announced bin Laden's death, he declared: 'Justice has been done.' The formula inevitably roused controversy in Europe, in view of the fact that bin Laden was killed during a military operation, and so was never literally brought to justice.[94] While Europeans also refer to justice in reaction to the Islamist attacks – several of the messages quoted above demonstrate as much – it is much less often mentioned than values such as love or life (970 times in the messages in response to the Madrid bombings, as against, as we have noted, 2,200 references to love, and more than 2,500 to life). This is because, in the logic of agape, rather than seeking to obtain justice or ensure that justice is done, it is above all important to work for peace among human beings by promoting, in one's world, the supreme values of love, respect for others and, ultimately, respect for life itself.

A sacralization of life

If the Europeans' reaction to 9/11 as well as the Madrid and London attacks demonstrated such an attachment to peace and a refusal to enter into a logic of confrontation, this was indeed because they felt, as many of their messages remind us, that the right to life of all human beings on this earth is inalienable, and that no cause could justify its being taken from them.[95] And even if terrorists do not respect this right, we cannot flout it too, unless we contradict ourselves. It is ultimately only with a

173

view to the preservation of that right that the promotion of humanistic values takes on real meaning, as one Spaniard explained after the Madrid bombings:

> Beyond any belief, religion, country, skin colour, or opinion, we all inhabit the same planet, the same universe, and ultimately, we are all entitled to life; we must protect life, we cannot go against it, because to do so would be to go against ourselves. We must defend life, but not with its main enemy, violence, but rather with kindness, generosity, tolerance, solidarity, and respect ... Madrid and the whole of Spain defend life. NO TO TERRORISM! YES TO LIFE!!![96]

While it was less prevalent in the reactions to the London bombings, this invocation of life as supreme value was still found in them, for example in this message, found among the many calls to defend freedom:

> Is there anything more diverse than this life and this universe?
> Is there anything more precious than this life and this universe?
> The earth rotates on a single axis, yet we are still on a journey.
> The fundamental fact is, as we meet we import our souls on one another.
> Can we as a human race show only goodness or mercy on one another?
> The answer is if we so wished, we could. For it is within us all.
> Evil has no place on this Earth.
> Respect for life and each other will bring about change for the good of all.
> My sincerest Condolences.[97]

As far as can be seen from the books of condolences collected in the London Metropolitan Archives, such messages are most often left by nationals of continental Europe rather than British or American people. While the vast majority of messages in the London books of condolences that mention freedom are written in English, a message like the following one, for example, is written in French:

> Pour la Vie et Pour l'Amour [For Life and for Love].[98]

And this, while written in English, is signed by a German woman:

> Like after any attack there will be a before and an after July the 7th. But just as for NY and Madrid we will grow stronger of those attacks and may understand the real meaning of love, solidarity and what is

to be alive. And thus, please keep enjoying life and trusting in human kindness.

Love and compassion,

Flora (from Munich).[99]

Similarly, it was a Polish woman who, after visiting Ground Zero, wrote:

We are all human being. We all have right to live. Do not forget about love to other people. We have only one world to share![100]

The gap between the Anglo-American and European views on the Islamist attacks in Western countries since 9/11 is hence also reflected in the values invoked by the former and the latter. To put it in a nutshell, these attacks were seen as targeting mainly freedom in the eyes of the Americans, and mainly life in the eyes of the Europeans – even if political leaders did not mention this value in their public reactions. This is clear from two further messages received after the London bombings by the mayor of Bassetlaw, in Nottinghamshire, sent from the two cities with which that town is twinned. The first was a fax sent by the mayor of Farmer's Branch, Texas, which states:

These cowardly acts upon innocent citizens will serve only to underscore our collective resolve to defy those who would presume to harm freedom-loving people everywhere.[101]

Conversely, in the second, an email sent by the mayor of Garbsen, Germany, the London bombings were described as 'a malicious attack against life and peaceful co-existence of nations in the world'.[102]

In retrospect, Americans and Europeans tend consequently to associate different values with the memory of 9/11. In 2008, after visiting Ground Zero, a Californian left a message at the 9/11 Tribute Center that concluded by stating that 9/11 was an attack 'on all the Americans and people who believe in freedom'.[103] But a Spaniard wrote:

Events like what happened in this city or took place in Madrid (2004) and in London demonstrate that humanity must reflect on its own future. We must all become aware of the true meaning of life.[104]

This divergence was not so clear in 2001. In Europe too, as we have seen, 9/11 was widely perceived as an attack on freedom, reminding people of the Second World War. However, in several messages of Operation 'Fraternally', it was life, rather than freedom, that was already

175

presented as the main issue. For Sophie, for example, this value judgement proceeds from a cosmopolitical point of view:

> The atrocities that have been committed are unspeakable, just as those that have been occurring for months in Algeria, Palestine, Israel, and in all countries where life is undermined in the name of intolerable fanatical ideologies. It is no longer the time to talk about countries, ethnicities, races, religions, borders ... we are all just men and women, nothing else. The only thing worth fighting for is life and in no case can this happen by dealing death. Suffering is universal.[105]

Another, more succinct, message ends with these words: 'Against terrorism, against the contempt for life'.[106] And in yet another, we read: 'All human life is sacred.'[107]

This last formula is worth remembering, as it sums up what is ultimately at stake here: a sacralization of human life, which leads to the perception that any attack on the life of any human being whatsoever is a sacrilege. At the end of the nineteenth century, Émile Durkheim was already pointing out in *Suicide* that 'man has become a god for men. Therefore, any attempt against his life suggests sacrilege.'[108] The founding father of French sociology saw this as a consequence of the secularization of European societies which led them to recognize no longer the supreme value that the human person is in him- or herself:

> The human person has become the thing to which the social consciousness of the European peoples has become more attached than to any other; as a result, it has acquired an incomparable value.[109]

One can, of course, take a critical look at this development, as did the philosopher Walter Benjamin, for whom '[t]he proposition that existence stands higher than a just existence is false and ignoble, if by existence we mean nothing other than mere life'.[110] But the fact remains, as we noted at the end of the previous chapter in connection with the values that seem to symbolize European cities, that this sacralization of life has quite real effects in European societies. Hence the tone of the reactions observed there after an Islamist attack, but also the fact that the death penalty has been abolished in Europe, unlike in other countries in the world,[111] and that the movement opposing the war in Iraq was particularly well supported in Europe.[112]

It is because the reason behind their reactions to the attacks of 9/11 and those in Madrid and London also led them to oppose the war in Iraq that some Europeans were able to equate the victims of these attacks and the innocent civilians killed in Baghdad or elsewhere in the world, and to wonder about the merits of the minutes of silence that they are required to devote to some people, but not others.[113] And this conviction that all human life, of whatever kind, is sacred, that no life is more sacred than another, is also what explains that we may have felt embarrassed to find that the murder of well-known cartoonists affected us more directly than the murder of people who were not well known, and to endeavour to make up for this moral failing by uttering the slogan 'I am Charlie' in the form of a list of the names of all the victims, in alphabetical order, as *Libération* did, for example, on its front page for 11 January 2015: 'I am Frédéric Boisseau, Philippe Braham, Franck Brinsolaro, Jean Cabut known as Cabu …'

— 9 —

THE ATTACKS IN PERSONS

The 'I' of 'I am Charlie' gave rise to much discussion. Some saw it as the culmination of an individualism exacerbated by social media, an extra proof of the narcissism of the 'Me Generation', the last avatar of postmodern egocentrism; others viewed it as a major sociopolitical invention, the sign of a historic turning point. By modifying the modalities of public reactions to terrorist attacks, social media have in fact only made obvious a tendency already massively at work in the reactions to the 9/11, Madrid and London attacks. Tens of thousands of people in Europe had already expressed their support for the victims in the first person singular and in their name, rather than using a 'we'. Some did so in just a few words, as they would these days in a tweet, others in several pages, explaining in detail to the victims what personal reasons they had to feel concerned by what had happened to them, relating their own feelings basically in the same way that we do to our friends.

Doubtless this may be regarded as an additional demonstration of what Eva Illouz identifies as a new culture of 'affect' peculiar to individualist and capitalist societies,[1] but the mechanism behind this demonstration remains to be explored. These personal reactions to terrorist attacks express a solidarity based on the feeling of a direct connection between singular human lives: the lives of the victims and the life of the person who is sorry for their fate. The condition sine qua non for us to react to an attack – or any other disaster – in this way is that its victims should appear to us as singular human lives, people *in their own right*, just like us. If we could say 'I'm Charlie', this is because the cartoonists at *Charlie Hebdo* were known, because their faces and their names were familiar to us, with many of us – even outside of France[2] – having the feeling of a personal, direct connection with Charb, Cabu or Wolinski, as if they were pretty much a part of our lives. But when we are confronted by a mass attack striking ordinary, nameless people, this singular-ized perception of the victims is not self-evident.

The singularization of the victims

In September 2015, the photograph of little Alan Kurdi lying on a beach in Turkey, which has become iconic of the tragedy of migrants in the Mediterranean, reminded us of how compassion needs singularity. It can only be triggered by the suffering of one or a few persons perceived as singular, and not by the suffering of a mass of indistinct individuals, however many they may be, and however horrible may be their suffer-ing.[3] If a public of singular people, as I proposed calling it, can therefore be formed in reaction to a terrorist attack, this is primarily because their victims appear to us as singular persons, with faces, names and life stories of their own – a perception that is constructed by society and the media.

Giving victims a face

Shortly after the Madrid bombings, someone posted on the Internet forum of the newspaper *Libération* a very long message in which can be read:

> I have engraved for ever in my memory the image of that young man, sitting on the ground, his face covered in blood, leaning against a tree, his right eye completely swollen, trying to call his family with a mobile that was not working. I have since learned that his name was Sergio, that he was 22 years old and a student. The good news is that he is recovering from his injuries and that he has not lost his eye.[4]

The photograph mentioned here is one of those most reproduced in the aftermath of this attack.[5] The newspapers which published it on their front pages received so many calls about it that they carried out an investigation to identify the young man in the photo, to find him and to inquire about his health. They quickly learned that he was Sergio Gil, a resident of the Santa Eugenia area, then aged 19 years (and not 22, as the author of the message quoted above asserted), and that he had been released from hospital after a week. In France, two articles were devoted to him on 25 March 2004, one in *Libération* (which had published his photograph on its front page),[6] the other in *Le Parisien-Aujourd'hui* in France, which depicted him as 'a quiet worker who has become a symbol'.[7] This media overexposure meant that Sergio received many messages of support, and even gifts from strangers.[8] The same was true

179

after the London bombings: the photograph of a woman holding a protective mask with both hands on her burned face while a man holds her
in his arms to guide her steps was the focus for particular attention,[9] so
that the young woman, Davinia Turrell, and the man who rescued her,
Paul Dadge, were featured in numerous press articles and TV reports in
the following months and years. And like them, several other victims of
this attack saw their lives splashed across the pages of the English
tabloids.[10]

None of the 9/11 victims, on the other hand, embodied the tragedy in
person. The 'icons' of these attacks are the towers of the World Trade
Center themselves. So, in September 2001, the singularization of the
victims happened in other ways: the countless appeals for information
posted after the attacks in every part of New York by the relatives of
missing persons.[11] It is estimated that between 500 and 700 families put
up some 100,000 notices in the city.[12] The same phenomenon was
observed in Madrid and London in the vicinities hit by the attacks and
in the most frequented areas of both cities.[13] But in New York, its magnitude was such that it was impossible to walk through Manhattan
without being confronted by these small handcrafted posters all based
on the model of the personal information sheet: a photo and the word
'Missing', then family name and first name, height and weight, colour
of skin, eyes and hair, and any distinguishing features. Often, there was
also a description of the clothes worn by the missing person on the day
of the attacks, as well as the tower, the floor and the company where he
or she worked. By publicly giving a name, a face and a body to each
person presumed missing or dead after the collapse of the towers of the
World Trade Center, these notices helped to restore their individual singularity. Also, the photographs used in these posters had nothing to do
with frozen identity photos. They showed each victim in an attitude and
a context that rendered them immediately familiar, as Fraenkel notes:

> Mike smiles at us, Ansha laughs, Bob is tender, Audrey is sticking out her
> tongue. Some are accompanied by their children or surrounded by friends:
> in this case, their faces are shown by a red circle. [...] This is why these
> faces are so close to us: I can see my husband, my wife and daughter, my
> best mate, my childhood friend, my mother, my cousin. And because the
> disaster envelops the whole city, weighs on every street, I feel connected
> to all these missing persons, they become *my* missing persons.[14]

These notices did not merely make the human record of the collapse of
the towers of the World Trade Center less abstract: they also challenged
the New Yorker passers-by, impelling them to feel concerned. All these
missing were also *our missing*.

But this statement is not only valid for people present in New York in September 2001, given that the media broadcast in profusion, in the days that followed the attacks, images of the people searching for their loved ones and their appeals for information. The viewer, therefore, was confronted with the faces of the missing and directly addressed. One Frenchwoman wrote:

> I've been in a state of collapse, wiped out, terrified for 3 days, impossible to get rid of these terrible images and the cries of the witnesses of this atrocious act of barbarism.
>
> Something in me is broken, bruised ... I have trouble thinking about anything other than all the horrible anguish and suffering experienced by thousands of New Yorkers. This wait, this doubt ... They are looking for a son, a daughter, a father, a mother, a brother, a sister, a friend, a husband, a wife.
>
> I do not know the USA. I have neither family nor friends there. Yet I weep with you and I suffer with each and every one of you. [...] The suffering that I experience is real, profound, sincere, and it has nothing to do with any mere mark of respect or politeness, it is *spontaneous*.[15]

In addition, over the following days the media set up a 'blow by blow account of the suffering',[16] with ever more testimonies of survivors and portraits of missing persons. Each time, 'the victims are individualized, given their precise names and described by one or more aspects of their social identity'.[17] And their lives are recounted to us, both after the attacks of 9/11 and after those in Madrid and London.

Relating ordinary lives

It was not only the image of Sergio Gil published on the front pages of several newspapers in the aftermath of the Madrid bombings that had such an impact on the author of the message posted on the forum of *Libération* that I quoted above. This message went on to say:

> I have read the story of the 199th victim. Her name was Patricia: she was seven months old, she was blonde and had blue eyes, her parents Yolanda and Wiesław were Polish emigrants who had settled in Spain eight years ago, where they lived happily while working hard: Wiesław worked in the building, he was 34 years old. Yolanda, she was a domestic worker, she was 28 years old.[18]

The next few lines provided a detailed account of the tragic story of Patricia, the youngest victim of the Madrid bombings, to whom several

181

articles were devoted in the Spanish press: it had been difficult for her mother to have this child, Patricia had been given a chain bracelet that enabled her to be recognized at the morgue, her aunt had had a premonition on the morning of the attacks, her father had been killed on the spot, her mother seriously injured, her grandparents were just about to arrive from Poland to get to know their granddaughter, and so on. The author of this message was not the only person to have been touched by this story. In Atocha station, someone left a piece of paper on which was drawn a broken heart in red, with these words: 'In memory of the youngest victim of 11 March'.[19] And among the messages recorded via the computer system set up in June 2004 was one that read:

> I felt sorry for all the victims, but especially for the one who was not yet born and for the nine-month-old baby they did not even allow to blow out his first birthday candle. We send our best wishes to all of you who need to be brave as you have left a part of yourselves here, after suffering the loss of those who have departed.[20]

Like those on the front pages of newspapers, some victims thus attract more media attention than others after terrorist attacks, either because of their age (like the baby here), their nationality (foreign media focus immediately upon the nationals of their own country), or a backstory that is deemed particularly touching (couples that are separated just before getting married or becoming parents) or edifying (such as that of Shahara Islam, a young Muslim victim of the London bombings, whose portrait was set alongside that of the terrorist who had killed her, in the *Guardian* of 14 July 2005). But beyond these individual cases, each of the victims of the attacks in Madrid and London was entitled to an obituary with a photo published in the national press – except when their families refused to give permission.[21]

It was far from obvious that this would happen. The Spanish and British press followed the example of the *New York Times* after 9/11, which on 15 September 2001 started to publish its *Portraits of Grief* – an initiative for which it was awarded the Pulitzer Prize in 2002. It continued to do so until the end of 2001, i.e. for three and a half months, in its supplement devoted to 9/11, 'A Nation Challenged', then once a week, every Sunday, in its obituaries, until the spring of 2002. These portraits then continued to appear at a random rate, as new victims were identified by personal effects or human remains found among the debris at Ground Zero.[22] All of these portraits, finally, were reproduced in a monumental book, *Portraits – 9/11/01*, first published for the first anniversary of 9/11, in 2002, and then reissued in an enlarged version the following year.[23]

Yet their compilation has a strange effect. Taken one by one, each of these portraits restores the singularity of a person: his or her character traits, plans and life story. But once they have been united, what emerges from them is a strange sense of redundancy. All these singular lives appear to resemble each other:

> [T]he stories were almost all versions of the same story – happy people, fulfilled in their jobs, fountains of love and charity, pillars of their family and community. The assembled miniature biographies told the story of a flourishing civil society indifferent to race, gender, and economic category. Everyone under the roofs of the Twin Towers was happy and getting happier.[24]

In fact, these obituary portraits, while endeavouring to restore each victim in his or her singularity, conform at the same time to an implicit standard, in relation to which certain biographical features are highlighted, and others passed over in silence. They aim to make each victim a 'Good American', each embodying in his or her way the American Dream. The philosopher Judith Butler, in a still-celebrated critique of these *Portraits of Grief*, even concludes that each of these obituaries must be considered as 'an act of nation-building',[25] a way of recomposing the unity of the American nation under attack, stating who belonged to it and who did not.

These portraits, she points out, create a 'hierarchy in mourning',[26] since making public the names, faces and life stories of the deceased is also a way of indicating which lives deserve to be mourned and, at the same time, to condemn to even greater oblivion those who were not that lucky or did not fall within the normative framework of this public statement. The implicit prevalence of marital and heterosexual norms, for example, implies that the legitimate husbands and wives of the heterosexual and married victims of 9/11 were naturally included in the community of public mourning, while the partners of homosexual victims were usually absent, as were lovers or so-called 'illegitimate' children. From these portraits, moreover, were excluded all the victims of 9/11 who had not been and would never be identified: illegal immigrant workers in the World Trade Center, homeless people living in its basements, unnamed and faceless people not on the official list of the victims of 9/11.[27] Finally, and most importantly, one of the essential remarks of *Precarious Life* consists in denouncing the fact that, while the officially registered victims of 9/11 had the right to their portrait in the *New York Times*, tens of thousands of civilians killed by the US military in Afghanistan and Iraq had been ignored in the US media; and in showing that one phenomenon is a counterpart of the other.

Judith Butler's approach is much more critical than empathetic. Thus, she does not dwell on the fact that foreigners were also sometimes affected by these portraits of 'good Americans', without this feeling being reducible to a simple form of Americanophilia. She thus abstains from giving a detailed analysis of what, in these obituary portraits, could give rise to forms of identification with the victims that did not involve a sense of national belonging. She comes close to this at just one point, when she ponders what justifies the fact that an American like her can find it easier to mourn Daniel Pearl, the journalist from the *Wall Street Journal* murdered in February 2002 while investigating Islamist networks in Pakistan, rather than an Afghan civilian killed by an American bomb:

> Indeed, Daniel Pearl, 'Danny' Pearl, is so familiar to me: he could be my brother or my cousin; he is so easily humanized; he fits the frame, his name has my father's name in it. His last name contains my Yiddish name.[28]

A little further on, she adds:

> Mourning Daniel Pearl presents no problem for me or for my family of origin. His is a familiar name, a familiar face, a story about education that I understand and share; his wife's education makes her language familiar, even moving, to me, a closeness of what is similar.[29]

Judith Butler's sense of familiarity with Daniel Pearl was obviously fostered by the fact that they were both American nationals, but it cannot be reduced to that alone: both come from the same social background and from Jewish families, they were trained at the best American universities – Stanford for Daniel Pearl, Yale for Judith Butler – and work in intellectual professions. And one may ultimately wonder if all these added factors would not have impelled the one to feel concerned about the fate of the other, even had they not been of the same nationality. It is significant, however, that Judith Butler produced this analysis in connection with Daniel Pearl rather than with one of the victims of 9/11 whose portrait had been published by the *New York Times*. Her analysis of the *Portraits of Grief* was not based on a systematic study of their contents. Also, in order to understand how the publication of such portraits can foster personal reactions to terrorist attacks, we need to go further.

Providing occasions for concern

In their canonical form, as embodied in the *Portraits of Grief* in the *New York Times*, the obituary portraits published after terrorist attacks aimed to perform a twofold operation in just a few words (150 maximum for the *New York Times*): recomposing the unity of a singular life around a 'significant fact' or a 'character trait', and showing how this life was at the same time part of a mourning society.[30] The first movement lies in referring to the form of a *life story* that plays fully on 'the biographical illusion'[31] by being organized around a guiding principle that is taken as synthesizing in itself the whole person. The second movement consists in displaying, in each of these narratives, different forms of the social bond. These obituaries are not biographical records endeavouring to be the most comprehensive possible. They do not aim to sum up a person accurately; rather, they seek 'to give a snapshot of the personality of each victim, of a life lived',[32] and rely for this on two essential elements: an anecdote, on which the life story is centred, and a caption (or nickname) attached to the victim's name, which is not only a 'narrative program' but, even more than that, a 'promise of proximity'.[33]

The two elements are inseparable: the portrait of Marc Zeplin, for example, captioned 'He shoots! He scores!', is entirely structured around his passion for baseball;[34] that of James Lee Connor, 'Golf paved his way', tells of how Connor met his wife and future employer while playing golf.[35] Similarly, in *El País* after the Madrid bombings, we meet Nicoleta Deac, 'the girl with the ball', a young Romanian who had been working in Spain for four years, loved to play football and dreamed of opening a pizzeria;[36] Jorge Rodríguez Casanova, with his 'Zidane shirt', who was a young supporter of Real Madrid who 'loved Zidane more than anything', so that his parents decided to bury him with his Real Madrid shirt bearing the player's number ...[37] Though the portraits published on the BBC website after the London bombings did not have captions, they did at least have subheadings which also followed this logic of the 'snapshot' fleshed out with an anecdote:

A freelance picture editor with a wide circle of friends and a close-knit family, Miriam Hyman was born, graduated and died, all within one square mile in London.[38]

It was a measure of Phil Beer's outgoing personality that his family asked all mourners at his funeral to wear brightly coloured clothes.[39]

A village in Derbyshire came out to grieve together when one of its most cherished residents, Michael Stanley Brewster, known by many as Stan, was killed on 7 July 2005.[40]

And as we can see, these three examples are also evidence of the second movement performed by these obituary portraits: they emphasize the social integration of the deceased.

185

In the *Portraits of Grief*, Adeline Wrona identifies six types of social bond that are highlighted, all of them reflected in the portraits of victims of the Madrid and London bombings. The first type corresponds to the family circle, all the more ubiquitous as it is from the relatives of the deceased that biographical information about him or her is obtained. Then there is the circle of sociability which, especially in the portraits of victims of 9/11, is present through the recurrent evocation of festive meals, but may also include the mention of a liking for parties, outings or travels, as for Miryam, a victim of the Madrid bombings, who 'was always making preparations for dinners, birthdays and trips' and was a 'wonderful' dancer.[41] Then comes the world of work: the mention of a successful career, and hopes of a promotion, all of which makes it possible to refer to colleagues, clients or employees. Attachment to wearing a uniform also makes it possible to underline membership of a professional body, in particular for police officers and firefighters who lost their lives on 11 September 2001. The last three types of social bond, finally, are those created through sporting activities, religious practices or participation in a cultural community.

However, while the emphasis on these social bonds is part of the recreation of a vast 'living together' at the level of the countries struck, both after the 9/11 attacks and after those in Madrid and London, it likewise makes possible forms of concern which can rest on things other than a sense of shared national belonging. Surveying these portraits, a foreigner may very well feel more affected by the story of a victim because he or she practises the same profession, shares a common passion, is the same age or is in an identical family situation. This is particularly evident when the link between the victims and the concerned person stems from the fact that they belong to the same 'social circle',[42] one that goes beyond national borders, such as religious communities and certain professional or sporting communities. See, for example, these two messages from French men who reacted to 9/11 *as firefighters*:

Having spent my entire career with the PARIS FIRE BRIGADE, I can only express my emotion and admiration for these valorous firefighters who committed themselves with courage and abnegation to help the victims of this cowardly and appalling attack. 'Save Others or Perish' was our motto. Your men knew how to highlight this maxim and apply it with abnegation. I bow deeply before their remains.[43]

I am thinking of all those families who have lost one of their loved ones, in particular the Firemen, myself having been an auxiliary firefighter from 1941 (I was 15 years old) working on the bombed sites of railway hubs in the Paris region. My support and my prayers go out to all.[44]

An entire career as a firefighter in one case, a shorter experience but an event that happened at a decisive moment in a life – these proved, in the ordeal of the attacks of 9/11, to be the source of a feeling of personal concern. If we find here a sense of common belonging to the 'great family of firefighters', so to speak, this feeling is experienced in the singular mode of a *personal reason*, as a kind of elective affinity bringing the person concerned closer to *certain* victims in particular.

A factor of the same nature can be identified in the reactions aroused in Europe by the kidnapping and assassination of Daniel Pearl by members of Al-Qaeda, already mentioned. While Judith Butler could easily feel concerned by Pearl's fate, this was not true of everyone. Denis Jeambar complained about this in an editorial in *L'Express*:

> Daniel Pearl was an American, but *he was primarily a journalist* and, as such, a defender of these universal values, the freedom to think and publish. [...] French and European indignation, so prompt to express itself when it came to denouncing the treatment of the Taliban prisoners in Guantanamo, should thus have been voiced loud and clear. Alas! We did not hear a thing. Or hardly anything.[45]

The invocation of the values embodied by the profession of journalist, thereby placed on a pedestal as a herald (or even hero) of democracy, is part of a clear attempt to 'boost' the cause of Daniel Pearl and win him support. But the fact remains that if Denis Jeambar is indignant at the lack of impact this murder had in France, it is primarily because he is himself a journalist. It seems clear that outside the United States, those who shared with Daniel Pearl the status of journalist (or intellectual, if one thinks of the book Bernard-Henri Lévy wrote about him) were more inclined than others to feel concerned by his fate. So what applies to the 'great family of firefighters' also applies to the 'great family of journalists'. The attack on *Charlie Hebdo* brought this out even more clearly, as journalists from all over the world, those mainly concerned by the event, contributed to extending its scope – as the slogan 'I am Charlie' was itself launched by a journalist.

'The more we knew about them, the more we could wrestle with our own grief',[46] as Paul Auster wrote of the victims of 9/11. He is no doubt right: the portraits of the victims of terrorist attacks do not merely designate which lives deserved to be mourned, they also as it were allow the people who weep over these portraits to start to understand the source of their emotion. In modern societies, as Simmel was the first to point out, each individual is at the intersection of many 'social circles',[47] and there are thus many ways in which people can feel personally concerned by an event taking place thousands of kilometres away that does not affect them directly. Understanding why they are affected involves them identifying the 'social circle' linking them to this event and bringing them closer to those who are its victims. Hence individuals can be led to express solidarity with these victims by providing them with personal details about themselves. This explains the impression that some messages of reaction to terrorist attacks are replicating the anecdotal aspect of the portraits of victims published in the press. Indeed, anecdotes are more important than one might think.

Reacting as a singular person

Let us go back again to the message posted on the online forum of *Libération* six days after the Madrid bombings.[48] Its author, who signs as 'Fran', does not just mention the victims whose image or story have had a powerful impact on him. He also writes a few words about himself:

> I live in the Pyrénées-Orientales, Roussillon, right in the south, 30 km from the Spanish border. I own a house on the Costa Brava where I will spend a few days as soon as I can. On 11 March I was there.

One might think that this element is enough to explain why Fran was personally affected by the Madrid bombings. But the Costa Brava is closer to Barcelona or Perpignan than to Madrid, and not all those who lived there felt as concerned as he did – to such an extent that he took an interest in the stories of the victims, sought information about one of them whose photo he had seen, and posted a message of several paragraphs on an Internet forum. Fran knows this, and that is why his whole story tends to this conclusion:

> I can again see the Atocha station, from which, as a seven-year-old child, I left Madrid, the city where I was born fifty years ago. I can hear Rafaelillo, our neighbour from Tetuan, on the platform of the station, telling me never to forget my country and singing me a song entitled 'El Emigrante'. No, Rafaelillo, I have not forgotten. It's 5.20 a.m. and I can't sleep.

This is the key point: not only does Fran live near the Spanish border and possesses a house in Spain where he was on the day of the attacks, but above all, Spain is his country of origin, he was born in Madrid and left it as a child, from Atocha station, the epicentre of the bombings. The terrorist attack therefore concerns him personally because it suddenly brought back to the surface the memory of a decisive biographical event that happened where the bombs exploded. While he is not directly affected by the attack, and has no friends or family to mourn among the victims, Fran is concerned personally because, by striking the Atocha station, it is a significant place in his own life story that the terrorists have attacked. To explain this, he has no other means at his disposal than to relate this personal story.

It must be emphasized: at no time did Fran react to the Madrid bombings explicitly as a 'Spaniard'. Many others on the forum did so, but not him; and indeed, after reading these other messages, he wrote at the beginning of his: 'I was shocked by the testimony of our Spanish friends.' So one might deduce that he is of French nationality. But this is only a supposition, for all that we know from what he writes is where he lives, where he was on the day of the attack, and where he was born: nothing is said of any national belonging, to one country or to another. At no point did he write something like 'Although I have lived in France for years, today I feel more Spanish than ever.' Moreover, he does not say that he is a 'Madrilenian' any more than he calls himself 'Spanish'. What he feels about the attack is simply not any firm sense of collective belonging, but more a purely personal concern, which can be expressed only in the first person singular. That he devotes more than a quarter of his message to telling the story of Patricia and her parents thereby assumes its full meaning. What matters for him is not just the story of the youngest victim of the Madrid bombings, but the story of the daughter of a young couple of immigrants, who came from Poland to Spain, *just as* he had come from Spain to France. Her story attests to the fact that the terrorists were not so much attacking 'Spaniards' or 'Madrilenians' as, first and foremost, human individuals with different origins and singular lives. The singular story of the child of immigrants who lost their lives in the Madrid bombings is echoed by the singular story of a child born in Madrid who emigrated to France and who, now an adult, is horrified by the attack. A seven-year-old boy left his home town from the station where a seven-month baby has just lost her life: a personal sense of concern is woven by this shuttling backwards and forwards.

'All this is just to tell you that ...'

People who respond to a terrorist attack by giving details about themselves, such as Fran, are generally ambivalent about the attack and its victims; they have with these a relationship of both distance and closeness. They feel close *even though* something keeps them at bay. The narrative thus responds to the need to reduce the distance between the person concerned and the victims. In some cases, it is the social distance of the one who lives here, where the attack occurred, but was born elsewhere; in others, it is the geographical distance of the one who was born here but left to live elsewhere. The two kinds of distance imply that concern – or at the very least the intensity of its feelings – is not self-evident. A message written by a young student from Liverpool after the London bombings and specifying that he came from a north-western district of London also demonstrates this:

> The 7/7/05 was meant to be a day I would never forget, my girlfriend and fellow classmates were graduating to be Dr's that afternoon in Liverpool University. I turned on the radio that morning to hear devastating news, I was first shocked and confused, I then heard that a bomb had gone off at Edgware Road, where my Mum passes through every morning. I desperately tried ringing her, but it just rang out. My father would not answer nor my sister. I just broke down and cried, my girlfriend (Charlie) whose special day this was meant to be had to comfort me. I was so angry at the people who could cause/breed such mindless victimisation. I can only try and imagine what the victims' families are going through. My prayers and thoughts are with you, and I can only hope that we never have to go through anything like this.[49]

It is only through a narrative that this student can tell the victims how close he feels to them, even though he experienced the attacks at a distance, in Liverpool, because this feeling of closeness absolutely refuses to be circumscribed to a sense of belonging to the British nation, or even to the city of London where he was born. He insists more on the fact that, in this particular case, being a native of London means that he personally knows the places hit by the bombs, that his mother passes through one of them every morning, and that, on hearing the news of the attacks, he was first and foremost worried about her. His first experience of the event, from this point of view, was exactly the same as that of Londoners who did actually lose a loved one. And even if he was lucky enough not to be affected, the attacks had an even greater impact on him, because, in addition, it occurred on a day that had a special meaning for him.

Using a personal story to make explicit the specific reasons one has to feel deeply affected by a terrorist attack is a way of highlighting what links us to those who are victims and showing how close they are to us, in the same way that, in the obituary portraits of the deceased, highlighting their social ties through anecdotal narratives helps make them familiar to us. In the life stories told by the persons concerned by the attacks, many things are mere anecdotes and could for this reason seem, at first sight, inappropriate or out of place in a message of condolences. To explain to the New Yorkers he wrote to after 9/11 why he felt 'upset' – this is the term he used – by the tragedy that had struck them, a Frenchman named Patrick composed a meticulous narrative where he detailed, inter alia, his passion for jazz, a concert by Duke Ellington at the Salle Pleyel in 1969, and the unforgettable impression made on him that same year by Neil Armstrong's first steps on the Moon.[50] Another wrote:

> I sympathize with all the families of the deceased ... I know New York only through books, TV and cinema. How can anyone forget George Gershwin's magnificent music in *Rhapsody in Blue*, Cary Grant and Jean Fontaine at the top of the Empire State Building in *Love Affaire*[51] Grace Kelly/Frank Sinatra as sailors on leave in New York *On Town*,[52] Nathalie Wood[53] in *West Side Story*, Woody Allen in *Manhattan*. And the Hymn which will remain forever in the collective memory and that we will never be able to listen to without a pang: 'New York, New York' by the great Mr Frank Sinatra (of whom I am an unconditional admirer).[54]

All of which, intrinsically, have very little to do with 9/11, but nevertheless allow this Frenchman to explain to the New York victims why he feels close to them and particularly concerned by what has happened to them. Taking care to specify in parentheses that he is an 'unconditional admirer' of Frank Sinatra, whose name remains forever linked to what is probably the most famous song that has ever been written about New York, must be understood, in this context, as a way of attesting to the sincerity and strength of his attachment to a city he knows only through its cultural products.

In the same way, a French student from Rennes also wrote after 9/11:

> I also have to tell you that I experienced this attack as a violation of my person, for how could I not feel a bit American? I grew up with American movies and sports such as basketball and US football, and for me the biggest stars were almost all American, from the world of either sport or cinema. How could I not feel concerned when the freedom I enjoy today I owe to your country, but above all to those thousands of young Americans who died to deliver us from tyranny, a little more than fifty years ago?[55]

What may seem to be only insignificant details contribute in fact to personalize and modulate the expression of a solidarity which here follows a more impersonal pathway: the sense of a 'historic debt' owed by the French to the Americans, dating back to the Second World War. The link between these two ways of feeling concerned is also very clear from a message such as this one:

191

I am French, I am 27 years old and I was born in a city in the centre of France called Châteauroux. This city was after the war under the control of the Americans who had installed a base there and provided many of the inhabitants with work. Today, I live in Caen in Normandy.

In April 1992, I went to your country, to Boston, and spent a day in New York. I climbed up the Empire State Building and saw its two great towers soaring over Manhattan.

If I tell you all this, it is just to tell you that I feel concerned both at the historical level and by the sympathy I have for your people.[56]

'*All this is just to tell you that...*': the expression is worth dwelling on as it so clearly expresses what is at stake here. All these personal stories are not pointless: they have a specific purpose, which is to express to just the right extent the emotions of the person who feels concerned about the plight of the victims of the terrorist attack and to demonstrate that, in spite of the distance, such a person feels close to them. Remembering the historical ties between the French and the Americans does not in itself accurately express what this young resident of Caen feels about the victims of 9/11: this also relies on the fact that he visited New York and saw with his own eyes the Twin Towers. All the autobiographical details one can give in response to a terrorist attack, however confusing they at times may seem, make sense only in connection with this objective.

Thus Patrick, after having told in detail of his passion for American jazz musicians, also wrote:

All this is just to tell you how much what happened recently, on 11 September 2001, upset me.[57]

One could also quote many other messages from French people reacting to 9/11 that use this formula, but one of them in particular deserves closer attention: the one written by a young woman from Toulouse in the aftermath of the explosion at the AZF factory, which aroused fears in France that the attack in the United States ten days earlier might be replicated:

My name is Alexandra, I'm 17 years old. I'm in my first year of medical studies. My greatest dream would be to be a doctor and to be able to save all those people who died under the rubble of the Twin Towers. I do not know anyone there but the news has nevertheless been hard to take in. It could have been us, they could have killed us here. [...]

I live in Toulouse in France. Yesterday, a petrochemical plant exploded, there was a big tremor and a huge explosion. We were very scared, we thought it was a terrorist attack. [...]

There were 30 confirmed deaths and 100 injured: these figures are minimal compared to those in the US but they touched us deeply. I saw so many wounded, it was horrible. [...] I tell myself how lucky I was. My parents too, as a shopping centre almost collapsed on top of them, they ran to the cars. *All this is just to tell you that* I sympathize with you.[58]

This one-and-a-half-page letter is ultimately more about the explosion at the AZF factory than 9/11. Only by recounting in detail what she experienced the day before can Alexandra manage to express her feelings for the victims of 9/11. In fact, everything suggests that she would not have felt the need to write to them if she had not experienced this disaster and feared to fall victim to a terrorist attack in turn: 9/11 could have remained for her just another news item, certainly 'hard to take in', but not of personal concern to her. The interest of this latter case lies also in the way it reminds us that it is not so obvious that a terrorist attack, however murderous, spectacular and widely reported it may be, will touch us in anything other than a superficial way. So how are we to interpret the fact that some, like Patrick, write that they feel so 'upset'? Might this just be a word?

What being upset means

Who we are, including at the most intimate and personal levels, is closely connected to the society in which we live and the world around us. Any change, any event which occurs in this world is therefore likely to have an impact on our identity. And vice versa, as George H. Mead remarked, no one can hope to change society, and still less the world, without first changing oneself.[59] Feeling concerned by a terrorist attack, whether this occurs in our own country or elsewhere in the world, is therefore an experience which engages what George H. Mead calls our 'self' – witness the emotion we feel in such circumstances. And this experience is likely to have on us a more or less profound, more or less lasting impact:[60] the fact that some people may call themselves 'upset' does not refer to anything else. This upheaval is not only emotional, it is an upsetting of the *self*. This can be seen, for example, in the testimony of the sociologist Carolyn Ellis, who explained that, after 9/11, she had felt the need to reflect on herself, on her experiences and past ordeals, her relationship to others and the world, so that she could integrate what she felt on 9/11 into it, and give it meaning. She then began to write what became, in her own terms, an essay in 'autoethnography'.[61] It was a process of the same nature that led so many people concerned by the attacks of 9/11, or those in Madrid and London, to send their victims a personal message as a sign of solidarity.

For some, as we have seen, the experience of feeling concerned may involve nothing other than the reaffirmation, or activation, of a sense of common belonging. Carolyn Ellis notes that, on 11 September 2001, she felt 'American' as never before.[62] This already constitutes a modification of people's selves: this sense of common belonging then comes to the forefront of their identity, and relegates the rest to the background. No matter who these persons are: in the face of the attack, they first and foremost feel American, Madrilenians, Londoners, etc. For others, on the other hand, this experience is reflected in a deeper sense of upset, as their concern passes through a less obvious channel: it brings into play a part of themselves which might have hitherto seemed secondary, but which suddenly attains a particular importance, since it is through its intermediary that the 'intimate union', to use an eloquent expression of Dewey's,[63] is formed between these people and the situation. In the second case, it is *who* these people are that takes precedence over what they usually are; their singular emotion can thus no longer be expressed (solely) in an impersonal fashion. Expressing what they feel in the most adequate way requires them to provide a narrative of themselves, even if it is only two lines long. Paul Ricœur has demonstrated this: who a person is (what he calls their *ipse*-identity) and what he or she is (*idem*-identity) are two facets of the self which are irreducible to one another and which can be composed together only through a narrative.[64]

The narrative form is therefore self-evident when individuals, by trying to express their emotion, realize that they have reasons for being moved, which *belong only to them*, even if those reasons may be added to others which they share with thousands or millions of other individuals. Where, for example, one particular Londoner begins his message for the victims of the 7 July 2005 attacks by admitting that he does not know what to write because he cannot find words to express what he feels, then states that he is Irish and has lived in London for eight years,[65] this should not be interpreted as a way of 'filling' the space, writing something *despite everything*, for lack of knowing how to express his feelings in a better way. There is no better way for this adoptive Londoner to express *his* emotion, which is due to the special relationship he has with this city and its inhabitants, made of distance and closeness. By providing this brief narrative of himself, he finds precisely those words which he lacked. He comes up with a personal response to the collective ordeal and affirms his singular voice: it is therefore logical that he signs his message by giving his name and city of origin ('Elmar, Dublin – Ireland') rather than by an anonymous formula as others do.

We have already seen how foreigners who have settled in a city struck by a terrorist attack can react as inhabitants of this city but at the same time may need to give a brief personal narrative to explain why they feel all the more concerned in that this is actually the first time since they moved there that they feel they truly belong to it.[66] This type of reaction, which combines a feeling of belonging with a feeling of singularity, has its counterpart in people originating from the city that has been struck, but who moved away a long time ago. While their 'roots' may have faded over the years spent abroad, losing the importance they once had in their daily lives, these roots are suddenly brought back into the foreground by the feeling of being concerned:

> I'm a Madrilenian and I live in Italy ... Since 11/03/04, I feel more Spanish. We will not forget you.[67]

In this sense, the experience of being concerned seems to be experienced as a kind of biographical turning point, including by persons not originally from the cities and countries under attack. Martine, a resident of the Paris region, wrote two days after 9/11:

> I can say that since Tuesday, 11 September at 8.55 am, I have been an American ... at heart.[68]

And this is not just a simple word, for if 9/11 marks a turning point for her, this is because it brings her previous experiences to the forefront and suddenly gives new importance to what hitherto were merely biographical details. Her declaration therefore calls for a narrative that supports and justifies it:

> I experienced this tragedy practically live on television, and my heart will bear its imprint forever. I felt helpless and thought to myself: this is war ... For me, N.Y. was a memory of youth, I went there in 1977, at 20, I had been shopping at the World Trade Center ... Now, I have American family in Santa Clara, CA. I was there again this summer (via American Airlines).[69]

Even the name of the airline used on her last trip to the United States now has a particular significance, since two of the planes hijacked by the terrorists on 11 September 2001 belonged to the fleet of American Airlines. A personal sense of concern draws on this too, however parenthetically: the writer feels that she is close to the victims because she belongs to the community of users of the same air carrier.

Of course, the real scope of these biographical turning points does not fail to raise questions: they are expressed under the impact of emotion, so can we really imagine that they are deep and lasting? Does this Frenchwoman still feel American at heart today? She might well have demonstrated against the war in Iraq a year and a half later and then felt less American than ever; then maybe she rejoiced at the election of Barack Obama in 2008 and again felt empathy with the United States. We can also imagine that the Madrilenian woman who lives in Italy has, since 2004, experienced events that have led her to feel henceforth more Italian than at the time of the Madrid bombings. Living a self-reconfiguration in the event of an ordeal that concerns us does not in any way prejudice future reconfigurations. This is the whole problem of self-constancy in the mode of ipseity: our ability to keep promises has, according to Paul Ricœur, the function of regulating this.[70] Hence, some testify to their solidarity with the victims by making them a promise – and the message of solidarity then becomes a matter of giving one's word. We can already put this interpretation on the innumerable messages that end with a formula such as 'We will not forget you.' But some people go further, like this Londoner in July 2005:

> At 09:47 am in Tavistock Place on 7th July 2005 I had just walked past the bus as it exploded. I am lucky and grateful to be alive. I think of you poor souls who died instantly. I will do my best to be a better person in your honour. God rest your souls and may the angels watch over you for evermore.[71]

Or a Frenchman after the Madrid bombings:

> *To all the dead*
> I commit myself to Change
> Your death will not be in vain.[72]

It seems, then, that in such cases, which are singularly rare, the experience of being concerned can produce, even more than a biographical turning point, something which is tantamount to an 'existential revolution'[73] (note the way that the word 'Change' is capitalized in the second message): the self which is concerned posits an act that will provide a basis for the future – one that will, it is hoped, live up to the event.

The self and the test of emotion

In order to understand how feeling concerned by a terrorist attack engages the self, one last type of message, just as rare, still needs to be taken into consideration. Contrary to all of those messages quoted so far, this type shows what might at first glance be taken for an indifference to the suffering of the victims. But being indifferent, strictly speaking, would mean not reacting to what has happened to them, let alone taking the time to write to them. These messages attest, therefore, to a form of misalignment between the self and the situation that concerns it, which makes us view them as unseemly or shocking. One of them, the email sent by an Australian woman to the embassy of the United Kingdom in Ireland two weeks after the London bombings, seems to have aroused some discomfort in the secretary who received it, since, instead of classifying it with the other messages, she forwarded it to a colleague:

> I don't know anyone in London, in fact I don't really know any one in Australia either who wants to talk to me.
>
> I feel sorry for those who died in London though, but you know the last thing I heard about London was some time ago when there was a news report about a fellow on a bus who literally tore the eyes out of another man's head with his hand, because he felt like it, it seemed to be.
>
> Ever since then, I have thought that maybe London hasn't been a good place to go. And now it isn't. Perhaps that is why it has happened.
>
> Or perhaps it is just a sign of the times, when things get boring, noone has a job they like and life drags on.
>
> I can't say, because unless I am depressed, I mean really depressed I can't feel sorry enough for myself to approach anyone else, because they all seem so mean lately.[74]

Although the title of the message is 'Expressing condolences', this seems to be a radically misleading description of what the message is doing. A hasty 'I feel sorry for those who died' is immediately counterbalanced by remarks that may seem out of place, or even incoherent, and the message ends with the admission of an inability to feel sorry if only for oneself, and all the more so for others. We are faced with the message of someone trying to express condolences to the victims of the attack, but who openly states that she is unable to do so, given her depression and lack of human contact.

This case shows that the experience of concern not only engages the self but as it were submits it to an ordeal, puts it to the test. Someone who is separated from interactions with others and the recognition that these interactions should bring, and who in consequence lacks self-esteem, just like someone in a situation of psychological distress, whose self is 'broken' or 'cracked', may not be able to sympathize adequately with the fate of the victims. Thus one Londoner writes:

I can find no words to express my sadness for all those people who died for no point at all. I only wish it was me – who have no reason to live.[75]

Likewise, someone affected by a recent bereavement ends up talking more about this personal mourning than what he feels for the people killed in the London bombings:

Today is the first anniversary of the death of my best friend, Lindi ***. There is so much pain with loss. My friend was killed in a senseless road traffic accident. I miss her. Today and always. Love and peace and truth will always endure.[76]

In a book of condolences for the victims of the London bombings, in fact, not a word in this message is explicitly intended for them: this cannot fail to attract attention. We might almost have the impression that the book of condolences is being hijacked to commemorate someone whose death has no connection with this attack.

Finally, it is probable that the secretaries of the Mémorial de Caen in charge of receiving the letters of Operation 'Fraternally' also experienced some discomfort in September 2001 when they came across this message:

My heart is full of hate:

childhood raped, woman in difficulty loving a homosexual man.

This duel of love and hatred,

I live it, in myself, every day.

Before hoping that the problems on a human scale may be solved, I pray to the Heavens to help me find once again the strength to lay down my arms of anger, resentment and repression towards my beloved, to open myself up, as if giving birth to Love, so that I can behave in a kindly way towards my neighbour and my children.[77]

One can, of course, take this message as the distress call of a distraught woman who is using Operation 'Fraternally' as an opportunity to launch a message in a bottle. But what resists this interpretation and arouses a certain discomfort are the words 'Before hoping that the problems on a human scale may be solved', which create a hierarchy between misfortunes, and view the author's problems as more important than those of the rest of humanity. In a message ostensibly addressed to the American people as a mark of solidarity with the victims of 9/11, this woman says very explicitly that she prefers to 'pray to the Heavens' to save her family rather than for those who perished in the attacks. So this woman, too, is not expressing her condolences, but a mere grievance: she is communicating the pain that dwells in her every day and rather than drawing on this in order to sympathize with the victims of 9/11, by establishing a parallel between her pain and theirs, she gives the opposite impression of contrasting them. In short, we might see this as a message of grievance-against-grievance.

This message, like the others, is undeniably personal: a singular person is engaged in it and confesses intimate things, opening up his or her heart. The problem is that this heart as it opens up does not actually turn towards anybody. The difference between these messages that appear inappropriate or embarrassing and the other self-narratives produced in reaction to terrorist attacks lies basically in the place occupied by victims to whom these messages are supposed to be addressed. If a detailed account of a passion for jazz or American movies seems less shocking, this is because it leads to the formula 'all this is just to tell you that ...' and serves to emphasize an emotional closeness to the victims of 9/11. These messages establish a person-to-person relationship that, in extreme cases, even takes the form of a promise. In this they attest to the fact that their authors have successfully passed what Luc Boltanski calls the 'test' of emotion, that is, they are able to exteriorize their interiority, so as to establish between themselves and their interlocutors a heart-to-heart relationship, 'from interiority to interiority'.[78] And, as Luc Boltanski suggests, it is precisely this which gives them their moving character, including for a third party.

In fact, at the beginning of the message he posted on the forum of *Libération* after the Madrid bombings, Fran begins by explaining that he has read all the other messages already posted, and he writes:

> I found some really nice answers, words of support and encouragement that honour their authors. I notice that women are more sensitive to the distress of our Spanish neighbours. They express a moving compassion in the face of anguish. I want first to congratulate, and then to thank, these anonymous people, they will recognize themselves. You're great![79]

Independently of the statement that women are more sensitive than men to the fate of victims (I will not risk generalizing this to the other sources discussed here), what should draw our attention is the phrase 'a moving compassion'. It sums up what is at stake: a successful expression of emotion must itself arouse emotion. In so doing, it must be able to provide comfort to the victims, and encourage a third party in turn to feel concerned. It is in the same sense that the experience of concern comprises a 'test' for the self: an already weakened self may well not be able to express its feelings adequately, while those who manage to 'find the right words' to do this emerge transformed: *therefore*, they have grown – which is the reason why Fran congratulates the authors of the messages that have moved him and calls them 'great'. Undoubtedly this is also what one might have thought about the upsurge of solidarity triggered by the January 2015 attacks in Paris: sometimes, people are great.

SOLIDARITY IN THE SINGULAR

Here is what a friend wrote to me in January 2015 to explain what she felt after the attack on the premises of *Charlie Hebdo*:

> *Charlie*, for me, was my teens and the birth of a political awareness (along with *Le Monde Diplo*, but that was a much more boring read!). It was a friend's tee-shirt with a drawing by Charb: 'Allô, is that the Préfecture? He's coming in going out coming in going out!'

For me, it was the front page of an issue published a few weeks after 9/11, with a drawing by Jul showing bin Laden singing the Georges Brassens song 'La mauvais réputation'; I'd had this image stuck up on the wall of my student digs for a long time. Neither she nor I could have predicted that these insignificant details of our lives – a friend's tee-shirt, one of many posters – would one day give us the feeling of being more closely concerned by a terrorist attack than other people. Being French, having lived in Paris, still living there, having been a reader of *Charlie*, or still being a reader – all this inclined us, of course, not to be indifferent to the events of January 2015. But it was under the impact of emotion that these two details come back to both of us, like significant elemnts that suddenly made sense, explaining our reactions, our feeling of being concerned in the first person singular, in other words having our own personal and unique reasons for feeling touched.

Thousands of people may have had a personal story to tell in order to explain what they feel after a terrorist attack: however, this does not mean that sociological analysis in this area is condemned to mere casuistry. Even if the factors highlighted by different groups to explain their sense of concern are each time experienced and presented as singular, the mass of the aggregated reactions does enable certain recurrent patterns, or types of factor, to emerge. The study of the reactions to the attacks of 9/11, Madrid and London makes it possible to detect three such patterns, which can be observed irrespective of whether the persons concerned live in the country struck by the terrorists or elsewhere. But there is nothing to say that they are specific to reactions to terrorist attacks. There are, on the contrary, quite good reasons to believe that they can be found at work in our reactions to other tragedies. What they allow us to grasp, at bottom, is a certain sensitivity to the suffering of others that is characteristic of 'singularist' societies,[1] where even our connection with other people proceeds from an exacerbated sense of 'I'.

The attachment to place

Sometimes the feeling of being personally affected by a distant event is due to something altogether coincidental and independent of the person, something that could easily be explained by circumstances. For example, one young Frenchwoman, Aurélie, tells the victims of 9/11 that when she heard the news about the World Trade Center and turned on the television, she was in the middle of babysitting and had just finished a 500-piece jigsaw depicting the skyline of New York that she had completed with the child she was looking after. 'The jigsaw will stay on the wall of my room forever', she concludes.[2] Had she been finishing a jigsaw puzzle depicting anything else, Aurélie would not have experienced 9/11 in quite the same way. But apart from such exceptional cases, the most common form of personal concern usually draws on structural elements that are part and parcel of our socio-biographical trajectories. The first and most obvious of these is some form of attachment to the place where the terrorist attack occurs. 'Place' does not just mean 'country' or 'city': if the attack occurs on the premises of a newspaper, everything that connects us closely or remotely to this newspaper involves this factor of concern. To have the front page of an issue of *Charlie Hebdo* stuck on my wall for a long time is a form of attachment to the place of an attack. To have friends living in the same neighbourhood as the paper's editorial office is another.

'This city will always be a part of me'

I have already mentioned several times in previous chapters the cases of people who feel personally concerned as a result of family roots linking them to the city and/or country struck by terrorists: the fact of being born there, or of having relatives from there. For example, after 9/11, a Frenchwoman from Toulon wrote:

My father was born in Philadelphia, I have family somewhere on that continent, and I feel very deeply affected.[3]

But this is not the only way that one can be attached to the place of a terrorist attack. Experiences play a part too, such as having spent part of your life there, even if only a few months, and remained marked by this period. This may explain why Peter, for example, felt more concerned than most New Yorkers by the Madrid bombings, almost as much as he had been by 9/11:

> After 11 September, I came to Madrid from NY to escape the pain and the sadness that I felt. For me, Madrid was a marvellous dream, and it was here that I had discovered how to be happy again. I am so sorry that you too have had to suffer terrorism. We must continue to seek peace. I love you, Madrid.[4]

Like him, many people go out of their way, in the messages they address to the victims of this attack, to note the importance of Madrid in their lives. Wilfy, a British woman, wrote for example:

> My heart goes out to all those that were directly affected. Madrid has been a big part of my life and this inconsideration for human life saddens me. My heart will always be in Finnegans, Plaza de salasas.[5]

And Hélène, a Frenchwoman, put it like this:

> I am French, but Madrid is my second city.[6]

Others sign collective messages indicating each time where they come from and where they live, in order to show clearly that they are all, in one way or another, attached to Madrid:

> Melika (Madrid/Paris), Matthieu (Paris and Madrid), Guillerme (Madrid/ Corunna), Mamá (Buenos Aires/Madrid).[7]

Finally, there is Hetty, a Dutch woman who explains that 'Spain has always been part of her life' since her studies in Madrid in 1963 and 1964 and her marriage in Alcala de Henares. She goes on to say that despite settling in Holland, she and her husband, originally from Guinea, insisted on returning to Alcala de Henares to have each of their three children baptized where they had been married. This attachment to the city of Alcala is now all the more important for her as it was from here that, on the morning of 11 March 2004, the terrorists and many of their victims began their journeys.[8]

Examples of this type could be multiplied, for the Madrid bombings as well as the London bombings:

> Even though I no longer live in London, I was here for two years, and became a part of it. It will always be part of me.[9]

> As a former Londoner, now living not far from New York City, the event have a special resonance.[10]

> The 7th July has brought me closer to my fellow Londoners than any event since I went to live abroad 13 years ago.[11]

After 9/11 as well, a Frenchman called Bernard explains that he feels concerned because he has 'two countries: France and the USA', then tells the victims his life story to support this assertion. In his teens, he saw his village liberated by General Patton's division (and drove a jeep for the first time in his life), he started to learn English and in 1951 was given a Marshall Plan scholarship to study agricultural techniques in the United States. He stayed there for a year, working on several farms, including one in the State of New York, before visiting a dozen other states. Thereafter, he had returned to the United States some twenty times.[12] Marie-France, a teacher from Toulouse, also tells how in the early stages of her career she was able to take part in an exchange programme funded by the New York postal services, which had enabled her to reside in Manhattan in summer 1973, while the Twin Towers were nearing completion.[13]

Student stays alone constitute a significant reason for feeling concerned, especially when they happened recently. Just as students who are nationals of the country that has been hit by an attack may take the initiative and organize demonstrations of solidarity in the countries where they happen to be at the time of the attack,[14] students who are foreigners to that country, but who had stayed there recently, are more likely to feel concerned:

> My name is Audrey, I'm French. I spent 3 months in Madrid. They were the most wonderful months of my life, with the magic of that city and its residents that I will never forget. That is why I wanted to pay tribute to those who died on 11 March and also to their loved ones. A kiss full of sunshine to all Madrilenians.[15]

And if, thousands of miles from London, a young Singaporean felt particularly affected by the 7 July 2005 attacks, this was also because he had studied in the British capital two years before:

204

London is very dear to my heart as I studied at UCL in 2002–2003. It was a shock to see familiar places like Russell Square and Tavistock Square caught up in the terrible attacks. My prayers go to the victims and their families and loved ones, and to all affected by the tragedy. Stay strong, London, and continue to be the vibrant city that you are.[16]

This attachment to the cities or countries hit by the terrorist attacks, an attachment rooted in the fact of having been born there or having passed part of your life there, may be all the stronger as it usually involves knowing people who live there, family, friends, or even just acquaintances.

'My sister lives there'

You will recall the student living in Liverpool quoted in the previous chapter, who said how he had been worried about his parents in London on the day of the attack.[17] Like him, many people who experience terrorist attacks at a distance feel personally concerned because they fear that something has happened to people they know, and their first reflex is then to try and join them. On 14 March 2004, Margaret, living in Sutherland in Scotland, send a message to Sonia, an old friend of hers from Madrid, when she couldn't get through by phone:

I really must write to find out that you are all safe in view of the terrible atrocity which struck Madrid on Thursday 11 of March.[18]

Her friend Sonia then came to leave a message at the Atocha station so that everyone could learn about the expression of condolences addressed also to those 'Madrilenian compatriots'. She was far from being the only one to have done such a thing: Isabel, for example, went to Atocha and left a photocopy of a German letter accompanied by its translation into Spanish and a small note stating that the author of the letter, Isle, is a German who is 90 years old and has always loved Spain:

Dear Isabel,

The news that reached us yesterday from Madrid shocked me so much that I am writing to you to pass on to the Spanish nation, and in particular to those people who have been wounded by this terrible attack, my most sincere condolences. I feel united with them.[19]

In one of London's registers of condolences, someone also took the trouble to copy by hand the electronic message received from a South African girlfriend.[20] Past relationships are thus transformed not only into

205

factors of concern but also into vectors of solidarity, serving as a way of transmitting to the victims of the attacks the compassion of those who are concerned by what is happening to them – in the same way as twinning links at the institutional level.[21]

But this means that it is not necessary to know a city personally to feel attached to it: you just need to know people there or have friends or family living or staying there. One French couple felt all the more empathy with New Yorkers as their son had arrived there a few days before 9/11:

We have a son: Xavier, 22, who has been in New York for a week living at ___ (*postal address*). He is supposed to be there for about 3 months. What is he going to do?

We were among those anguished parents waiting for the reassuring phone call. And it came at around 9.30 p.m. We then thought about those people who were less lucky than us.[22]

Christine, a woman in a similar situation, also writes:

I was very affected by this tragedy [...]. My sister happened to be in New York on that day. She was 200 m from the World Trade Center, in the subway. She was going to see the Statue of Liberty. She was very shocked to experience this on her first day in the United States. She had been planning to visit the 2 twin towers that day, Tuesday, 11 September 2001. I am thinking of all the victims and their families.[23]

And after the London bombings, Caroline, a Frenchwoman who had moved to Ireland, also sent the UK embassy a message, stating:

My sister leaves in London, it could have been her.[24]

Even if she hadn't been there on that day, Caroline would most likely still have felt personally concerned. In any case, Gisèle, a resident of Troyes who was on vacation in the Haute-Vienne when 9/11 occurred, took the trouble to send a card to the victims because, she explains:

I have a sister who lived for a few years in New York but she moved away. She could have been among those innocent victims.[25]

Finally, there is the remarkable case of a Frenchwoman who, from her village in the Vendée, wrote to the victims of 9/11:

In my living room, I have the photo of my eldest son, Druand, 29 years old today, who together with his partner saw in the New Year 2000 photographed on the terrace of the World Trade Center, it was very cold, a beautiful blue sky, New York behind them ... All this will ensure that, every day, I remember the horror that you have gone through.[26]

While this woman has probably never even been to New York and knows no one there, this ordinary family photo in her living room makes the place of the attacks familiar to her. This photo is, so to speak, the small door through which the world-historical event came into her private life and concerned her personally. And it should be emphasized that if this Frenchwoman feels concerned by 9/11, this is not through any sensitivity peculiar to her person (apart from the sensitivity she feels about anything affecting her son, closely or not), but through a third element – in this case a photo displayed in her living room – that suddenly turns out to be relevant as a factor of concern with regard to 9/11.

'I feel as if I were still there'

It is more than likely that, on 11 September 2001, this woman's son immediately remembered that photo taken at the top of the World Trade Center in the winter cold and that New Year's Day celebrated in New York a year and a half before the attacks. Tourist visits are of course another important factor of attachment to the place of a terrorist attack, a factor that is very often mentioned in the reactions to 9/11 in particular. For example, Pascale addresses to the victims a short and conventional message of condolence, taking care to add:

In addition, I am touched because I visited New York in 1994 and loved the city.[27]

Among Europeans passing through the 9/11 Tribute Center at Ground Zero, those who had visited New York in the past and remember the Twin Towers before their destruction mention it each time. One Italian man, for example, writes:

I went up the Tower in 1991 and there I thought how the man is great to think and build so beautiful things. Never I should have thought be able to destroy too.[28]

Jean-Claude, from the Paris region, also writes:

I am here today with my wife more than 10 years after having visited WTC. I wanted to tell to all Americans and especially for victims and parent's victims of this disaster how I am proud to be not French today

207

but American. Even if I am French living in Paris my heart is so close of you.[29]

And Stefan, from Hamburg:

> Today, I have come back to the place that, in 1999, left me with a completely different set of memories. I still cannot understand what happened in 2001. Feelings overwhelm me, I am on the edge of tears.[30]

It would, however, be unreasonable to assert that visits we make as tourists over the course of our lives help to make us a priori more sensitive to the dramatic events that may occur in all the countries we have visited. It is only in a certain situation, in the face of a given event, that a trip we made in the past may prove to be a relevant factor of concern. And again, as in the case of the photo displayed in a living room, this particular attachment formed through a journey can be incarnated in a certain object. An American living in Massachusetts says, on a visit to Ground Zero:

> Today is June 18, 2008 and this is my first visit to WTC since 1996. In 1996, I purchased a key chain of the WTC towers and kept it on my one piece of luggage. In April of 2002, I was in Florence, Italy and waited three days for my lost luggage. It finally appeared after spending time at an airport in Beirut, thanks to Air France. When my bag was returned, the keychain was gone – what a loss … I still miss my keychain & what it represented.[31]

What might again seem an insignificant anecdote turns out to be relevant, as it explains the personal relationship that one American man continues to have with 9/11.

It is not insignificant, moreover, that this American states that this is the first time he has been back to the site of the World Trade Center since one previous trip made five years before the attacks. Kat, a German woman, also indicates that her previous trip to New York in 1998 had been the first:

> I've been on the Twin Towers back in 1998 – my first visit to the USA – first time to NYC. I've always loved New York and always will! I still can't believe what happened and it still makes me cry.[32]

Thus, the persons concerned by terrorist attacks as a result of tourist visits can be divided into two categories. On the one hand, there are all those who are especially attached to the place of the attacks since they have been there several times. They usually have the special feature of stating in their message, out of solidarity, that they are determined not to be frightened by the terrorists and will continue to come as often as possible. We could quote many instances of this, but we will just mention the two most emblematic. An English couple, after the Madrid bombings, left the following message in Atocha Station:

> We love your country & people! Have visited 63 veces [*times*]! This wont stop us![33]

And after the London bombings, a Finnish man wrote:

> I've visited this city annually for ages now but no bombs or terrorists will scare me away.[34]

On the other hand, there are all those who, like Kat, had visited the site of the attacks only once before the fateful day. That just makes the visit all the more important and memorable, especially if it took place shortly before.

Jocelyne and Jeannine, after taking part in an organized trip to North America, successively wrote:

> In late May, I realized my dream by visiting part of Canada, Washington and New York. These two cities had a very great impact on me. [...] I feel as if I were still there and I'm still struggling to realize what has happened.

> It was my dream come true, three months ago, I will never forget the beauty of Washington that delighted me, the majesty of New York struck me dumb, and I can't imagine the horror of right now.[35]

Moreover, Peggy, a Dutch woman, returned to New York in 2007 and was all the more moved as her previous visit had taken place two days before 9/11:

> I just want to say that this tribute and visiting the WTC means a lot to me. Because this is the first time I visit NY after the attack in 2001 and all the memories are coming back. Actually I visited the World Trade center in 2001, 2 days before it happened ... So I just needed to pay my respect.[36]

A Greek woman in a similar situation also wrote:

> On 9/11 my nephew called and told me to turn on the television. The previous day I returned with my husband from New York where we had gone on vacation. I couldn't believe my eyes. That which had happened

was unbelievably tragic. So many innocents. Why? Why? Why? What did they do?[37]

The feeling of being personally affected by a terrorist attack is thus also due to a temporal factor. Firstly because the impression that you might have been among the victims is all the stronger when you visited the place struck by the terrorists two days ago rather than two years ago, but mostly because we grant dates a certain importance and a coincidence between them may give the impression of a temporal short-circuit bringing us symbolically closer to the attack and to the victims; witness the words of a Spanish couple:

> On our first trip to New York, we visited the Twin Towers. It was one of the most emblematic places in the city. In the video we made on 11 September 1991, just ten years before they were destroyed, you can still admire them and contemplate the magnificent view from the top. It's a real tragedy. [...] We are truly sorry about what happened, with all our heart.[38]

It is this second factor as such that we must now explore in greater depth.

The coincidence of dates

In one of the registers of condolences opened in London after the attacks of 7 July 2005, a Polish couple writes:

> And so, we're here to commemorate those,
> who had a bad luck on that day. We arrived to London also on 7/7 ...
> May it won't happen again.[39]

The only personal element in their message is the mention of the date on which the couple arrived in London. How is this to be explained? One might have thought that, if they had arrived two days earlier or later, they would not have taken the trouble to indicate the date. If they consider it appropriate to do so here, this is because they arrived in London on the very day of the attacks. The event coincided with their arrival in the city, and they attribute to this coincidence a particular significance (which is also evidenced by the dots, '...', after '7/7'), as if it somehow brought them closer to the victims, just as, in the previous message, the Spanish tourists stated that they had made a video of the World Trade Center exactly ten years to the day before 9/11.

The fact is, dates seem important to us – especially as some of them have a special personal meaning for us. Take for example the Liverpool student cited earlier[40] who began by stating that 7 July 2005 was meant to be an important date for him because his girlfriend had her PhD viva on that day. A German woman visiting Ground Zero in 2008 also says that 9/11 had a particular impact on her not only because she had been to the top of the towers in the past, but also because it was a special day for her and her family:

> I will never forget that day: on 11/09/2001, we organized a really nice party to celebrate our daughter Karen starting secondary school. I still can't really get my head around what happened. In 1986, I visited the observation deck of the World Trade Center.[41]

Many messages, such as this one, indicate a sense of personal concern underpinned or reinforced by a coincidence between the date of a terrorist attack and that of a celebration or memorable personal event. And the commonest case is undoubtedly that of a coincidence with one's birthday.

'My birthday will never be the same again'

She was born on 11 September: this is the first thing that Iris, who lives in China, highlights to explain her reaction to the attacks on the United States:

> My birthday is September 11th. Twenty minutes before the first plane crashed into the WTC, a friend was calling me from MA. & then we hung up & we went to class. When the news broke out, I didn't even know how to respond. What I thought of was my friend who just called me. So I tried to ring him, but time & time again the line couldn't get through. I was in fear, although I was miles away, in China.[42]

This message contrasts sharply with others left at the 9/11 Tribute Center by tourists from countries just as far from the epicentre of 9/11 as China, but who found it difficult to feel concerned by the event. For example Akiko, from Japan, wrote:

> When I got to know about 9/11 on TV, it was something irrelevant to me: it happened somewhere else and had nothing to do with me.[43]

And Robert, an Australian:

> I'll say honestly, as an Australian, this event never fully hit home with me. As most things that I watch from here come from Hollywood, and this event had always felt like a movie.[44]

Of course, the difference between the way these people experienced 9/11 and the way Iris did also stems from the fact that Iris has a friend in the

US and was talking to him by phone just before the attacks. One personal connection, perhaps even several, thus link her to the stricken country.

It is very common, however, that the coincidence of a terrorist attack with a birthday will be presented as the sole reason for considering yourself to be affected by it more than are other people. Here are just three examples:

> For all the families, friends, and acquaintances of the victims who have lost a part of their hearts on this day that has brought unhappiness to so many. We will always remember it, and especially myself, given that 11 March is the date of my birthday, and will always have this bad memory for me. We will keep you in our hearts.[45]

> From this year onwards, my birthday will never be the same again ...[46]

> Since Tuesday, the date of 11 September will remain in our memories, not as the date of my birthday but as a worldwide time of mourning. That day, we all became 'Americans'.[47]

The phenomenon is not confined to the younger generation, as one might imagine. In connection with the Madrid bombings, one Spanish woman wrote:

> It was my saddest birthday (my 74th).[48]

And an American man born on 11 September 1944 wrote about 9/11:

> I've never celebrated my Birthday since. I now know what my parents felt on 12-7-41.[49]

Aneta, a woman from Alsace living a few kilometres from the German border, also wrote:

> 11 September 2001: it was my 49th birthday and, I think, the saddest one of my life. I know no one in America but I weep for the dead and their families.[50]

Finally, Anne, a Parisian, on the eve of the 'Day of Mourning and Solidarity' with the victims of 9/11 observed in the European Union, wrote:

> It will be the day of my birthday, and at noon, when we observe the minutes of silence, I shall be exactly 47 years of age.[51]

To understand where this phenomenon comes from, we need to place the importance we attach to birthdays in a certain context. According to the historian Jean-Claude Schmitt, our preoccupation with knowing the exact day of our birth is thoroughly modern: it appeared only at the end of the Middle Ages. And the ritual celebration of that day every year became widespread and started to take the form that we know (with cake and candles) only in the nineteenth century.[52] The melody of the song 'Happy Birthday To You' goes back to 1893 and its lyrics to 1924, the French equivalent 'Joyeux anniversaire, nos vœux les plus sincères' to 1951.[53] The particular attention that we pay to birthdays is specific to our very singularist society in which each person is no longer valued simply as a human being endowed with reason (which corresponds to the classical individualism of the liberal thinkers and the philosophers of the Enlightenment, or what Simmel calls 'the individualism of simili-tude'), but as a personality unique in the world, born at a precise date (what Simmel calls 'an individualism of dissimilitude').[54] One of the first demonstrations of this singularism on an artistic and cultural level was German romanticism and, according to the available historical docu-ments, Goethe seems to have been particularly concerned about his birthday and its celebration: the first birthday cake was probably served on his fifty-third birthday, in 1802.[55] From this comes our feeling nowa-days that what coincides with our birthday has a profound resonance with our singular person, and touches on our 'deep nature'.[56]

'That day, I turned twenty'

However, it is clear that not all individuals born on 11 September or 11 March responded in a personal way to the terrorist attacks on those dates in 2001 and 2004. We can assume that the weight of the factor of concern depends on the degree to which a person is aware of his or her singularity and endeavours to cultivate it. Artists, who strive to achieve the highest level of expression and recognition for their individual sin-gularity,[57] would thus seem be particularly exposed to this phenomenon. Hence Richard Ashcroft, singer and leader of a British rock band that was in the charts in the 1990s, The Verve, said in a 2004 interview:

> I had my 30th birthday on 9/11 with my child. For anyone around the world with an ounce of feeling in their bones it was a huge moment, and it was weird because a lot of the songs I wrote beforehand seemed to refer-ence the event somehow.[58]

This example also testifies to the way that two other factors can play a part. There is first of all the fact of reaching on that day an age to which a particular importance is ascribed. This may be for social reasons: the entry into a new decade of one's life, or a turning point such as becoming an adult, for example.[59] But this may also be for personal reasons, such as having a member of one's family who passed away at that age, for example. The second factor, then, is learning the news of the event on the same day and not belatedly, which then makes the celebration of the birthday problematic.

These two factors emerge very clearly from the way one young person from Metz, in France, uses an Internet forum to relate the circumstances in which he learned the news of 9/11:

> I go home and I see this crazy stuff on the TV [. . .]. Just then, the phone . . . I pick up and hear: 'HAPPY BIRTHDAY!'
>
> My grandmother.
>
> I tell her:
>
> 'But Granny, who cares about my birthday, it's the end of the world!'
>
> 'Happy Birthday!!'
>
> 'Look, Granny, are you completely bonkers or what?!'
>
> 'HAPPY BIRTHDAY MY JOJO!!'
>
> In short . . . On 11 September 2001, I turned 20.
>
> I also remembered, just then, Pierre Bachelet: 'Quand on aura 20 ans, en l'an 2001'.[60] I remember, we sang that at school when we were kids. I never thought this day would turn out the way it did.[61]

As this testimony shows, not without a certain humour, the seriousness of the situation we experience live is such that it naturally overshadows the birthday, and the experience is all the more memorable as it comes up against generational expectations forged in childhood through a popular song.

In some cases, this coincidence may leave traces on the person and make the celebration of his or her birthday problematic in the longer term, too. Individuals shocked by a terrorist attack may react immediately by asserting that they never want to celebrate their birthday again, while others look back and say they have never celebrated it since that fateful day. But this long-term effect, of course, depends on the extent of the attack and its impact on the social environment of each individual concerned: we are much more likely to observe it in an American born on 11 September, or even a Madrilenian born on 11 March, than in a French person born on 7 July (even if that person may for this reason have felt more concerned than others by the London bombings in 2005). Regarding 9/11, the meaning which henceforth attaches to that date in the United States is such that adolescents and young adults appear to experience their date of birth as a 'stigma'. This has led one American woman for whom this is the case to create a website so that people confronted with the problem can share their experiences and give each other support.[62]

The importance we attach to the dates of our birthdays is such that the coincidence between one of them and the occurrence of a terrorist attack is capable of operating as a factor of personal concern even when the date in question is not that of the anniversary of our actual day of birth. It can also be the date of birth of one of our parents, for example:

I will never forget you. 11 March, my father's birthday.[63]

Or that of a friend:

On 11 September 2001, it was my best friend birthday, he's 20. How can we forget a moment like this. All world can remember his birthday date now. [...] I never forget.[64]

Or the date of a wedding anniversary:

The 9/11/01 was my wedding anniversary. I lived in NYC for two years and have been on the Twins. Nobody in Switzerland could believe that the pictures we saw where real. [...] My wife and I will always think of all victims on our wedding day. We also will never forget.[65]

Finally, as can be imagined, many parents mention a coincidence with the birthday of their child. The most striking example in this respect is undoubtedly that of a Spanish couple who write after the Madrid bombings, on behalf of their baby born on 11 September 2003:

I was born on 11 September and the anniversary of my sixth month was painful. My family sees hope in the fact that those who are born today will always remember, thanks to this date, all these 'angels' who watch over us. I do not want to have to remember other dates.[66]

Others, more simply, say how much their child, at an age when the celebration of birthdays is of particular importance, has been deeply affected by the misfortune that occurred on that day:

My son, Stéphane, turned 10 on 11 September 2001. Instead of his cartoons, he saw the unnameable. His childhood heart was overwhelmed, his innocence was wounded.

215

We wept together, united by the same sadness, the same feeling of horror. We are still weeping for America, for all that chaos, those innocent dead, these families destroyed; we are united in the same grief and we are praying for them, very hard.[67]

'My brother died today'

One final case still deserves mention: that where the terrorist attack coincides not with a date of birth, but with the anniversary of a death – indeed, the word *anniversarium* in the Middle Ages referred to the day of death, not the day of birth.[68] Thus, when he visited Ground Zero in 2008, Ian, from Southampton, wrote:

My father died on 9-11-01 in a hospital in England 'with his family around him'. God Bless those who never had that opportunity. None of them will be forgotten.[69]

Similarly, in September 2001, French people reacted in these terms:

All my sympathy to the American people. The death of my grandmother on this same day is nothing compared to this global catastrophe.[70]

My 48-year-old brother died on Tuesday, 11 September. And despite our pain, we thought of all these innocent victims, all those unhappy people.[71]

The way in which, in each of these messages, the two events are connected is particularly interesting. It is reminiscent of the famous passage in the *Theory of Moral Sentiments* where Adam Smith explains that it would be quite natural for a European to be more concerned and moved by the loss of his little finger than by the deaths of millions of Chinese caused at the same time by an earthquake, if he had never seen them at any time in his life. And if he does not yield to this natural inclination, says Adam Smith, this is only because he is endowed with a moral sense, by virtue of which he knows that such selfishness would make him feel ashamed.[72] Emphasizing that the death of a relative is *nothing compared to* the suffering of thousands of Americans, or that *despite* the pain that one feels for the loss of this loved one, one still sympathizes with their fate, seems clearly to be part of the 'moral sense' of which the Scottish philosopher speaks. However, his analysis does not explain the sense of personal concern established through the coincidence between the two events. In his logic, these events are contrasted, in the sense that one affects us directly while the other does not affect us in the slightest (it is for this reason that he insists on the fact that the European must never have seen a Chinese at any time in his life)[73] – they literally have nothing to do with each other, and only our moral sense explains why we care, *despite* what affects us, about the event that does not affect us. However, these reactions to 9/11 are testimony to the fact that it is also *because* Europeans are affected at the same time by the death of a loved one that they feel personally affected by what the victims of the attacks on the other side of the Atlantic are going through – an emotional mechanism peculiar to singularist societies that Adam Smith could scarcely envisage in the eighteenth century.

Going through a bereavement just when a terrorist attack occurs can also intensify a feeling of concern on an impersonal basis, such as the sense of fraternity between Americans and French forged during the Liberation:

> My husband has just passed away. He had participated in the liberation of France with all these young Americans. We are all brothers.[74]

But above all, it makes suffering more 'real' when it affects men who are strangers to us, and helps us to imagine what they are enduring thousands of kilometres away, and to feel empathy with them in spite of the distance. This explains the words of Christian:

> When we talk about war dead at the level of the nation, we are talking about thousands of dead, anonymous dead. When we talk about war dead at the level of the citizen, we are talking about units, on the level of a single person and his or her family. In the latter case, war is given its true sense of destruction. It wreaks havoc on the level of human beings. So my thoughts are with those thousands of bereaved families, whose happiness in living has been destroyed until the day they die, because one of their loved ones has died. I am currently experiencing this situation with the recent deaths of my wife and my 19-year-old son, and I can understand only too well what these thousands of families will have to experience and go through. May God give you much courage.[75]

When collective mourning thus coincides with personal mourning, the sense of concern also rests on a third and last factor, distinct from the two previous ones: the homology of experiences.

The homology of experiences

A homology of lived experiences can sometimes be enough to produce a sense of personal concern about a terrorist attack independently of any coincidence of dates. This is especially so in the case of persons who have also lost a loved one, for example in a car crash, and even more so, it seems, when this death is related to a disaster that, like the attack, was something of a public event.[76] In her attempt at an autoethnography, Carolyn Ellis notes that 9/11 upset her even more as it stirred up the memory of her brother's death in the crash of Air Florida Flight 90 which was headline news in January 1982.[77] She says how she felt more empathy with the families bereaved by the terrorist attacks in that she had an intimate knowledge of what they were experiencing. Similarly, in a register of condolences for the victims of the London bombings, Sophie recalls that behind every human life lost there is a broken family, and she signs off with the words:

> Lost a brother in the King's Cross Fire of 1987.[78]

A Dutch man also wrote:

> I know what it's like. My brother is missing now for nearly 11 years, he is missed after the Estonia Ferry disaster and we still don't know what happened.[79]

A fortiori those who have already had to suffer from a terrorist attack at some point in their lives react in the same way.

'I know what it's like'

In an article in *Midi Libre* devoted to a demonstration of solidarity organized in Béziers in the aftermath of the Madrid bombings, José, who is interviewed in the procession, explains:

> I am here in solidarity. Because it is the whole of humanity that is affected. But also because I am thinking about all the victims of terrorism. In Casablanca I lost two French friends and a dozen Moroccan acquaintances.[80]

Here we see how an impersonal concern, based on a common membership in 'humanity', can be combined with a more personal concern resting on the fact that you know what it means to be the victim of a terrorist attack.

Bearing in mind that in 2004, 30 per cent of Spaniards felt they had been closely or distantly affected at least once in their lives by a terrorist act,[81] it is hardly surprising that many of them expressed their solidarity with the victims of the Madrid bombings by referring to a similar homology of experiences. To give only two examples:

218

In my time, I too had to endure it from very close up, a long time ago, fifteen years. I understand your pain and your feeling of helplessness ... There's only one thing left we can do for them ... be as happy as we can ... that's definitely what they would have wanted.[82]

I'm sorry for all the dead and the wounded. I know what it is to suffering a terrorist attack on your own flesh, I suffered the attacks of 9/11.[83]

And this was also true for those who were not Spanish. Passing through Atocha Station four months after the attack, Marina wrote:

I am a Paraguayan and I do not know anyone who was involved on that sad day, but I did lose a friend on 9/11, and it's true that it hurts ...[84]

The reference to the 9/11 experience is also found in reactions to the London bombings. Colleen, an American woman living in Massachusetts, says that not only is England one of her favourite destinations, that she has already visited it on several occasions and hopes to do so again, but also that what she saw on television on 7 July 2005 reminded her of 9/11; and she adds:

Having gone through 9/11 and lost 2 friends, I know how devastating a senseless act like this is.[85]

Similarly, a man from New York says that he feels all the more concerned as he not only witnessed 9/11 but also lived in London at the time of the IRA bombings.[86]

Others also say they suffered from the bombing of Harrods in 1983, the Lockerbie disaster in 1988, or the attacks on the Paris RER in 1995 and 1996. But the most frequently quoted terrorist attack in these London registers is undeniably that of 11 March 2004 in Madrid. Almost all Spaniards make reference to it. To have experienced this attack, especially if they were directly affected, allows them to tell Londoners and victims of the London bombings that they know what they are feeling and can thus sympathize all the more with them:

I lived through 11 March and I know how London is feeling at a similar time.[87]

We are very sorry, we are with you, we know what you have been through because we also lived through it in Madrid.[88]

My condolences to London, my name is Patricia and I am from Madrid, I know what you have been through, and sincerely, I believe that in this kind of ordeals, we are all united, we stand as one against the terrorists.[89]

219

I am deeply sorry what's happened to Londoners. I am also from country where was similar problems, myself and my family lost one member of the family which is my father. I can understand what is going on. Deeply sorry ...[90]

The fact of having lived through the Madrid bombings, and of enduring terrorist acts for many years in addition, seems to have made the Spaniards particularly sensitive, perhaps more than other Europeans, to the London bombings, even though there are no particular historical or cultural links between Spain and the United Kingdom or between Madrid and London. This is also shown, negatively, by the fact that we some-times find towards the end of the registers of condolences opened in London City Hall in July 2005 messages from tourists (especially French) who confuse these registers with visitors' books and so leave in them messages congratulating the mayor on the beauty of his city or the reno-vation of certain buildings, while no Spanish people seem to have fallen prey to such a misunderstanding – as if they had been somewhat more attentive to what had struck London that summer.

'Now I realize'

Concern that stems from a homology of experiences, however, does not work only one way, but can also operate retrospectively. As we saw in the previous chapter, a young Frenchwoman from Toulouse felt person-ally concerned by 9/11 ten days later when she experienced the explo-sion at the AZF factory, thought she too was going to be the victim of a terrorist attack and was afraid she would lose her parents. In exactly the same way, when visiting Ground Zero in 2008, a young American who had started at the University of Virginia Tech in September 2001 said that she now felt more empathy with the victims of 9/11 as she had since experienced the killings that occurred on the university campus on 16 April 2007.[91] Here again, the same phenomenon can be observed as the result of another terrorist attack. Two English boys just ten or so years old in September 2001 also said, on the occasion of their visit to Ground Zero in 2008, that they were all the more affected by 9/11 as they had since experienced the London bombings. As one of them wrote:

I was 11 when this happened, and had just finished my second day of High School. I came home and the TV was on: my mum was watching the news, and they were interviewing passers-by as it happened. I look back on it now and feel I witnessed a piece of history that joins the other unspeakable tragedies that we have scarred into our pasts. [...] After the 7/7 bombings in my own country, I feel that I can share the fear and pain of feeling vulnerable, but I also see that humanity is full of love and in such times of uncertainty, I believe love can save us.[92]

Even more interesting in this regard is Josette's message. It is highly unusual in that she did not write it at the time, after her visit to the 9/11 Tribute Center, but carefully composed it before coming to Ground Zero, on a spare sheet of paper which she then folded and slipped into an envelope on which she wrote 'In Remembrance of 9/11 and (for me) 7/7'. The letter is worth quoting at length:

> I do not know what to say. It's been quite hard to take it all in.
>
> When I heard about the two towers, it was my birthday, 11th September.
>
> I was about 12, and I had come home from school and walked into my lounge, everyone was here, staring at the News Channel.
>
> I'll admit, I didn't think *too* much about it (tried not to anyhow), as my thoughts were so daunting.
>
> I didn't understand what it felt like, until 7/7.
>
> I live in Britain, and I was on holiday with my mates and we heard about the bombs in London.
>
> I froze, and some idiot turned off the TV and we told him to switch it back.
>
> We rung our families; my dad was okay, along with my sister, the one person which *has* to be in my life. She was safe.
>
> It ended up a few of my cousins and my uncle were on *one* of the trains. They too were fine, luckily.
>
> To think, the smallest things make the bigger difference.
>
> 'Little things count'
>
> We should appreciate that more often.
>
> With love and thoughts.[93]

This message addressed to the victims of 9/11 shows clearly how the awareness of having lived through a historical event, that is to say, not just being a distant onlooker, but being *concerned* by it personally, can arise retrospectively.

In his discussion of the relationship between memory and history, the sociologist Maurice Halbwachs noted that it was not enough to teach children retrospectively that what they had witnessed *was historical* for them to keep a precise and lasting personal memory of it; a child needed also to have immediately felt that what was happening had disturbed the adults and disrupted their social environment. In other words, the child must have felt somehow concerned by the event, so as

221

to catch a glimpse of the vastness and complexity of the world of adults beyond the world of children.[94] This is what Josette found 'daunting' on 11 September 2001 and led her to take her mind off the attacks as much as possible. But her reaction was doubtless all the more intense as that day was her birthday and the last thing she was expecting was to find her family's attention monopolized by the television when she got home. It matters little, Halbwachs says, if children do not straight away understand the meaning and scope of the event that has disrupted their social environment, as long as they experience the disturbance and remain affected by it: they will always be able to understand it later on.[95] So, for Josette, 9/11 assumed its full meaning only six years later, when she herself lived through the London bombings and realized what it meant to be the target of a terrorist attack and to fear for your relatives. And that is why, as she writes on her envelope, for her, the two events are inseparable: 9/11 would most likely not have had the same impact on her if she had not then experienced the attacks of 7/7 in London.

This last example bears clear witness to this, but it was already perceptible through many of the messages quoted above: factors of concern are also frames of memory. Everything suggests that the more an event concerns us, especially on a personal level, the more we have a clear recollection of the circumstances in which we experienced it. We know that 9/11 is one of those events that form the subject matter of what psychologists call 'flashbulb memories'.[96] So, like many people, I can still tell you precisely where, when and how I learned that planes had crashed into the towers of the World Trade Center. And it is more than likely that it will be the same in fifteen years for the attack on *Charlie Hebdo*. I can also remember clearly the Madrid bombings and other events such as the announcement of the results of the first round of presidential elections on 21 April 2002.[97] But my memories are already much more blurred for the London bombings, for example. It would be different, in all likelihood, for a Londoner. It is difficult for psychologists to determine why we preserve flashbulb memories of some events rather than others and, with regard to 9/11 in particular, why some individuals have much more accurate flashbulb memories of it than others, including New Yorkers and Americans.[98] The key to the riddle actually lies in the experience of concern proper to each individual.

The philosopher Avishai Margalit has noted that '[t]he significance of the event for us depends on our being personally connected with what happened'.[99] For this reason, he explains:

> It is not surprising that blacks in the United States have much better flashbulb memories than whites of the assassination of Martin Luther

King, Jr., while whites have better flashbulb memories of John Kennedy's assassination.[100]

And because one day in June 1963, just five months before being assassinated, John Kennedy had proclaimed himself a 'Berliner' in a momentous speech, it is also plausible, Margalit points out, that Berliners have a flashbulb memory of this assassination that is clearer than that of other Europeans, simply because at the time they had good reason to feel more concerned by the event. But we can go even further than the philosopher does, for the experience of concern proper to each person, as we have just seen, is also due to personal factors. While most French people, and perhaps especially most Parisians, will keep for a long time a precise recollection of the circumstances under which they learned that a massacre had taken place on the premises of *Charlie Hebdo*, a young student in journalism who turned twenty on that day will remain, without a shadow of a doubt, marked by it for life.

CONCLUSION
'THERE'S SOMETHING OF CHARLIE IN ALL OF US'

At the beginning of the year 2015, the French experienced what Durkheim calls a moment of 'collective effervescence'.[1] As they faced up to the ordeal of the terrorist attacks, they gathered in the streets and drew together; their interactions and thoughts intensified, their emotions were heightened. Some will have seen this as the quasi-mechanical activation of a sense of the univocal 'we', founded on the mere fact that the French felt themselves to be under attack as French people, a pure reflex of national unity – as the strange expression of a republican 'surge' suggests. These interpretations are rather like suggesting that contemporary French society was similar to that of the Aborigines of Australia, studied by Durkheim in *The Elementary Forms of Religious Life*. They ignore a fundamental sociological law, brought to light by the founding father of French sociology more than a century ago: in modern societies, mechanical solidarity, based on the simple fact of belonging to the same group, is forever retreating in the face of organic solidarity, which proceeds from the differentiation of individuals within the group. Collective consciousness collapses, yielding to the affirmation of singularities, and thus also of individual forms of dissent.[2] Social cohesion, therefore, is no longer as immediate, or obvious, in them as it can be among the Aborigines. And that is precisely why terrorist attacks are ordeals for modern societies – in fact, they are unique to these societies.[3]

This does not mean that there is no longer any form of mechanical solidarity in modern societies. The reactions to these attacks formulated in an impersonal and anonymous way are evidence of this: many people forced to undergo the ordeal of terrorism feel that they are being carried along by a 'we' that goes beyond them and into which they merge. There is no reason to deny that Americans never felt so American as on 9/11, and the French probably never felt as French as in January 2015. But mechanical solidarity can play a part, even in the case of the inhabitants of countries struck by terrorists, on other levels than the national one: that of public transport users, for example, where these are targeted, that of a professional community (firefighters on 9/11, journalists in the case of the attack on *Charlie Hebdo*), that of the cities attacked (in Europe or the West), and finally, at the level of humanity as such. Of course, when terrorists attack national symbols and buildings, as on 11 September 2001, the sense of belonging takes precedence over others and tends to block them out them. Still, the momentum of collective solidarity that can be observed in our societies in response to an attack always proceeds from an aggregation of different meanings of 'we', and not just from the activation of a straightforward feeling of common belonging. And if this is correct, it is because we are no longer confined to allegiance to a single group; the process of social differentiation characteristic of modern societies implies, on the contrary, that we play a part in a multitude of social circles, at the intersection of which each one of us asserts himself or herself as a singular individual. That is also why, at the same time as involving a multiplicity of meanings of 'we', our reactions to attacks demonstrate a heightened sense of 'I', which leads us to sympathize with the fate of the victims on the basis less of a shared belonging than of a shared singularity. The slogan 'I am Charlie' has become the visible symbol of this phenomenon, symptomatic of the importance assumed in our societies by organic solidarity.

This, then, is what causes our feeling of being shell shocked by the news of a terrorist attack, and means that we are not left indifferent: a complex interweaving of feelings at once impersonal and personal, of the different meanings of 'we' and of 'I' whose proportion varies in each of us. That is why the idea of 'shell shock' can take so many forms. We are 'all shell shocked' by the terrorist attack, but for different reasons and to varying degrees. Although we go through this ordeal together, we all have our own experience of it. If, however, we tend to interpret our reactions to the Islamist attacks carried out in the West since 2001 mainly in terms of the national *imaginaire*, this is because it occupies a central place in the political and media discourses that provide a framework for these attacks and thus affect the way in which we perceive them. The recurrent analogies drawn in Europe between these attacks and 9/11 are a clear clue, with 9/11 appearing as a 'new Pearl Harbor', as the archetype of an attack that roused national unity. This being so, if these political and media discourses shape our reactions to the attacks, we remain capable of critical distance and reflexivity with regard to normative injunctions to feel concerned and in solidarity with the victims in one way or another. The discussions after 9/11 on the relevance of the slogan 'We are all Americans' are an illustration of this. The voices that were raised, after the march on 11 January 2015, to denounce a 'political recuperation' of the spontaneous upsurge of solidarity created by the attack on *Charlie Hebdo* is another. And the recurrent questions about the merits of the minutes of silence that the public authorities ask us to observe are yet another.

These debates also testify to the fact that the transformation of the relations between 'we' and 'I' is, in Europe, accompanied by a change in the relations between 'we' and 'they'. Even when they are attacked on their own soil, in their cities, most Europeans expressing concern about these attacks refuse to recognize that they have enemies and to enter into a logic of 'the war of civilizations'. Rightly or wrongly, the idea that seemed to predominate after the Madrid and London bombings was that these terrorist attacks would never have happened if Spain and the United Kingdom, instead of taking part in the war in Iraq, had remained faithful to the principle of resolving the terrorist problem that respected international law, resorting to military force only with the agreement of the United Nations, so as to preserve as far as possible the conditions of peace in the world.[4] Thus the forms of 'we' involved by the reactions of Europeans to 9/11 and the attacks in Madrid and London become more notable for the compassion they feel for the victims than for the anger or hatred they might feel for a 'they' embodied by the Muslims in whose name the terrorists claim to be acting – and this also means that the spread of Islamophobia arises mainly from other causes.[5] Aggregated with each other, these 'we's give shape to a community of suffering and mourning that has fuzzy outlines, and may sometimes seem to extend to the whole of humanity. It is necessary, again, to see this as an effect of the progress of organic solidarity which, according to Durkheim, leads us to recognize as a supreme value only the respect for every human person, and to set our social life, including on a national scale, in the ideal perspective of universal human brotherhood.[6]

Extending the analysis of Durkheim in the late 1980s, Norbert Elias pointed out that the realization of this ideal – i.e. the emergence of a sense of 'we' on the scale of humanity – was made desirable by the emergence of global issues that de facto concerned the whole of humanity, but is still very difficult to envisage, precisely because it cannot rely on the dialectic of 'we' and 'they'.[7] While all earlier forms of social integration, from tribal communities to national societies, assert themselves in opposition to an 'other' outside the group, this is indeed impossible at the level of ultimate integration, namely humanity – if we rule out the possibility of an attack by extraterrestrials ... This last hypothesis may obviously raise a smile, yet it was with the utmost seriousness that the German sociologist Ulrich Beck was able to describe 9/11 as 'an attack from our "internal Mars"'.[8] His words express the full ambiguity of the relation of Europeans to Islamist attacks. On the one hand, Islamists are equated with extraterrestrials, strangers to humanity: new barbarians, in short, against whom civilized people must unite. But on the other hand, Islamic terrorism is clearly presented as an *internal* problem, inside the world of men, internal to humanity, which therefore calls for a cosmopolitical response rather than a war if it is to be solved in the long term.

A multitude of meanings of the 'we' whose aggregation comprises a community with fuzzy and potentially universal boundaries; a sense of solidarity with the victims of the attacks that also involves an intensification of the sense of 'I'; and a reluctance to endorse a split between 'us and them': what emerges, in short, from this picture is an impersonal 'one', as in 'one is', 'one feels'. If we go back to the beginning of chapter 6, which opened with a message posted on Facebook by a French student on the evening of the attack on *Charlie Hebdo*, we will see that it is precisely by using such an impersonal form that the student manages to express what he is feeling on that evening. 'But everyone is to some extent affected by an event like that', he wrote, before adding a little further on: 'I am Charlie. There's something of Charlie in all of us (*On est tous un peu Charlie*).' *There's something of Charlie in all of us*: these words, however uncertain ('something'), are potentially universal, open to all, and at the same time exposed to the risk of occidentalo-centrism. There may be more of Charlie in some of 'us' than in others, and each of us is Charlie in our own way. This is no homogeneous 'us'. But nor is it a simple juxtaposition of 'I's indifferent to each other and reacting in an egocentric way to the attacks.[9]

Re-reading this student's message, we can also see that the emotions he is feeling as he stands outside the French embassy in Madrid mingle with a feeling of belonging to France, since he says he shed a tear while waiting for the Marseillaise to be sung.[10] But it would be mistaken to see in it the simple activation of a pre-existing sense of patriotism in him, since he himself is surprised at his reaction: basically, he does not really know why he started crying, since none of the victims were close or distant acquaintances. He would not have put it that way if he had immediately felt that the attack concerned him *as a Frenchman*. It was in the moment, in a particular situation, that he felt moved by the French national anthem, and what he felt at the time was intimately linked to that situation: that is to say not only to the fact that journalists had just been murdered in France, but also that he himself was in Spain, in front of the French embassy, amidst people who were crying too. That is another reason why this feeling was fleeting. This student will no doubt remember this experience intensely for the rest of his life; there is little likelihood, on the other hand, that he will always feel *more French*

227

because he experienced it. The same could be said for millions of people who took part in the republican march on 11 January 2015.

Which brings us, finally, to the question that has ceaselessly cropped up since then in France: what is left of 'the spirit of January 11'? What *can* be left of it? The feelings that we experience when we face the ordeal of terrorist attacks are destined to disappear, as social life resumes its normal course and we 'move on to something else', in plain and simple terms.[11] The only way to make them last, unless new attacks occur, is to remember them regularly through commemorative ceremonies. If the spirit of 9/11 has managed to endure in the United States, this is because it is the subject of national commemorations every year, a ritual that is now an integral part of American civil religion. It is unlikely that this will ever be the case in France for the attacks of January 2015. Firstly, because 9/11 in this respect is a completely separate case, due to the fact that it was experienced in the United States as a declaration of war. The Madrid bombings, for example, may have caused considerable shock in Spain, but have never been the subject of a consensual national commemoration which could revive the 'spirit of Atocha', and so their public memory tends now to be maintained only by associations of victims and the Madrid authorities.[12] Secondly, the families of the victims of the attack on *Charlie Hebdo* would oppose commemorations taking the form of a national homage, just as, after the attack, they refused to attend a ceremony in the courtyard of Les Invalides, deeming it to go against the spirit of the newspaper and the convictions of the cartoonists killed.

Ceremonies to commemorate the attacks on 7, 8 and 9 January will take place, there is no doubt of that, but their scope will inevitably be limited. Most of the millions of French people who came out onto the streets in reaction to these attacks will pay them little attention. However, they will always remember what they experienced during those January days. And if by any sad chance an attack of the same nature were to occur in France tomorrow, they would feel just as concerned.

Paris, 13 October 2015

AFTERWORD TO THE ENGLISH EDITION

In this book, my aim was to grasp the pattern underlying the great impulses of solidarity and compassion observed in Western societies in reaction to mass terrorist attacks. I tried to clarify their sources and their causes and to show how ambiguous they can also be. But it is quite obvious that this way of reacting to a terrorist attack is not the only one. Not everyone goes out onto the streets to reflect on the events or pay tribute to the victims; not everyone leaves them a message of support. Some may remain relatively indifferent to the event, and others may sympathize with the cause of the terrorists. There are also reactions that are not expressed publicly, that remain confined to family meals and armchair debates, and to which the sociologist can have access only indirectly. While I felt it was necessary and urgent to examine first of all what constituted the most widespread and discussed aspects of the social response to an attack, I do not pretend to have exhausted the subject. On the contrary, much more research is needed to produce a fully fledged 'sociology of terrorist attacks'.

Some of this research is already under way. As I said in the preface, many mass attacks have, alas, been committed in Western societies since the book was written, most of which were claimed by ISIS: in Paris, of course, but also in Brussels, Orlando, Nice, Berlin and even Stockholm and Manchester. So the work continues, more than ever. At first it was solitary, but it has now become collective. While an international network of researchers interested in these questions is taking shape, I and my colleagues have set up in France a team engaged in project 'REAT' ('Social REsponse to terrorist ATtacks'), supported by the CNRS:[1] working together means that the amount of material collected can be increased and a greater number of sources investigated, several fields can be explored at the same time, and what is happening simultaneously in several places and in different social environments can be observed. Ultimately, I hope that this work will allow us to propose a more complete and systematic view (in terms of both time and space) of the process of social reaction to terrorist attacks than I could achieve in this book.

The questions which concern us are therefore those which the reader may have asked himself or herself in the course of the preceding pages. To what extent can we say, for example, that women are more likely than men to feel concerned by a terrorist attack and to sympathize publicly with the plight of its victims? Is reacting to an attack on a personal level, emphasizing 'I' rather than 'we', a matter of which generation one belongs to? Or does it depend rather on level of education and social class? And since when have people reacted to attacks in this way? We saw in this book that expressing support for the victims of a terrorist attack by saying '*I am* ...' pre-existed the appearance of social networks and the 'I am Charlie' phenomenon. But did people actually say this twenty-five years ago? And more than a century ago, at the time of the anarchist attacks? Furthermore, how do people react to attacks in certain sectors of society that are more directly involved or targeted than others? How do they react to Islamist attacks when they are Muslims? How do they react to anti-Semitic attacks when they are Jewish? Or to attacks targeting children, like those in Nice or Manchester, when they are parents? And how are such attacks experienced by people who live in the neighbourhoods from which those who perpetrate them originally came?

In a sense, this book raises perhaps more questions than it answers. But if it could, in so doing, help us to gain more perspective on how we collectively confront and respond to terrorist attacks, and thus stop us being drawn into the maelstrom created in their wake, then it will not have been written in vain.

SELECTIVE BIBLIOGRAPHY

General works

Alexander, Jeffrey C., Ron Eyerman, Bernard Giesen, Neil J. Smelser and Piotr Sztompka (eds.), *Cultural trauma and collective identity* (Berkeley, CA: University of California Press, 2004).

Anderson, Benedict, *Imagined communities: Reflections on the origin and spread of nationalism* (London: Verso, 2016).

Arendt, Hannah, *On revolution*, new edition (London: Faber & Faber, 2016).

Barthe, Yannick, Damien de Blic, Jean-Philippe Heurtin, Éric Lagneau, Cyril Lemieux, Dominique Linhardt, Cédric Moreau De Bellaing, Catherine Rémy and Danny Trom, 'Sociologie pragmatique: Mode d'emploi', *Politix*, 26 (103), 2013, pp. 175–204.

Beck, Ulrich, *Cosmopolitan vision* (Cambridge: Polity, 2014).

Benjamin, Walter, 'Critique of violence', in *On violence: A reader*, ed. Bruce B. Lawrence and Aisha Karim (Durham, NC: Duke University Press, 2007), pp. 268–85.

Bidet, Alexandra, Louis Quéré and Gérôme Truc, 'Ce à quoi nous tenons: Dewey et la formation des valeurs', in J. Dewey, *La formation des valeurs*, tr. A. Bidet, L. Quéré and G. Truc (Paris: La Découverte, 2011), pp. 5–64.

Billig, Michael, *Banal nationalism* (London: Sage, 1995).

Boltanski, Luc, *Distant suffering: Morality, media and politics*, tr. Graham Burchell (Cambridge: Cambridge University Press, 1999).

Boltanski, Luc, *On critique: A sociology of emancipation*, tr. Gregory Elliot (Cambridge and Malden, MA: Polity, 2011).

Boltanski, Luc, *Love and justice as competences: Three essays on the sociology of action*, tr. Catherine Porter (Cambridge: Polity, 2012).

Boltanski, Luc and Marie-Noël Godet, 'Messages d'amour sur le *Téléphone du Dimanche*', *Politix*, 8 (31), 1995, pp. 30–76.

Boltanski, Luc and Laurent Thévenot, *On justification: Economies of worth*, tr. Catherine Porter (Princeton, NJ, and Oxford: Princeton University Press, 2006).

Bourdieu, Pierre, 'The biographical illusion', in *Identity: A reader*, ed. Jessica Evans, Paul du Gay and Peter Redman (London: Sage, 2000), pp. 299–305.

Brown, Steven D., 'Two minutes of silence: Social technologies of public commemoration', *Theory & Psychology*, 22 (2), 2012, pp. 234–52.

Cefaï, Daniel, *Pourquoi se mobilise-t-on? Les théories de l'action collective* (Paris: La Découverte, 2007).

Cefaï, Daniel, 'Public, socialisation et politisation: Mead et Dewey', in A. Cukier and E. Debray (eds.), *La théorie sociale de George Herbert Mead* (Paris: Le Bord de l'Eau, 2014), pp. 340–66.

Coulmas, Peter, *Les citoyens du monde: Histoire du cosmopolitisme*, tr. J. Étoré (Paris: Albin Michel, 1995 [1990]).

Dayan, Daniel and Elihu Katz, *La télévision cérémonielle: Anthropologie et histoire en direct* (Paris: PUF, 1992).

Dewey, John, 'Creative democracy: The task before us', in *The Later Works, 1925–1953*, 17 vols., ed. Jo Ann Boydston (Carbondale, IL: Southern Illinois University Press, 1981–91), vol. 14 (1939–1941).

Dewey, John, *La formation des valeurs*, tr. A. Bidet, L. Quéré and G. Truc (Paris: La Découverte, 2011).

Dewey, John, *The public and its problems: An essay in political inquiry*, ed. Melvin L. Rogers (University Park, PA: Pennsylvania State University Press, 2012).

Durkheim, Émile, *Leçons de sociologie* (Paris: PUF, 1995 [1950]).

Durkheim, Émile, 'Détermination du fait moral', in *Sociologie et philosophie* (Paris: PUF, 1996 [1924]), pp. 49–90.

Durkheim, Émile, *Suicide: A study in sociology*, tr. John A. Spaulding and George Simpson, ed. George Simpson (London: Routledge, 2002).

Durkheim, Émile, *The elementary forms of religious life*, tr. Carol Cosman, ed. Mark S. Cladis (Oxford: Oxford University Press, 2008).

Durkheim, Émile, *The division of labour in society*, 2nd edition, tr. W. D. Halls, ed. Steven Lukes (Basingstoke: Palgrave Macmillan, 2013).

Edkins, Jenny, *Missing: Persons and politics* (New York, NY: Cornell University Press, 2011).

Elias, Norbert, 'Changes in the we–I balance', in *The society of individuals*, tr. Edmund Jephcott, ed. Michael Schröter (New York, NY, and London: Continuum, 2001), pp. 153–238.

Fassin, Didier, 'L'ordre moral du monde: Essai d'anthropologie de l'intolérable', in P. Bourdelais and D. Fassin (eds.), *Les constructions de l'intolérable* (Paris: La Découverte, 2005), pp. 17–50.

Fassin, Didier, *Humanitarian reason: A moral history of the present*, tr. Rachel Gomme (Berkeley, CA: University of California Press, 2011).

Fassin, Didier and Richard Rechtman, *The empire of trauma: An inquiry into the condition of victimhood*, tr. Rachel Gomme (Princeton, NJ: Princeton University Press, 2009).

Favre, Pierre (ed.), *La manifestation* (Paris: Presses de Sciences Po, 1990).

Favre, Pierre, 'Les manifestations de rue entre espace privé et espaces publics', in P. Favre, O. Fillieule and F. Jobard (eds.), *L'atelier du politiste* (Paris: La Découverte, 2007), pp. 193–213.

Fillieule, Olivier, *Stratégies de la rue: Les manifestations en France* (Paris: Presses de Sciences Po, 1997).

Fillieule, Olivier and Christophe Broqua, 'Raisons d'agir et proximité à la maladie dans l'économie de l'engagement à Aides, 1984–1998', in A. Micoud and M. Peroni (eds.), *Ce qui nous relie* (La Tour d'Aigues: Éditions de l'Aube, 2000), pp. 283–315.

Filloux, Jean-Claude, 'Personne et sacré chez Durkheim', *Archives de Sciences Sociales des Religions*, 69, 1990, pp. 41–53.

Forman-Barzilai, Fonna, *Adam Smith and the circles of sympathy: Cosmopolitanism and moral theory* (Cambridge: Cambridge University Press, 2010).

Fraenkel, Béatrice, 'Actes d'écriture: Quand écrire c'est faire', *Langage & Société*, 121–2, 2007, pp. 101–12.

Garfinkel, Harold, *Studies in ethnomethodology* (Cambridge: Polity, 1984).

Goffman, Erving, *The presentation of self in everyday life* (Edinburgh: University of Edinburgh Social Sciences Research Centre, 1956).

Goffman, Erving, *Frame analysis: An essay on the organization of experience* (Harmondsworth: Penguin, 1975).

Göle, Nilüfer, *Musulmans au quotidien: Une enquête européenne sur les controverses autour de l'Islam* (Paris: La Découverte, 2015).

Hajjat, Abdellali and Marwan Mohammed, *Islamophobie: Comment les élites françaises fabriquent le 'problème musulman'* (Paris: La Découverte, 2013).

Halbwachs, Maurice, *The collective memory*, tr. Francis J. Ditter, Jr. and Vida Yazdi Ditter (New York, NY, and London: Harper & Row, 1980).

Halbwachs, Maurice, 'L'expression des émotions et la société', *Vingtième Siècle*, 123, 2014, pp. 39–48.

Hughes, Everett C., 'Cycles, turning points, and careers', in *Men and their work* (Glencoe, IL: Free Press, 1958), pp. 11–22.

Illouz, Eva, *Consuming the romantic utopia: Love and the cultural contradictions of capitalism* (Berkeley, CA, and London: University of California Press, 1997).

Katz, Elihu and Tamar Liebes, '"No more peace!" How disaster, terror and war have upstaged media events', *International Journal of Communication*, 1, 2007, pp. 157–66.

Kurasawa, Fuyuki, 'L'humanitaire, manifestation du cosmopolitisme?', *Sociologie et Sociétés*, 44 (1), 2012, pp. 212–37.

Kurasawa, Fuyuki, 'The sentimentalist paradox: On the normative and visual foundations of humanitarianism', *Journal of Global Ethics*, 9 (2), 2013, pp. 201–14.

Latté, Stéphane, *Les 'victimes': La formation d'une catégorie sociale improbable et ses usages dans l'action collective*, PhD thesis, Paris, EHESS, 2008.

Latté, Stéphane, 'La "force de l'événement" est-elle un artefact? Les mobilisations de victimes au prisme des théories événementielles de l'action collective', *Revue Française de Science Politique*, 62 (3), 2012, pp. 409–32.

Laurens, Henry, 'Le terrorisme comme personnage historique', in H. Laurens and M. Delmas-Marty (eds.), *Terrorismes: Histoire et droit* (Paris: CNRS Éditions, 2010), pp. 9–66.

Legewie, Joscha, 'Terrorist events and attitudes toward immigrants: A natural experiment', *American Journal of Sociology*, 118 (5), 2013, pp. 1199–1245.

Levinas, Emmanuel, 'Peace and proximity', in *Basic philosophical writings*, ed. Adriaan T. Peperzak, Simon Critchley and Robert Bernasconi (Bloomington, IN: Indiana University Press, 1996), pp. 161–70.

Lévy, Jacques, 'Un "nous" sans "eux": Manufactures de la société-monde', in A. Caillé and S. Dufoix (eds.), *Le tournant global des sciences sociales* (Paris: La Découverte, 2013), pp. 288–311.

Linhardt, Dominique, '*Guerrilla diffusa*: Clandestinité, soupçon et provocation dans le conflit entre organisations révolutionnaires subversives et l'État ouest-allemand (années 1970)', *Politix*, 19 (74), 2006, pp. 75–102.

Linhardt, Dominique, 'Épreuves d'État: Une variation sur la définition wébérienne de l'État', *Quaderni*, 78, 2012, pp. 5–22.

Linklater, Andrew, 'Distant suffering and cosmopolitan obligations', *International Politics*, 44 (1), 2007, pp. 19–36.

Livet, Pierre, *Émotions et rationalité morale* (Paris: PUF, 2002).

Malandain, Gilles, 'Les sens d'un mot: "Attentat", de l'Ancien Régime à nos jours', *La Révolution Française*, 1, 2012, available online at http://lrf.revues.org/368.

Margalit, Avishai, *The ethics of memory* (Cambridge, MA, and London: Harvard University Press, 2002).

Mariot, Nicolas, 'Les formes élémentaires de l'effervescence collective, ou l'état d'esprit prêté aux foules', *Revue Française de Science Politique*, 51 (5), 2001, pp. 707–38.

Mariot, Nicolas, *Bains de foule: Les voyages présidentiels en province, 1888–2002* (Paris: Belin, 2006).

Mariot, Nicolas, 'La réflexivité comme second mouvement', *L'Homme*, 203–4, 2012, pp. 369–98.

Martuccelli, Danilo, *La société singulariste* (Paris: Armand Colin, 2010).

Mauss, Marcel, 'L'expression obligatoire des sentiments: Rituels oraux funéraires australiens' (1921), in *Œuvres*, vol. 3: *Cohésion sociale et divisions de la sociologie* (Paris: Éditions de Minuit, 1969), pp. 269–79.

Mead, George H., *Mind, self, and society*, ed. Charles W. Morris, Daniel R. Huebner and Hans Joas (Chicago, IL: University of Chicago Press, 2015).

Merrimann, John, *The dynamite club: How a bombing in fin-de-siècle Paris ignited the age of modern terror* (Boston, MA, and New York, NY: Houghton Mifflin Harcourt, 2009).

Nussbaum, Martha C., 'Emotions as judgments of value', *Yale Journal of Criticism*, 5, 1992, pp. 201–12.

Olson, Mancur, *The logic of collective action: Public goods and the theory of groups*, revised edition (Cambridge, MA, and London: Harvard University Press, 1971).

Oxaal, Ivar, Michael Pollak and Gerhard Botz (eds.), *Jews, antisemitism and culture in Vienna* (London: Routledge & Kegan Paul, 1987).

Passeron, Jean-Claude, *Le raisonnement sociologique: Un espace non poppérien de l'argumentation* (Paris: Albin Michel, 2006 [1991]).

Portis, Larry, 'La sociologie consensuelle et le terrorisme: De la propagande par le fait à Unabomber', *L'Homme et la Société*, 123–4, 1997, pp. 57–74.

Quéré, Louis, 'Pour un calme examen des faits de société', in B. Lahire (ed.), *À quoi sert la sociologie?* (Paris: La Découverte, 2002), pp. 79–94.

Quéré, Louis, 'Le public comme forme et comme modalité d'expérience', in D. Cefaï and D. Pasquier (eds.), *Les sens du public: Publics politiques, publics médiatiques* (Paris: PUF, 2003), pp. 113–34.

Quéré, Louis, 'Entre fait et sens, la dualité de l'événement', *Réseaux*, 139, 2006, pp. 183–218.

Renan, Ernest, *Qu'est-ce qu'une nation?* (Paris: Mille et Une Nuits, 1997 [1887]).

Ricœur, Paul, *Oneself as another*, tr. Kathleen Blamey (Chicago, IL, and London: University of Chicago Press, 1992).

Rimé, Bernard, *Le partage social des émotions* (Paris: PUF, 2005).

Scheff, Thomas J., *Emotions, the social bond, and human reality: Part/whole analysis* (Cambridge: Cambridge University Press, 1997).

Schmitt, Jean-Claude, *L'invention de l'anniversaire* (Paris: Éditions Arkhê, 2009).

Simmel, Georg, 'The metropolis and mental life', in *The sociology of Georg Simmel*, tr. and ed. Kurt H. Wolff (New York, NY, and London: Free Press, 1950).

Simmel, Georg, 'L'individualisme moderne' (1917), in *Philosophie de la modernité*, tr. J.-L. Vieillard-Baron (Paris: Payot, 2004), pp. 201–31.

Simmel, Georg, *Sociology: Inquiries into the construction of social forms*, 2 vols., tr. and ed. Anthony J. Blasi, Anton K. Jacobs and Mathew Kanjiranthinkal (Leiden and Boston, MA: Brill, 2009).

Singly, François de, *L'individualisme est un humanisme* (La Tour d'Aigues: Éditions de l'Aube, 2005).

Smith, Adam, *The theory of moral sentiments*, ed. Ryan Patrick Hanley (New York, NY: Penguin, 2009).

Tassin, Étienne, *Un monde commun: Pour une cosmo-politique des conflits* (Paris: Seuil, 2003).

Taylor, Charles, *The sources of the self: The making of the modern identity* (Cambridge: Cambridge University Press, 1989).

Thévenot, Laurent, *L'action au pluriel: Sociologie des régimes d'engagement* (Paris: La Découverte, 2006).

Truc, Gérôme, 'Analyser un corpus illisible? Le logiciel Alceste confronté à des registres de condoléances', *Langage & Société*, 135, 2011, pp. 29–45.

Truc, Gérôme, *Le 11-Septembre européen: La sensibilité morale des Européens à l'épreuve des attentats du 11 septembre 2001, du 11 mars 2004 et du 7 juillet 2005*, PhD thesis, Paris: EHESS, 2014.

Walzer, Michael, *On toleration* (New Haven, CT, and London: Yale University Press, 1997).

Zask, Joëlle, 'Le public chez Dewey: Une union sociale plurielle', *Tracés*, 15, 2008, pp. 169–89.

On 9/11

Anker, Elisabeth, 'Villains, victims and heroes: Melodrama, media and September 11', *Journal of Communication*, 55 (1), 2005, pp. 22–37.

Archibugi, Daniele, 'Terrorism and cosmopolitanism', *Social Science Research Council*, 2001, available online at http://www.ssrc.org/sept11/essays/archibugi_text_only.htm.

Brassett, James, 'Cosmopolitan sentiments after 9–11?', *Journal of Critical Globalisation Studies*, 2, 2010, pp. 12–29.

Butler Judith, *Precarious life: The powers of mourning and violence* (London and New York, NY: Verso, 2004).

Chermak, Steven, Frankie Y. Bailey and Michelle Brown (eds.), *Media representations of September 11* (London and Westport, CT: Praeger, 2003).

Chéroux, Clément, *Diplopie: L'image photographique à l'ère des médias globalisés. Essai sur le 11 septembre 2001* (Cherbourg-Octeville: Le Point du Jour, 2009).

Collins, Randall, 'Rituals of solidarity and security in the wake of terrorist attack', *Sociological Theory*, 22 (1), 2004, pp. 53–87.

Conway, Andrew R. A., Linda J. Skitka, Joshua A. Hemmerich and Trina C. Kershaw, 'Flashbulb memory for 11 September 2001', *Applied Cognitive Psychology*, 23 (5), 2009, pp. 605–23.

Crettiez, Xavier and Isabelle Sommier, 'Les attentats du 11 septembre: Continuité et rupture des logiques du terrorisme', *Annuaire Français des Relations Internationales*, 3, 2002, pp. 58–69.

Dayan, Daniel (ed.), *La terreur spectacle: Terrorisme et télévision* (Brussels: De Boeck/INA, 2006).

Delage, Christian, 'Une censure intériorisée? Les premières images des attentats du 11 septembre 2001', *Ethnologie Française*, 36 (1), 2006, pp. 91–9.

Délano, Alexandra and Benjamin Nienass, 'Invisible victims: Undocumented migrants and the aftermath of September 11', *Politics & Society*, 42 (3), 2014, pp. 399–421.

Derrida, Jacques and Jürgen Habermas, *Philosophy in a time of terror: Dialogues with Jürgen Habermas and Jacques Derrida*, interviewed by Giovanna Borradori (Chicago, IL, and London: University of Chicago Press, 2003).

Ellis, Carolyn, 'Shattered lives: Making sense of September 11th and its aftermath', *Journal of Contemporary Ethnography*, 31 (4), 2002, pp. 375–410.

Fraenkel, Béatrice, *Les écrits de septembre: New York 2001* (Paris: Textuel, 2002).

Fragnon, Julien, 'Quand le 11-Septembre s'approprie le onze septembre: Entre dérive métonymique et antonomase', *Mots*, 85, 2007, pp. 83–95.

Frau-Meigs, Divina, *Qui a détourné le 11 septembre? Journalisme, information et démocratie aux États-Unis* (Brussels: De Boeck/INA, 2005).

237

Gluck, Carole, '11 septembre: Guerre et télévision au XXIe siècle', *Annales: Histoire, Sciences Sociales*, 58 (1), 2003, pp. 135–62.

Greenberg, Bradley S. (ed.), *Communication and terrorism: Public and media responses to 9/11* (Cresskill, NJ: Hampton Press, 2002).

Held, David, 'Cosmopolitanism after 9/11', *International Politics*, 47, 2010, pp. 52–61.

Hirst, William, Elizabeth A. Phelps, Randy L. Buckner, Andrew E. Budson et al., 'Long-term memory for the terrorist attack of September 11: Flashbulb memories, event memories, and the factors that influence their retention', *Journal of Experimental Psychology*, 138 (2), 2009, pp. 161–76.

Kirshenblatt-Gimblett, Barbara, 'Kodak moments, flashbulb memories: Reflections on 9/11', *Drama Review*, 47 (1), 2003, pp. 11–48.

Lagarde, François, 'Penser l'impensable: Le 11 Septembre des penseurs français', *French Politics, Culture & Society*, 23 (2), 2005, pp. 91–100.

Lamy, Aurélia, *La médiatisation de l' 'Apocalypse': Le traitement médiatique des attentats du 11 septembre 2001 aux États-Unis dans la presse et à la télévision françaises (11–18 septembre 2001)*, PhD thesis, Metz, Université Paul-Verlaine, 2005.

Lamy, Aurélia, 'Récits médiatiques, mémoires électives. De la construction de l'événement à celle de l'oubli: L'exemple du 11 septembre 2001', Espacestemps.net, 21 November 2007, available online at http://www.espacestemps.net/document3673.html.

Luminet, Olivier and Antonietta Curci, 'The 9/11 attacks inside and outside the US: Testing four models of flashbulb memory formation across groups and the specific effects of social identity', *Memory*, 17 (7), 2009, pp. 742–59.

Méchet, Philippe and Dominique Reynié, 'Les opinions publiques face à la crise du 11 septembre 2001', in B. Cautrès and D. Reynié (eds.), *L'opinion européenne 2002* (Paris: Presses de Sciences Po, 2002), pp. 39–48.

Morris-Suzuki, Tessa, 'Le missile et la souris: Mouvements virtuels pour la paix dans un âge de terreur', *Annales: Histoire, Sciences Sociales*, 58 (1), 2003, pp. 163–78.

Pludowski, Tomasz (ed.), *How the world's news media reacted to 9/11: Essays from around the world* (Spokane, WA: Marquette Books, 2007).

Ramel, Frédéric, 'Presse écrite et traitement immédiat du 11 septembre: Un imaginaire occidental réactivé?', *Mots*, 76, 2004, pp. 113–26.

Riley, Alexander T., *Angel patriots: The crash of United Flight 93 and the myth of America* (New York, NY, and London: New York University Press, 2015).

Samaras, Iathanassios N., 'Représentation du 11-Septembre dans quatre journaux grecs: Une question de cadrage', *Questions de Communication*, 8, 2005, pp. 367–89.

Sather-Wagstaff, Joy, *Heritage that hurts: Tourists in the memoryscapes of September 11* (Walnut Creek, CA: Left Coast Press, 2011).

Sémelin, Jacques, 'Le 11 septembre comme massacre: La rationalité délirante et la propagation de la peur', *Vingtième Siècle*, 76, 2002, pp. 15–24.

Simko, Christina, 'Rhetorics of suffering: September 11 commemorations as theodicy', *American Review of Sociology*, 77 (6), 2012, pp. 880–902.

Simpson, David, *9/11: The culture of commemoration* (Chicago, IL: University of Chicago Press, 2006).

Taylor, Diana, 'Lost in the field of vision', in *The Archive and the repertoire: Performing cultural memory in the Americas* (Durham, NC, and London: Duke University Press, 2003), pp. 237–64.

Tiryakian, Edward A., 'Durkheim, solidarity, and September 11', in J. C. Alexander and P. Smith (eds.), *The Cambridge companion to Durkheim* (Cambridge: Cambridge University Press, 2005), pp. 305–21.

Wagner-Pacifici, Robin, 'Theorizing the restlessness of events', *American Journal of Sociology*, 115 (5), 2010, pp. 1351–86.

White, Geoffrey M., 'National subjects: September 11 and Pearl Harbor', *American Ethnologist*, 31 (3), 2004, pp. 293–310.

Wrona, Adeline, 'Vies minuscules, vies exemplaires: Récit d'individu et actualité. Le cas des *portraits of grief* parus dans le *New York Times* après le 11 septembre 2001', *Réseaux*, 132, 2005, pp. 93–110.

Zelizer, Barbie and Stuart Allan (eds.), *Journalism after September 11* (London and New York, NY: Routledge, 2002).

On the 11 March 2004 attacks in Madrid and the 7 July 2005 attacks in London

Ansiedad y Estrés, 10 (2–3), 2004 ('La reacción humana ante el trauma: Consecuencias del 11 de marzo de 2004').

Brassett, James, 'Cosmopolitanism vs. terrorism? Discourses of ethical possibility before and after 7/7', *Millennium: Journal of International Studies*, 36 (2), 2008, pp. 311–37.

Closs Stephens, Angharad and Nick Vaughan Williams (eds.), *Terrorism and the politics of response* (London and New York, NY: Routledge, 2009).

European Monitoring Centre on Racism and Xenophobia, *The impact of 7 July 2005 London bomb attacks on Muslim communities in the EU* (Luxembourg: Office for Official Publications of the European Communities, 2006), available online at https://fra.europa.eu/sites/default/files/fra_uploads/197-London-Bomb-attacksEN.pdf.

Gil Calvo, Enrique, *11/14-M, el cambio trágico: De la masacre al vuelco electoral* (Madrid: Adhara, 2005).

Hermès, 46, 2006 ('Événements mondiaux, regards nationaux').

Kelsey, Darren, *Media, myth and terrorism: A discourse-mythological analysis of the 'Blitz Spirit' in British newspaper responses to the July 7th bombings* (New York, NY, and Basingstoke: Palgrave Macmillan, 2015).

Mewes, Jan, *11. März 2004 – Madrid im Spiegel der Presse: Eine vergleichende Inhaltsanalyse der Berichterstattung über den Terroranschlag in den Printmedien 'Frankfurter Allgemeine Zeitung', 'Frankfurter Rundschau' und 'New York Times'* (Munich: GRIN, 2007).

Ortiz García, Carmen, 'Pictures that save, pictures that soothe: Photographs at the grassroots memorials to the victims of the March 11, 2004 Madrid bombings', *Visual Anthropology Review*, 29 (1), 2013, pp. 57–71.

Páez, Darío, Nekane Basabe, Silvia Ubillos and José Luis González-Castro, 'Social sharing, participation in demonstrations, emotional climate and coping with collective violence after the March 11th Madrid bombings', *Journal of Social Issues*, 63 (2), 2007, pp. 323–37.

Papin, Delphine, 'Les attentats de Londres, révélateur du malaise de la nation britannique', *Hérodote*, 120, 2006, pp. 190–9.

Reading, Anna, 'The London bombings: Mobile witnessing, mortal bodies and globital time', *Memory Studies*, 4 (3), 2011, pp. 298–311.

Sánchez-Carretero, Cristina, 'Trains of workers, trains of death: Some reflections after the March 11 attacks in Madrid', in J. Santino (ed.), *Spontaneous shrines and the public memorialization of death* (New York, NY, and Basingstoke: Palgrave, 2006), pp. 333–47.

Sánchez-Carretero, Cristina (ed.), *El Archivo del Duelo: Análisis de la respuesta ciudadana ante los atentados del 11 de marzo en Madrid* (Madrid: CSIC, 2011).

Sánchez-Carretero, Cristina, Antonio Cea, Paloma Díaz-Mas, Pilar Martínez and Carmen Ortiz, 'On blurred borders and interdisciplinary research teams: The case of the "Archive of Mourning"', *Forum: Qualitative Social Research*, 12 (3), 2011, available online at: http://nbn-resolving.de/urn: nbn: de: 0114-fqs1103124.

Teruel Rodríguez, Laura, 'La cobertura del 11M–15M en la prensa noruega: Una perspectiva mediática desde el norte de Europa', *Revista Latina de Comunicación Social*, 60, 2005, available online at http://www.ull.es/publicaciones/latina/200521teruel.htm.

Tota, Anna Lisa, 'Terrorism and collective memories: Comparing Bologna, Naples, Madrid 11 March', *International Journal of Comparative Sociology*, 46 (1–2), 2005, pp. 55–78.

Truc, Gérôme, 'Le politique aux marges de la commémoration: Une ethnographie des cérémonies de commémoration officielle des attentats du 11 mars 2004 à Madrid', in M. Berger, D. Cefaï, C. Gayet-Viaud and J. Stavo-Debauge (eds.), *Du civil au politique: Ethnographies du vivre-ensemble* (Brussels: Peter Lang, 2011), pp. 205–27.

Truc, Gérôme, 'Les victimes du terrorisme comme citoyens affectés: L'enjeu politique de la mobilisation des victimes du 11-Mars' (forthcoming).

Vara Miguel, Alfonso, Jordi Rodríguez Virgili, Elea Giménez Toledo and Montserrat Díaz Méndez (eds.), *Cobertura informativa del 11-M* (Pamplona: EUNSA, 2006).

On death, collective mourning and the relation to suffering in the Western world

Arboit, Gérald, 'Rôles et fonctions des images de cadavres dans les médias: L'actualité permanente du "massacre des Saints Innocents"', *Annuaire Français de Relations Internationales*, 4, 2003, pp. 828–48.

Baudot, Pierre-Yves, 'Épitaphes oubliées: Les registres de condoléances à la mort d'un Président de la République', *Mots*, 84, 2007, pp. 71–84.

Capdevila, Luc and Danièle Voldman, *Nos morts: Les sociétés occidentales face aux tués de la guerre (XIXe–XXe siècles)* (Paris: Payot, 2002).

Clavandier, Gaëlle, *La mort collective: Pour une sociologie des catastrophes* (Paris: CNRS Éditions, 2004).

Doss, Erika, *The emotional life of contemporary public memorials: Towards a theory of temporary memorials* (Amsterdam: Amsterdam University Press, 2008).

Gervereau, Laurent, *Montrer la guerre? Information ou propagande* (Paris: CNDP, 2006).

Grider, Sylvia, 'Spontaneous shrines: A modern response to tragedy and disaster', *New Directions in Folklore*, 5, 2001, pp. 1–9.

Hallin, Daniel C., *The 'uncensored war': The media and Vietnam* (New York, NY, and Oxford: Oxford University Press, 1986).

Margry, Peter Jan and Cristina Sánchez-Carretero (eds.), *Grassroots memorials: The politics of memorializing traumatic death* (New York, NY: Berghahn, 2010).

Santino, Jack (ed.), *Spontaneous shrines and the public memorialization of death* (New York, NY, and Basingstoke: Palgrave, 2006).

Solomon-Godeau, Abigail, 'Photographier la catastrophe', *Terrain*, 54, 2010, pp. 56–65.

Sontag, Susan, *Regarding the pain of others* (London: Penguin, 2003).

Stora, Benjamin, *Imaginaires de guerre: Les images dans les guerres d'Algérie et du Viêt-nam* (Paris: La Découverte, 2004).

Taïeb, Emmanuel, 'Faut-il montrer les images de violence?', *La Vie des Idées*, 7 July 2015, available online at http://www.laviedesidees.fr/Faut-il-montrer-les-images-de-violence.html.

Walter, Tony, 'From cathedral to supermarket: Mourning, silence and solidarity', *Sociological Review*, 49 (4), 2001, pp. 494–511.

Walter, Tony (ed.), *The mourning for Diana* (Oxford and New York, NY: Berg, 1999).

On Europe

Balibar, Étienne, *L'Europe, l'Amérique, la guerre* (Paris: La Découverte, 2003).

Belot, Céline, 'Le tournant identitaire des études consacrées aux attitudes à l'égard de l'Europe: Genèses, apports, limites', *Politique Européenne*, 30, 2010, pp. 17–44.

Cautrès, Bruno, '"Plus on se connaît, plus on s'aime?"', *Politique Européenne*, 26, 2008, pp. 165–90.

Cicchelli, Vincenzo, *L'esprit cosmopolite: Voyages de formation des jeunes en Europe* (Paris: Presses de Sciences Po, 2012).

Derrida, Jacques and Jürgen Habermas, 'February 15, or what binds Europeans together: A plea for a common foreign policy, beginning in the core of Europe', tr. Max Pensky, *Constellations*, 10 (3), 2003, pp. 291–7, available online at http://platypus1917.org/wpcontent/uploads/archive/rgroups/2006-chicago/habermasderrida_europe.pdf.

Duchesne, Sophie, 'L'identité européenne, entre science politique et science fiction', *Politique Européenne*, 30, 2010, pp. 7–16.

Duchesne, Sophie and Virginie Van Ingelgom, 'L'indifférence des français et des belges (franco-phones) pour leurs voisins européens: Une pièce de plus au dossier de l'absence de communauté politique européenne?', *Politique Européenne*, 26, 2008, pp. 143–64.

Foret, François, *Légitimer l'Europe: Pouvoir et symbolique à l'heure de la gouvernance* (Paris: Presses de Sciences Po, 2008).

Goody, Jack, *The theft of history* (Cambridge: Cambridge University Press, 2006).

Le Galès, Patrick, *Le retour des villes européennes* (Paris: Presses de Sciences Po, 2003).

Lefort, Claude, 'L'Europe, civilisation urbaine', *Esprit*, 303, 2004, pp. 225–43.

Reynié, Dominique, *La fracture occidentale: Naissance d'une opinion européenne* (Paris: La Table Ronde, 2004).

Roudometof, Victor and William Haller, 'Cosmopolitan trends across world regions: Discerning a European exceptionalism', in R. Robertson and A. S. Krossa (eds.), *European cosmopolitanism in question* (Basingstoke: Palgrave Macmillan, 2012), pp. 126–50.

Truc, Gérôme, 'Aux victimes du terrorisme, l'Europe reconnaissante? Portée et limites de la Journée européenne en mémoire des victimes du terrorisme', *Politique Européenne*, 37, 2012, pp. 132–54.

Wallerstein, Immanuel, *European universalism: The rhetoric of power* (New York, NY: New Press, 2006).

NOTES

Preface

1. Mahmood Mamdani, *Good Muslim, bad Muslim: America, the Cold War, and the roots of terror* (New York: Doubleday, 2004).
2. Norbert Elias, *Involvement and detachment*, revised English edn (Dublin: University College Dublin Press, 2007).
3. http://www.mirror.co.uk/news/politics/general-election-manchester-bombing-attack-10479733.

Introduction Terrorist attacks as a test

1. Marie Fatayi-Williams, 'Foreword', in A. Closs Stephens and N. Vaughan Williams (eds.), *Terrorism and the politics of response* (London and New York: Routledge, 2009), p. xii.
2. The term 'attack' (*attentat*) is used here in the sense, now current, of 'terrorist act' – that is, a random act of violence whose aim is to terrorize a population for political purposes, even though it initially had a much broader sense, as shown by the expression 'attack on modesty' (*attentat à la pudeur*, meaning 'molestation'). It was long used as a generic term, the scholarly equivalent of 'crime' (the French dictionary *Littré* defines an attack (*attentat*) as a 'criminal enterprise, against the law'), accompanied by a figurative use – now almost never found – designating an act that contravenes reason or violates morality (see Gilles Malandain, 'Les sens d'un mot: 'Attentat', de l'Ancien Régime à nos jours', *La Révolution Française*, 1, 2012, available online: http://lrf.revues.org/368).

NOTES TO PP. 2–5

3. See Louis Quéré, 'Pour un calme examen des faits de société', in B. Lahire (ed.), *À quoi sert la sociologie?* (Paris: La Découverte, 2002), pp. 79–94.
4. Emmanuel Todd, *Who is Charlie? Xenophobia and the new middle class*, tr. Andrew Brown (Cambridge: Polity, 2015).
5. On the notion of 'test' (in the sense of 'ordeal') in sociology, see Yannick Barthe et al., 'Sociologie pragmatique: Mode d'emploi', *Politix*, 26 (103), 2013, pp. 175–204. [The French word used by Truc for 'test' is *épreuve*: it can mean an 'ordeal', a 'trial', or something which 'puts X to the test'; I have used 'test' because the author is here partly drawing on the work of Luc Boltanski, where *épreuve* is generally translated as 'test'. (Translator's note)]
6. Dominique Linhardt, 'Épreuves d'État: Une variation sur la définition wébérienne de l'État', *Quaderni*, 78, 2012, pp. 5–22.
7. See Alexandra Bidet, Louis Quéré and Gérôme Truc, 'Ce à quoi nous tenons: Dewey et la formation des valeurs', in J. Dewey, *La formation des valeurs*, tr. A. Bidet, L. Quéré and G. Truc (Paris: La Découverte, 2011), pp. 5–64.
8. Émile Durkheim, *The division of labour in society*, 2nd edition, ed. Steven Lukes, tr. W. D. Halls (Basingstoke: Palgrave Macmillan, 2013). The book was first published as *De la division du travail social*, in 1893.
9. See 'La décennie Ben Laden', *Le Monde*, special issue, July–September 2011.
10. Rick Coolsaet, 'Au temps du terrorisme anarchiste', *Monde diplomatique*, 606, September 2004, p. 26.
11. John Merrimann, *The dynamite club: How a bombing in fin-de-siècle Paris ignited the age of modern terror* (Boston, MA, and New York, NY: Houghton Mifflin Harcourt, 2009).
12. 'Nouvel attentat anarchiste', *Le Temps*, 14 February 1894, p. 1.
13. Larry Portis, 'La sociologie consensuelle et le terrorisme: De la propagande par le fait à Unabomber', *L'Homme et la Société*, 123–4, 1997, pp. 57–74 at p. 57. (See also Larry Portis, 'La terreur et la sociologie', *Divergences*, 14, 2008, available online: http://divergences.be/spip.php?rubrique347.) There are traces of this view in *La psychologie des foules* by Gustave Le Bon, published 1895 (English tr. *The crowd: A study of the popular mind* (Harmondsworth: Penguin, 1977)), and in Gabriel Tarde: see in particular Gabriel Tarde, 'Les crimes de haine', *Archives d'Anthropologie Criminelle*, 9 (51), 1894, pp. 241–54.
14. Edward A. Tiryakian, 'Durkheim, solidarity, and September 11', in J. C. Alexander and P. Smith (eds.), *The Cambridge Companion*

to Durkheim (Cambridge: Cambridge University Press, 2005), pp. 305–31.

15. See for example Julian E. Barnes, 'As demand soars, flag makers help bolster nation's morale', *New York Times*, 23 September 2001, available online: http://www.nytimes.com/2001/09/23/business/nation-challenged-proud-spirits-demand-soars-flag-makers-help-bolster-nation-s.html.

16. Bradley S. Greenberg and Linda Hofschire, 'Summary and discussion', in B. S. Greenberg (ed.), *Communication and terrorism: Public and media responses to 9/11* (Cresskill, NJ: Hampton Press, 2002), p. 320.

17. Tiryakian, 'Durkheim, solidarity, and September 11', pp. 316–17.

18. See Cristina Sánchez-Carretero, Antonio Cea, Paloma Díaz-Mas, Pilar Martínez and Carmen Ortiz, 'On blurred borders and interdisciplinary research teams: The case of the "Archive of Mourning"', *Forum: Qualitative Social Research*, 12 (3), 2011, available online: http://nbn-resolving.de/urn:nbn:de:0114-fqs1103124.

19. I will return at greater length to these messages and the method used to analyse them in due course.

Chapter 1   Under attack

1. Dominique Linhardt, '*Guerrilla diffusa*: Clandestinité, soupçon et provocation dans le conflit entre organisations révolutionnaires subversives et l'État ouest-allemand (années 1970)', *Politix*, 19 (74), 2006, pp. 75–102 at p. 76.

2. Harold Garfinkel, *Studies in ethnomethodology* (Cambridge: Polity, 1984), pp. 35–75.

3. Xavier Crettiez and Isabelle Sommier, 'Les attentats du 11 septembre: Continuité et rupture des logiques du terrorisme', *Annales Français des Relations Internationales*, 3, 2002, pp. 58–69 at p. 62.

4. Erving Goffman, *Frame analysis: An essay on the organization of experience* (Harmondsworth: Penguin, 1975), p. 21.

5. Isaac Joseph, *Erving Goffman et la microsociologie* (Paris: PUF, 1998), p. 123.

6. Goffman, *Frame analysis*, p. 304.

7. All these factual elements are quoted from the official report drawn up by the 9/11 Commission, available online: http://www.9-11commission.gov/report/911Report_Exec.pdf. I am aware of the criticism that has been levelled at this report, but it

seems to me that even those most sceptical about the so-called 'official' version of the 9/11 attacks can acknowledge that, in Peter Dale Scott's words, 'in many areas the report gives a useful and accurate summary of events' (Peter Dale Scott, *The road to 9/11: Wealth, empire, and the future of America* (Berkeley, CA, and London: University of California Press, 2007), p. 196).

8. See the video available online: https://www.youtube.com/watch?v=2Qg-rdCQ5dc. For a detailed account of the first images of 9/11 broadcast by CNN, see Paddy Scannell, 'Quelle est la réalité du malheur?', in D. Dayan (ed.), *La terreur spectacle: Terrorisme et télévision* (Brussels: De Boeck/INA, 2006), pp. 25–39; Amy Reynolds and Brooke Barnett, '"America under attack": CNN's verbal and visual framing of September 11', in S. Chermak, F. Y. Bailey and M. Brown (eds.), *Media representations of September 11* (London and Westport, CT: Praeger, 2003), pp. 85–102.

9. Greg Myers, '*Vox populi*: Les micros-trottoirs du 11 septembre', in Dayan, *La terreur spectacle*, pp. 187–98.

10. As we now know, the only person who, with a professional camera and from Manhattan itself, filmed the moment American Airlines Flight 11 crashed into the north tower was Jules Naudet, a French documentary maker who was making a film report on New York's firefighters with his brother. Their film subsequently became a unique document on 11 September (Jules and Gédéon Naudet, *9/11*, CBS Television, 2002).

11. Special edition, France 3, 11 September 2001, 3.49 p.m.–4.03 p.m., verbatim at 1'50. See the video online: http://www.dailymotion.com/video/x6al45_france3-15h-49-16h03-flash-special-1_news.

12. See Louis Quéré, 'Entre fait et sens, la dualité de l'événement', *Réseaux*, 139, 2006, pp. 183–218.

13. See David Carr, 'Y a-t-il une expérience directe de l'histoire? La chute du mur de Berlin et le 11 septembre 2001', *A Contrario*, 13, 2010, pp. 83–94.

14. More than two weeks after the attacks, on 7 October, in a televised address in which he announced the participation of French military forces in the war waged by the United States in Afghanistan, President Jacques Chirac was still speaking of the 'six thousand innocent people who had died' (Mikaël Guedj and Yoanna Sultan-R'bibo, *11 septembre: Paris, 14 h 46* (Paris: Stock, 2001), p. 173). It would take several months before the final toll was known, actually half Chirac's figure (2,973 dead according to the official report; four more deaths have since been added to this total, thus bringing it to 2,977).

15. Bob Woodward, *Bush at War* (New York, NY: Simon & Schuster, 2002), p. 37.
16. See Geoffrey M. White, 'National subjects: September 11 and Pearl Harbor', *American Ethnologist*, 31 (3), 2004, pp. 293–310.
17. Robert Kagan, 'A declaration of war', in the *Washington Post*, 11 September 2001, available online at: http://www.washingtonpost.com/wp-srv/nation/articles/kagan11.htm.
18. Televised address by President George W. Bush, 12 September 2001, transcript available online: http://news.bbc.co.uk/2/hi/americas/1540544.stm.
19. Adopted unanimously in less than half an hour, this resolution was subsequently the subject of much debate and criticism: see in particular Monique Chemillier-Gendreau, 'Démission du Conseil de sécurité', *Le Monde Diplomatique*, 572, November 2001, p. 18, and Olivier Corten and François Dubuisson, 'Opération "liberté immutable": Une extension abusive du concept de légitime défense', *Revue Générale de Droit International Public*, 106, 2002, pp. 51–77.
20. In a telephone conversation with the mayor of New York and the governor of the State of New York; the transcript is available online: http://georgewbush-hitehouse.archives.gov/news/releases/2001/09/20010913-4.html.
21. Randall Collins, 'Rituals of solidarity and security in the wake of terrorist attack', *Sociological Theory*, 22 (1), 2004, pp. 53–87 at pp. 57–8.
22. President George W. Bush, 'Address to the Joint Session of the 107th Congress', speech given in the Capitol, Washington, DC, 20 September 2001, available online: https://georgewbush-whitehouse.archives.gov/infocus/bushrecord/documents/Selected_Speeches_George_W_Bush.pdf.
23. Daniel Dayan and Elihu Katz, *La télévision cérémonielle: Anthropologie et histoire en direct* (Paris: PUF, 1992); Elihu Katz and Tamar Liebes, '"No more peace!": How disaster, terror and war have upstaged media events', *International Journal of Communication*, 1, 2007, pp. 157–66.
24. Robin Wagner-Pacifici, 'Theorizing the restlessness of events', *American Journal of Sociology*, 115 (5), 2010, pp. 1351–86.
25. *The 9/11 Commission report: Final report of the National Commission on Terrorist Attacks upon the United States* (Washington, DC: National Commission on Terrorist Attacks upon the United States, 2004), pp. 45–6, available online: http://govinfo.library.unt.edu/911/report/911Report.pdf, pp. 45–6.

26. *9/11 Commission report*, p. 337.
27. Special edition, France 3, 11 September 2001, 3.49 p.m.–4.03 p.m., verbatim between 11' and 12'.
28. Special news flash, France 2, 11 September 2001, 3.33 p.m.–5.39 p.m., verbatim between 15' and 17'. See the video available online: http://www.dailymotion.com/video/xb3pj4_france2-15h33-17h39-flash-special-1_news.
29. See Elisabeth Anker, 'Villains, victims and heroes: Melodrama, media and September 11', *Journal of Communication*, 55 (1), 2005, p. 22–37.
30. Reynolds and Barnett, '"America under attack"', p. 92.
31. Reynolds and Barnett, '"America under attack"', p. 93.
32. Quoted in N. R. Kleinfield, 'A creeping horror and panicked flight as towers burn, then slowly fall', *New York Times*, 12 September 2001.
33. Carole Gluck, '11 septembre: Guerre et télévision au XXIe siècle', *Annales: Histoire, Sciences Sociales*, 58 (1), 2003, pp. 135–62 at p. 137.
34. See Emily S. Rosenberg, *A date which will live: Pearl Harbor in American memory* (Durham, NC, and London: Duke University Press, 2003); Clement Chéroux, *Diplopie: L'image photographique à l'ère des médias globalisés. Essai sur le 11 septembre 2001* (Cherbourg-Octeville: Le Point du Jour, 2009), pp. 92–8.
35. Rosenberg, *A date which will live*, p. 170.
36. On this film, see Geoffrey M. White, 'Disney's *Pearl Harbor*: National memory at the movies', *Public Historian*, 24 (4), 2002, pp. 97–115.
37. See Susan D. Moeller, *Shooting war: Photography and the American experience of combat* (New York, NY: Basic Books, 1989).
38. Chéroux, *Diplopie*, pp. 24–7.
39. Chéroux, *Diplopie*, pp. 58–60.
40. Marie-Monique Robin, *Les 100 photos du siècle* (Paris: Éditions du Chêne, 1999), p. 27.
41. See Chéroux, *Diplopie*, pp. 60–74.
42. Special newsflash, France 2, 11 September 2001, 3.33 p.m.–5.39 p.m., verbatim between 15' and 17'. The same thing could be observed on the BBC: see Gwen Bouvier, '"Breaking news": The first hours of BBC coverage of 9/11 as a media event', in T. Pludowski (ed.), *How the world's news media reacted to 9/11: Essays from around the world* (Spokane, WA: Marquette Books, 2007), pp. 69–74.

43. Annabelle Sreberny, 'Pour qui nous prenons-nous? La distance journalistique et le problème du pronom', in Dayan, *La terreur spectacle*, pp. 229–41.
44. Frédéric Ramel, 'Presse écrite et traitement immédiat du 11 septembre: Un imaginaire occidental réactivé?', *Mots*, 76, 2004, pp. 113–26.
45. Special edition, France 3, 11 September 2001, 3.49 p.m.–4.03 p.m., verbatim at 12'.
46. *Le Figaro*, 14 September 2001, p. 20.
47. She later turned this into a pamphlet that amounted to a declaration of war on Islam: Oriana Fallaci, *The rage and the pride* (New York, NY: Rizzoli, 2002). On the reception and impact of this book in Italy, see Bruno Cousin and Tommaso Vitale, 'Le magistère intellectuel islamophobe d'Oriana Fallaci: Origines et modalités du succès italien de la "Trilogie sur l'Islam et sur l'Occident" (2001–2006)', *Sociologie*, 5 (1), 2014, pp. 61–79.
48. Denis Jeambar and Alain Louyot, 'Guerre contre l'Occident', *L'Express*, 2619, 13–19 September 2001, p. 13 and pp. 17–18.
49. Samuel P. Huntington, *The clash of civilizations and the remaking of world order* (New York, NY: Simon & Schuster, 1996). The book was immediately translated into most European languages, including French (*Le choc des civilisations*, tr. J.-L. Fidel et al. (Paris: Odile Jacob, 1997, 1st edn 1996)). For a critique of Huntington's ideas in the context of the post-9/11 period, see Marc Crépon, *L'imposture du choc des civilisations* (Paris: Éditions Pleins Feux, 2002).
50. Quoted in René-Éric Dagorn, 'Huntington ou la culture de l'ennemi', Espacestemps.net, 5 March 2003, available online: http://www.espacestemps.net/articles/huntington-ou-la-culture-de-lennemi.
51. Dominique Dhombres, 'La prédiction de Samuel Huntington: Le début d'une grande guerre', *Le Monde*, 13 September 2001, p. 19.
52. *Le Monde*, 13 September 2001, p. 8.
53. *Le Monde*, 13 September 2001, p. 8. See also Gerhard Schröder, *Ma vie et la politique*, tr. G. Bégou et al. (Paris: Odile Jacob, 2006), p. 122 and p. 126; originally published in German as *Entscheidungen: Mein Leben in der Politik*, 3rd edn (Hamburg: Hoffmann und Campe, 2006).
54. The exact number of messages inventoried was 4,723. The last was dated 12 October 2001, but the flood of messages started to dry up after 26 September.
55. These figures have been obtained by including only messages whose authors explicitly give their ages, or provide sufficient clues for this to be worked out.

NOTES TO PP. 25–28

56. Mémorial de Caen, OF (Operation 'Fraternally'), message without date.
57. Mémorial de Caen, OF, message without date.
58. Mémorial de Caen, OF, message of 25 September 2001.
59. Philippe Méchet and Dominique Reynié, 'Les opinions publiques face à la crise du 11 septembre 2001', in B. Cautrès and D. Reynié (eds.), *L'opinion européenne 2002* (Paris: Presses de Sciences Po, 2002), p. 40.
60. Méchet and Reynié, 'Les opinions publiques', p. 40.
61. President Johannes Rau, speech in Berlin on 14 September 2001, available online: www.welt.de/print-welt/article476104/Rau-Wir-muessen-den-Terrorismus-bekaempfen.html.
62. Schröder, *Ma vie et la politique*, p. 122.
63. 'Conclusions and Plan of Action of the Extraordinary European Council Meeting (21 September 2001)', available online: http:// europa.eu/rapid/press-release_DOC-01-13_fr.doc, or: http://www. cvce.eu/en/obj/conclusions_and_plan_of_action_of_the_extraor-dinary_european_council_meeting_21_september_2001-en-a012ede7-96d9-4c37-a7ce-cae949ddf401.html.
64. Jeambar and Louyot, 'Guerre contre l'Occident', p. 18 (my emphasis).
65. *Le Monde*, 13 September 2001, p. 7; *Paris Match*, 2730, 20–7 September 2001, p. 63.
66. Chéroux, *Diplopie*, p. 83.
67. Aurélia Lamy, *La médiatisation de l'*'Apocalypse'*: Le traitement médiatique des attentats du 11 septembre 2001 aux États-Unis dans la presse et à la télévision françaises (11–18 septembre 2001)*, PhD thesis, Metz, Université Paul Verlaine, 2005, p. 163.
68. Ramel, 'Presse écrite et traitement immédiat du 11 septembre', p. 119.
69. Michael Bromley and Stephen Cushion, 'Media fundamentalism: The immediate response of the UK national press to September 11', in B. Zelizer and S. Allan (eds.), *Journalism after September 11* (London and New York, NY: Routledge, 2002), pp. 160–77. However, the British press was, in Europe, the most likely to be closer to the way the US media reported 9/11 as an act of war against the United States rather than as an apocalypse: see Brian McNair, 'UK media coverage of September 11', in Pludowski, *How the world's news media reacted to 9/11*, pp. 29–37.
70. Chéroux, *Diplopie*, p. 84.
71. François Lagarde, 'Penser l'impensable: Le 11 Septembre des penseurs français', *French Politics, Culture & Society*, 23 (2), 2005,

pp. 91–100. It is worth remembering the opening of Alexandre Adler's book *J'ai vu finir le monde ancien* (Paris: Grasset, 2002): 'Yes, it was indeed an Apocalypse, [...] this terrible spectacle of 11 September' (p. 7).

72. See Michaël Foessel, *Après la fin du monde: Critique de la raison apocalyptique* (Paris: Seuil, 2012).
73. *Paris Match*, 2730, 20 September 2001, p. 42.
74. John Berger, 'The first fireball', *Guardian*, 29 June 2002, available online: https://www.theguardian.com/world/2002/jun/29/usa.japan.
75. Gérald Arboit, 'Rôles et fonctions des images de cadavres dans les médias: L'actualité permanente du "massacre des Saints Innocents"', *Annuaire Français de Relations Internationales*, 4, 2003, pp. 828–48 at p. 830.
76. Serge July, 'Le nouveau désordre mondial', *Libération*, 13 September 2001, p. 48. For a critical analysis of this comparison, see Antoine Bousquet, 'Time Zero: Hiroshima, September 11 and apocalyptic revelations in historical consciousness', *Millennium: Journal of International Studies*, 34 (3), 2006, pp. 739–64.
77. Special edition, TF1, 11 September 2001, 5.24 p.m., quoted in Lamy, *La médiatisation de l'*'Apocalypse', p. 31.
78. *Paris Match*, 2730, 20–7 September 2001, p. 67.
79. Only 6 per cent of them were in favour of military reprisals, and 29 per cent in favour of their country supporting the US in the event of military intervention. See Méchet and Reynié, 'Les opinions publiques', pp. 40–3.
80. Iathanassios N. Samaras, 'Représentation du 11-Septembre dans quatre journaux grecs: Une question de cadrage', *Questions de Communication*, 8, 2005, pp. 367–89.
81. 'Le massacre des innocents', *Le Monde*, 16–17 September 2001, p. 18.
82. 'Manichéisme', *Le Figaro*, 14 September 2001, p. 20.
83. 'Les valeurs d'Occident', *Le Monde*, 16–17 September 2001, p. 18.
84. Victor Roudometof and William Haller, 'Cosmopolitan trends across world regions: Discerning a European exceptionalism', in R. Robertson and A. S. Krossa (eds.), *European cosmopolitanism in question* (Basingstoke: Palgrave Macmillan, 2012), p. 147.
85. Tzvetan Todorov, *Duties and delights: The life of a go-between. Interviews by Catherine Portevin*, tr. Gila Walker (Longford: Seagull, 2008), pp. 402–3.
86. Méchet and Reynié, 'Les opinions publiques', p. 40.

87. See *Le Monde*, 12 September 2001, p. 8; *Frankfurter Allgemeine*, 14 September 2001, p. 9, and 15 September 2001, p. 7; *Der Spiegel*, 15 September, 38 (of 2001), p. 35.
88. See chapter 8.
89. Mémorial de Caen, OF, message of 19 September 2001.
90. Mémorial de Caen, OF, message of 19 September 2001.
91. Mémorial de Caen, OF, message of 14 September 2001.
92. President Johannes Rau, speech in Berlin on 14 September 2001.
93. Jacques Derrida and Jürgen Habermas, *Philosophy in a time of terror: Dialogues with Jürgen Habermas and Jacques Derrida*, interviewed by Giovanna Borradori (Chicago, IL, and London: University of Chicago Press, 2003).
94. Daniele Archibugi, 'Terrorism and cosmopolitanism', *Social Science Research Council*, 2001, available online: http://www.ssrc.org/sept11/essays/archibugi_text_only.htm. For a later defence of this cosmopolitan response to 9/11 that takes account of the results of the war on terrorism, see David Held, 'Cosmopolitanism after 9/11', *International Politics*, 47, 2010, pp. 52–61. And for a critical discussion, see James Brassett, 'Cosmopolitan sentiments after 9–11?', *Journal of Critical Globalisation Studies*, 2, 2010, pp. 12–29.
95. See Étienne Balibar, *L'Europe, l'Amérique, la guerre* (Paris: La Découverte, 2003), pp. 15–35.
96. 'Conclusions and Plan of Action of the Extraordinary European Council Meeting (21 September 2001)'.
97. See Jacques Sémelin, 'Le 11 septembre comme massacre: La rationalité délirante et la propagation de la peur', *Vingtième Siècle*, 76, 2002, pp. 15–24; Jacques Sémelin, *Purifier et détruire: Usages politiques des massacres et génocides* (Paris: Seuil, 2005), pp. 414–31.
98. Jean-Marie Colombani, 'Nous sommes tous Américains', *Le Monde*, 13 September 2001, p. 1 and p. 18.
99. Quoted in in Guillaume Soulez, 'Choc en retour: Les téléspectateurs et le 11 septembre 2001', in Dayan, *La terreur spectacle*, p. 226.
100. 'Réflexions après l'attentat: Le syndrome post-11-Septembre. Entretien avec Alain Joxe, Pierre Hassner et Mohammad-Reza Djalili (propos recueillis par S. Cypel et D. Vernet)', *Le Monde*, 24 September 2001, reissued in the collective work *11 septembre, un an après* (Paris and La Tour d'Aigues: Le Monde and Éditions de l'Aube, 2002), p. 103.
101. Jean-Paul Dollé, 'Nous ne sommes pas tous Américains, nous sommes New-Yorkais', *L'Infini*, 78, 2002, p. 101 (my emphasis).

102. Toni Negri, 'Ruptures dans l'Empire, puissance de l'exode (entretien avec G. Cocco et M. Lazzarato)', *Multitudes*, 7, 2001, p. 80.
103. 'Daniel Cohn-Bendit: "Nous sommes tous madrilènes" (propos recueillis par H. Vernet)', *Le Parisien-Aujourd'hui en France*, 13 March 2004, p. 5.
104. Colombani, 'Nous sommes tous Américains'.
105. Dollé, 'Nous ne sommes pas tous Américains'.
106. See Alexander T. Riley, *Angel patriots: The crash of United Flight 93 and the myth of America* (New York, NY, and London: New York University Press, 2015).
107. Lamy, *La médiatisation de l'"Apocalypse"*, pp. 134–7. See also Aurélia Lamy, 'Récits médiatiques, mémoires électives. De la construction de l'événement à celle de l'oubli: L'exemple du 11 septembre 2001', Espacestemps.net, 21 November 2007, available online: http://www.espacestemps.net/articles/recits-mediatiques-memoires-electives.
108. Myers, *'Vox populi'*, p. 195.
109. Lamy, *La médiatisation de l'"Apocalypse"*, p. 136.
110. Pascal Lardellier, *11 septembre 2001 … Que faisiez-vous-ce jour-là?* (Grolley: Éditions de l'Hèbe, 2006), p. 152.
111. Julien Fragnon, 'Quand le 11-Septembre s'approprie le onze septembre: Entre dérive métonymique et antonomase', *Mots*, 85, 2007, pp. 83–95.

Chapter 2 Experiencing your 'own' 9/11

1. See '"Charlie Hebdo": Hollande face à son 11-Septembre', *Le Parisien*, 8 January 2015, available online: http://www.leparisien.fr/charlie-hebdo/charlie-hebdo-hollande-face-a-son-11-septembre-08-01-2015-4429399.php.
2. See Tania Roy, '"India's 9/11": Accidents of a moveable metaphor', *Theory, Culture & Society*, 26 (7–8), 2009, pp. 314–28.
3. The facts and the number of casualties given here follow the conclusions of the National Court and the Supreme Court of Spain, available online: http://www.asociacion11m.org/juicio-11m-sumario-20-04.php.
4. Cathy Ceïbe, '"D'un seul coup, des scènes de guerre"', *L'Humanité*, 12 March 2004, p. 3.
5. *ABC*, special edition, 11 March 2004, p. 12; *El Mundo*, special edition, 11 March 2004, p. 1.
6. J.-F. Gintzburger, '11 mars 2004, 11 septembre de l'Espagne', *La Voix du Nord*, 13 March 2004.

7. Resolution No. 1530, 11 March 2004. In connection with this resolution, Sylvia Desazars de Montgailhard speaks of an 'unusual example of a collective diplomatic error', one which forced Spain a few days later to present an official apology to the United Nations, and cost the Spanish ambassador to the UN his job (Sylvia Desazars de Montgailhard, *Madrid et le monde: Les tourments d'une reconquête* (Paris: Autrement, 2007), p. 142).

8. *Le Monde*, 12 March 2004, pp. 1–2.

9. José María Aznar, speech from the Palace of Moncloa, Madrid, 11 March 2004, available online: http://www.elmundo.es/elmundo/2004/03/11/espana/1079016264.html.

10. Remarks quoted in *Le Monde*, 13 March 2004, p. 7. In his memoirs, Javier Rupérez also noted that, when he made these declarations, he was completely convinced that ETA was indeed behind the attack (Javier Rupérez, *Memoria de Washington: Embajador de España en la capital del Imperio* (Madrid: La Esfera de los Libros, 2011), p. 286).

11. Juan Juaristi, 'Madrid, 11 de marzo', *ABC*, 12 March 2004, p. 3.

12. Gérard Chaliand, 'Réflexions sur le "11 septembre des Espagnols"', *Le Figaro*, 13 March 2004, p. 15.

13. '"Tous unis contre la terreur"', *Le Monde*, 13 March 2004, p. 6; '"Notre 11 septembre"', *Le Monde*, 13 March 2004, p. 7.

14. Robert Belleret, 'Stupeur, indignation, colère et chagrin submergent les espagnols', *Le Monde*, 13 March 2004, p. 4.

15. Daniel Vernet, 'Le 11 Septembre de l'Europe', *Le Monde*, 13 March 2004, p. 16.

16. *France-Soir*, 12 March 2004, p. 2 (my emphasis).

17. Quoted in 'World press in shock over Madrid blasts', *BBC News*, 12 March 2004, available online: http://news.bbc.co.uk/go/pr/fr/-/2/hi/europe/3505082.stm.

18. Quoted by AFP in 'L'hypothèse d'Al-Qaida se renforce dans la presse européenne', press dispatch of 13 March 2004.

19. 'Tragédie européenne', *Le Monde*, 13 March 2004, p. 16.

20. 'Statement by Pat Cox on the terrorist attacks in Spain', Strasbourg, 11 March 2014, available online: http://www.europarl.europa.eu/former_ep_presidents/president-cox/press/en/cp0100.htm.

21. See Gérôme Truc, 'Aux victimes du terrorisme, l'Europe reconnaissante? Portée et limites de la Journée européenne en mémoire des victimes du terrorisme', *Politique Européenne*, 37, 2012, pp. 132–54.

22. Michel Barnier, 'Prévenir un "11 septembre européen"', *Le Figaro*, 15 September 2003, p. 13.

23. Vernet, 'Le 11 Septembre de l'Europe'.
24. 'Javier Solana: "Ici, en Europe, on va souffrir"', *La Dépêche du Midi*, 14–15 March 2004, p. 6.
25. Timothy Garton Ash, 'Is this Europe's 9/11?', *Guardian*, 13 March 2004, available online: http://www.guardian.co.uk/politics/2004/mar/13/spain.world.
26. Tenth Session of the Parliamentary Grand Commission on France-Russia, Paris, 13–15 May 2004, speech by Jean-Louis Debré, president of the National Assembly, available online: http://www.assemblee-nationale.fr/12/rap-dian/dian044-2004.asp.
27. 'Le 11-Mars en procès à Madrid', *Le Monde*, 15 February 2007, p. 1.
28. This was the view taken by Sergio Romano in particular, in an editorial in *Corriere della Sera* published on 12 March 2004. The next day, in *Le Monde*, Xavier Crettiez replied that 'this speculation is absurd', given that ETA was a 'totally paranoid' organization (interview by A. Chemin, *Le Monde*, 13 March 2004, p. 8).
29. Alain Duhamel, 'L'Europe en première ligne', *Nice-Matin*, 13 March 2004, p. 1 and p. 18.
30. Alain Duhamel, 'L'Espagne au secours de l'Europe', *Libération*, 17 March 2004, p. 36.
31. Aurélie Aubert, 'France: La construction d'un public européen', *Hermès*, 46, 2006, pp. 85–8.
32. Interview with Noëlle Lenoir, Minister for Foreign Affairs, Radio Classique, 15 March 2004, transcription available online: http://discours.vie-publique.fr/notices/043000853.html.
33. Cristina Hermeziu, 'Roumanie: La dimension d'un drame national', *Hermès*, 46, 2006, pp. 101–5.
34. Sixteen Romanians, four Bulgarians, four Poles, two Ukrainians and one French person.
35. Fausto Colombo, 'Italie: Une analogie avec l'Espagne', *Hermès*, 46, 2006, pp. 79–84.
36. Laura Teruel Rodríguez, 'La cobertura del 11M–15M en la prensa noruega: Una perspectiva mediática desde el norte de Europa', *Revista Latina de Comunicación Social*, 60, 2005, available online: http://www.ull.es/publicaciones/latina/200521teruel.htm.
37. Victor F. Sampedro Blanco, Raquel Rodriguez, José M. García de Madariaga and Fernando Tucho, 'El 11-M y el 14-M en la prensa de referencia anglosajona (EE.UU. y Reino Unido)', in A. Vara Miguel, J. Rodríguez Virgili, E. Giménez Toledo and M. Díaz Méndez (eds.), *Cobertura informativa del 11-M* (Pamplona: EUNSA, 2006), pp. 255–73.

38. Jan Mewes, *11 März 2004 – Madrid im Spiegel der Presse: Eine vergleichende Inhaltsanalyse der Berichterstattung über den Terroranschlag in den Printmedien 'Frankfurter Allgemeine Zeitung', 'Frankfurter Rundschau' und 'New York Times'* (Munich: GRIN, 2007).
39. From 12 to 21 March 2004, 150 articles were published on the Madrid attack in *Le Monde* and *Le Figaro*, as against 62 in the *Süddeutsche Zeitung* and the *Frankfurter Allgemeine Zeitung*. See Manuel Martínez Nicolás, María Luisa Humanes and Pablo Francescutti, 'Amenazas y consensos: La cobertura del 11-M y del 14-M en la prensa de referencia francesa y alemana', in Vara Miguel, Virgili, Gimenéz Toledo and Díaz Méndez, *Cobertura informativa del 11-M*, pp. 275–80.
40. 'Je crois que bcp [beaucoup] d'entre nous sont avec vous', message posted on the forum of *Libération*, 12 March 2004.
41. 'Paroles de françaises venues par simple solidarité', Radio France, 12 March 2004.
42. '3 questions à … Jean-François Daguzan', *France-Soir*, 12 March 2004, p. 5.
43. See Anna Lisa Tota, 'Terrorism and collective memories: Comparing Bologna, Naples, Madrid 11 March', *International Journal of Comparative Sociology*, 46 (1–2), 2005, pp. 55–78.
44. See chapter 10.
45. 'Réaction au témoignage de Françoise Rudetzki dans l'émission "Tout le monde en parle" – Attentats de Madrid', message posted on the forum of the website sos-attentats.org on 14 March 2004.
46. *La Provence*, 15 March 2004, p. 25 (my emphasis).
47. The facts and the number of casualties are quoted from the report prepared for the House of Commons, dated 11 May 2006, available online: https://www.gov.uk/government/publications/report-of-the-official-account-of-the-bombings-in-london-on-7th-july-2005.
48. Most of the victims of the Lockerbie bombing were US citizens (189 to be precise, as against 43 British nationals), as the aircraft attacked belonged to the US company Pan American.
49. 'London terror attack "inevitable"', *BBC News*, 16 March 2004, available online: http://news.bbc.co.uk/2/hi/uk_news/politics/3515312.stm.
50. See the official list of victims of British nationality released by the Foreign and Commonwealth Office in September 2002, available online: http://www.guardian.co.uk/world/2002/sep/10/september11.uk.

51. Jean-Pierre Langellier, 'À Londres en deuil, l'hymne américain devant Buckingham', *Le Monde*, 15 September 2001, p. 1.
52. Opened in July 2010, this memorial has since been extended to include the victims of 11 September who were nationals of other Commonwealth countries (Canada and Australia, initially); accordingly, it was officially renamed in May 2012 as the 'Queen Elizabeth II September 11th Garden'.
53. Anna Reading, 'The London bombings: Mobile witnessing, mortal bodies and globital time', *Memory Studies*, 4 (3), 2011, pp. 298–311 at p. 304.
54. See Darren Kelsey, *Media, myth and terrorism: A discourse-mythological analysis of the 'Blitz Spirit' in British newspaper responses to the July 7th Bombings* (New York, NY, and Basingstoke: Palgrave Macmillan, 2015).
55. See 'What the papers say', *Guardian*, 8 July 2005, available online: http://www.guardian.co.uk/media/2005/jul/08/pressandpublishing.terrorism1.
56. Quoted in Rowland Manthorpe, 'Spirit of the Brits', *Guardian*, 1 July 2006, available online: http://www.guardian.co.uk/books/2006/jul/01/featuresreviews.guardianreview29.
57. André Gunthert, 'Comment "Zero Dark Thirty" écrit l'histoire', *Culture Visuelle* (blog), 17 February 2013, available online: http://culturevisuelle.org/icones/2630#more-2630.
58. 'In the face of danger', *Guardian*, 8 July 2005, available online: http://www.guardian.co.uk/world/ 2005/jul/08/terrorism.july71.
59. Of course, at the time of the Second World War, London could already be considered a cosmopolitan city, but the mythologized version of the ordeal of the Blitz specifically helped impose the representation of an ethnically homogeneous British capital, populated mainly by white Protestants. See Paul Gilroy, *After Empire: Melancholia or convivial culture?* (Abingdon: Routledge, 2004), p. 95.
60. Ken Livingstone, 'London will not be divided', speech delivered via videolink from Singapore on 7 July 2005, available online: http://www.independent.co.uk/news/uk/home-news/ken-livingstones-speech-77-bombings-from-singapore-speak-to-those-come-to-london-10370832.html.
61. Delphine Papin, 'Les attentats de Londres, révélateur du malaise de la nation britannique', *Hérodote*, 120, 2006, pp. 190–9.
62. See Virtudes Téllez, 'Respuesta de los musulmanes a los atentados del 11 de marzo', in C. Sánchez-Carretero (ed.), *El Archivo del Duelo: Análisis de la respuesta ciudadana ante los atentados del 11 de marzo en Madrid* (Madrid: CSIC, 2011), pp. 167–8; Anna

Caresche and Carole Da Costa Dias, *El Islam: Una realidad social en España* (Madrid: Liga Española Pro Derechos Humanos, 2010).

63. European Monitoring Centre on Racism and Xenophobia, *The impact of 7 July 2005 London bomb attacks on Muslim communities in the EU* (Luxembourg: Office for Official Publications of the European Communities, 2006), available online: https://fra.europa.eu/sites/default/files/fra_uploads/197-London-Bomb-attacks-EN.pdf.

64. See Angharad Closs Stephens, 'Seven million Londoners, one London: National and urban ideas of community', in Closs Stephens and Vaughan Williams, *Terrorism and the politics of response*, pp. 68–70.

65. Léo Benedictus, 'Every race, colour, nation and religion on earth', *Guardian Unlimited*, 21 January 2005, available online: http://www.guardian.co.uk/uk/2005/jan/21/britishidentity1.

66. See the piece available online: http://www.guardian.co.uk/britain/london/0,,1394802,00.html.

67. Maxine Frith, 'The world city: One in three Londoners was born overseas', *Independent*, 14 November 2006, available online: http://www.independent.co.uk/news/uk/this-britain/the-world-city-one-in-three-londoners-was-born-overseas-424239.html.

68. See table 1, p. 47.

69. *Paris Match*, 2930, 13–20 July 2005, p. 52.

70. Ben Hoyle and Devika Bhat, 'A grieving world in one city as many nations suffer loss', *The Times*, 11 July 2005, p. 8.

71. *Report of the official account of the bombings in London on 7th July 2005*, commissioned by the House of Commons, 11 May 2006, p. 1.

72. Andrew Linklater, 'Distant suffering and cosmopolitan obligations', *International Politics*, 44 (1), 2007, pp. 19–36 at p. 19; James Brassett, 'Cosmopolitanism vs. terrorism? Discourses of ethical possibility before and after 7/7', *Millennium: Journal of International Studies*, 36 (2), 2008, pp. 311–37.

73. Brassett, 'Cosmopolitanism vs. terrorism?', p. 313.

74. Tony Blair, declaration on the London bombings, Gleneagles (Scotland), 7 July 2005, reported for instance in the *Guardian* (https://www.theguardian.com/uk/2005/jul/07/july7.terrorism).

75. Brassett, 'Cosmopolitanism vs. terrorism?', p. 313.

76. Martin Karbovski, 'Notre 11-Septembre à nous', *Courrier International*, 1134, 26 July 2012, p. 17.

77. Maxime Behar, 'Pourquoi la Bulgarie?', *Courrier International*, 1134, 26 July 2012, p. 17.

Chapter 3 To show, or not to show, violence

1. See Emmanuel Taïeb, 'Faut-il montrer les images de violence?', *La Vie des Idées*, 7 July 2015, available online: http://www.laviede-sidees.fr/Faut-il-montrer-les-images-de-violence.html.
2. See chapter 1.
3. François Jost, 'Les images du 11 septembre sont-elles des images violentes?', in Dayan, *La terreur spectacle*, pp. 63–73.
4. Phil Nesbitt, 'Designing for a tragedy', in American Press Institute, *Crisis journalism: A handbook for media response* (New York, NY: American Press Institute, 2001), p. 19.
5. Barbie Zelizer, 'Photographie, journalisme et traumatisme', in Dayan, *La terreur spectacle*, p. 145.
6. Zelizer, 'Photographie', p. 148. See also Arboit, 'Rôles et fonctions', p. 830.
7. See chapter 1.
8. Chéroux, *Diplopie*, pp. 26–7.
9. Zelizer, 'Photographie', p. 145.
10. Susan Linfields, 'Jumpers', *New York Magazine*, available online: http://nymag.com/news/9-11/10th-anniversary/jumpers.
11. See Tom Junod, 'The falling man', *Esquire*, 140 (3), September 2003, available online: http://www.esquire.com/features/ESQ0903-SEP_FALLINGMAN.
12. On this photo and the controversy it aroused, see Daniel Girardin and Christian Pirker (eds.), *Controverses: Une histoire juridique et éthique de la photographie* (Lausanne: Actes Sud/Musée de l'Élysée, 2008), pp. 286–9.
13. Chéroux, *Diplopie*, pp. 38–39.
14. Christian Delage, 'Une censure intériorisée? Les premières images des attentats du 11 septembre 2001', *Ethnologie Française*, 36 (1), 2006, pp. 91–9.
15. See Divina Frau-Meigs, *Qui a détourné le 11 septembre? Journalisme, information et démocratie aux États-Unis* (Brussels: De Boeck/INA, 2005).
16. Chéroux, *Diplopie*, p. 46
17. Chéroux, *Diplopie*, p. 48.
18. Chéroux, *Diplopie*, p. 48.
19. Mission report for Reporters sans frontières, 11 October 2001, quoted in Lamy, *La médiatisation de l'"Apocalypse"*, pp. 477–8.
20. See Lamy, *La médiatisation de l'"Apocalypse"*, p. 522, and Daniel Psenny, 'Polémique autour de la "censure" des images', *Le Monde*, 23 September 2001, media supplement, p. 6.

21. *Paris Match*, 2730, 20–7 September 2001, pp. 53–4.
22. Edition of 13 September 2001, p. 3.
23. Lamy, *La médiatisation de l''Apocalypse'*, p. 524.
24. Susan Sontag, *Regarding the pain of others* (London: Penguin, 2003), p. 63.
25. See chapter 2.
26. The sample analysed consists of 248 photographs published on the front page on 12 March 2004 (and, in some exceptional cases, on the evening of 11 March), in Spain (42 photos), the rest of Europe (45) and the United States (161).
27. Juan Varela, 'El dolor y la verdad de la imagen', *Sala de Prensa*, 66, April 2004, available online: http://www.saladeprensa.org/art546.htm.
28. Abd al Malik, '12 septembre 2001', *Gibraltar* (Atmosphériques, 2006).
29. 'Merci de ne pas censurer les morts', *Libération*, 13–14 March 2004, p. 9.
30. Remarks reported in *Télérama*, 19 September 2001, p. 92. Quoted in Lamy, *La médiatisation de l''Apocalypse'*, p. 524.
31. In France, some of them were published in *Paris Match*, 2861, 17–24 March 2004, pp. 34–49.
32. Chéroux, *Diplopie*, p. 40.
33. See Varela, 'El dolor y la verdad de la imagen', and Kenneth Irby, 'Beyond taste: Editing truth', *Poynter Online*, 30 March 2004, available online: http://www.poynter.org/content/content_view.asp?id=63131.
34. Todd Venezia, Niles Lathem and Aly Sujo, 'Spain reels from a "9/11"', *New York Post*, 12 March 2004, p. 4, available online: http://nypost.com/2004/03/12/spain-reels-from-a-911-death-toll-192-in-10-rail-blasts-scenes-of-horror-in-madrid-qaeda-among-prime-suspects-3.
35. Sontag, *Regarding the pain of others*, p. 64.
36. See chapter 1.
37. Chéroux, *Diplopie*, p. 77.
38. Laurent Gervereau, *Montrer la guerre? Information ou propaganda* (Paris: CNDP, 2006), pp. 62–4 and p. 98.
39. Robin, *Les 100 photos du siècle*, p. 21.
40. Gervereau, *Montrer la guerre?*, p. 93.
41. In France, they were published in the Communist periodical *Regards*, 148, 11 November 1936, under the title 'Nous accusons …'. On the history of these photographs, see Merche Fernández, 'La fotografía acusa', on the blog of the exhibition 'La maleta mexicana' at the Museu Nacional

d'Art de Catalunya, 30 November 2011, available online: http://maletamexicana.mnac.cat/2011/11/la-fotografia-acusa.
42. Angel Casaña, 'Las imágenes que acabaron con ETA', *La Foto* (blog), 21 October 2011: http://www.elmundo.es/blogs/elmundo/lafotodelasemana/2011/10/21/las-imagenes-que-acabaron-con-eta.html.
43. Arboit, 'Rôles et fonctions', p. 846.
44. Quoted in Irby, 'Beyond taste: Editing truth'.
45. Luc Boltanski, *Distant suffering: Morality, media and politics*, tr. Graham Burchell (Cambridge: Cambridge University Press, 1999), pp. 114–30.
46. See also Sontag, *Regarding the pain of others*, pp. 39–42.
47. Jean-Claude Passeron, *Le raisonnement sociologique: Un espace non poppérien de l'argumentation* (Paris: Albin Michel, 2006 [1991]), p. 424.
48. See the documentary film *Goya: El secreto de la sombra*, by David Mauas (2011).
49. See Fuyuki Kurasawa, 'L'humanitaire, manifestation du cosmopolitisme?', *Sociologie et Sociétés*, 44 (1), 2012, pp. 212–37, and Kurasawa, 'The sentimentalist paradox: On the normative and visual foundations of humanitarianism', *Journal of Global Ethics*, 9 (2), 2013, pp. 201–14.
50. Antonio Cea-Gutiérrez, 'Sistema y mentalidad devocional en las estampas del 11M: Imágenes, palabras, tiempos, lágrimas', in Sánchez-Carretero, *El Archivo del Duelo*, pp. 175–203.
51. Deborah Puccio-Den, *Les théâtres de 'Maures et Chrétiens': Conflits politiques et dispositifs de réconciliation (Espagne, Sicile, XVIIe–XXIe siècles)* (Turnhout: Brepols, 2009), p. 183.
52. See http://madridinmemoriam.org/, and Adán Burgos and David Burgos (eds.), *Madrid in Memoriam: Una iniciativa para el recuerdo* (Madrid: B & B Ediciones, 2005).
53. Sontag, *Regarding the pain of others*, p. 71.
54. See Daniel C. Hallin, *The 'uncensored war': The media and Vietnam* (New York, NY, and Oxford: Oxford University Press, 1986), and Benjamin Stora, *Imaginaires de guerre: Les images dans les guerres d'Algérie et du Viêt-nam* (Paris: La Découverte, 2004).
55. 'Since it had been developed in the mid-nineteenth century, pacifist pedagogy had always drawn on shocking images that generated strong emotions. *Krieg dem Kriege* by Ernst Friedrich in 1924 is no different from the *Disasters of War* by Francisco Goya in 1811–1812, or the edicts on tolerance of the seventeenth century'

(Arboit, 'Rôles et fonctions', p. 844). See also Luc Capdevila and Danièle Voldman, *Nos morts: Les sociétés occidentales face aux tués de la guerre (XIXe–XXe siècles)* (Paris: Payot, 2002), p. 36.

56. '17 h 30, sur le quai du massacre', *Paris Match*, 2410, 3–10 August 1995, pp. 56–65.

57. André Gunthert, '"Tous journalistes?" Les attentats de Londres ou l'intrusion des amateurs', *Actualités de la Recherche en Histoire Visuelle*, 19 March 2009, available online: http://www.arhv.lhivic. org/index.php/2009/03/19/956-tous-journalistes. (Reprinted in André Gunthert, *L'image partagée: La photographie numérique* (Paris: Textuel, 2015), pp. 43–53.)

58. See chapter 2.

59. There were also a few images of Underground train carriages destroyed by the bombs, taken after the event, once the rescue operations had been completed.

60. See *Paris Match*, 2930, 13–20 July 2005, pp. 46–9.

61. Peter Coulmas, *Les citoyens du monde: Histoire du cosmopolitisme*, tr. J. Étoré (Paris: Albin Michel, 1995 [1990]), p. 290.

Chapter 4   Demonstrating solidarity

1. The number of demonstrators in the streets of Spain on the evening of 12 March 2004 has sometimes been estimated at eleven million: this was the figure given by the government of José María Aznar and relayed by the Spanish media close to the People's Party, in particular the newspaper *El Mundo*. It was also the figure reported by CNN and it is currently found on Wikipedia (both in Spanish and in English). But the call to demonstrate was issued by José María Aznar himself, in the belief that the attack was attributable to ETA, so it is likely that the total number of demonstrators was exaggerated by government sources. That is why newspapers more distant from the government, such as *El País*, and the vast majority of the European press, stuck with the figure of eight million – still the largest number of people to have gathered for a demonstration in the streets of Spain, and indeed Europe (far more than the marches of 11 January 2015).

2. See chapter 2.

3. Ernest Renan, *Qu'est-ce qu'une nation?* (Paris: Mille et Une Nuits, 1997 [1887]), p. 32.

4. See Pierre Favre (ed.), *La manifestation* (Paris: Presses de Sciences Po, 1990).

5. It is still possible today to find images of these gatherings on the Internet. See especially http://www.youtube.com/watch?v=lZiHN3z2o08; http://www.september11news.com/InternationalImages.htm.

6. The Deutsche Bank building in New York was located directly opposite the World Trade Center and four Germans were on board the planes hijacked by the terrorists. Thus, in the first hours after the attacks, the Germans, like the British, feared they would be mourning several hundred of their own dead. In the end, there were only eleven Germans among the people who died in the 11 September attacks.

7. Pierre Favre, 'Manifester en France aujourd'hui', in Favre, *La manifestation*, p. 15.

8. Olivier Fillieule, *Stratégies de la rue: Les manifestations en France* (Paris: Presses de Sciences Po, 1997), p. 43.

9. Jack Santino (ed.), *Spontaneous shrines and the public memorialization of death* (New York, NY, and Basingstoke: Palgrave, 2006); Erika Doss, *The emotional life of contemporary public memorials: Towards a theory of temporary memorials* (Amsterdam: Amsterdam University Press, 2008); Peter Jan Margry and Cristina Sánchez-Carretero (eds.), *Grassroots memorials: The politics of memorializing traumatic death* (New York, NY: Berghahn, 2010).

10. Sylvia Grider, 'Spontaneous shrines: A modern response to tragedy and disaster', *New Directions in Folklore*, 5, 2001, pp. 1–9; Tony Walter, 'From cathedral to supermarket: Mourning, silence and solidarity', *Sociological Review*, 49 (4), 2001, pp. 494–511.

11. See Adrian Kear and Deborah Lynn Steinberg (eds.), *Mourning Diana: Nation, culture and the performance of grief* (London: Routledge, 1999); Tony Walter (ed.), *The mourning for Diana* (Oxford and New York, NY: Berg, 1999).

12. Ewa Klekot, 'Mourning John Paul II in the streets of Warsaw', *Anthropology Today*, 2 (4), 2007, pp. 3–6.

13. See more generally the analysis by Pierre-Yves Baudot, 'Le 11-janvier: Crise ou consensus?', *La Vie des Idées*, 15 September 2015, available online: http://www.laviedesidees.fr/Le-11-janvier-crise-ou-consensus.html.

14. See chapter 1.

15. On the role of the Internet in pacifist activities after 11 September, see Tessa Morris-Suzuki, 'Le missile et la souris: Mouvements virtuels pour la paix dans un âge de terreur', *Annales: Histoire, Sciences Sociales*, 58 (1), 2003, pp. 163–78.

16. Marianne Debouzy, 'Le militantisme politique aux États-Unis au lendemain du 11 septembre 2001', *Transatlantica*, 1, 2008, available online: http://transatlantica.revues.org/2883.

17. Fillieule, *Stratégies de la rue*, pp. 180ff.

18. Gaëlle Clavandier, *La mort collective: Pour une sociologie des catastrophes* (Paris: CNRS Éditions, 2004), p. 47.

19. Émile Durkheim, *Suicide: A study in sociology*, tr. John A. Spaulding and George Simpson, ed. George Simpson (London: Routledge, 2002), p. 299.

20. Danielle Tartakowsky, 'Manifestations: L'émotion est dans la rue', *Sciences Humaines*, 141, 2003, p. 49.

21. See Benjamín Tejerina, 'Protest cycle, political violence and social movements in the Basque country', *Nations and Nationalism*, 7 (1), 2001, pp. 39–57.

22. Laurent Favreuille, '"Madrid n'est pas si loin que ça ..."', *La Nouvelle République du Centre-Ouest* (Vienne edition), 13 March 2004, p. 3.

23. Charles Tilly, *The contentious French* (Cambridge, MA, and London: Belknap Press of Harvard University Press, 1986).

24. Enrique Gil Calvo, *11/14-M, el cambio trágico: De la masacre al vuelco electoral* (Madrid: Adhara, 2005), pp. 149–56.

25. José María Benegas, *Diccionario Espasa terrorismo* (Madrid: Espasa, 2004), p. 75.

26. Dominique Reynié, *La fracture occidentale: Naissance d'une opinion européenne* (Paris: La Table Ronde, 2004), p. 43.

27. Voir María Luz Morán, 'Viejos y nuevos espacios para la ciudadanía: La manifestación del 15 de febrero de 2003 en Madrid', *Política y Sociedad*, 42 (2), 2005, pp. 95–113.

28. Reynié, *La fracture occidentale*, p. 164. On the extent of this opposition movement in Spain, see also Denis Rolland (ed.), *L'Espagne et la guerre du Golfe. D'Aznar à Zapatero: Démocratie, violence et émotion* (Paris: L'Harmattan, 2005).

29. It is known today that the idea of carrying out this attack predated the war in Iraq: it probably originated in December 2001 in Karachi, with an ex-member of an Al-Qaeda cell in Spain that was dismantled after 9/11, who wanted to take revenge. It is true, however, that while this project was being planned by members of the Moroccan Islamic Combatant Group it was endorsed by Al-Qaeda's leadership at the end of 2003, once Spain had engaged in the war in Iraq (bin Laden explicitly threatened Spain in a video broadcast by Al Jazeera on 18 October 2003). See the probably definitive study by Fernando Reinares, *¡Matadlos! Quién estuvo*

detrás del 11-M y por qué se atentó en España (Madrid: Galaxia Gutenberg, 2014).

30. *Barometer of the Real Instituto Elcano de Estudios Internacionales y Estratégicos*, 6th wave, Madrid, June 2004, p. 25.
31. Francisco J. Llera and Alfredo Retortillo (eds.), 'Los Españoles y las víctimas del terrorismo', *Opiniones y Actitudes*, 50, 2005, pp. 84–5.
32. This can be done quite easily by working through local press archives. Although police sources are generally more reliable for information about demonstrations, as the media ignore many of them, this is no longer the case when these sources are reporting on an event that has hit the headlines: 'a small demonstration that ordinarily would not have been the subject of even the shortest news flash will be mentioned if it relates to an international event that momentarily comes to the fore' (Pierre Favre, 'Les manifestations de rue entre espace privé et espaces publics', in P. Favre, O. Fillieule and F. Jobard (eds.), *L'atelier du politiste* (Paris: La Découverte, 2007), pp. 193–213 (p. 203).
33. 'Madrid: Entre silence et indignations', *Le Télégramme de Brest*, 14 March 2004.
34. 'Les Rennais solidaires de l'Espagne', *Ouest-France*, Saturday 13 March, p. 11.
35. 'Une manifestation dans le silence en hommage aux victimes de l'attentat de Madrid a eu lieu hier soir', *Le Progrès*, 13 March 2004, p. 11.
36. 'Attentats de Madrid: Manifestation de solidarité à Copenhague', AFP release, 12 March 2004.
37. 'La solidaridad con Madrid da la vuelta al mundo', *El Mundo*, 14 March 2004 (available online: http://www.elmundo.es/elmundo/2004/03/12/internacional/1079124771.html); 'En Liverpool', message posted on the *El Mundo* forum, 12 March 2004.
38. 'Des hommages à "Charlie Hebdo" dans de nombreuses villes étrangères', *Le Monde*, 11 January 2015, available online: http://www.lemonde.fr/societe/article/2015/01/11/des-hommages-a-charlie-hebdo-dans-de-nombreuses-villes-etrangeres_4553751_3224.html.
39. 'Paroles de trois françaises venues par simple solidarité', Radio France, 12 March 2004.
40. INSEE, 2009 census.
41. 'Viva España!', *L'Est Républicain*, 14 March 2004.
42. See Nicolas Mariot, 'La réflexivité comme second mouvement', *L'Homme*, 203–4, 2012, pp. 369–98.

43. Mancur Olson, *The logic of collective action: Public goods and the theory of groups*, revised edition (Cambridge, MA, and London: Harvard University Press, 1971).

44. For an overview of this problem, see Daniel Cefaï, *Pourquoi se mobilise-t-on? Les théories de l'action collective* (Paris: La Découverte, 2007).

45. Darío Páez, Nekane Basabe, Silvia Ubillos and José Luis González-Castro, 'Social sharing, participation in demonstrations, emotional climate and coping with collective violence after the March 11th Madrid bombings', *Journal of Social Issues*, 63 (2), 2007, pp. 323–37. (See also, based on the same research: Nekane Basabe, Darío Paéz Rovira and Bernard Rimé, 'Efectos y procesos psicosociales de la participación en manifestaciones después del atentado del 11 de marzo', *Ansiedad y Estrés*, 10 (2–3), 2004, pp. 247–63.)

46. Paéz et al., 'Social sharing', p. 334.

47. See also Bernard Rimé, *La partage social des émotions* (Paris: PUF, 2005), p. 357.

48. This is, moreover, a common presupposition of all the articles contained in the special issue of the Spanish social psychology review *Ansiedad y Estrés* devoted to 'The human response to trauma: The consequences of 11 March 2004' (10 (2–3), 2004).

49. See Stéphane Latté, 'La "force de l'événement" est-elle un artefact? Les mobilisations de victimes au prisme des théories événementielles de l'action collective', *Revue Française de Science Politique*, 62 (3), 2012, pp. 409–32.

50. See Didier Fassin and Richard Rechtman, *The empire of trauma: An inquiry into the condition of victimhood*, tr. Rachel Gomme (Princeton, NJ: Princeton University Press, 2009), p. 15.

51. Neil J. Smelser, 'September 11, 2001 as cultural trauma', in J. Alexander, R. Eyerman, B. Giesen, N. J. Smelser and P. Sztompka (eds.), *Cultural trauma and collective identity* (Berkeley, CA: University of California Press, 2004), pp. 264–82.

52. Jeffrey C. Alexander, 'Toward a theory of cultural trauma', in Alexander et al., *Cultural trauma and collective identity*, pp. 1–30.

53. This flaw is also brought out in Chris Rumford, 'Finding meaning in meaningless times: Emotional responses to terror threats in London', in Closs Stephens and Vaughan-Williams, *Terrorism and the politics of response*, p. 168.

54. See Marcel Mauss, 'L'expression obligatoire des sentiments: Rituels oraux funéraires australiens' (1921), *Œuvres*, vol. 3: *Cohésion sociale et divisions de la sociologie* (Paris: Éditions de Minuit, 1969), pp. 269–79; Maurice Halbwachs, 'L'expression

des émotions et la société' (1947), *Vingtième Siècle*, 123, 2014, pp. 39–48.

55. Collins, 'Rituals of solidarity and security', p. 62.
56. Collins, 'Rituals of solidarity and security', p. 62.
57. Michel Offerlé, 'Descendre dans la rue: De la "journée" à la manif', in Favre, *La Manifestation*, p. 109.
58. Favre, 'Les manifestations de rue', p. 199. See also Clark McPhail, *The myth of the madding crowd* (New York, NY: Aldine de Gruyter, 1991).
59. This is a classic example of the local rootedness of transnational social movements. See Sidney Tarrow, *The new transnational activism* (Cambridge and New York, NY: Cambridge University Press, 2005), especially ch. 3, 'Rooted cosmopolitans and transnational militants' (pp. 35–58).
60. Matthew Parris, 'From a rural view, it is too easy to blame those with darker skin', *The Times*, 11 July 2005, p. 10.
61. Benedict Anderson, *Imagined communities: Reflections on the origin and spread of nationalism* (London: Verso, 2016).
62. We will be returning to this in chapter 8.
63. For an overview, see Sophie Duchesne, 'L'identité européenne, entre science politique et science fiction', *Politique Européenne*, 30, 2010, pp. 7–16; Céline Belot, 'Le tournant identitaire des études consacrées aux attitudes à l'égard de l'Europe: Genèses, apports, limites', *Politique Européenne*, 30, 2010, pp. 17–44.
64. Sophie Duchesne and Virginie Van Ingelgom, 'L'indifférence des français et des belges (francophones) pour leurs voisins européens: Une pièce de plus au dossier de l'absence de communauté politique européenne?', *Politique Européenne*, 26, 2008, pp. 143–64 at pp. 160–1.
65. See the 1 April 2004 editions of the newspapers *Libération*, *Le Figaro* and *Le Monde*.
66. Data from *Eurobarometer* 60 (1), Autumn 2003, quoted in Bruno Cautrès, '"Plus on se connaît, plus on s'aime?"', *Politique Européenne*, 26, 2008, pp. 165–90 at p. 172 and p. 179.
67. Cautrès, '"Plus on se connaît, plus on s'aime?"', p. 187.
68. Marquis de Molins, 'Paris-Murcie, 1829–1879', in É. Lebey (ed.), *Paris-Murcie: Journal Publié au Profit des Victimes des Inondations d'Espagne par le Comité de la Presse Française*, single issue, December 1879, pp. 6–7.
69. Victor Hugo, 'Fraternité', in Lebey, *Paris-Murcie*, p. 3.
70. 'Danielle Segalen: "Je dis chapeau aux Espagnols" (propos recueillis par S. Prévost)', *Télégramme de Brest*, 11 April 2004.

71. 'Sommières: Marche silencieuse de solidarité', *Midi-Libre*, 16 March 2004.
72. 'Émotion à Saint-Joseph', *L'Yonne Républicaine*, 13 March 2004.

Chapter 5 Observing silence

1. Luc Boltanski, *On critique: A sociology of emancipation*, tr. Gregory Elliot (Cambridge and Malden, MA: Polity, 2011).
2. Steven D. Brown, 'Two minutes of silence: Social technologies of public commemoration', *Theory & Psychology*, 22 (2), 2012, pp. 234–52.
3. On this distinction, see McPhail, *The myth of the madding crowd*, p. 177.
4. See chapter 1.
5. Éric Leser, 'New York a célébré dans l'émotion une journée "de prière et du souvenir"', *Le Monde*, 16–17 September 2001, p. 7.
6. See for example 'Hommage de l'Europe aux victimes des attentats de New York', France 2, 14 September 2001, 8 p.m. news programme, available online: http://www.ina.fr/art-et-culture/musees-et-expositions/video/1803131003074/hommage-de-l-europe-aux-victimes-des-attentats-de-new-york.fr.html.
7. See 'Décret du 12 septembre 2001 portant déclaration de deuil national' and 'Circulaire du 12 septembre 2001 relative au jour de deuil national en hommage aux victimes des attentats commis aux États-Unis d'Amérique le 11 septembre 2001', published in the *Journal Officiel de la République Française*, 13 September 2001.
8. Guedj and Sultan-R'bibo, *11 septembre: Paris, 14 h 46*, pp. 87–8.
9. Christophe Châtelot, 'Le monde entier exprime sa solidarité à l'égard des victimes américaines', *Le Monde*, 14 September 2001, p. 15. Furthermore, the page on which this article appeared had the general heading 'Un deuil mondial' ('Worldwide mourning').
10. The sequence was broadcast again in 'La minute de silence observée dans le monde', France 2, 14 September 2001, 8 p.m. news programme, available online: http://www.ina.fr/economie-et-societe/justice-et-faits-divers/video/1803131003008/la-minute-de-silence-observee-dans-le-monde.fr.html.
11. For example: '800 million Europeans express their solidarity with the American people', *Le Monde*, 15 September 2001, p. 8. This figure corresponds to the number of the inhabitants in the forty-three countries represented in the Council of Europe in 2001.

12. Simon Loubris, 'Trois minutes de silence', *Café Babel*, 18 March 2004, available online: http://www.cafebabel.fr/article/711/trois-minutes-de-silence.html.
13. François Foret, *Légitimer l'Europe: Pouvoir et symbolique à l'heure de la gouvernance* (Paris: Presses de Sciences Po, 2008).
14. Remarks reported in Bruno Le Maire, *Des hommes d'État* (Paris: Grasset, 2007), pp. 109–10.
15. 'Toute la France s'est associée à la peine des Américains', *Le Monde*, 15 September 2001, p. 8.
16. Nicolas Mariot, *Bains de foule: Les voyages présidentiels en province, 1888–2002* (Paris: Belin, 2006); 'Les formes élémentaires de l'effervescence collective, ou l'état d'esprit prêté aux foules', *Revue Française de Science Politique*, 51 (5), 2001, pp. 707–38. There is a similar critique of the 'illusion of unanimity' in the observation of collective gatherings in McPhail, *The myth of the madding crowd*.
17. 'While we can expect to find natural movement back and forth between cynicism and sincerity, still we must not rule out the kind of transitional points that can be sustained, on the strength of a little self-illusion': Erving Goffman, *The presentation of self in everyday life* (Edinburgh: University of Edinburgh Social Sciences Research Centre, 1956), pp. 12–13. See also Isaac Joseph, 'Erving Goffman et le problème des convictions', in R. Castel, J. Cosnier and I. Joseph (eds.), *Le parler frais d'Erving Goffman* (Paris: Éditions de Minuit, 1989), pp. 13–30.
18. Georg Simmel, *Sociology: Inquiries into the construction of social forms*, 2 vols., tr. and ed. Anthony J. Blasi, Anton K. Jacobs and Mathew Kanjiranthinkal, vol. 1 (Leiden and Boston, MA: Brill, 2009), pp. 415–48.
19. See Mauss, 'L'expression obligatoire des sentiments'.
20. 'Pas de rassemblement à Belley', *Le Progrès*, 16 March 2004, p. 9.
21. 'Sélestat: Nous sommes tous des Espagnols!', *Dernières Nouvelles d'Alsace*, 16 March 2004.
22. 'Colmar: Une manifestation privée de voix', *Dernières Nouvelles d'Alsace*, 16 March 2004; *Le Progrès*, 16 March 2004, p. 12.
23. Cécile Maillard, 'À midi, les sirènes puis le silence', *France-Soir*, 15 March 2004, p. 4.
24. 'Solidaires des victimes espagnoles', *L'Est Républicain*, 16 March 2004.
25. 'Mulhouse: Trois minutes de solidarité', *Dernières Nouvelles d'Alsace*, 16 March 2004.
26. *Le Progrès*, 16 March 2004, p. 6.

27. 'Attentats de Madrid: Pas de minute de silence chez Doux', *Télégramme de Brest*, 16 March 2004.
28. 'L'hommage aux victimes de Madrid', *Midi-Libre*, 16 March 2004, p. 5.
29. 2,116 immigrants born in Spain, out of a total of 255,080 inhabitants (INSEE, 2009 census).
30. 'Trois minutes en hommage aux victimes madrilènes', *Le Progrès*, 16 March 2004, p. 11.
31. '12 h 00 à la gare de Valenciennes', *La Voix du Nord*, 16 March 2004.
32. 'Trois minutes de recueillement', *L'Est Républicain*, 16 March 2004.
33. Marie Berthoumieu, 'Silence troublé gare Montparnasse', *France-Soir*, 16 March 2004, p. 3.
34. 'Difficile de sacrifier la pause déjeuner', *La Voix du Nord*, 16 March 2004.
35. 'Trois minutes de recueillement', *L'Est Républicain*, 16 March 2004.
36. 'Trois minutes de silence', *La Provence*, 16 March 2004, p. 32.
37. 'Trois minutes de recueillement', *L'Est Républicain*, 16 March 2004.
38. We find here an equivalence between human beings with regard to a principle of common humanity, characteristic of critical operations calling for justification: see Luc Boltanski and Laurent Thévenot, *On justification: Economies of worth*, tr. Catherine Porter (Princeton, NJ, and Oxford: Princeton University Press, 2006).
39. 'Solidarité limitée?', message posted on the *Libération* forum on 15 March 2004.
40. London Metropolitan Archives, LMA/4469/A/01/022/02. The garden to which this message refers is a site dedicated to the victims of the London attacks in the Victoria Embankment Garden, marked by a tree planted in their memory.
41. London Metropolitan Archives, LMA/4469/A/01/022/02.
42. Christian Laporte, 'Trois minutes de silence', *Le Soir*, 14 September 2001.
43. Gérard Prémel is the author of several literary works and one of the founders of the review *Hopala! La Bretagne au Monde*. A former student of the École des Hautes Études en Sciences Sociales, he holds a PhD in sociology, and has also conducted sociological work within the framework of the AREAR (Atelier de Recherche sur l'Environnement, l'Aménagement et la Régionalisation), a community study centre created in 1992. (See his biography on

271

the website of the Association des Écrivains Bretons: http://www. ecrivainsbretons.org/Premel-Gerard.html.)

44. Gérard Prémel, 'Nos "frères humains"', *Ouest-France* (Ille-et-Vilaine edition), 21 September 2001.
45. *Libération*, 18 March 2004, p. 18; *Le Figaro*, 17 March 2004, p. 13.
46. 'L'école face au terrorisme' (debate of the bureau of the Cercle de Recherche et d'Action Pédagogiques, remarks noted and edited by P. Madiot), *Les Cahiers Pédagogiques*, 423, April 2004, available online: http://www.cahiers-pedagogiques.com/L-Ecole-face-au-terrorisme. All the following quotations are taken from this.
47. See chapter 9.
48. See chapter 2.
49. Maillard, 'À midi, les sirènes puis le silence'.
50. Laurent Thévenot, *L'action au pluriel: Sociologie des régimes d'engagement* (Paris: La Découverte, 2006), pp. 219ff.
51. Thévenot, *L'action au pluriel*, p. 221.

Chapter 6   Terrorist attacks and their publics

1. On the theory of the public on which this analysis is based, see John Dewey, *The public and its problems: An essay in political inquiry*, ed. Melvin L. Rogers (University Park, PA: Pennsylvania State University Press, 2012); Joëlle Zask, 'Le public chez Dewey: Une union sociale plurielle', *Tracés*, 15, 2008, pp. 169–89; and Louis Quéré, 'Le public comme forme et comme modalité d'expérience', in D. Cefaï and D. Pasquier (eds.), *Les sens du public: Publics politiques, publics médiatiques* (Paris: PUF, 2003), pp. 113–34.
2. 'Expression et recueillement au Capitole: "Madrid, nous pleurons avec toi!"', *Dépêche du Midi*, 16 March 2004, p. 25.
3. 'Et hommages dans le Val-de-Marne', *Le Parisien-Aujourd'hui en France*, 14 March 2004, p. 3.
4. Mémorial de Caen, OF, message dated 13 September 2001, translated from French.
5. Mémorial de Caen, OF, message with no date, translated from French.
6. Mémorial de Caen, OF, message dated 14 September 2001, translated from French.
7. Archivo del Duelo, DP-2595, translated from Spanish.
8. This is also shown by the sudden rapid growth in the number of letters received in these periods by newspapers, even when they

do not launch a specific appeal to their readers. Two weeks after 11 September, *Télérama* reported that it had received 'within a week the equivalent of one month's mail' (Soulez, 'Choc en retour: Les téléspectateurs et le 11 septembre 2001', p. 226).

9. London Metropolitan Archives, LMA/4469/A/03/038.
10. See the fine, richly illustrated study by Béatrice Fraenkel, *Les écrits de septembre: New York 2001* (Paris: Textuel, 2002).
11. There are many photographs documenting the phenomenon in the group 'London Bomb Blasts' on Flickr: http://www.flickr.com/groups/bomb.
12. For a detailed description and numerous illustrations, see Sánchez-Carretero, *El Archivo del Duelo*.
13. François Musseau, 'À Madrid, une semaine après les attentats: Mots pour maux', *Libération*, 19 March 2004, pp. 38–9. [The prase *mots pour maux* is a pun, meaning literally 'words for evils'. (Translator's note)]
14. Joy Sather-Wagstaff, *Heritage that hurts: Tourists in the memory-scapes of September 11* (Walnut Creek, CA: Left Coast Press, 2011), pp. 119–29.
15. See Krystyna Sanderson, *Light at Ground Zero: St. Paul's chapel after 9/11* (Baltimore, MD: Square Halo Books, 2003).
16. Its original name was 'Tribute WTC Visitor Center'. See http://tributewtc.org.
17. In all likelihood, this arrangement, designed primarily to channel the presumed need to write of certain visitors to Ground Zero, may also encourage those who would not necessarily have had the idea of leaving a note. One might also think that it contributes to a form of 'standardization' of messages. However, the fact that visitors to the 9/11 Tribute Center are provided with calling cards does not stop some of them writing just one sentence occupying the whole card, while others join together several cards or end their messages on other pieces of paper, when what they have to say exceeds the available space. Similarly, in the book of condolences containing pre-formatted pages, some do not hesitate to go beyond the box reserved for their message and annex the following box(es), or slip into the book a message written previously on a piece of paper and placed in an envelope.
18. Tribute WTC Visitor Center, *9/11: The world speaks* (Guilford, NC: Lyons Press, 2011). Some of these are also available online: http://tributewtc.org/exhibits/visitors-write-about-911.
19. 'Más cercanos', which means 'closer', suggests that this system brings the authors of the messages closer to the victims of the attacks, but also alludes to the names of the suburban trains hit

by the bombs, known in Spain as 'Cercanías' (literally, 'close' trains).

20. See Béatrice Fraenkel, 'Actes d'écriture: Quand écrire c'est faire', *Langage & Société*, 121–2, 2007, pp. 101–12.

21. Pierre-Yves Baudot, 'Épitaphes oubliées: Les registres de condoléances à la mort d'un président de la République', *Mots*, 84, 2007, pp. 71–84 at p. 71.

22. The messages written in response to the death of Lady Diana, for example, were sorted into those that expressed sympathy for Diana, those that blamed those responsible, those that had been written by children, those addressed to Dodi Al-Fayed, those with a religious dimension, etc. (Brian Jones, 'Books of condolence', in Walter, *The mourning for Diana*, pp. 203–14). It is also the method used by S. Hazareesingh in his study of the books of condolences opened at the death of General de Gaulle: see Sudhir Hazareesingh, 'Mort et transfiguration: La renaissance du mythe gaullien en novembre 1970', *Parlement(s)*, 13, 2010, pp. 24–36.

23. This is what Béatrice Fraenkel does in her study of the writings that flooded the streets of New York in the wake of 11 September (Fraenkel, *Les écrits de septembre*); the same procedure is adopted by Baudot in his analysis of the books of condolences opened after the death of French presidents (see Baudot, 'Épitaphes oubliées').

24. For further discussion on the various possible methodological options and the use of Alceste software to analyse post-attack messages, I refer the reader to my article: Gérôme Truc, 'Analyser un corpus illisible? Le logiciel Alceste confronté à des registres de condoléances', *Langage & Société*, 135, 2011, pp. 29–45.

25. For a presentation of the principle of analysis on which the Alceste software is based, see Max Reinert, 'Postures énonciatives et mondes lexicaux stabilisés en analyse statistique de discours', *Langage & Société*, 121–2, 2007, pp. 189–202. And for a comparison with other existing computerized methods of textual analysis, see Didier Demazière, Claire Brossaud, Patrick Trabal and Karl Van Meter (eds.), *Analyses textuelles en sociologie: Logiciels, méthodes, usages* (Rennes: Presses Universitaires de Rennes: 2006).

26. Fraenkel, *Les écrits de septembre*, p. 61.

27. This set of messages is part of the Archivo del Duelo, an archive created by anthropologists at the Consejo Superior de Investigaciones Científicas, now part of the collections of the historical archives of the Spanish railways in Madrid.

28. The size of the initial corpus exceeded that which the academic version of the software could cope with (3 MB), so this first analysis was carried out by Max Reinert, creator of the software. All the subsequent analyses were carried out by me.

29. Indeed, 'in practice, the number of classes has little meaning: what counts is the form of the tree of classification and the stability of the classes obtained' from the hierarchical top-down classification (France Guérin-Pace, 'La statistique textuelle: Un outil exploratoire en sciences sociales', *Population*, 4, 1997, p. 869). But here the classes obtained prove to be very stable and hierarchized in the same order by the software.

30. In the following discussion, I begin by giving each time excerpts from the messages considered by Alceste to be the most characteristic of each class (on the basis of a chi-squared test). All have been translated from Spanish. For a more detailed presentation of each analysis and their results, the reader is referred to Truc, 'Analyser un corpus illisible?', and Truc, *Le 11-Septembre européen: La sensibilité morale des Européens à l'épreuve des attentats du 11 septembre 2001, du 11 mars 2004 et du 7 juillet 2005*, PhD thesis, Paris, EHESS, 2014, pp. 280ff.

31. This analysis of binary correspondences, also carried out by the Alceste software, was applied to a table crossing the 'uce's characteristic of each class and the words appearing at least four times in the corpus. In figure 29, for the sake of clarity, we have retained only the words of which the chi square of association with a class is greater than or equal to 45.

32. See Stéphane Latté, *Les 'victimes': La formation d'une catégorie sociale improbable et ses usages dans l'action collective*, PhD thesis, Paris, EHESS, 2008.

33. See Gérôme Truc, 'Les victimes du terrorisme comme citoyens affectés: L'enjeu politique de la mobilisation des victimes du 11-Mars' (forthcoming).

34. Of course, subjective considerations are not the only ones at issue here: the definition of who is a 'victim' and who is not essentially depends on the law and on psychological expertise, and is the subject of political struggles. On this point, as well as Latté's thesis, see Fassin and Rechtman, *The empire of trauma*, and Sandrine Lefranc and Lilian Mathieu (eds.), *Mobilisations de victimes* (Rennes: Presses Universitaires de Rennes, 2010).

35. In the following pages, the signatures of the cited messages will be indicated, as is conventional, between brackets, so an absence of final parentheses indicates a message without a signature. In order to comply with the legislation on personal data, surnames

and postal and electronic addresses have been deleted, here as in the rest of the book.

36. Archivo del Duelo, EP, message recorded at Atocha on 27 September 2004, translated from Spanish.
37. Archivo del Duelo, EP, message recorded at Atocha on 22 February 2004, translated from Spanish.
38. Archivo del Duelo, EP, message recorded at Atocha on 30 September 2004, translated from Spanish.
39. Archivo del Duelo, EP, message recorded on the website mascercanos.com on 23 June 2004, translated from Spanish.
40. Archivo del Duelo, DP-2571.
41. Durkheim, *The division of labour in society*, pp. 88–90.
42. Durkheim, *The division of labour in society*, pp. 57–60 and pp. 119–20.
43. Mémorial de Caen, OF, message dated 22 September 2001, translated from French.
44. Archivo del Duelo, EP, message recorded at Atocha on 16 June 2004, translated from Spanish.
45. London Metropolitan Archives, LMA/4469/A/01/021/04.
46. Archivo del Duelo, EP, message recorded at Atocha on 21 June 2004, translated from Spanish.
47. Archivo del Duelo, EP, message recorded at Atocha on 24 November 2004, translated from Spanish.
48. Archivo del Duelo, EP, message recorded on the website mascercanos.com on 9 June 2004, translated from Spanish.
49. London Metropolitan Archives, LMA/4469/A/01/021/02.
50. Fraenkel, *Les écrits de septembre*, p. 64.
51. Georg Simmel, 'The metropolis and mental life', in *The sociology of Georg Simmel*, tr. and ed. Kurt H. Wolff (New York, NY, and London: Free Press, 1950), p. 413.
52. London Metropolitan Archives, LMA/4469/A/01/020.
53. Cristina Sánchez-Carretero, 'Trains of workers, trains of death: Some reflections after the March 11 attacks in Madrid', in Santino, *Spontaneous shrines and the public memorialization of death*, pp. 333–47.
54. London Metropolitan Archives, LMA/4469/A/01/022/01.
55. Carolyn Ellis, 'Shattered lives: Making sense of September 11th and its aftermath', *Journal of Contemporary Ethnography*, 31 (4), 2002, pp. 375–410 at p. 397.
56. London Metropolitan Archives, LMA/4469/A/01/022/01.
57. Archivo del Duelo, EP, message recorded at Atocha on 11 March 2005, translated from Spanish.

58. Archivo del Duelo, EP, message recorded at Atocha on 2 September 2004, translated from Spanish.
59. Archivo del Duelo, EP, message recorded at Atocha on 6 July 2004, translated from Spanish.
60. Archivo del Duelo, EP, message recorded at Santa Eugenia on 11 June 2004, translated from Spanish.
61. London Metropolitan Archives, LMA/4469/A/01/022/01.
62. Archivo del Duelo, DP-6106, translated from Spanish.
63. London Metropolitan Archives, LMA/4469/A/01/021/04.
64. Archivo del Duelo, EP, message recorded on the website mascercanos.com on 11 June 2004, translated from Spanish.
65. Archivo del Duelo, EP, message recorded at Atocha on 25 June 2004, translated from Spanish.
66. Archivo del Duelo, EP, message recorded at Atocha on 15 June 2004, translated from Spanish.
67. Archivo del Duelo, EP, message recorded on the website mascercanos.com on 4 October 2004, translated from Spanish.
68. Archivo del Duelo, DP-2468, translated from Spanish.
69. Archivo del Duelo, DP-0620, translated from Spanish.
70. Archivo del Duelo, DP-1369, translated from Spanish.
71. London Metropolitan Archives, LMA/4469/A/01/021/02.
72. London Metropolitan Archives, LMA/4469/A/01/027, translated from French.
73. London Metropolitan Archives, LMA/4469/A/01/022/01, translated from Spanish.
74. On Arendt's notion of 'love of the world' and its link with cosmopolitanism, see Étienne Tassin, *Un monde commun: Pour une cosmo-politique des conflits* (Paris: Seuil, 2003).
75. Archivo del Duelo, EP, message recorded on the website mascercanos.com on 10 June 2004, translated from Spanish.
76. London Metropolitan Archives, LMA/4469/A/01/022/02.
77. London Metropolitan Archives, LMA/4469/A/01/021/02.

Chapter 7 The meanings of 'we'

1. Vincent Daoud, 'Wikipédia au risque de l'événement', *Sociopublique* (blog), 30 June 2015, available online at: https://sociopublique.wordpress.com/2015/06/30/wikipedia-au-risque-de-levenement.
2. See Vincenzo Cicchelli, *L'esprit cosmopolite: Voyages de formation des jeunes en Europe* (Paris: Presses de Sciences Po, 2012), pp. 217–43.

3. Norbert Elias, 'Changes in the we-I balance', in *The Society of Individuals*, ed. Michael Schröter, tr. Edmund Jephcott (New York, NY, and London: Continuum, 2001), pp. 153–238 at p. 226.
4. London Metropolitan Archives, LMA/4469/A/01/021/02, translated from Spanish.
5. Archivo del Duelo, EP, message recorded at Atocha on 13 August 2004, translated from Spanish.
6. Archivo del Duelo, EP, message recorded at Atocha on 23 September 2004, translated from Spanish.
7. Archivo del Duelo, EP, message recorded at Atocha on 22 June 2004, translated from Spanish.
8. Archivo del Duelo, EP, message recorded on the website mascercanos.com on 10 June 2004, translated from Spanish.
9. Archivo del Duelo, EP, message recorded at Atocha on 8 August 2004, translated from Spanish.
10. Archivo del Duelo, EP, message recorded on the website mascercanos.com on 12 August 2004, translated from Spanish.
11. Archivo del Duelo, EP, message recorded at Atocha on 18 August 2004, translated from French.
12. Archivo del Duelo, EP, message recorded on the website mascercanos.com on 11 June 2004, translated from French.
13. Archivo del Duelo, DP-3011, translated from Spanish.
14. London Metropolitan Archives, LMA/4469/A/01/022/02, translated from Spanish.
15. London Metropolitan Archives, LMA/4469/A/01/023. The formula 'One London, One Europe' refers to the slogan 'One City, One World' promoted by the then mayor of London, Ken Livingstone, in the wake of the attack.
16. Archivo del Duelo, EP, message recorded at Atocha on 6 July 2004, translated from French.
17. Archivo del Duelo, EP, message recorded at Atocha on 1 September 2004, translated from French.
18. Émile Durkheim, *Leçons de sociologie* (Paris : PUF, 1995 [1950]), pp. 107–9, and Durkheim, 'Pacifism and patriotism' (1908), tr. Neville Layne, *Sociological Inquiry*, 43 (2), 1973, pp. 99–103. The expressions 'open patriotism' and 'humanist patriotism' come from Jean-Claude Filloux, commenting on these texts by Durkheim: see Jean-Claude Filloux, *Durkheim et le socialisme* (Geneva: Droz, 1977), pp. 353–63.
19. Archivo del Duelo, FD-1459, translated from Spanish; DP-0649, translated from Spanish; DP-4004; and EP, message recorded at Atocha on 17 June 2004, translated from Spanish.

20. Archivo del Duelo, DP-4699, translated from Spanish; DP-1952; FD-1493, translated from Spanish; DP-2314, translated from Spanish; DP-2963, translated from Spanish.
21. This, of course, must be related to the great autonomy of the Spanish provinces, and the very low sense of national belonging encountered in some of them, such as Catalonia or the Basque Country.
22. Archivo del Duelo, EP, message recorded at Atocha on 9 June 2004, translated from Spanish.
23. Archivo del Duelo, EP, message recorded at Atocha on 18 August 2004, translated from Spanish.
24. Archivo del Duelo, EP, messages recorded at Atocha on 13, 14, 22, 26 and 27 June, 21 July and 20 August 2004, translated from Spanish.
25. Archivo del Duelo, DP-3280, translated from Spanish.
26. Archivo del Duelo, EP, message recorded at Atocha on 11 June 2004, translated from Spanish.
27. Archivo del Duelo, EP, message recorded at Atocha on 9 June 2004, translated from Spanish.
28. Archivo del Duelo, EP, message recorded at Atocha on 14 June 2004, translated from Spanish.
29. Archivo del Duelo, EP, message recorded at Atocha on 22 June 2004, translated from Spanish.
30. Archivo del Duelo, DP-4852, translated from French.
31. Archivo del Duelo, DP-1934, translated from French.
32. Quoted in Alan Hamilton, 'Cities stand still and silent to send defiant message', *The Times*, 15 July 2005, p. 9.
33. London Metropolitan Archives, LMA/4469/A/01/023, translated from Spanish.
34. We here encounter, in a different way, the distinction made in the preceding chapter between messages expressing a collective grief and those sending condolences to the victims, linked to a feeling of greater or lesser proximity to the attack.
35. See chapter 4.
36. See Thomas J. Scheff, *Emotions, the social bond, and human reality: Part/whole analysis* (Cambridge: Cambridge University Press, 1997).
37. Archivo del Duelo, EP, message recorded on the website mascercanos.com on 9 June 2004, translated from Spanish.
38. London Metropolitan Archives, LMA/4469/A/01/020.
39. London Metropolitan Archives, LMA/4469/A/01/024.
40. London Metropolitan Archives, LMA/4469/A/01/028.
41. London Metropolitan Archives, LMA/4469/A/01/021/03.

42. In the same way, the cartoonist Art Spiegelman, despite having moved to New York at the age of nine and spending the greater part of his life there, testified in *In the Shadow of No Towers* (London: Viking, 2004) that it was only at the time of 11 September that, for the very first time, he became aware of his attachment to this city, and realized that he was not a pure 'uprooted cosmopolitan' as he had hitherto thought.
43. London Metropolitan Archives, LMA/4469/A/01/028.
44. London Metropolitan Archives, LMA/4469/A/01/021/04.
45. London Metropolitan Archives, LMA/4469/A/01/026.
46. London Metropolitan Archives, LMA/4469/A/01/020.
47. London Metropolitan Archives, LMA/4469/A/01/020.
48. Simmel, 'The metropolis and mental life'.
49. Archivo del Duelo, DP-4162, translated from Spanish.
50. Archivo del Duelo, DP-5839, translated from Spanish.
51. Sánchez-Carretero, 'Trains of workers, trains of death', p. 340.
52. London Metropolitan Archives, LMA/4469/A/01/022/03.
53. 'Réaction au témoignage de Françoise Rudetzki dans l'émission "Tout le monde en parle" – Attentats de Madrid', message posted on the forum of the website sos-attentats.org, 14 March 2004, translated from French.
54. Archivo del Duelo, EP, message recorded on the website mascercanos.com on 9 June 2004, translated from Spanish.
55. 9/11 Tribute Center, VC, message as of March 2008, translated from Spanish.
56. London Metropolitan Archives, LMA/4469/A/01/020.
57. Archivo del Duelo, DP-4386.
58. London Metropolitan Archives, LMA/4469/B/03/009.
59. London Metropolitan Archives, LMA/4469/A/01/028.
60. London Metropolitan Archives, LMA/4469/A/01/021/01.
61. London Metropolitan Archives, LMA/4469/A/01/024.
62. See chapter 2.
63. London Metropolitan Archives, LMA/4469/A/01/022/02.
64. London Metropolitan Archives, LMA/4469/B/03/17.
65. Another social phenomenon, light years away from reactions to terrorist attacks, also, in its own way, brings this out. In his study of the 'remote' supporters of the Marseilles Olympics, i.e. supporters who do not live in Marseilles and are not from that city, Ludovic Lestrelin has shown that it is possible to identify with a city simply through the values it symbolizes, and not exclusively from any territorial roots one may have there. The 'national imaginary', on the other hand, is so made that it seems very difficult to 'deterritorialize' a national identity; and this is

why 'remote support' is a phenomenon peculiar to the football clubs of the major European metropolises (Barcelona, Madrid, Munich, Milan, Marseilles, etc.), something which does not exist for national teams except in a trivial way. See Ludovic Lestrelin, *L'autre public des matchs de football: Sociologie des support-ers à distance de l'Olympique de Marseille* (Paris: Éditions de l'EHESS, 2010).

66. Simmel, *Sociology*, vol. 1, p. 448.
67. London Metropolitan Archives, LMA/4469/A/01/020.
68. Claude Lefort, 'L'Europe, civilisation urbaine', *Esprit*, 303, 2004, pp. 225–43.
69. Max Weber, *The city*, tr. and ed. Don Martindale and Gertrud Neuwirth (New York, NY: Free Press, 1966).
70. Marc Bloch, *Feudal society*, tr. L. A. Manyon (Abingdon and New York, NY: Routledge, 2014).
71. Aldo Schiavone, *The end of the past: Ancient Rome and the modern West*, tr. Margery J. Schneider (Cambridge, MA, and London: Harvard University Press, 2000), p. 30.
72. On this point, see also his Marc Bloch lecture of 2009 on the theme of 'The fragility and fertility of democracies' (available online in French as 'Fragilité et fécondité des démocraties': http://cmb.ehess.fr/320), in which he affirms that 'urban civilization, which is gradually taking hold in Europe, involves a humanist conception of the city that underlies the history of egalitarian democracy'.
73. Lefort, 'L'Europe, civilisation urbaine', p. 230.
74. See also Coulmas, *Les citoyens du monde*.
75. Simmel, 'The metropolis and mental life', p. 419. On this subject, see Alain Bourdin, *La métropole des individus* (La Tour d'Aigues: Éditions de l'Aube, 2005), pp. 17–21.
76. Stefan Zweig, *The world of yesterday: An autobiography* (London: Cassell, 1943). On Vienna at the turn of the century, see also the fine work *Jews, antisemitism and culture in Vienna*, ed. Ivar Oxaal, Michael Pollak and Gerhard Botz (London: Routledge & Kegan Paul, 1987).
77. London Metropolitan Archives, LMA/4469/A/01/021/04.
78. Crettiez and Sommier, 'Les attentats du 11 septembre', p. 66.
79. See chapter 1.
80. Dollé, 'Nous ne sommes pas tous Américains, nous sommes New-Yorkais', p. 101.
81. See chapter 2.
82. See Immanuel Wallerstein, *European universalism: The rhetoric of power* (New York, NY: New Press, 2006).

83. See Jack Goody, *The theft of history* (Cambridge: Cambridge University Press, 2006), especially ch. 8, 'The theft of institutions, towns, and universities' and ch. 9, 'The appropriation of values: humanism, democracy, and individualism', pp. 215–66.
84. Patrick Le Galès, *Le retour des villes européennes* (Paris: Presses de Sciences Po, 2003), pp. 57–8.

Chapter 8   The values at stake

1. Pierre Livet, *Émotions et rationalité morale* (Paris : PUF, 2002), p. 177–8. See also Martha C. Nussbaum, 'Emotions as judgments of value', *Yale Journal of Criticism*, 5, 1992, pp. 201–12.
2. Durkheim, *The division of labour in society*.
3. President François Hollande, 'Allocution à la suite de l'attentat au siège de *Charlie Hebdo*', 7 January 2015, available online: http://www.elysee.fr/declarations/article/allocution-a-la-suite-de-l-attentat-au-siege-de-charlie-hebdo.
4. President François Hollande, 'Adresse à la nation suite aux événements des 7 et 8 janvier 2015', 9 January 2015, available online: http://www.elysee.fr/declarations/article/adresse-a-la-nation-a-la-suite-des-evenements-des-7-et-8-janvier-2.
5. See chapter 2.
6. Quoted in Elaine Ganley, 'Europe remembers Madrid train victims', Associated Press dispatch, 15 March 2004. Prodi was here reproducing verbatim the values enumerated in Article I-2 of the Draft European Constitutional Treaty, then under debate, and which are now included in Article 2 of the Treaty on European Union.
7. See President George W. Bush, 'Address to the nation on the September 11 attacks', 11 September 2001, and 'Address to the joint session of the 107th Congress', 20 September 2001, available online: http://georgewbush-whitehouse.archives.gov/infocus/bush-record/documents/Selected_Speeches_George_W_Bush.pdf. See also the open letter (known in English as 'What we're fighting for') issued by the Institute for American Values, signed by some sixty American intellectuals and published in France by *Le Monde* as 'Lettre d'Amérique' on 15 February 2002.
8. See Luc Boltanski, 'Public denunciation', in *Love and justice as competences: Three essays on the sociology of action*, tr. Catherine Porter (Cambridge: Polity, 2012), pp. 169–258.
9. John Dewey, 'Creative democracy: The task before us', in *The Later Works, 1925–1953*, 17 vols., ed. Jo Ann Boydston (Carbondale,

IL: Southern Illinois University Press, 1981–91), vol. 14 (1939–1941), p. 227.

10. Bidet, Quéré and Truc, 'Ce à quoi nous tenons'.
11. London Metropolitan Archives, LMA/4469/A/01/022/01.
12. London Metropolitan Archives, LMA/4469/A/01/024.
13. Archivo del Duelo, EP, message recorded at Atocha on 16 August 2004, translated from Spanish.
14. Fraenkel, *Les écrits de septembre*, p. 71.
15. Archivo del Duelo, EP, message recorded at Santa Eugenia on 17 December 2004, translated from Spanish.
16. Archivo del Duelo, EP, message recorded at Atocha on 2 July 2004, translated from Spanish.
17. Archivo del Duelo, EP, message recorded on the website mascercanos.com on 9 June 2004, translated from Spanish.
18. London Metropolitan Archives, LMA/4469/A/01/027.
19. London Metropolitan Archives, LMA/4469/A/01/026.
20. London Metropolitan Archives, LMA/4469/A/01/022/03.
21. This is what John Dewey calls the 'means–end continuum'. Values and ideals are not necessarily 'ends in themselves' that can be taken for granted: in the field of human experience, everything that resembles an end in itself can very well be seen, from another point of view, as a means to something else. See John Dewey, *Theory of valuation* (Chicago, IL: University of Chicago Press, 1939).
22. Archivo del Duelo, EP, message recorded on the website mascercanos.com on 11 June 2004, translated from Spanish.
23. Archivo del Duelo, EP, message recorded at Atocha on 16 January 2005, translated from Spanish.
24. Archivo del Duelo, EP, message recorded on the website mascercanos.com on 22 July 2004, translated from Spanish.
25. London Metropolitan Archives, LMA/4469/A/01/023.
26. This is a breakdown of the 58,732 digital messages collected from June 2004 to March 2005 via the Espacio de Palabras (see chapter 6). Given the size of the corpus, the spelling and typing errors contained in the messages and the different languages used, these figures are approximate and should be seen as mere indicators.
27. The word 'life' is of course also used in these messages to designate the lives lost by those killed in the attacks. It was used 14,923 times. To distinguish the cases in which it is used to designate a value, I have restricted myself to occurrences of the word in the singular and with an article, as (in French) 'la vie'.
28. Hollande, 'Allocation suite à l'attentat au siège de *Charlie Hebdo*'.
29. Bush, 'Address to the joint session of the 107th Congress'.

30. 9/11 Tribute Center, VC, message as of May 2008, translated from French.
31. See chapter 2.
32. London Metropolitan Archives, LMA/4469/A/01/021/02.
33. London Metropolitan Archives, LMA/4469/A/01/021/04.
34. London Metropolitan Archives, LMA/4469/A/01/024.
35. London Metropolitan Archives, LMA/4469/A/01/020.
36. Ken Livingstone, 'London will not be divided', available online: http://www.independent.co.uk/news/uk/home-news/ken-living-stones-speech-77-bombings-from-singapore-speak-to-those-come-to-london-10370832.html.
37. See Closs Stephens, 'Seven million Londoners, one London: National and urban ideas of community', p. 73.
38. Paul Valéry, 'Fluctuations sur la liberté' (1938), in Œuvres, vol. 2 (Paris: Gallimard, 'Bibliothèque de la Pléiade'), 1960, p. 951.
39. Yves Citton, 'Vers une Europe post-identitaire', Multitudes, 14, 2003, p. 65.
40. Archivo del Duelo, EP, message recorded at Atocha on 10 June 2004, translated from Spanish.
41. Archivo del Duelo, EP, message recorded on the website mascercanos.com on 18 June 2004, translated from Spanish.
42. Archivo del Duelo, EP, message recorded at Atocha on 25 November 2004, translated from Spanish.
43. Archivo del Duelo, EP, message recorded on the website mascercanos.com on 11 June 2004, translated from Spanish.
44. Archivo del Duelo, EP, message recorded on the website mascercanos.com on 9 June 2004, translated from Spanish.
45. Archivo del Duelo, EP, message recorded on the website mascercanos.com on 9 June 2004, translated from Spanish.
46. Archivo del Duelo, EP, message recorded at Atocha on 17 August 2004, translated from Spanish.
47. London Metropolitan Archives, LMA/4469/A/01/020, translated from Spanish.
48. Archivo del Duelo, EP, message recorded on the website mascercanos.com on 12 June 2004, translated from Spanish.
49. Archivo del Duelo, EP, message recorded at Atocha on 21 November 2004, translated from Spanish.
50. Archivo del Duelo, EP, message recorded on the website mascercanos.com on 15 June 2004, translated from Spanish.
51. Michael Billig, Banal nationalism (London: Sage, 1995).
52. Archivo del Duelo, EP, words excerpted from messages recorded, respectively, in order of quotation, on the website mascercanos.

com on 14 June 2004, at Atocha on 28 December 2004, at Atocha on 1 January 2005, at Atocha on 2 October 2004, at Atocha on 26 July 2004, at Atocha on 1 January 2005, on the website mascercanos.com on 11 June 2004, at Atocha on 12 September 2004, on the website mascercanos.com on 13 June 2004, on the website mascercanos.com on 13 June 2004, at Santa Eugenia on 17 June 2004, at Atocha on 20 January 2005, at Atocha on 16 July 2004, at Atocha on 28 October 2004, at Atocha on 11 August 2004, all translated from Spanish. All these quotations are just examples – each of these expressions is used in many of the messages.

53. Archivo del Duelo, EP, message recorded at Atocha on 21 August 2004, translated from Spanish.
54. Archivo del Duelo, EP, message recorded at Atocha on 8 August 2004, translated from Spanish.
55. Archivo del Duelo, EP, message recorded at Atocha on 10 June 2004, translated from Spanish.
56. See chapter 1.
57. Mémorial de Caen, OF, letter as of 26 September 2001, translated from French.
58. Mémorial de Caen, letter as of 13 September 2001, translated from French.
59. London Metropolitan Archives, LMA/4469/A/01/022/01.
60. Archivo del Duelo, EP, message recorded at Atocha on 17 July 2004, translated from Spanish.
61. Archivo del Duelo, EP, message recorded at Atocha on 5 December 2004, translated from Spanish.
62. Archivo del Duelo, EP, message recorded on the website mascercanos.com on 14 November 2004, translated from Spanish.
63. Archivo del Duelo, EP, message recorded at Atocha on 8 November 2004, translated from Spanish.
64. Archivo del Duelo, EP, message recorded at Atocha on 3 October 2004, translated from Spanish.
65. Archivo del Duelo, EP, message recorded at Atocha on 31 October 2004, translated from Spanish.
66. Archivo del Duelo, EP, message recorded on the website mascercanos.com on 14 June 2004, translated from Spanish.
67. London Metropolitan Archives, LMA/4469/A/01/024.
68. London Metropolitan Archives, LMA/4469/A/01/020, translated from Catalan.
69. Simmel, 'The metropolis and mental life', p. 413.
70. Michael Walzer, *On toleration* (New Haven, CT, and London: Yale University Press, 1997), pp. 10–11.

71. Jacques Derrida, 'Autoimmunity: Real and symbolic suicides – a dialogue with Jacques Derrida', in Derrida and Habermas, *Philosophy in a time of terror*, pp. 85–136 at p. 126.
72. Derrida, 'Autoimmunity, pp. 126–7 (translation slightly modified).
73. Derrida, 'Autoimmunity, p. 127.
74. Archivo del Duelo, EP, message recorded at Atocha on 25 September 2004, translated from Spanish.
75. Archivo del Duelo, EP, message recorded at Atocha on 10 July 2004, translated from Spanish.
76. Archivo del Duelo, EP, message recorded at Santa Eugenia on 29 July 2004, translated from Spanish.
77. London Metropolitan Archives, LMA/4469/A/01/027.
78. London Metropolitan Archives, LMA/4469/A/01/024.
79. Archivo del Duelo, DP-2930, translated from Spanish.
80. London Metropolitan Archives, LMA/4469/A/01/022/01.
81. London Metropolitan Archives, LMA/4469/A/01/022/03. [As often in these messages, the sense is clear even though the original is in idiosyncratic English. (Translator's note)]
82. On this point, see part II of Coulmas, *Les citoyens du monde*, pp. 91ff.
83. See Michel Messier, *Agapè: Recherches sur l'histoire de la charité* (Montreal: Fides, 2007), and, for a sociological use of this notion, L. Boltanski, '*Agapè*: An introduction to the states of peace', in Boltanski, *Love and justice as competences*, pp. 89–128.
84. 9/11 Tribute Center, VC, message as of 17 July 2007, translated from French.
85. Emmanuel Levinas, 'Peace and proximity', in *Basic philosophical writings*, ed. Adriaan T. Peperzak, Simon Critchley and Robert Bernasconi (Bloomington, IN: Indiana University Press, 1996), pp. 161–70 at p. 167.
86. Ceslas Spicq, *Agapè dans le Nouveau Testament*, vol. 1: *Analyse de textes* (Paris: Gabalda, 1958), p. 186.
87. Nilüfer Göle, *Musulmans au quotidien: Une enquête européenne sur les controverses autour de l'Islam* (Paris: La Découverte, 2015), p. 12.
88. See chapter 6.
89. Archivo del Duelo, DP-3017, translated from Spanish.
90. Archivo del Duelo, EP, message recorded at Atocha on 7 July 2004, translated from Spanish.
91. Archivo del Duelo, EP, message recorded at Atocha on 12 February 2005, translated from Spanish.
92. Archivo del Duelo, EP, message recorded at Atocha on 25 June 2004, translated from Spanish.

93. Boltanski, *Love and justice as competences*, pp. 156–9.
94. See Jonathan Chalier, 'Questions sur la mort de Ben Laden', *Études*, 418 (4), 2013, pp. 453–60.
95. On this conviction, which is also the principle behind humanitarian commitment, see Didier Fassin, 'L'ordre moral du monde: essai d'anthropologie de l'intolérable', in P. Bourdelais and D. Fassin (eds.), *Les constructions de l'intolérable* (Paris: La Découverte, 2005), pp. 17–50, and Fassin, *Humanitarian reason : A moral history of the present*, tr. Rachel Gomme (Berkeley, CA: University of California Press, 2011).
96. Archivo del Duelo, DP-2922, translated from Spanish.
97. London Metropolitan Archives, LMA/4469/A/01/024.
98. London Metropolitan Archives, LMA/4469/A/01/022/03, translated from French.
99. London Metropolitan Archives, LMA/4469/A/01/021/02.
100. 9/11 Tribute Center, VC, message as of 2006, translated from Polish.
101. London Metropolitan Archives, LMA/4469/A/02/053.
102. London Metropolitan Archives, LMA/4469/A/02/053.
103. 9/11 Tribute Center, VC, message as of 9 February 2008.
104. 9/11 Tribute Center, VC, message as of 12 June 2008, translated from Spanish.
105. Mémorial de Caen, OF, message without date, translated from French.
106. Mémorial de Caen, OF, message as of 15 September 2001, translated from French.
107. Mémorial de Caen, OF, message without date, translated from French.
108. Durkheim, *Suicide*, p. 299.
109. Émile Durkheim, 'Détermination du fait moral', in *Sociologie et philosophie* (Paris: PUF, 1996 [1924]), pp. 49–90 at p. 84. However, this idea was far from being specific to Durkheim: it goes back at least to Kant and reflects the influence on Durkheim of the personalism of Charles Renouvier: see Jean-Claude Filloux, 'Personne et sacré chez Durkheim', *Archives de Sciences Sociales des Religions*, 69, 1990, pp. 41–53.
110. Walter Benjamin, 'Critique of violence', in *On violence: A reader*, ed. Bruce B. Lawrence and Aisha Karim (Durham, NC: Duke University Press, 2007), pp. 268–85 at pp. 283–4.
111. Matthew D. Mathias, 'The sacralization of the individual: Human rights and the abolition of the death penalty', *American Journal of Sociology*, 118 (5), 2013, pp. 1246–83.
112. See Jacques Derrida and Jürgen Habermas, 'February 15, or what binds Europeans together: A plea for a common foreign policy,

beginning in the core of Europe', tr. Max Pensky, *Constellations*, 10 (3), 2003, pp. 291–7, available online: http://platypus1917. org/wp-content/uploads/archive/rgroups/2006-chicago/habermas-derrida_europe.pdf.

113. See chapter 5.

Chapter 9   The attacks in persons

1. Eva Illouz, *Cold intimacies: The making of emotional capitalism* (Cambridge: Polity, 2013), p. 5.
2. See for example the piece by the Spanish philosopher Fernando Savater, 'Merci à Georges Wolinski ... et aux autres', *Libération*, 18 January 2015, available online: http://www. liberation.fr/chroniques/2015/01/18/merci-a-georges-wolinski-et-aux-autres_1183387.
3. See Hannah Arendt, *On revolution*, new edition (London: Faber & Faber, 2016).
4. 'Une superbe journée de printemps ...', message posted on the forum of *Libération* on 17 March 2004.
5. See chapter 3, pp. 68–72.
6. Blandine Grosjean, 'Le garçon au téléphone portable', *Libération*, 25 March 2004, p. 39.
7. Pascale Egré, 'Sergio Gil, 19 ans, un ouvrier discret devenu un symbole', *Le Parisien-Aujourd'hui en France*, 25 March 2004, p. 19.
8. Joaquín Manso, '"Veo la foto y pienso: Esto yo no lo he vivido"', *El Mundo*, 11 March 2013, p. 1 and p. 14.
9. See chapter 3, pp. 80–2.
10. See the testimony and the critical analysis of one of these victims, who is also a sociologist of the media: John Tulloch, *One day in July: Experiencing 7/7* (London: Little, Brown, 2006).
11. Fraenkel, *Les écrits de septembre*, pp. 41–7; and Diana Taylor, 'Lost in the field of vision', in *The Archive and the repertoire: Performing cultural memory in the Americas* (Durham, NC, and London: Duke University Press, 2003), pp. 237–64.
12. Barbara Kirshenblatt-Gimblett, 'Kodak moments, flashbulb memories: Reflections on 9/11', *Drama Review*, 47 (1), 2003, pp. 11–48 at p. 30.
13. On the case of Madrid, see Sánchez-Carretero, *El Archivo del Duelo*, and Carmen Ortiz García, 'Pictures that save, pictures that soothe: Photographs at the grassroots memorials to the victims of the March 11, 2004 Madrid bombings', *Visual Anthropology*

Review, 29 (1), 2013, pp. 57–71. On the case of London, see Jenny Edkins, *Missing: Persons and politics* (New York, NY: Cornell University Press, 2011), pp. 84–106.

14. Fraenkel, *Les écrits de septembre*, p. 43.
15. Mémorial de Caen, message without a date, translated from French.
16. Dayan, *La terreur spectacle*, p. 169.
17. Lamy, *La médiatisation de l'"Apocalypse'*, p. 458.
18. 'Une superbe journée de printemps …', message posted on the forum of *Libération* on 17 March 2004. Just as he was mistaken about Sergio Gil's age, the author of the message presented Patricia as the '199th victim', whereas the number of people killed in the trains was later established as 191.
19. Archivo del Duelo, DP-3279, translated from Spanish.
20. Archivo del Duelo, EP, message recorded on the site mascercanos. com on 10 June 2004, translated from Spanish.
21. In *El País* and *El Mundo* for the Madrid attacks (http://www.elpais. com/comunes/2004/11m/index.html; http://www.elmundo.es/documentos/2004/03/espana/atentados11m/victimas.html), *The Times*, the *Guardian* and the BBC website (http://news.bbc.co.uk/2/shared/spl/hi/uk/05/london_blasts/victims/) for the London attacks.
22. All are still available online: http://www.nytimes.com/interactive/us/sept-11-reckoning/portraits-of-grief.html?_r=0.
23. *Portraits – 9/11/01: The collected portraits of grief from the New York Times* (New York, NY: Times Books, 2003 [2002]).
24. David Simpson, *9/11: The culture of commemoration* (Chicago, IL: University of Chicago Press, 2006), p. 95.
25. Judith Butler, *Precarious life: The powers of mourning and violence* (London and New York, NY: Verso, 2004), p. 34.
26. Butler, *Precarious life*, p. 32.
27. See Edkins, *Missing*, pp. 22–6, and Alexandra Délano and Benjamin Nienass, 'Invisible victims: Undocumented migrants and the aftermath of September 11', *Politics & Society*, 42 (3), 2014, pp. 399–421.
28. Butler, *Precarious life*, p. 37.
29. Butler, *Precarious life*, p. 38.
30. I am here drawing on Adeline Wrona, 'Vies minuscules, vies exemplaires: Récit d'individu et actualité. Le cas des *portraits of grief* parus dans le *New York Times* après le 11 septembre 2001', *Réseaux*, 132, 2005, pp. 93–110.
31. Pierre Bourdieu, 'The biographical illusion', in *Identity: A reader*, ed. Jessica Evans, Paul du Gay and Peter Redman (London: Sage, 2000), pp. 299–305.

32. Wrona, 'Vies minuscules', p. 100.
33. Wrona, 'Vies minuscules', p. 101.
34. 'Marc Zeplin: He shoots! He scores!', *New York Times*, 13 January 2002.
35. 'James Lee Connor: Golf paved his way', *New York Times*, 23 October 2001.
36. 'Nicoleta Deac: La chica del balón', *El País*, 19 March 2004.
37. 'Jorge Rodríguez Casanova: Una camiseta de Zidane', *El País*, 13 March 2004.
38. 'Obituary: Miriam Hyman', *BBC News*, 20 January 2011.
39. 'Obituary: Philip Beer', *BBC News*, 3 August 2005.
40. 'Obituary: Michael Brewster', *BBC News*, 26 November 2010.
41. 'Miryam Pedraza Rivero: Eso que llaman duende', *El País*, 21 March 2004.
42. Georg Simmel, 'The intersection of social circles', in *The sociology of Georg Simmel*, pp. 305–44.
43. Mémorial de Caen, OF, message without date, translated from French.
44. Mémorial de Caen, OF, message without date, translated from French.
45. Denis Jeambar, 'Regrets', *L'Express*, 2643, 28 February–6 March 2002, p. 5 (my emphasis).
46. Janny Scott, 'Closing a scrapbook full of life and sorrow', *New York Times*, 31 December 2001, available online: http://www.nytimes.com/2001/12/31/nyregion/a-nation-challenged-the-por-traits-closing-a-scrapbook-full-of-life-and-sorrow.html.
47. Simmel, 'The intersection of social circles'.
48. 'Une superbe journée de printemps ...', message posted on the forum of *Libération* on 17 March 2004. See above, p. 182 and p. 184.
49. London Metropolitan Archives, LMA/4469/A/01/027.
50. Mémorial de Caen, OF, message as of 16 September 2001, translated from French.
51. [I.e., *An Affair to Remember*. (Translator's note)]
52. [*On the Town*. (Translator's note)]
53. [Natalie Wood. (Translator's note)]
54. Mémorial de Caen, OF, message as of 22 September 2001, translated from French.
55. Mémorial de Caen, OF, message as of 18 September 2001, translated from French.
56. Mémorial de Caen, OF, message as of 14 September 2001, translated from French.

57. Mémorial de Caen, OF, message as of 22 September 2001, translated from French.
58. Mémorial de Caen, OF, message without a date, translated from French (my emphasis).
59. George H. Mead, *Mind, self, and society*, ed. Charles W. Morris, Daniel R. Huebner and Hans Joas (Chicago, IL: University of Chicago Press, 2015), p. 451.
60. See Daniel Cefaï, 'Public, socialisation et politisation: Mead et Dewey', in A. Cukier and E. Debray (eds.), *La théorie sociale de George Herbert Mead* (Paris: Le Bord de l'Eau, 2014), pp. 340–66 at pp. 344–7.
61. Ellis, 'Shattered lives', p. 397.
62. Ellis, 'Shattered lives', p. 389.
63. John Dewey, *Art as experience* (New York, NY: Perigee Books, 1980 [1934]), p. 71.
64. See Paul Ricœur, *Oneself as another*, tr. Kathleen Blamey (Chicago, IL, and London: University of Chicago Press, 1992), p. 3.
65. London Metropolitan Archives, LMA/4469/A/01/023.
66. See chapter 7, p. 153.
67. Archivo del Duelo, DP-1444, translated from Spanish.
68. Mémorial de Caen, OF, electronic message as of 13 September 2001, translated fron French.
69. Mémorial de Caen, OF, electronic message as of 13 September 2001, translated fron French.
70. Ricœur, *Oneself as another*, pp. 42–50.
71. London Metropolitan Archives, LMA/4469/A/01/022/01.
72. Archivo del Duelo, DP-4112, translated from French.
73. Cefaï, 'Public, socialisation et politisation', p. 346.
74. London Metropolitan Archives, LMA/4469/A/03/038.
75. London Metropolitan Archives, LMA/4469/A/01/023.
76. London Metropolitan Archives, LMA/4469/A/01/022/01.
77. Mémorial de Caen, OF, message as of 16 September 2001, translated from French.
78. Boltanski, *Distant suffering*, p. 82. The notion of 'test of emotion' is discussed at greater length in a late work: Luc Boltanski and Marie-Noël Godet, 'Messages d'amour sur le *Téléphone du Dimanche*', *Politix*, 8 (31), 1995, pp. 30–76, reprinted as 'La présence des absents' at the end of the second edition of the French original, *La souffrance à distance* (Paris: Gallimard, 2007), pp. 347–433.
79. 'Une superbe journée de printemps …', message posted on the forum of *Libération* on 17 March 2004.

Chapter 10 Solidarity in the singular

1. Danilo Martuccelli, *La société singulariste* (Paris: Armand Colin, 2010).
2. 9/11 Tribute Center, VC, message as of 21 June 2008, translated from French.
3. Mémorial de Caen, OF, message without date, translated from French.
4. Archivo del Duelo, EP, message recorded at Atocha on 20 January 2005, translated from Spanish.
5. Archivo del Duelo, EP, message recorded on the website mascercanos.com on 11 June 2004.
6. Archivo del Duelo, EP, message recorded at Atocha on 17 August 2004.
7. Archivo del Duelo, DP-1925.
8. Archivo del Duelo, DP-4677.
9. London Metropolitan Archives, LMA/4469/A/01/021/03.
10. London Metropolitan Archives, LMA/4469/A/01/021/04.
11. London Metropolitan Archives, LMA/4469/A/01/022/01.
12. Mémorial de Caen, OF, message as of 2 October 2001.
13. Mémorial de Caen, OF, message as of 16 September 2001.
14. See chapter 4.
15. Archivo del Duelo, EP, message recorded on the website mascercanos.com on 10 August 2004, translated from Spanish.
16. London Metropolitan Archives, LMA/4469/A/01/027.
17. See pp. 189–90.
18. Archivo del Duelo, DP-4379.
19. Archivo del Duelo, DP-0650, translated from Spanish.
20. London Metropolitan Archives, LMA/4469/A/01/023.
21. See chapter 4.
22. Mémorial de Caen, OF, message without date, translated from French.
23. Mémorial de Caen, OF, message without date, translated from French.
24. London Metropolitan Archives, LMA/4469/A/03/038, original spelling preserved.
25. Mémorial de Caen, OF, message as of 15 September 2001, translated from French.
26. Mémorial de Caen, OF, message without date, translated from French.
27. Mémorial de Caen, OF, message without date, translated from French.

28. 9/11 Tribute Center, VC, message as of 2007, original syntax preserved.
29. 9/11 Tribute Center, VC, message as of 5 July 2008, original syntax preserved.
30. 9/11 Tribute Center, VC, message as of May 2008, translated from German.
31. 9/11 Tribute Center, VC, message as of 18 June 2008.
32. 9/11 Tribute Center, VC, message as of 20 May 2008.
33. Archivo del Duelo, DP-3076, original spelling preserved (*veces* (Sp.) = 'times').
34. London Metropolitan Archives, LMA/4469/A/01/027.
35. Mémorial de Caen, OF, messages as of 22 October 2001, translated from French.
36. 9/11 Tribute Center, VC, message as of 2007, original syntax preserved.
37. 9/11 Tribute Center, VC, message as of 2 August 2007, translated from Greek.
38. 9/11 Tribute Center, VC, message as of 15 October 2008, translated from Spanish.
39. London Metropolitan Archives, LMA/4469/A/01/023, original syntax preserved.
40. See pp. 189–90.
41. 9/11 Tribute Center, VC, message as of 16 May 2008, translated from German.
42. 9/11 Tribute Center, VC, message as of 7 April 2008.
43. 9/11 Tribute Center, VC, message as of 2006, translated from Japanese.
44. 9/11 Tribute Center, VC, message as of 2008.
45. Archivo del Duelo, EP, message recorded at Atocha on 16 September 2004, translated from Spanish.
46. Archivo del Duelo, EP, message recorded at Atocha on 7 October 2004, translated from Spanish.
47. Mémorial de Caen, OF, message as of 15 September 2001, translated from French.
48. Archivo del Duelo, EP, message recorded on the website mascercanos.com on 10 June 2004, translated from Spanish.
49. 9/11 Tribute Center, VC, message without date.
50. Mémorial de Caen, OF, message without date, translated from French.
51. Mémorial de Caen, OF, message as of 13 September 2001, translated from French.
52. Jean-Claude Schmitt, *L'invention de l'anniversaire* (Paris: Éditions Arkhê, 2009).

53. Schmitt, *L'invention de l'anniversaire*, p. 15. Schmitt also notes that there is no mention of any festivities for birthdays in the *Manuel de folklore français contemporain* by Arnold Van Gennep published in 1937.
54. Georg Simmel, 'L'individualisme moderne' (1917). This distinction is also drawn by François de Singly, who contrasts an 'abstract individualism' and a 'concrete singularism': see in particular François de Singly, *L'individualisme est un humanisme* (La Tour d'Aigues: Editions de l'Aube, 2005).
55. Schmitt, *L'invention de l'anniversaire*, p. 109.
56. Charles Taylor, *The sources of the self: The making of the modern identity* (Cambridge: Cambridge University Press, 1989), p. 376.
57. Nathalie Heinich, *L'élite artiste: Excellence et singularité en régime démocratique* (Paris: Gallimard, 2005).
58. Thomas Beller, 'A conversation with Richard Ashcroft', *Mr. Beller's Neighborhood* (blog), 3 August 2004, available online: http://mrbellersneighborhood.com/2004/03/a-conversation-with-richard-ashcroft.
59. See Everett C. Hughes, 'Cycles, turning points, and careers', in *Men and their work* (Glencoe, IL: Free Press, 1958), pp. 11–22.
60. ['When we turn twenty, in 2001', a very popular song in France in the 1980s. Pierre Bachelet was a romantic French singer-songwriter. (Translator's note.)]
61. Message posted on the forum of the website KerMetz.org on 13 September 2007: http://www.kermetz.org/forum/viewtopic.php?f=7&t=2544&start=15.
62. 'Birthday Spirit: A site for people born on September 11': http://birthdayspirit.org.
63. Archivo del Duelo, EP, message recorded at Atocha on 15 July 2004, translated from Spanish.
64. 9/11 Tribute Center, VC, message as of 21 June 2008.
65. 9/11 Tribute Center, VC, message without date, spelling and syntax of original preserved.
66. Archivo del Duelo, EP, message recorded on the website mascercanos.com on 31 October 2004, translated from Spanish.
67. Mémorial de Caen, OF, message as of 14 September 2001, translated from French.
68. Schmitt, *L'invention de l'anniversaire*, pp. 49–50.
69. 9/11 Tribute Center, VC, message as of 26 April 2008.
70. Mémorial de Caen, OF, message as of 14 September 2001, translated from French.
71. Mémorial de Caen, OF, message as of 18 September 2001, translated from French.

72. See Adam Smith, *The theory of moral sentiments*, ed. Ryan Patrick Hanley (New York, NY: Penguin, 2009).
73. See Fonna Forman-Barzilai, *Adam Smith and the circles of sympathy: Cosmopolitanism and moral theory* (Cambridge: Cambridge University Press, 2010), p. 51.
74. Mémorial de Caen, OF, message without date, translated from French.
75. Mémorial de Caen, OF, message without date, translated from French.
76. This observation should be compared with certain results established in the sociology of activism. Olivier Fillieule and Christophe Broqua, for example, showed that what motivated some people to engage in the fight against AIDS was their degree of closeness to the disease, and that besides a 'direct' closeness (being HIV positive oneself) or an 'affective' closeness (having relatives who were HIV positive or had died of AIDS), it was possible to identify a 'more distant' closeness, based on an analogy between forms of physical and social suffering and those inflicted by the experience of AIDS. See Olivier Fillieule and Christophe Broqua, 'Raisons d'agir et proximité à la maladie dans l'économie de l'engagement à Aides, 1984–1998', in A. Micoud and M. Peroni (eds.), *Ce qui nous relie* (La Tour d'Aigues: Éditions de l'Aube, 2000), pp. 283–315.
77. Ellis, 'Shattered lives', p. 397 and pp. 398–9.
78. London Metropolitan Archives, LMA/4469/A/01/023. The fire in King's Cross station on 18 November 1987 was an accident that cost thirty-one lives and left a hundred injured.
79. London Metropolitan Archives, LMA/4469/A/01/026. The shipwreck of the *Estonia* on 28 September 1994 in the Baltic Sea killed 852 people (of the 989 on board), the majority of whom were Swedish nationals.
80. Patricia Guipponi, 'La communauté espagnole entre douleur et révolte', *Midi-Libre* (Béziers edition), 13 March 2004, p. 3.
81. Llera and Retortillo, *Los Españoles y las víctimas del terrorismo*, p. 108.
82. Archivo del Duelo, EP, message recorded on the website mascercanos.com on 22 June 2004, translated from Spanish.
83. Archivo del Duelo, EP, message recorded on the website mascercanos.com on 29 August 2004, translated from Spanish.
84. Archivo del Duelo, EP, message recorded at Atocha on 5 July 2004, translated from Spanish.
85. London Metropolitan Archives, LMA/4469/A/03/038.
86. London Metropolitan Archives, LMA/4469/A/01/022/01.

87. London Metropolitan Archives, LMA/4469/A/01/022/02, translated from Spanish.
88. London Metropolitan Archives, LMA/4469/A/01/021/03, translated from Spanish.
89. London Metropolitan Archives, LMA/4469/A/01/020, translated from Spanish.
90. London Metropolitan Archives, LMA/4469/A/01/022/01.
91. 9/11 Tribute Center, VC, message as of 5 March 2008. With a death toll of thirty-two, the bloodbath at the University of Virginia Tech is one of the most serious episodes of civilian shootings in US history.
92. 9/11 Tribute Center, VC, message as of 18 April 2008.
93. 9/11 Tribute Center, VC, message as of 19 March 2008.
94. See Maurice Halbwachs, *The collective memory*, tr. Francis J. Ditter, Jr. and Vida Yazdi Ditter (New York, NY, and London: Harper & Row, 1980).
95. Halbwachs, *The collective memory*.
96. See Roger W. Brown and James Kulick, 'Flashbulb memories', *Cognition*, 5 (1), 1977, pp. 73–99, and Martin A. Conway, *Flashbulb memories: Essays in cognitive psychology* (Hove: LEA, 1995). An up-to-date inventory of research on this subject can be found in Olivier Luminet and Antonietta Curci (eds.), *Flashbulb memories: New issues and new perspectives* (New York, NY: Psychology Press, 2009).
97. [This was when Jean-Marie Le Pen, the National Front leader, unexpectedly beat the Socialist Lionel Jospin into third place. (Translator's note)]
98. Among a large number of publications, reference may be made to: Andrew R. A. Conway, Linda J. Skitka, Joshua A. Hemmerich and Trina C. Kershaw, 'Flashbulb memory for September 11, 2001', *Applied Cognitive Psychology*, 23 (5), 2009, pp. 605–23; Olivier Luminet and Antonietta Curci, 'The 9/11 attacks inside and outside the US: Testing four models of flashbulb memory formation across groups and the specific effects of social identity', *Memory*, 17 (7), 2009, pp. 742–59; William Hirst, Elizabeth A. Phelps, Randy L. Buckner, Andrew E. Budson et al., 'Long-term memory for the terrorist attack of September 11: Flashbulb memories, event memories, and the factors that influence their retention', *Journal of Experimental Psychology*, 138 (2), 2009, pp. 161–76.
99. Avishai Margalit, *The ethics of memory* (Cambridge, MA, and London: Harvard University Press, 2002), p. 53.
100. Margalit, *The ethics of memory*, p. 53.

Conclusion 'There's something of Charlie in all of us'

1. Émile Durkheim, *The elementary forms of religious life*, tr. Carol Cosman, ed. Mark S. Cladis (Oxford: Oxford University Press, 2008).
2. See Durkheim, *The division of labour in society*, especially pp. 134–5.
3. See Henry Laurens, 'Le terrorisme comme personnage historique', in H. Laurens and M. Delmas-Marty (eds.), *Terrorismes: Histoire et droit* (Paris: CNRS Éditions, 2010), pp. 9–66.
4. The same type of argument was heard after the attack on *Charlie Hebdo*, voiced by those who considered that the paper had gone too far down the road of provocation with its caricatures of Muhammad and that, while this could not in any way justify the terrorists, the state of the world since 9/11 and the underlying threat of a 'war of civilizations' should have encouraged the publication to be more 'responsible'. See for example Jean Delumeau, '"Nous nous trouvons devant une régression de civilisation" (propos recueillis par J. Cordellier)', *Le Point*, 2209, 15 January 2015, pp. 50–1.
5. See Abdellali Hajjat and Marwan Mohammed, *Islamophobie: Comment les élites françaises fabriquent le 'problème musulman'* (Paris: La Découverte, 2013) and Thomas Delthombe, *L'Islam imaginaire: la construction médiatique de l'islamophobie en France, 1975-2005* (Paris: La Découverte, 2005). In the case of the United States, see Christopher A. Bail, *Terrified: How anti-muslim fringe organizations became mainstream* (Princeton: Princeton University Press, 2014). A study based on the statistical data also showed that hostility towards immigrants, while sporadically increasing in certain European regions in the wake of the Bali attacks in 2002 or in Madrid in 2004, depends mainly on changes in the level of unemployment. See Joscha Legewie, 'Terrorist events and attitudes towards immigrants: A natural experiment', *American Journal of Sociology*, 118 (5), 2013, pp. 1199–1245.
6. Durkheim, *The division of labour in society*, pp. 315–16.
7. Elias, 'Changes in the we-I balance'.
8. Ulrich Beck, *Cosmopolitan vision* (Cambridge: Polity, 2014), p. 35.
9. On this pluralist and open conception of the 'us' inspired by the impersonal French pronoun *on* ('one' in the sense of 'people in general') see Jacques Lévy, 'Un "nous" sans "eux": Manufactures

de la société-monde', in A. Caillé and S. Dufoix (eds.), *Le tournant global des sciences sociales* (Paris: La Découverte, 2013), pp. 288–311.

10. See p. 122.

11. See Christina Simko, 'Rhetorics of suffering: September 11 commemorations as theodicy', *American Review of Sociology*, 77 (6), 2012, pp. 880–902, and, on American civil religion in general, the classic article by Robert N. Bellah, 'Civil religion in America', *Dædalus*, 96 (1), 1967, pp. 1–21.

12. Gérôme Truc, 'Le politique aux marges de la commémoration: Une ethnographie des cérémonies de commémoration officielle des attentats du 11 mars 2004 à Madrid', in M. Berger, D. Cefaï, C. Gayet-Viaud and J. Stavo-Debauge (eds.), *Du civil au politique: Ethnographies du vivre-ensemble* (Brussels: Peter Lang, 2011), pp. 205–27.

Afterword

1. See http://reat.hypotheses.org. Research carried out as part of this collective project has already led to new books being published: Sarah Gensburger, *Mémoire vive. Chroniques d'un quartier: Bataclan 2015–2016* (Paris: Anamosa, 2017); Fabien Truong, *Radicalized loyalties* (Cambridge: Polity, 2018).

INDEX

Note: page numbers in italics denote illustrations or tables

cartoonists 39, 58, 65, 140, 177,
178, 228
see also Charlie Hebdo
Casablanca bombings 57
Caserio, Sante 4
casualties of terrorism 46, 47, 51,
54–5, 84, 261–2n6
see also civilian deaths
Cautrès, Bruno 96
Ceibe, Cathy 40
censorship 61, 62, 66–7
Chapatte cartoon 65
Charleston Gazette 22
Charlie Hebdo
criticized 294–5n4
demonstrations 83, 85
emotional closeness 121
freedom of expression 95, 159,
160, 161, 163
as French 9/11 13, 49, 50, 142
journalists on 187–8
media coverage 58
minutes of silence 100, 110
naming of victims 177
official response 102
personal connections with 178–9,
201–2
Place de la République 85, 123
recollection of 223
solidarity 226
see also 'I am Charlie'
Chéroux, Clément 21, 60, 61, 63,
71
Chirac, Jacques 104–5, 110,
245n14
Christianity 169, 171, 172–3
cities
Europe 155–6, 175
twinned 98, 206
see also metropolises
citizen of the world 32, 138–9, 145,
156
see also cosmopolitanism
Citton, Yves 164
civilian deaths 17, 30, 31, 32–3,
111, 183, 245n14
see also casualties of terrorism

clash of civilizations 24, 27, 56,
110, 144–6
closeness, cultural/emotional 115,
116, 121, 292–3n76
CNN 14–15, 20, 31, 35, 41–2
Cohn-Bendit, Daniel 36
coincidence of dates 210–17
USS *Cole* 19
collective action 87, 91–2, 106
collective consciousness 75, 103,
176, 224
collective mourning 101–9, 108
collective trauma 92–5
Collins, Randall 93–4
Colombani, Jean-Marie 35, 36–7
compassion 32–3, 82, 113, 167,
179, 199, 206, 226
Consejo Superior de Investigaciones
Científicas 6
Coppola, Francis Ford: *Apocalypse
Now* 29
Il Corriere della Sera 24, 29, 58, 62
cosmopolitanism
Berlin 156
Bush 56
Europe 157–8
framing 54
humanity 152
individualism 32, 157
Islamism 53–7, 157–8
London 55, 156
minutes of silence 111, 114
national identity 151–2
9/11 attack 32–5
pacifism 78
terrorism 56, 157
Council of Europe 103
Cox, Pat 42–3
Crettiez, Xavier 157, 254n28
cultural trauma theory 93
Cyprus 31

Dadge, Paul 180
Daily Express 52
Daily Mail 29
Daily Mirror 52
Daily News, Los Angeles 70